ARCHITECTURAL HERITAGE
OF THE CARIBBEAN

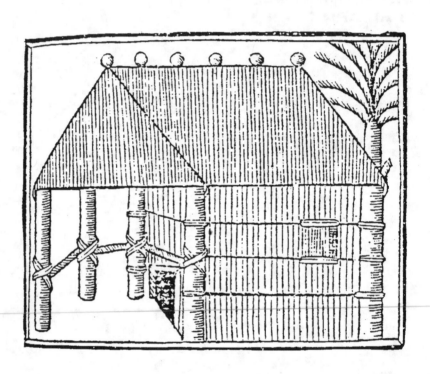

ARCHITECTURAL HERITAGE OF THE CARIBBEAN

An A-Z of Historic Buildings

16 Colour plates and 120 Line Drawings

ANDREW GRAVETTE

Line Drawings by Andrew Gravette and Pamela Gosner

 Ian Randle Publishers *Kingston*

 Signal Books *Oxford*

 Markus Wiener Publishers *Princeton*

First published in Jamaica 2000 by
Ian Randle Publishers, 206 Old Hope Road, Kingston 6
ISBN 976-8123-91-5 paperback
A catalogue record for this book is available from the National Library of Jamaica.

© Andrew Gravette 2000

The right of Andrew Gravette to be identified as author of this work has been asserted by
him in accordance with the Copyright, Designs and Patents Act 1988.

First published 2000 in the UK and Europe
by Signal Books Ltd, 9 Park End Street, Oxford OX1 1HH, United Kingdom

ISBN 1-902669-08-8 Hardback
ISBN 1-902669-09-6 Paperback

A British Library Cataloguing in Publication Data record is available for this
book.

First published in the United States of America 2000 by
Markus Wiener Publishers Inc., 231 Nassau St., Princeton, NJ 08540

       Library of Congress Cataloging-in-Publication Data
Gravette, A. G. (Andrew Gerald)
   Architectural heritage of the Caribbean: an A-Z of historic buildings /
   Andrew Gravette ; line drawings by Andrew Gravette and Pamela Gosner.
    p. cm.
   Includes bibliographical references and index.
   ISBN 1-55876-237-X (hardcover) — ISBN 1-55876-238-8 (alk. paper)
   1. Architecture—Caribbean Area. 2. Historic buildings—Caribbean Area. I. Title
NA791 .G73 2000
720'.9729—dc21   00-021293

Book and cover design by Prodesign Ltd., Red Gal Ring, Kingston, Jamaica
Cover artwork by Elizabeth Manson-Bahr

Printed in the USA

Contents

Colour Plates

THE PRINCE OF WALES'S INSTITUTE OF ARCHITECTURE

THE ARCHITECTURAL HERITAGE OF THE CARIBBEAN

I am delighted to introduce the 'Architectural Heritage of the Caribbean'.

The region has much to offer both students of ethnic and colonial architecture, and the discerning traveller - and this book caters for both interests.

Thoroughly researched, it fills a gap in the study of worldwide architecture. This book offers the academic and casual visitor alike a unique insight into the varied architectural treasures of the Caribbean.

Only art, literature and historic architecture really give us a perception of past lives and times, and through this book we can appreciate the true history of the Caribbean and the way its people lived and worked.

Today, just as tourism is essential to the economy of the Caribbean, so is the reconstruction and preservation of its historic buildings. I am therefore pleased to endorse this comprehensive work on the Caribbean's historic architecture which I am sure will contribute substantially to the universal awareness of this region's rich heritage.

Professor Richard Hodges OBE FSA
Director

Preface

The Alpha and Omega of New World architecture, the Caribbean boasts the first European-built religious, educational, military, civil and domestic structures in the Americas. Five centuries later, construction continues at a frenetic pace. With the boom in tourism, the foundations of a new hotel are being laid almost every week. From the rotting timbers of Columbus's first stockade, to the megalithic edifice of the ultra-modern Columbus Lighthouse, the 500-year span of European Caribbean architecture presents a unique cultural legacy.

With thirty main islands spread across 2,500 miles of sea, the Caribbean is a treasure-chest of architectural gems, each deserving more documentation than one book can comfortably contain. Although the origin of the region's historic heritage dates back more than 3,000 years, developed architecture was first imported from late-medieval Europe with the Spanish explorers and *conquistadores* in the late 1400s. Over the following 500 years, British, Danish, Dutch, French, Scandinavians and North Americans have all made their mark in the Caribbean, leaving behind them, on independence, a wealth of architectural treasures. To these multifaceted influences must be added those of Africa and Asia, reflections of the region's cruel history of slavery and servitude.

Nowhere else on earth can boast such a melting-pot of architectural styles, ranging from Mudéjar mansions to Islamic mosques, from Gothic cathedrals to Georgian great houses. The variety of architectural styles mingles Italianate and Romanesque with Baroque and Art Nouveau, while palatial Palladian mansions rub shoulders with tropical Regency halls. Victorian churches, straight out of a typical English village, stand a short distance from a windmill, reminiscent of a painting by some Dutch master. The work of 19th-century French architect Gustave Eiffel can be seen just an hour's flight away from fortifications built by the 17th-century Italian designer, Cristoforo de Roda. In Havana is a faithful replica of the Capitol building in Washington DC, and a copy of the Sacré Coeur in Paris stands amid lush tropical vegetation just outside the capital of Martinique.

An estimated 25,000 buildings of architectural and historic importance dot the islands of the Caribbean, and naturally no one book can do the region's structural heritage full justice. While recently compiling a book on the architecture of Cuba alone, the author documented just over 5,000 significant historic buildings. Therefore, this book has been confined to parameters which encompass the more architecturally important structures of historic and social note, and those which typify a particular style or use, or reflect an island's domestic or economic development. Apart from forts, churches, commercial, domestic, public and plantation buildings, several monuments, gateways and other edifices of interest have also been included to give an overall impression of the Caribbean's architectural diversity.

Defining Heritage

Most modern structures, particularly those built after the 1950s, are omitted from this book, although a few might soon be considered important by heritage committees. Some buildings, like the Columbus Lighthouse in the Dominican Republic, deserve mention, if only to contrast modern architectural technology with that of the earliest New World structures in nearby Santo Domingo. For the most part, however, I am more concerned with the colonial, pre-independence period in most islands, or, in the case of nations such as Haiti, the Dominican Republic or Cuba, with the buildings that predate the last half century.

This book also looks at the homes of 'ordinary' people and their tastes. By no means least significant in the rich tapestry of the Caribbean's architectural heritage is the wealth of vernacular structures, which reflect the development of the social order of the region. From simple case and 'chattel' houses like those on Antigua and Barbados, to elaborately embellished town or country residences, like those on Haiti and Guadeloupe, true Caribbean architecture contrasts with those early buildings which replicate traditional European styles. It is in the detail of these locally designed structures that we see how the influence of European architecture has been adapted and refined to suit the needs and climate of the tropical Caribbean.

In this book, which is designed for the student of architecture and the casual visitor alike, I have endeavoured to present an inclusive architectural picture of the Caribbean. My intention is not to provide an analytical framework, but rather to describe selectively the most salient examples of the region's historic buildings. The book should serve as an introduction its varied architecture, and whet the appetite for a closer look at the story of the Caribbean through its architectural heritage.

Andrew Gravette
June 1999

Acknowledgments

The author and publishers would like to extend their thanks to all those Tourist Boards, National Trusts, local agencies and others, which have assisted in the research for this book and contributed pictures and other material. In particular, thanks are due to the Bahamas Tourist Office, Jamaica Tourist Board, Puerto Rico Tourism Co., Saba Tourist Office and US Virgin Islands Division of Tourism, as well as Manning, Selvage & Lee on behalf of the Barbados Tourism Authority. The publishers' gratitude is also extended to Catriona Davidson for her photographs. All reasonable efforts have been made to trace the sources of those illustrations and diagrams not originated by the author. The publishers are also grateful to Passeggiata Press for permission to reproduce the drawings by Pamela Gosner from *Caribbean Georgian* on pages 23, 34, 40, 42, 43, 52, 77, 81, 111, 116, 158, 163, 189, 194, 198, 206, 213, 218, 221, 229, 233, 235, 241, 242, 244, 251, 269, 273, 303, 304, 306, 308, 310, and 312. The publishers would also like to thank John Murray (Publishers) Ltd for permission to use the extract by Patrick Leigh Fermor on page 105; and A. P. Wall Ltd for permission to reproduce the extract by Jan Morris on page 296.

Part One

History and Development

Climate and Geography

The first consideration when addressing the architecture of the Caribbean region is its weather and the prevailing conditions which affect all who live in the area. Being tropical, and ranging across 15 degrees of Latitude, the Caribbean Sea covers an area of almost 750,000 square miles, subject to strong winds and high tides, often brought about by hurricanes, when rainfall can be extremely heavy. Several of the islands are also currently volcanically active, and earthquakes periodically strike on some islands. Many Caribbean islands have both large, low-lying areas, and high peaks or mountain ranges. Some are of entirely volcanic origin, and others are comprised of ancient limestone and fossilized coral, providing a mixture of natural building materials, including wood, which once covered most of the Caribbean islands. In past days, before colonization by the Europeans, the islands in the Caribbean were carpeted in dense, high forests, consisting of ancient hardwoods and rain forest. On many islands, mangrove swamps protected the coastlines, which were often fine, sandy beaches, built up over many millions of years by the erosion of coral reefs and rocky shorelines.

The temperature and rainfall of a region are naturally vital in determining styles of habitation. The islands lie in the Tropics between ten degrees south and the Tropic of Cancer, and temperatures seldom exceed 30 degrees C (86F) or drop much below 20 degrees C (68F). The conservation of warmth is hence not a priority in Caribbean architecture, while the encouragement of ventilation most definitely is. The low-lying islands of the region are usually the driest, with the higher terrain catching rain-laden winds, and rainfall can vary dramatically from 12 inches per month down to almost zero precipitation. This results in a marked difference in habitation styles between the drier and wetter islands as well as between the hotter islands to the south and those in the cooler north.

Another factor that features prominently in the design of shelter is wind velocity. The Caribbean is one of those regions which experiences periods of high winds. In pre-Columbian times the indigenous peoples of the Caribbean recognized the awesome power of these winds, naming the all-powerful storm *huracan*. Today, we continue to call these cyclonic winds hurricanes, often baptizing the most destructive with human names for the record. Some island architecture has evolved in a way that minimizes the damage hurricanes can cause. Often the simplest wooden houses survive most effectively, since they can be reconstructed relatively easily. And the sold stone structures built by European colonists several centuries ago continue to show their remarkable resilience, where more modern buildings prove vulnerable. Despite this, some formidable hurricanes in the course of the 1980s and 1990s caused considerable structural damage to many Caribbean islands, even where buildings were designed to withstand most onslaughts.

Two further natural phenomena are even less predictable than hurricanes and are even more difficult to protect against. Earthquakes in the Caribbean are mercifully few and far between and are mostly confined to seabed seismic activity. Yet one such quake completely engulfed the 'pirate capital' of Port Royal, Jamaica, in 1692, while Santiago de Cuba has intermittently been subject to earth tremors. More destructive perhaps have been volcanic eruptions. Two eruptions, at either end of the 20th century, have marked Caribbean history, the first at St Pierre in Martinique destroying an entire city and its population in 1902. More recently, the eruption of Montserrat's Soufrière Hills volcano from 1995 onwards has caused loss of life and enormous disruption, putting the future of this tiny British colony in doubt.

Fire, too, has been the scourge of Caribbean architecture. There is hardly a town or city in the region that has not at one time been engulfed by fire, encouraged by strong winds and primarily wooden buildings. Towns such as Castries in St Lucia have been repeatedly razed to the ground, sometimes quite deliberately in the course of conflict. Haiti lost much of its 17th- and 18th- century architecture in the tumultuous civil war between 1791 and 1804.

Past geological action and the varied vegetation of the Caribbean have hence contributed to the style of architecture on each island. Building materials include different sorts of wood according to what is – and has been – available, including local hardwoods and palms. Stone ranges from soft coral limestone to extremely hard igneous rock, while fossil coral rock is also used as a building material in the larger islands of the Greater Antilles and Barbados. Imported materials have added variety to local resources, and the region's architectural repertoire encompasses iron, bricks, tiles, marble and granite.

The biggest influence, of course, is man, and human activity, social and economic, has reshaped the original wilderness of the Caribbean into what we know today. It remains a primarily agricultural region, as it was from within a few decades of European colonization, and industrial development has been restricted to a few larger islands, such as Cuba, Jamaica and Trinidad. There are fewer than twenty towns or cities with any significant population in the whole of the Caribbean, and many people continue to inhabit small villages or towns. The largest city is Havana, with over two million inhabitants. Conversely, on Haiti, less than a quarter of the population live in an urban area.

Before Columbus

The mainland of South America has been occupied by humans since 30,000 BC, from which time the first evidence of human settlement dates. Wooden stakes, lashed together and found in Monte Verde, 500 miles south of Santiago de Chile, are considered to be the remnants of America's first settled habitations. The first arrivals on the southerly islands of the Caribbean came from the Orinoco River region of what is now Venezuela. Unrest in the social structure of the tribal make-up there precipitated a northerly migration of forest-dwelling tribes into the Caribbean Sea.

For over 6,000 years, the indigenous peoples of South America had lived in comparative harmony with nature, undisturbed and unaware of the worlds and civilizations beyond the great seas to the east and west. In pre-Columbian times, to the east of the forest regions of tropical South America, Arawak tribes inhabited the river basins of the Orinoco and the northern Amazon. In appearance, these dark-haired, cinnamon-coloured jungle-dwellers, were comparatively short, with round faces and almond-shaped eyes. They lived in thatched huts, made of bent branches, covered in leafy boughs; they slept in hammocks, cultivated certain plants for food and medicine, created clay ceramics, and travelled in canoes made from deftly carved tree trunks. Their slash-and-burn agricultural practices meant that their villages were relocated at regular intervals as the forest soil fertility had a limited time-span. Edible roots and tubers like cassava, wild beans, groundnuts, wild fruit and vegetables, supplemented their varied diet, including those plants that they cultivated. The Arawaks lived off the land, stunning parrots from the trees by burning pepper under their roosts, shooting wild game-birds, peccaries, tapir, forest deer, monkeys, iguana, snakes and fish with powerful bows and arrows, using natural poisons. These forest tribes had few enemies; the word Taino (a sub-division of the Arawak people) meant 'men of the good'. Their only fears were of their gods of nature, forest snakes and the panther, until the advent of the most dangerous of all animals – man, in the image of the Carib.

It was from the forests to the south-east of the Orinoco, in the depths of Amazonia, that the warlike tribes of the Warru and Caribs emerged. The Caribs were shorter than the Arawaks, copper-coloured, with wiry black hair cut in a fringe-style around the head. Their homes were temporary, leaf-covered frameworks of rounded branches. They settled only briefly in jungle clearings and generally followed the trails of the animals which they hunted with blowpipe darts and bows and arrows, using the poison curare to kill their prey. This people allegedly engaged in cannibalism – the word is derived from their name – but evidence suggests that this was a purely ceremonial practice, intended to pass on to victorious warriors their dead victims' qualities of bravery.

It is not known what prompted the tribes to infringe on each other's territory. However, a time came when the aggressive Caribs, driving north from the Amazonian floodwaters, began turning their weapons on their neighbours. Eventually the unwanted attentions of the Caribs forced the forest-dwellers to drift north from their homelands.

For many generations, the Arawaks slowly moved north, until

around the same time as the Romans began subduing the English, in about 100 AD, the Arawaks reached the Caribbean coast of South America. These peaceful tribes, pursued by the Caribs, then began a saga of island-hopping from the south to the north. The transportation they used was the Amerindian canoe, often containing up to 200 paddlers. For two centuries, the Caribs relentlessly harassed the fleeing Arawaks, pursuing them through the island chain, until, around the third century AD, the first of the hunter-gatherer tribes reached the islands of the Greater Antilles, now Puerto Rico, Hispaniola, Jamaica and Cuba. It was here that the Arawaks, followed by the Tainos (a people of Arawak extraction), found the vast forests of the islands, ideal refuges from the warring Caribs. A wave of Tainos reached the larger islands in around 700 AD, with another group arriving in 1250 and yet another in around 1450. By the end of the 15th century, the Caribs were beginning to make raids on Puerto Rico and Jamaica, although they never established a permanent footing in either island.

The Arawaks having brought with them their hunting, fishing, and gathering skills, and the Tainos their ceramic expertise, the two peoples settled down to recreating their lifestyles from their South American homeland. With them came the basics of survival, including their foodstuffs, cooking methods and living styles, which adapted ideally to the conditions which they found in the Caribbean islands. They discovered, however, that they were sharing the islands with two much more primitive groups of cave-dwellers who had arrived more than 4,500 years before. These were known as the Ciboney and Gunahatabey Amerindians, a people who dwelt mostly in caves and coastal caverns, living off shellfish. The Tainos co-existed in harmony with the Ciboney on each of the larger islands of Puerto Rico, Hispaniola and Cuba, both always wary of the predatory Caribs. On the Bahamian archipelago lived the Lucayans, another people belonging to the Arawak group, who were peaceful and skilled at fishing and boat-building.

Even with the advent of a number of migrating peoples, from both the Central American mainland and particularly from the Arawak river cultures of South America, little changed on the Caribbean islands. Almost impenetrable forest clad every island with soil enough to support it, and many islands were ringed with a protective barrier of mangrove. Early human occupation did little to alter the forested nature of the Caribbean islands.

The end of the 15th century saw the Caribbean islands divided between the Lucayans living on the Bahamas, the Taino, Arawak, Ciboney and Guanahatabey occupying those islands in the far north of the Caribbean – Cuba, Hispaniola and Puerto Rico – and the ferocious Caribs living in the Lesser Antilles and close to conquering some of the larger islands. When Europeans arrived in the region, they discovered a variety of peoples living in an assortment of habitations, all designed and adapted to the special conditions of the Caribbean.

We have mostly cursory descriptions of how indigenous communities lived from contemporary reports by the earliest Europeans explorers. On his first voyage to the New World, in 1492, Christopher Columbus sent two of his men on a brief excursion into the interior of Cuba, meeting with Arawak tribespeople and noting their particular style of housing. Columbus was also the first European to visit the coast of South America on his third voyage in 1498. Although he did not land on that coast, his companion, the Spanish navigator Alonso de Ojeda explored the coastline extensively the following year. Probably the most accurate description of Amerindian dwellings was made by Sir Francis Drake, when, in the late 1500s he made several expeditions to the north coast of South America, detailing the indigenous way of life. His diarist recorded in words and pictures leaf-thatched, woven cane-walled huts, with conical roofs.

Over several thousand years, indigenous Amerindian domestic buildings had evolved very slowly. In an area in the north of South America, the Paraujano tribes lived in *barbacoas*, or stilt houses, built over the water. It was during the 1499 excursion by Ojeda's Italian navigator, Amerigo Vespucci, that he remarked on these dwellings that apparently (and improbably) reminded him of Venice and led him to name the area Venezuela or 'little Venice'. A related Arawak society also existed on neighbouring Aruba and had evolved communities of similar communal stilt-houses, known as *ajoupas*. There were also the *caneyes*, or conical, pointed-roofed, thatched family huts, favoured by forest-dwellers, and *carbets*, or large, round, palm-thatched communal huts, used by more sedentary peoples. The *kabays*, or *mouina*, tent-shaped, thatched dwellings without windows, but with a single, small entrance, easy and quick to erect, were the preference of forest tribes such as the Caribs who were constantly on the move.

The Bohío

The most distinctive dwelling of the Amerindians was the *bohío*, a rudimentary hut, but so perfectly compatible with the Caribbean climate that the basic design was to influence Spanish Caribbean architecture for the next 500 years. Arriving in the islands, the Arawaks had found the terrain and flora to be markedly different from the dense jungles which encroached on their original habitat.  Mountains, hills, and open plateaux replaced the monotony of South America's flat riverside jungles. The materials available for constructing houses were also different to those to be found on the mainland. Even the sixty species of palm tree differed substantially from the trees of the Arawaks' South American homeland. Dominating much of the Caribbean landscape, was the stately Royal Palm (*Roystonea regia*). It was around this magnificent tree that the Amerindians' distinctive architecture was woven.

The groups of houses which Columbus and his band found on Cuba and Hispaniola, the second large island on which he landed on his first voyage, were bohíos, made entirely from parts of the Royal Palm and providing all the raw materials from which the perfect shelter could be constructed. The collection of indigenous constructions had a design evolved over many centuries and as ideally suited to the Caribbean climate as the Spaniards' own *haciendas* were to the European climate. The Royal Palm has a straight, silvery trunk which can grow to 100 ft, culminating in an exuberant burst of green fronds, or *pencas*, which sprout with every new moon from their thick green bases, known as *yaguas*. The palm's trunk was found to be resistant to insect attack and rotting, yet was easy to carve and shape.

Primitive bohíos were initially rounded huts formed of posts, with either woven walls or walls made of reeds or straight sticks, lashed or sewn together between the posts. The roofs were conical, formed of palm frond thatch or reeds. As it evolved, the basic design of the indigenous houses resembled the traditional tent shape. A rude ridge framework was initially constructed out of strips of the palm's trunk, a dense, fibrous material which has enormously supple qualities. Open at both ends, this framework was thatched with the palm fronds. The triangular open ends of the tent-shaped hut were then filled with walls made from strips of the yaguas, the thick palm frond bases, which are elastic and waterproof. These were woven

together with lengths of fibre, stripped from the centre of the palm frond and from strips of the palm's bark. The front wall of the bohío included a doorway which could be closed with a square frame made in the same way as the walls.

Some of the migrating Arawaks brought with them their design for stilt houses built over the water on lakesides. These communities found that the Royal Palm also provided excellent materials for this house design, the barbacoa. Even the stilts were fashioned out of the Royal Palm trunk, a wood which became stronger as it absorbed water and was resistant to rot. These barbacoas were two-storey structures, with the living quarters on the top platform and another platform at water level, used during the day for working and preparing food. This lower platform also served as a canoe mooring and a place for fabricating fishing nets and weaving fish traps, and ladders connected the two levels. The stilt-based barbacoas were linked to each other and to the land by wooden walkways and woven bridges. More than 500 years later, when some Cuban families were dividing the high-ceilinged rooms of Havana's early colonial mansions into two levels because of overcrowding they named the family units barbacoas.

In a climate where fierce sun necessitated cool shade, tropical downpours of torrential rain made shelter vital, and the uniquely Caribbean hurricane made protection from high winds essential, the Amerindian bohío proved ideal. It was as cool, dry and almost as wind-proof as those caves and grottoes which the early Ciboney Amerindian tribes had originally inhabited. It took a short time to construct, and all the building material came from just one source. So perfectly adapted to the Caribbean climate was the design of the Amerindian bohío and the materials from which the primitive structure was made, that, many years after the indigenous population had been exterminated, the bohío remained a feature of the landscape of the Greater Antilles.

First European Settlement

The first European settlers were mostly, but not exclusively, Spanish. They had come with Columbus in 1492 from such diverse European locations and environments as Catalonia, Estremadura, the Basque region, Galicia, Andalusia, France and Italy. From the high plateau of Spain to the Mediterranean coastlands, from the mountains of the Sierra Nevada to the low estuaries of the Atlantic coast, the new settlers were used to their regional house styles, which all differed according to the local climate. Once in the Caribbean, they were faced with an architectural challenge.

Confronted with the rigours of a tropical climate, but, most importantly, with a potentially antagonistic indigenous people, the colonists were forced to make immediate decisions. How would they structure their first settlement in the New World? Would it be modelled on the villages in their homeland Spain, or designed to adapt to the pressures of the local environment? Here, the work-force – and the natural resources available – took precedence. Their predicament, in any case, was dire. One of their three ships had been wrecked; they had landed off a sandy beach, on a reef-bound shore on the north coast of what Columbus had named Hispaniola, (the part now known as Haiti). The local Arawaks, seemed peaceful (they were later provoked into violent hostility), and the building force and materials were both limited.

The coastal area to be built on was wooded, with dense forest down to the sea. The builders were shipwrights and indigenous villagers, the area to be developed needed possible fortification, and not one of the new arrivals had any experience in construction. Columbus decided to commandeer a small Amerindian village, close to a river, as the area was already cleared and could be easily defended. The first solution was to retrieve, with the assistance of the Arawaks, the timbers of the wrecked *Santa Maria*, Columbus's flagship. With the timbers from the small ship, the Spaniards were able to construct a basic stockade. This consisted of a palisade of wooden stakes as a defensive ring around a small area of ground near the river, with a square, timbered structure forming a fort. Columbus grandly called the first Spanish settlement in the New World, La Navidad, or Christmas, as it was founded on the day the settlers first said Mass, Christmas Day. However, most of the dwellings, except for the small fort, were native bohíos.

La Navidad survived for just a few months after Columbus had sailed back to Spain. The 39 European defenders of the little settle-ment were soon killed by warriors from the indigenous communi-ties whom they had abused and provoked beyond endurance, and when Columbus arrived back the following year, he found the village burned and razed to the ground. Columbus then selected a new location on which to build a stronger and more permanent township, a short distance to the east, on a little bay. The Spaniards on Columbus's second voyage in 1493 numbered some 1,200 sailors, soldiers, builders, farmers and specialists in numerous other trades, a contingent designed for colonization. It was decided to build this second settlement from stone. Within a few weeks, the new town of La Isabela had a church, a storehouse, and a public meeting place, or town hall, all built of stone. There is no remaining evidence of the design of these first European buildings in the New World, but it is documented that the living quarters were all made of wood and thatched with palm leaves and grass. Unusually, the settlers did not wall in their town or build any defensive structures.

A hurricane devastated La Isabela in 1495, and the Spanish colonists decided to abandon the site, which was found to be unhealthy and mosquito-ridden, and establish a new town on the south coast of Hispaniola, on the banks of the Ozama River. Bartolomé Columbus, the Admiral's brother, moved the entire Spanish contingent to a place he named Nueva Isabela, later to be called Santo Domingo, in 1496.

Adapting the Bohío

As the process of colonization gathered pace, Spanish homesteaders adapted the traditional Amerindian bohío to their own designs. Settlements spread outwards from Santo Domingo and into the other islands of the Greater Antilles. In Cuba, the Spanish conquistador Diego de Velázquez established the first seven European townships of Baracoa, Santiago de Cuba, Bayamo, Puerto Principe (now Camagüey), Sancti Spritus, Trinidad and Havana. Around these centres, settlers began to cultivate the land, while others prospected for precious metals.

With a shortage of building materials in the countryside with which to construct stone or adobe houses like those in Spain, farmers or *campesinos* adopted the design techniques of the Amerindians. As the Spanish were more used to houses with walls, they first imbedded four corner posts in the planned rectangle of their house. Four walls were then constructed between these corner posts in the same way, and of the same material, as that which the Amerindians had used to construct the walls of their bohíos. A framework of lathes made from strips of the Royal Palm trunk was erected above the walls, with sides sloping outwards from a central

ridge. From the ridge downwards, the palm fronds or pencas provided an excellent thatch, proven over centuries by the Amerindians. The ridge was then neatly finished by interweaving with fibres from the centre of the palm's pencas. A doorway was naturally left in one side of the oblong bohío and a door fitted which hinged on loops made from the same material.

As time passed, this mud-floored, one-roomed hut was stylized to include a rude window, and the walls were sometimes daubed with mud or clay. In some cases, the walls were composed of a lattice-work of twigs and branches, covered in wattle and daub and then whitewashed to resemble more closely the style of house that the Spanish settlers were used to in their homeland. Some bohíos were made large enough to incorporate divisions, making two or more rooms. However, the basic design of the one-roomed bohío predominated. These can still be seen in more remote rural areas of Cuba, Hispaniola and Puerto Rico. They have no sanitation, and many still have only a packed earthen floor. But some campesino bohíos are now fully fitted out and some even have air-conditioning and television.

The demand for more space and comfort gradually produced a further modification to the original bohío design. The next major architectural refinement was the addition of a verandah or porch to the front of the structure, giving shelter above the doorway and single window, if any. This was made by erecting two or more poles a few feet out from the front wall of the hut, and extending the thatched roof out to the supports, strengthened by the framework of palm lathes and lined underneath by lengths of yaguas. Usually this addition to the roof had a much shallower pitch than that of the main roof. Soon, the Amerindian bohío became Hispanicized, looking very similar to basic farm buildings in the remote country-side of Spain.

The more ingenious small farmers added a low wooden platform under the porch, sometimes creating a small enclosure around the

Shingled case

front of the bohío with railings. Some homesteaders built low walls around the verandah, creating a small area in which they could sit in the cool of the evening after a day's work on the land. Nevertheless, the basic style remained, the roof still being thatched with palm fronds. Yet even this gradually changed as some carpenters fashioned roofing tiles from the trunk wood of the Royal Palm. The more wealthy, and those who had access to imported tiles, built their roof extensions from ceramic tiles. In some places, where clay was available, these tiles were replaced by locally-made Spanish-style interlocking tiles. In some cases, wooden slates or rough shingles were used as a cheaper tiling material for the verandah overhang. But many owners kept the thatched main roofs, finding the insulation more comfortable, efficient and economical than covering the entire roof with tiles.

In other parts of the Caribbean, the basic bohío walls were later replaced by wooden planking or shingles, and often a wooden floor would be added, usually raised off the ground. Raised floors were particularly important in those islands where vermin, and especially snakes, were prevalent. Thus, the original bohío became the standard blueprint for the basic home or *case* throughout the region. Moreover, the design was found to stand up to quite high winds, whereas the modernized version, with wooden walls and tiled or corrugated iron roofs, was less resistant to Caribbean squalls and hurricanes. It was soon discovered that during high winds the airier style of the early bohío allowed the air pressures on the outside and inside to equalize, whereas the closed construction of the newer case could disintegrate in a hurricane.

On the outskirts of townships, where there was access to more sophisticated building materials, farm workers built their own particular version of the bohío. Constructed in much the same way as the indigenous dwelling, the workers used wooden planking to build the walls of their houses, incorporating a railed porch. With board planks forming the walls, it was also much easier to incorporate windows and also a more conventional doorway. These buildings were often divided internally into two or more rooms during their construction. Wooden-planked flooring was also added, sometimes even incorporating a rear, as well as a front, porch. With the advent of corrugated iron, some builders used this material for roofing, even though palm fronds and tiling remain popular roof materials to this day.

Settlement of the Lesser Antilles was piecemeal, beginning with the arrival of the English, French and Dutch in the mid-17th century. Small, European-style buildings were built in the little trading or farming communities which sprang up. Most of these structures were timber-framed, wattle and daub, or tapia-walled dwellings. Most were single-storey with windows and doors, and a small window under the ridged roof at both ends. The main difference between these European dwellings and the bohío was that indigenous builders used unfinished boughs for their home's framework, where the Europeans cut and shaped their timber with metal tools. The walls, in the case of the bohío, were also formed from vegetation, whereas the walls of the Europeans' buildings were more solid, with mud and stone infill. Many European homes were thatched in the same way as the bohío, although some were roofed with tiles imported as ship's ballast.

Building in Stone

Back in Columbus's first permanent settlement of Santo Domingo on Hispaniola, the experience of fire damage and the vulnerability of wooden structures turned Spanish architects to consider stronger structures. They also wanted to recreate the familiar buildings of Spain in their new lands. By the early 1500s, the Spanish also had recruited a large number of slaves, mostly indigenous men, who could be instructed to quarry local stone building blocks. The first stone structure in this town was the Church of the Virgin of the Rosary, erected in the original location of Nueva Isabela, across the river from the present city. The second important building was the military Tower of Homage, begun in 1502 after the settlement was shifted to the west bank of the Ozama. In 1507, the first brick-built building in the Americas was constructed from ballast brought over on trading galleons. This edifice, La Atarazana, was built as an arsenal and a customs house, and the following year, the first hospital, the St Nicolás de Bari hospice was built.

However, it was not until 1510 that the first stone house was built in the New World, proving that the Spanish adaptation of the traditional local building style proved adequate and comfortable for at least the first twenty years of European occupation. The Alcázar, America's first European palace, was completed in 1514 from massive blocks of coral limestone. It took 1,500 Amerindian and

Spanish worker almost four years to build the Alcázar, Don Diego Columbus's house, which was designed in a mixture of Gothic, Mudéjar and Italian Renaissance styles, with 22 rooms and 72 doors and windows.

Three Architectural Styles Evolve

The early Spanish preponderance for constructing towns in their new colonies in the Caribbean originated from the need to defend their settlers, firstly from the indigenous population, and later from itinerant raiders, pirates and hostile navies. The main towns of all the colonial islands were built around a military or religious centre, with the administrative buildings ranged around a square or plaza. The houses of the rich faced into a cathedral or church square, with lesser buildings occupying a characteristic grid system of streets branching out from these squares. Almost all were built in a coastal location, usually with the advantage of a harbour and port. One topographical feature which figured in the selection of a harbour settlement was a protective promontory. The promontory, usually with a high headland known as a *morro*, was ideal for defensive structures such as those of San Juan and Havana. Havana was a classic natural location, with a deep, wide bay to one side of the town and a narrow entrance that could be easily defended. Bays of this nature were known as *bolsas* or bags, because of their narrow mouths.

The architecture of the Caribbean's colonial towns and cities varies considerably. From the earliest Spanish settlements on the three main islands of Cuba, Hispaniola and Puerto Rico, to the British, French, Dutch and Danish occupancies in the smaller islands, architecture generally reflected the European mode of the time. Some of the earliest architectural styles can be seen in the Dominican Republic, with Gothic, Romanesque and Plateresque influences dating from the early 1500s. Spanish Baroque of the late 17th and early 18th century is also well represented on the larger Caribbean islands. The British, for their part, brought their stately Georgian and Victorian architecture to many of the smaller islands, while the French, Dutch and Danish imported elements of their homelands, ranging from French roof styles to traditional Dutch and Danish gables.

Outside the Caribbean's towns and cities, the very nature of the islands dictated rural architectural development. Being predominantly agricultural economies, two separate styles of building development emerged. As the demand for natural and raised products like logwood dyes, hides, tallow and timber overtook the initial gold-rush of the 16th century, the population not involved in the exploration and exploitation of Central and South America, turned to the land. Peasant farming saw a growth in isolated housing and an infrastructure of small villages. These buildings took their architectural style from elements of indigenous building combining them with imported techniques.

Within the first century of European occupation, the fertile soil and ideal climatic conditions of the Caribbean islands were found to be perfect for the raising of sugar cane. Because of the extensive way sugar cane is cultivated and its labour-intensive harvesting, enormous swaths of forest were cleared to provide space for the plantations. Many thousands of square miles of forest gave way to cane fields on Hispaniola, Puerto Rico and Cuba, spreading in the course of the 17th century to almost every cultivable island of the Caribbean archipelago. The massive encroachment of the sugar industry throughout the Caribbean brought with it a peculiar architectural style unique to the crop. The sugar plantation was to influence the entire development of the Caribbean islands and its population.

During the 16th and 17th centuries settlers in the Spanish islands had been concentrating on raising herds of cattle, cultivating tobacco and producing timber. However, the growing market in sugar, as well as the burgeoning trade in supplying molasses to the newly established colonies in North America, brought a new interest in the potential of the four largest Caribbean islands. The small sugar estates were quickly enlarged, and more forest was felled to make way for the cane fields. In the early 18th century, European financiers ploughed money into the development of vast sugar cane plantations throughout Cuba, Hispaniola and Puerto Rico. In return, many *peninsulares*, or Spanish-born colonists, became extremely rich. By the middle of the 18th century, sugar plantations had spread to every island of the Caribbean and sugar became 'King' in the region. The sugar baron hierarchy was established and was to rule the land for the next three hundred years.

Planters also developed other cash crops, such as coffee, cacao, cotton, citrus fruits, dyes, spices, herbs, and pharmaceutical products. Every crop was accompanied by its own specialized architecture, housing the processing machinery as well as the workers, estate owner or manager. No crop, however, had such an impact, architecturally, as sugar.

By the end of the 16th century, then, there were three distinctive architectural trends in the Caribbean. The colonial towns and cities had styles derived from the European trends of the time. The plantation introduced the first industrial-scale architecture, concerned with mass production and technology. And the peasant style of building was established, owing its origins to the indigenous inhabitants of the region. From these three areas evolved a new,

Caribbean, style of architecture, drawing on a vast gamut of influences. Spanish, British, French, Dutch, Danish, Swedish, Italian, African, Asian, and American styles all lent something of their own to the new synthesis. In some cases, buildings almost identical to those of the immigrants' homes were constructed in the Caribbean. In others, domestic style was modified to suit the tropical climate and environment. Occasionally buildings evolved independently from any influence outside the Caribbean.

It is difficult, therefore, to discriminate, and say that the architecture of the Caribbean either begins with the advent of Europeans or with the introduction of Africans, or that Caribbean style evolved entirely from indigenous building and construction methods. The Caribbean is as much a melting pot of architectural styles as it is a meeting of the cultures, beliefs, languages, habits and social structure of the Caribbean peoples themselves. It is a pot-pourri of architectural styles, evolved by the close juxtaposition of cultures from around the world and with a piquancy of its own, the Caribbean touch, making it unique in the world.

Part Two

Influences and Evolution

The region's history of discovery, colonization and conflict determined the architectural development of each individual Caribbean island, territory and township. Naturally, as the region's first imperial nation, Spain had most influence on its early architecture. For exactly 130 years from 1492, the Spanish had virtually dominated the settlement of the Caribbean, hampered only by the attentions of roving pirates and buccaneers, who set up primitive homesteads on isolated islets. As a result, almost all the permanent European structures erected since Columbus first landed in the Caribbean up until the 1620s were Spanish.

Yet the English, French, and Dutch were swiftly to make their mark in the region while Spain was busy plundering Central and South America. The English settled in St Kitts and Barbados, gradually claiming territories such as Antigua. In 1655 they took Jamaica from the Spanish, founding their largest island colony. The French, meanwhile, laid claim to Martinique and Guadeloupe, while the Dutch, perhaps the most accomplished of contemporary seafaring nations, took a series of small islands and developed them as trading posts. In their wake came the smaller powers: Denmark and Sweden.

Imperial competition introduced different architectural influences, but so too did mass migration. The estimated 15 million Africans who crossed the infamous 'middle passage' during three centuries of transatlantic slavery brought with them techniques and styles from their homelands. In the course of time, they were joined by many other communities of settlers and labourers: migrants from the North American colonies, Jewish refugees, Indian indentured workers, and Chinese, all contributing their particular styles to the rich architectural blend which we now find throughout the Caribbean.

Before exploring individual islands, it is perhaps useful to trace some of the many influences that have shaped Caribbean buildings, from 16th-century Spain to 1930s Americana. A selection of individual and highly representative buildings from different periods and territories can help in following this evolution. Important, too, has been the role of agriculture and other economic activities in shaping the Caribbean landscape.

Spanish Colonial Architecture

Spanish American church architecture of the 16th century was a mixture of functional and decorative styles usually of Gothic influence, with traditional decorations around the windows and dorways. The cathedral of Santo Domingo, for example, typically combines Italian Renaissance decoration with Gothic rigidity. Cross-vaulting was favoured, due to costly experience of earthquakes, particularly in Santiago de Cuba, and pillars, arcades and arches were popular features. Many features were added in subsequent decades, including Mudéjar wood-block ceilings, neo-Classical towers, domes and pillars, and Plateresque facades, forming an eclectic style known as *mestizaje*. Juan de Herrera, the official ecclesiastical architect, established an architectural style in 16th-century Spain, to be copied in the New World by Francisco Becerra.

> **Gothic**
>
> Mostly associated with church architecture
>
> Main features: pointed arches, rib vaulted ceilings, flying buttresses, height and impression of weightlessness
>
> Stylized elegance and emphasis on line and silhouette

As had already occurred in Hispaniola, Puerto Rico and Jamaica, the main preoccupation in early colonial Cuba was the search for the gold and silver which the conquistadores believed the island's mountains and hills held. The gold-rushes on most of the larger islands were short-lived, but attracted many weathy speculators to the colonies. Seven settlements were established on the island of

Cuba, each designed to a typical Spanish colonial template, established in Santo Domingo and in San Juan. In some cases, as in Havana, three squares would be laid out. These consisted of a military square, an administrative square and an ecclesiastical square. In other instances, such as Santiago de Cuba, one square would be flanked by the religious, governing and military structures. The priorities in town construction, were the church, the army garrison and the government building or administrative centre.

A single example of the Spanish town mansion, Diego Velázquez's villa on Plaza Céspedes in Santiago de Cuba, demonstrates how imported architectural designs from the Old World combined with modifications which climate demanded. Gold and copper were still being mined from the mountains above Santiago de Cuba when Velázquez began the construction of his impressive residence at the corner of the city square. The year was 1516, and Governor Velázquez intended that he should be housed in a mansion befitting that of the most influential individual in the New World. Much of the raw material for his mansion was imported from Spain. However, the precious woods of Cuba proved excellent materials from which to build the framework, the flooring and the embellishments which made this one of the grandest colonial mansions ever built in the Americas.

Built as a semi-fortress, Velázquez's villa was constructed on the traditional Spanish plan. It is austere and plain from the outside, but is striking within its high, whitewashed walls. The Spanish design of Andalusia and Castile ideally suited the hot Cuban climate, which made shade and shelter a priority. A large courtyard

Velázquez house, Santiago de Cuba

was laid out in the centre of the structure, which was enclosed on all four sides by the residential buildings. Facing the courtyard, the two-storey quadrangled building was surrounded by a wide verandah and cloister-like roofing overhangs.

A balcony runs around the inside of this building, overlooking the cobbled courtyard and railed around with finely turned Cuban hardwood supports. The entire grand palace design was built with cool and shade in mind. Wide doors, opening out onto the patio, provided a through-draught of air, while high windows in the outside wall ensured excellent air-conditioning. The deep long windows around the second storey, on the outside of the building, were enclosed on three sides by fretwork screens, copying the Moorish style. The windows could be closed from the inside with shutters. It had only been 24 years since the centuries-old Moorish occupation of the Spanish peninsula had finally been terminated by King Ferdinand and Queen Isabela, and many buildings in Spain had adopted Arab architectural features. Under the second-storey windows, which were topped by narrow, tiled roofs of their own and stood out from the wall of the house with their wooden fretwork screens, smaller windows, also with their own tiled roofing and screens, let light and air into the lower-floor rooms. Spanish architects adapted Moorish ideas by designing small, barred windows into door structures and often fitting shutters and wooden jalousies to the double-hinged full or half-doors which allowed privacy but encouraged refreshing breezes. In some Spanish-style buildings in the larger Caribbean islands, Moorish-style wind tunnels were built into the pitched and tiled roofs. This idea was perfected by the Moors, who had introduced ornate fenestration and cooling turrets which kept their Spanish interiors ventilated by any breezes which could be funnelled through the internal rooms. Before the introduction of mechanical fans, several of these innovations were introduced by local architects to encourage cooling draughts of air to pass through buildings.

On the side of Velázquez's villa, facing the main plaza, a small, open balcony was added in front of a second-floor doorway for observation and oratory purposes. The rooms were large and airy, with high ceilings and huge doors. The interior design was spectacularly ornate, with impressive hardwood ceilings, great cedar beams, carved embellishments and finely panelled doors. As in this case, many early colonial buildings were also constructed with a large gateway, closed by huge, heavy doors, through which the occupier could drive his carriage directly into the courtyard. This gave access to an integral carriage-house built into the main structure.

Unfortunately, many of the houses and mansions in the larger Caribbean islands which date from Velázquez's time and the following century, no longer exist intact. This is partly because most of the towns and cities went through several periods of economic decline and neglect and partly because many settlements were regularly ransacked and razed to the ground by pirates. Often, the building materials remaining after these attacks were cannibalized or recycled to build more modern structures. Tastes change, and towns also adapted the design of their buildings to suit climate, new trade patterns or changing aesthetic norms, and building design sometimes varied dramatically over the years. The dates of the affluence of a particular community or township can often be traced through its architecture.

The 17th and 18th centuries saw a rise of Baroque church architecture, with tapered pillars, spiral columns and decorated altars and retables. The Spanish penchant for coloured tiles (*azulejos*), was also replicated in New World architecture. The material used for many religious structures in the Hispanic islands of the Caribbean was the readily available fossilized coral, known as ironshore or *coquina*, a soft, porous limestone-like stone, comprised of millions of compressed coral skeletons and mollusc shells.

Baroque

Exuberant decoration, curviform arches and columns, extravagant ceilings and details

A reaction against simplicity of Classicism

Strongly Catholic imagery

In the later 18th century, contracts for public buildings and new churches went to popular Italian, French and Spanish architects, thus introducing a variety of neo-Classical styles into the Caribbean.

Neo-Classical

Dominant in Europe from the late 18th century to mid-19th century

Inspiration of Roman and Ancient Greek models, base on symmetry, simplicity and grandeur

Spreads to North America and Caribbean, most visible in Georgian pillars

British Building

Of the fifteen islands or island groups which were once British, the first island to be claimed was St Lucia in 1605, when the attempted settlement established by 67 English adventurers was quickly abandoned. Another failed attempt at English settlement had already been made by Captain Leight in what is now French Guyane, on the South American mainland. The third British claim was Barbados in 1615. This was followed in 1623 by the claim on St Kitts, and, in 1625, Tobago. However, no permanent settlement had been secured by the English until the early 1620s.

The first British buildings in the Caribbean were constructed in St Kitts, the 'Mother Colony' of the English. Fifteen settlers, under Sir Thomas Warner, arrived on St Kitts, in 1623, and established the first English base in the Caribbean further south from the landing at Sandy Point at a place named Old Road Town. Elsewhere in the West Indies, an English attempt at establishing a second foothold in Barbados was made in 1625 by Captain John Powell. This was followed by a more serious effort, in 1627, financed by Sir William Courteen. The site of the first major English building in the Caribbean, at Holetown, the initial settlement, is marked by the 1874 St James's Church. The original wooden church was said to have been erected in the 1660s. One of the finest examples of early English colonial architecture is St Nicholas Abbey on Barbados, a Jacobean great house built between 1650 and 1660 (see pages 110–11).

Jacobean

Refers to the reign of James I (1603-25)

Relatively plain exterior, with large windows, heavy and symmetrical

Preference for brick over stone and widespread use of gables

In 1628, settlers moved onto Nevis from nearby St Kitts, founding Jamestown, which was englufed in a tidal wave in 1690. St Thomas' Church, one of the earliest British churches in the West Indies, was built on Nevis in 1643. The 1640 Church of St Anthony, on Montserrat, predates it, but was reconstructed in 1730. Many early planters arrived in Barbados from the Guianas in South America, followed by colonists from Bristol, who established Speightstown, earning it the nickname of 'Little Bristol'. By 1625, the English had joined the Dutch in settling the Virgin Isands, with the English establishing themselves on St Croix. English settlers had gained Barbuda by 1628, and in 1632 a group of colonists from St Kitts, established themselves on Antigua and Montserrat.

During the first forty years of British colonization in the smaller islands of the Caribbean, the major structures were churches and plantation houses. By the 1640s, antagonism between French and British colonists necessitated the construction of defence buildings. It was from the 1650s that British building in the Caribbean began in earnest. Other foreign European countries were infiltrating the region, following the Spanish lead, and vying for their own place on the map. The Dutch and French were establishing themselves in the Caribbean, both on the sea and land, securing islands which the Spanish had either ignored, overlooked, or been deterred from settling because of the hostile presence of Caribs.

Defensive structures were a priority, as pirates and enemy action, as well as the understandably aggressive behaviour of indigenous groups, put any potential colony at risk. The first of these British fortifications in the Caribbean was Fort Charles, built on St Kitts in the 1650s to defend the inhabitants of Old Road Town from French raiders. At this time, many plantation mills were also being constructed as fortified buildings. Fort Ashby on nearby Nevis followed in the later half of the 1600s, and Fort Recovery on Tortola was built in 1660. A fort was built above Plymouth on Montserrat in 1664, followed by Brimstone Hill Fort on St Kitts in 1690 The Brimstone Hill fortress took 100 years to build, and is one of the largest fortifications in the Caribbean.

Unlike the Spanish and French settlers in the region, who quickly adapted to their new environment, the early English arrivals initially felt that the West Indies was a temporary posting. They were, in any case, a mixed collection of individuals. The majority of early colonists were either indentured workers, contracted to labour for five years on the plantations (the Welshman and future pirate, Henry Morgan, was one such contract worker), or were convicted criminals and other undesirables, shipped to the colonies as cheap labour. Then there were the wealthy, funded by investors gambling on quick returns, who sought to recreate their familiar northern European surroundings. Indeed, many prospecting gentry sailed to the Caribbean to lay claim to land, then returning with a plantation manager left behind to look after sugar or cotton production. The labour force had little to look forward to, apart from escape, usually into piracy, and the landed gentry and plantation managers lived for their eventual repatriation to England.

While the workers plotted release from their toil on the sugar plantations, the rich and powerful made the most of what they considered a temporary exile in the unhealthy and uncomfortable tropics. Determined to live in some style, they recruited architects and the best stone masons from the metropole, ordering re-creations of their temperate homeland among the Caribbean palms. No expense was spared in making the plantation owner's life agreeable, and some of these efforts were nothing short of incongruous in the circumstances. Food and drink took priority, with immense quantities of both being imported to provide feasts of incredible self-indulgence. One plantation master of the 18th century reputedly had a marble pond built in his garden, into which, for one party, he had poured 1,200 bottles of Malaga wine, 1,200 bottles of rum, the juice from 2,600 lemons, boiling water, sugar and 200 powdered nutmegs!

Apart from such social excesses, the 18th-century British plantocracy's architectural ostentation was also legendary, as grandiose mansions dominated each estate, competing in their Palladian splendour. On the whole, the British colonies were more oriented towards the rural great house than the town house, and it is noticeable that former British settlements like Kingston or Bridgetown lack much of the sophistication of cities such as Havana or Basse-Terre. The British colonial elite preferred its luxuries in the countryside and, as a result, its towns – mostly ports and trading centres – remained architecturally humdrum in comparison to those of the urban-minded Spanish. For a century the dominant style was Georgian, with the emphasis on the well-proportioned elegance to be found in English country houses. But the desire to replicate the familiar took another form, and parishes were founded in the colonies, each with its own church. In Barbados, arguably the most 'English' of Caribbean islands, the dual influence of country house and parish church is most strongly in evidence.

Georgian

Relating to period from George I to George IV (1714-1830)

Imitation of Classical style, but on smaller scale, with columns and pediments

Plain exteriors, sash windows, elaborate interiors

This island boasts many excellent examples of British colonial architecture, and they stand as testament to the stubborn attitude of early planners and builders. In attempts to replicate the styles of their home country, they often made little concession to local climate and conditions. Many mansions were hastily erected, their owners soon finding the buildings stiflingly hot in the tropical humidity. The settlers' places of worship were similarly vulnerable to an alien climate. Across Barbados numerous churches were erected in a style familiar to the British-born builders, only to suffer damage or destruction in a succession of hurricanes.

St Michael's Cathedral in Bridgetown, Barbados, is a good example of the determination of the settlers to surround themselves with the trappings of the 'old country'. It was the island's first site of worship, initially built of wood until replaced by a new structure between 1661 and 1665. Deciding to abandon wood in favour of something more permanent, the authorities called in stone masons. What followed, however, was a catalogue of mishaps. The vaulted barrel roof, with no centre supports, pushed the cathedral's walls outwards, necessitating the erection of buttresses, which, in the English Gothic period, would have been integral to the original plans. Under the great roof span, the north wall and porch had to be demolished and rebuilt, and problems constantly dogged successive builders until a hurricane in 1780 toppled the entire structure.

In the process of rebuilding, it was realized that a squat, square tower was much less susceptible to storm damage, and architects in 1784 looked back to Gothic English style for their inspiration. The only Georgian element employed in the new building was the porch detail. This cathedral represented the first instance of Gothic revival in the whole of the British West Indies, and it was not for another fifty years that neo-Gothic church architecture became fashionable. This trend, in the 1820s, led to many replicas of English Gothic-style churches being constructed on the sites of earlier wooden buildings throughout the island. The legacy of this passion for neo-Gothic religious architecture is imprinted on the Barbadian countryside, with delightful replicas of English village churches sheltering under palm trees and surrounded by tropical vegetation.

St Michael's Cathedral, Barbados

The French Presence

Following the Spanish into the New World, the French were the first European nation to make their presence known in the Americas. Although the Portuguese had speculated on challenging Spanish superiority, the papal Treaty of Tordesillas (1494) precluded their incursion into the New World apart from their colonization of the eastern part of South America, now known as Brazil. It was the French Crown which commissioned the first challenge to the Spanish in their exclusive New World territories in the early 1500s, even though the French sea-going forces were mostly manned by mercenaries, often Italian. It is interesting to note that the Spanish subsequently used Italian architects to devise the defences of their strategic harbours in the Americas, and also that Spain had commissioned an Italian to discover the rich new lands in the west!

The French, although making an impact on Spanish shipping in the Caribbean by attacking treasure fleets, did not establish themselves on land until the late 1500s. French pirates and buccaneers, together with cattle hunters, built a stockaded settlement on Tortuga, a small isolated island off the north-east coast of Hispaniola. This was probably one of the first French structures to be built in the Caribbean. Several times, the Spanish, then in control of Hispaniola, tried to oust the itinerant settlers from the island, as they posed a threat to Spanish shipping. For a while, a group of English buccaneers held the island, and in 1630 and 1634 the Spanish made concerted efforts to disperse the settlers. In the 1640s, a French Protestant leader, Le Vasseur, sailed for Tortuga from French-held St Kitts and established a stone-built fort in the island, which he named the 'dovecote'. Meanwhile, in the smaller islands to the east, France had established colonies on Guadeloupe and Martinique by 1635, and taken part of St Kitts from the English in 1625. In all these places, settlers were to quick to build forts.

Unlike the mostly reluctant early English settlers, many of the French arriving in the Caribbean were keen to make the best of their lot and to put down more permanent roots. The majority of French colonists were neither indentured labourers or criminals, but volunteers, some of noble background, who had paid the Compagnie des Isles d'Amérique for their passage. Later, galley slaves were freed on condition that they joined the workforce, and they were accompanied, in turn, by significant numbers of military personnel, traders and even missionaries.

Not only did the French set about fortifying their new possessions, but they also began building trends that were, in many cases, more appropriate to the climate than the British equivalents. This was perhaps because some of the French settlers already had experience of warmer climates than the British and adapted architectural details from Mediterranean traditions. One early French-built structure in St Kitts should be mentioned, however, as it seemingly contradicts this theory.

In the 1640s, the French Governor of the Antilles, the Chevalier Knight of Malta, Phillipe de Longvilliers de Poincy, decided to build the greatest house ever to be constructed in the Lesser Antilles, on a 1,000-ft high hill just outside Basseterre. His grandiose, oblong, four-storey Château La Fontaine, in red brick and stone, surmounted by a lookout post, was set in vast, Louis XIII-style formal gardens, with high double walls surrounding the grounds and the estate. His aim was to create a Caribbean Versailles ahead of its time, but the building is now in ruins, devastated by an earthquake in 1690. Since plundered for building material, the remains, including the chapel, grotto, entrance to underground stables and steps, can be traced in the Fountain Estate, now private property. De Poincy is remembered, however, as his name was given to the flamboyant tree's flower, the royal poinciana.

French town houses, St Pierre, Martinique

> ### Louis XIII
> **Refers to reign of French King (1601-43)**
> **French château style, with restrained exteriors windows emphasized and formal gardens**
> **Ornate interiors, featuring gilt and carvings**

Subsequent French plantation houses were much less ambitious and included details like dormer windows, verandahs, balconies and louvred shutters, all contributing to the provision of shade and ventilation. Wherever the French settled, they took their distinctive architectural innovations with them, like the fish-scale tiles, typical in the roofs of early French buildings. These tiles, specially made in potteries in the French islands, are still notable in places such as Grenada, St Lucia and Dominica, which the French temporarily colonized in the 18th and early 19th centuries.

Many early French houses were elaborately decorated in fretwork and 'gingerbread', and were well suited to the climate with the introduction of latticed hoods over windows, 'cooler windows' and diagonal work 'ventilators' in wood. The French were certainly more innovative in their building styles than the British, continually adapting their architecture to develop an attractive yet practical building style. Their urban architecture was also more developed, although little of this remains from the 17th and 18th centuries, especially the rococo phase. The city of St Pierre was one of the finest and most elegant of Caribbean settlements, with all the refinements of a European urban centre, until its appalling destruction in 1902. Fires and hurricanes have ravished Fort-de-France, and Port-au-Prince in Haiti has been submerged under recent slum developments, but in a city like Cap-Haïtien it is still possible to see traces of French colonial flair.

Rococo

Fashionable in France between 1700 and 1750, a reaction to the Baroque pomp of Louis XIV period

Characterized by curved forms and gentle pastel colours

Emphasis on interiors, with use of metalwork

The French were also instrumental in importing iron and steel as building materials, and churches, public buildings and private residences in Martinique and Guadeloupe show their versatility. The idea of building in iron in lands which experienced violent storms and the occasional earthquake soon caught on, and cathedrals, market halls and great houses were constructed throughout the Caribbean from the 1870s onwards. Railings, balconies and brackets in ornamental cast iron also began to proliferate.

The Dutch and Scandinavians

The Dutch, adept slave traders, arrived in the Caribbean as a sea-borne force in the early 1600s. It was important for the Dutch to quickly establish centres near to the Spanish shipping routes, from where they could ply their trade. The Spanish supply routes from Europe to the New World followed the north coast of South America, with ships stopping at Margarita, Cubagua and South

American continental outposts such as Cartagena and Maracaibo. Thus the three islands of Aruba, Bonaire and Curaçao were ideal slave-trading bases for the Dutch merchants.

On a couple of the islands, potential Dutch colonists found that itinerant pirates had already built crude fortresses, like that at Bushiribana on Aruba (see page 83), one of the New World's oldest European structures outside Hispaniola. The Dutch immediately set about building their own defensive trading posts, centred around large forts. The first structure to be built by the Dutch in the Caribbean was that at Fort Kyk-over-al, in the Essequibo region of Guyana in 1621. This fort was used as a slave trading post, dealing not only in imported slaves from Africa, but also local slaves, whom the Dutch supplied to the Spanish.

The second Dutch foothold in the Caribbean was erected under Van Walbeeck of the Dutch West India Company, who built Fort Amsterdam in Curaçao in 1642. It was important to secure the three islands of Aruba, Bonaire and Curaçao, not only because of their convenient location to the Spanish sea routes, but because of the increasing presence of foreign European navies in the Spanish Main. The Dutch forts, although not as impressive as their Spanish counterparts, were substantially built in strategic locations, initially on Curaçao, the largest island of the three in the southern Caribbean.

Meanwhile, other Dutch adventurers in the employ of the Dutch West India Company, established in 1621, had secured an island in the Leewards, Sint Maarten, constructing a fort in 1620 to protect their shipping, which sheltered in the southern coves. The Company also found an ideally secluded harbour on a nearby island, Sint Eustatius, building Fort Oranje above a large deep bay in 1636. So, by the 1640s the Dutch controlled not only a base on the important Spanish routes in the southern Caribbean, but two strategic islands in the Leewards to the north.

Aruba and Bonaire, the other two islands of the south Caribbean, initially occupied by the Spanish but quickly secured by the Dutch, although important for their salt production, were not fortified by the Dutch colonists until the late 1700s. Fort Zoutman on Aruba, for example, was built in 1796 and is the island's oldest structure. Although the early Dutch fortifications on the three islands are interesting in themselves, it is the typical Dutch architectural styles found in the capitals of Aruba and Curaçao particularly that are outstanding. With the typical curvilinear gables and dormer pediments of the two- and three-storey merchants' houses built in the early 1700s, buildings like the 1708 Penha House in Curaçao's capital combine the architectural styles of Holland with the bright colours of the Caribbean.

Early Dutch Caribbean town architecture is distinctive and incongruous under the tropical sun. The first settlers copied more or less exactly the architectural styles of 17th-century Holland, with high-rise buildings crammed close together to save space and money. This parsimony seems curious in colonies where space was almost unlimited, but research suggests that the onus was put on the town planner to economize with space, especially in Curaçao's capital Willemstad, where the original plans allotted small building plots to the town's first families. During this period, much of the building material was imported from Holland, including decorative Dutch tiles.

Dutch Caribbean

Flat exteriors, with typical curved gables

Detailed brickwork, red-orange tiled roofs, use of pastel colours

Emphasis on commercial buildings, such as warehouses

Penha House, Curaçao

It was not until the early days of the 18th century that the Dutch colonists began adapting their architecture to the Caribbean climate. In order to expand their living space and provide much-needed shade, they began to build galleries onto the facades of their houses, a trend probably stemming from styles observed in the Spanish Caribbean colonies. Arcades and bulbous columned colonnades followed, while those buildings on the town's outskirts – where there was more space – added grand staircases and enclosed patios.

Inland, especially on Curaçao and Aruba, the 18th- and 19th-century plantation houses or *landhuizen* are constructed in a unique colonial style, with old Dutch facades, tiled roofs, central staircase and verandahs contrasting with the local peasant houses, which are basic thatched or iron-roofed, square-built huts. Even more basic are the tiny slave huts on Bonaire, built in the 1850s to house the workers on the nearby salt pans.

For six years from 1666-1672 Danish merchants, under the auspices of the Danish West Indies and Guinea Company, held the tiny island of St Thomas in the Virgin Islands group, moving onto nearby St Croix in 1733. Eventually Denmark held each of what are now the US Virgin Islands – St Croix, St Thomas and St John – selling them and their adjacent islets to the United States for $25 million in 1917. The Danish architectural influence on these islands was hence significant.

As soon as the Danes arrived on St Thomas, they began building Fort Christian, completed in 1671. By 1680, there were 46 sugar plantations on St Thomas, and 92 on St John by 1730, but it was on St Croix that the Danes' most prosperous plantations flourished, producing a wider and more opulent range of architectural styles than those of either St Thomas or St John. The well laid out towns of Christiansted and Fredriksted reflected the wealth of the southermost island of the Virgin group. Conversely, the town of Charlotte Amalie on St Thomas was not planned to the same extent, and St John, even now, has no settlement of any size larger than a village. Danish architects left a number of military installations on several Caribbean islands. Three of these are particularly outstanding: on St Thomas, Bluebeard's Castle or Fort Skytsborg, and Fort Christian, and on St Croix, Fort Frederik.

The Swedish have fleeting connections with the Caribbean, but their 93-year stay in command of tiny St Barts from 1784, when they bought it from France, gave them the opportunity to leave a certain Swedish stamp in the region. There is now, however, scant evidence of any Swedish occupation in the Caribbean after Mother Nature took her toll. When the Swedish arrived on St Barts, traded for valuable Baltic trading rights, they found that the French had left their architectural legacy in the main port, Le Carenage, which the Swedish re-named Gustavia after their King. Four forts were erected around the oblong-shaped inlet to protect the small settlement. But subsequent hurricanes, and a great fire in 1852, destroyed almost all traces of Swedish architecture, except stone dividing walls and the belfry of an early Swedish church.

The American Influence

Nowhere is the influence of North American architecture more striking than in the Bahamas, where the mixture of imported and local traditions can best be seen in Nassau. After the American War of Independence from 1776, rebels from the original thirteen states known as Loyalists because of their loyalty to King George I, fled to the Bahamas. The British had already colonized several of the 700 islands, with the first settlers coming from Bermuda in 1648. Around 8,000 Americans and their slaves established settlements throughout the Bahamas, creating plantations of cotton, and communities based on the cultivation of aloes and citrus fruits.

Lord Dunmore, the last Governor of Virgina, was one of the refugees, and proved to be one of the most prolific builders of that era. As Governor of the Bahamas, he built a number of fortifications and grand houses, including his own villa at Dunmore Town on Harbour Island, Eleuthera. The new population recreated their former plantation houses on the islands. Beautiful porticoed Carolina plantation-style mansions were erected alongside typically English village-style churches, and Georgian mansions rubbed shoulders with Louisiana-style villas. All the buildings acknowledged the tropical climate, with high ceilings, shutters and ventilation adaptations, although the typically English sash windows and overall design were retained in most cases.

By around 1800, the poor soil of the Bahamas led to the decline of agriculture and the plantations, and many Loyalists returned to mainland America or emigrated further south, establishing them-

Jacaranda House, Nassau

selves in the British islands of the Leewards and Windwards and on Jamaica. Some settlers reverted to the practice of wrecking, or ship-building. Some migrants even packed their clapboard houses onto schooners and resettled on the islands of the Florida Keys.

The variety of building styles on the 'Out Islands' varied greatly from those grand houses and public buildings in the large towns such as Nassau. Most of these simple buildings were wood framed, with weather-boarded walls, cranked, shingled roofs, and with English-style, sash windows. Cut limestone coral blocks supported the homes above the ground, while water shortages necessitated specialized guttering systems which channelled rainwater into underground cisterns. Many buildings also showed signs of the shipwright's skills, being pegged together with wooden dowels instead of nails, and with chamfered posts and curved supports, typical of shipbuilders' carpentry.

By the early 1900s, American entrepreneurs also migrated to Cuba, the Dominican Republic and Puerto Rico, with the lure of riches to be made in the sugar and tobacco businesses. Puerto Rico had fallen into US hands in 1898 after the Spanish-American War, while Cuba was effectively a US protectorate. The Marines were also to occupy the Dominican Republic (1916-1925) and Haiti (1915-1934), opening the way for huge US investments and the arrival of speculators of all sorts. They imported with them the fashionable building styles of mainland America, particularly noticable in cities such as San Juan and the more modern districts of Santo Domingo. In the 1920s, the advent of tourism brought more riches to the islands of the Greater Antilles, particularly to Havana, where vast hotels were built to house battalions of tourists. Cuba became an offshore playground for America's rich, famous and notorious, with both Irene Dupont, the explosives magnate, and Al Capone, the gangster, building mansions in resort areas. Dupont's 'Xanadu' and Capone's beachside retreat are typical of the period, both built in the eclectic styles of the 1920s and 1930s. From Art Nouveau and Art Deco styles, the buildings in Havana became more ambitious into the 1940s and 1950s, when investment in tourism and gambling boomed.

Asiatic Architecture

The first appearance of Islamic architecture in the Caribbean came not with the arrival of Muslims in the region, but with the first Spanish colonists. Mudéjar influences were incorporated into Spanish architecture as a direct result of 800 years of Moorish presence in the Iberian peninsula, which ended only in 1492. The first wave of Spanish builders hence brought with them a style that was a mixture of European Plateresque or late Gothic, Renaissance and Arabic architecture. It combined ornate Gothic with traditional features of Muslim design, in which the depiction of natural forms was forbidden. The main Arabic features of this synthetic style, which was an extension of the earlier Mozarabic style, adopted the *ajimeces* or horseshoe window arches and geometric wooden ceilings among others, but embellished them with Gothic and Plateresque decoration.

Mudéjar

Moorish influence adapted by Europeans

Particularly conspicuous in elaborate wooden ceilings, window surrounds and colonnades

Ornamental brickwork and tiling

By the 17th century, this architectural trend was abandoned in favour of the more popular Renaissance and Baroque. A number of examples of early Mudéjar nevertheless exist to this day in Cuba, the Dominican Republic and Puerto Rico in cathedrals, monasteries, convents and in some domestic and municipal buildings. But this mixed architectural style, as deployed by the early colonists, was not truly Islamic, for it appeared mostly in explicitly Christian buildings and only incorporated Islamic features by a quirk of history and culture.

The advent of emancipation in the 1830s and 1840s presented the Caribbean's plantation owners with an immense problem. Although many freed slaves opted to continue working on the plantations as paid labourers, many chose the independence of a small plot of land and a peasant existence. The resulting dearth of labour threatened to cripple the traditional plantation-based economy of the islands. Looking around for alternative sources of labour, the colonial authorities invited free African labourers, indentured Europeans and Americans to fill the shortage. But by far the biggest influx of new workers came from India, contracted as fixed-term

Islamic mosque, Trinidad

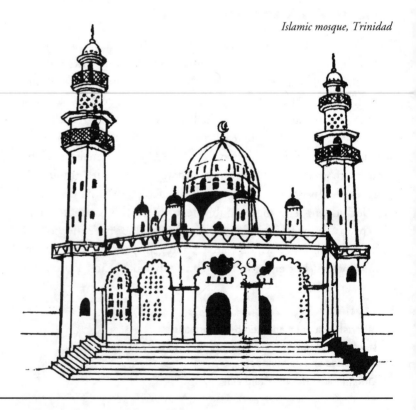

indentured labourers. From 1845 to 1917, some 150,000 Indians came to Trinidad alone, some returning home after their fixed term but the great majority remaining in the island. Chinese immigration also began in 1849, but the numbers were much smaller. Indian workers also arrived in significant numbers in mainland Guyana, Jamaica, Martinique, Guadeloupe and some smaller eastern Caribbean islands.

Initially, the Indian and Chinese communities had little influence on the region's architecture, mainly because they were poorly paid – and largely marginalized – indentured workers. But as the population became more established and wealthier, Indian Hindu temples and Muslim mosques were built, the most impressive being those in Trinidad and Martinique. These holy buildings were constructed in classic design, with minarets and domes intricately decorated with marble, multi-coloured tiles and mosaic work. Orn-- ately stylized verses from the Koran decorate mosque surfaces, and geometric designs predominate in pierced windows, ceilings and doors. Columns and arches replicate traditional Islamic architectural traits in use throughout the world, and glazed brickwork and tiling are prevalent in both mosques and temples. Hindu temples commemorate the religion's various deities, while Islamic mosques adhere to the traditional non-representation of natural forms.

The Hut, the *Case* and the Chattel

The most integral architectural feature of the Caribbean landscape is the dwelling of the majority of the populace, those who work the land. The rural hut is to be found all over the region, but it takes many forms, includes a range of details and reflects each island's particular historical and ethnic background. The agricultural nature of the islands and surrounding territories dictated the style of this vernacular architecture, based on local requirements, the availability of building materials and prevailing climatic conditions.

Basic requirements include – and have always included – living space, a cooking area, a cultivation area, a washing area, a space for domestic waste and an area for domestic animals. The dwelling must have ventilation, shade and shelter, protection from vermin and divisions for privacy. As many of the early basic huts or shelters were constructed by African slaves or the descendants of slaves, the experience of building shelters initially derived much from the African mainland. However, in some cases, particularly on those islands settled by the Spanish, the indigenous population had spent many centuries developing and improving a particular style of dwelling. On these islands, the attributes of indigenous dwellings were adopted by both European settlers and their African slaves alike.

African Influence

In the Spanish-occupied islands, both Europeans and slaves, used the Amerindian *bohío* style of construction, adapting it to their needs and requirements. However, in the islands occupied and developed by other European nations, a combination of African and European styles of building evolved. Naturally, as Europeans established themselves in the larger islands of the Caribbean before the advent of African slaves, their influence on the primitive country dwelling was substantial. Had Africans arrived in the Caribbean first, it is possible that the 'rondoval', or round, palm-thatched African mud hut and its integral compound, might have been prevalent. Certainly, elements of Africa's architecture and design sense found their way into Caribbean architecture, especially as the basic requirements for dwellings were similar to both regions.

It is important to look for any evidence of African architecture which was least influenced by European construction methods, to determine which other building elements arrived with the slave population from Africa. The best examples can be seen in those South American territories bordering the Caribbean Sea. In the 1700s, a group of African slaves escaped from French and English plantations in Suriname. They set up their independent black community on the banks of the Maroni River, living off the land. They were named Bosnegers or 'Wood Blacks'. From the indigenous Arawaks, with whom they mixed, they adopted some elements of construction, taking the low, ridge-roofed style of family day-hut, and rejecting the round, mud hut of their African ancestors and the round, wattle construction of the Arawaks' smaller sleeping huts.

Initially, the Bosnegers copied the Arawak communal hut design, known as the *ajoupa*, where the ridged, palm frond-thatched roof reached the ground each side, forming triangular gable ends. This meant that the shelter had to be accessed from one or another of the gable ends. In a community of these structures, the front or entrance gable end faced onto the main thoroughfare or central compound. The flooring was of packed mud, spread with regularly changed rushes or palm fronds. The Arawak ridge-roofed huts were not used for sleeping, but for shelter during daytime activities, being open to the elements on three or often four sides. The Bosnegers soon adopted the raised roof of the open Arawak day-huts, forming wattle or woven walls without daub, enclosing the structure on all four sides. The entrance to the hut was notably from the gable end, probably deriving from the design of the ajoupa. In most islands of the Caribbean, main access is predominantly from the long side of the hut. Thus, the earliest known dwellings of escaped African slaves took their building designs from both their African homeland, and from the indigenous Arawak population.

There is just one other example similar to the Bosnegers' adaptation of building design and the development of hut construction without European influence. In 1675, a cargo of African slaves bound for Barbados ran aground off St Vincent. The escaped slaves quickly mingled with the indigenous Caribs, known as the 'Yellow Caribs', becoming a mixed community known as 'Black Caribs'. For over a hundred years, the Black Caribs lived independently on St Vincent, with their lifestyle – and particularly their building skills – untainted by European influences. Towards the end of the 18th century, the fiercely independent Black Caribs were transported by the British to the island of Roatán, off Honduras, where they mixed with islanders of Mayan descent, evolving into a community known as Garifuna. On Roatán, the Garifuna adapted to a fishing-oriented style of living, adopting the local-style of stilt dwelling or the *barbacoa* found in many coastal areas of Caribbean South America inhabited by Caiquito tribes. These were primitive, thatched huts, often built over the water. Many Garifuna emigrated from Roatán to Belize in the 1830s, bringing with them elements of the building styles which had picked up attributes from the St Vincent Caribs, the coastal peoples of Honduras, the Caiquitos and their distant homeland of Africa. It was only when the Garifuna arrived in Belize that they were exposed to European construction techniques, quickly losing the ancient skills of basic hut building.

The black populations of the Caribbean islands, under the coercive influence of their European masters, incorporated architectural elements from both their own traditions and those which the

Europeans had brought with them. Just as the Bosnegers drew their building styles from their surroundings, so the island slaves borrowed from imported European designs. The wattle and daub of both African and early European construction was employed for walls and division building in the basic slave hut. Instead of the round African hut, wattle and daub lent itself more to a basic square-built construction. Palm-thatching was used for the roofing, which was initially pointed with four triangular sides.

Once board walls substituted wattle, the entrance became more emphasized, with the front of the hut remaining in one gable end. Instead of a beaten earth floor, an integral wooden floor was incorporated, enabling the building to be raised from the ground on supports and thereby deterring pests. Because of a preference for sleeping on mats on the floor (rather than beds or hammocks) in an environment infested with insects, rodents and snakes, the raised floor was a major innovation. The wood of the flooring also had to be raised to protect it from rot. The basic hut was used as sleeping quarters only, with washing, cooking and other domestic activities conducted out of doors. Outside areas were divided off for the kitchen, wash-area and domestic animal compounds, with rude wattle partitions forming windbreaks and giving a little privacy – much as compounds are divided in West Africa.

With the use of planking walls, windows could be let into the walls for ventilation. Previously, the wattle walls allowed breezes to circulate through the building. Solid, side-hinged shutters closed off the window openings from the outside, a typically African trait, as opposed to the use of jalousies, which allowed air to circulate but ensured privacy. The African preference for tightly shutting up living quarters was remarked upon by early diarists of social habits in the Caribbean colonies.

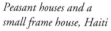

Peasant houses and a small frame house, Haiti

European Design

Basic building design elsewhere in the Caribbean, whether it was that of black slaves or struggling white settlers and labourers who lived independently of the plantation economy, borrowed heavily from European architecture. The style of hut building on the French-occupied islands shows heavy evidence of domestic features. The French-style basic hut is known as the *case*, or as in Guadeloupe the case *aménagée* or 'fitted out hut'. In Martinique, in particular, a traditional half-timbered style of hut building is evident, and on Martinique, Haiti and St Barthélémy the ground is prepared and foundations built before the structure is erected. In Guadeloupe, the preparation of a base is noticeably absent, as many huts are moveable in the style of chattel buildings. Foundation style depended primarily on the ground surface, whether rock or earth, and therefore varied from island to island.

The preparation of the base of the hut is typically European in origin. The inclement conditions of northern Europe dictated that the base be prepared so that surface water was diverted away from the floor of the hut. Thus, huts were built with their floors separated from the ground on pilings or on a gravel bed. As sanitation in the temperate climate was necessarily located indoors, waste was disposed of in a custom-built channel running under the floor of the hut. In the tropics, however, sanitation was predominantly outdoors, although surface water was avoided by raising the hut's floor. The wooden floor also had to be separated from the damp ground. In the French islands, the influence of ship-building techniques is also conspicuous. Characteristically, joints are mortise and tenon, with wooden pegs substituting nails. Indeed, some very large structure were built entirely without the use of iron nails, a structural method which allowed much more movement in adverse wind conditions, as with the movement in the framework of ships at sea. On most of the French-occupied islands of the Caribbean, roofs followed a traditional hipped style with four slopes, a predominant feature in the construction of huts in St Barthélémy. As this island was comparatively untouched by the sugar plantation industry, its architectural style evolved independently of the influences of other Caribbean islands.

The most conspicuous European feature of the Caribbean hut is the entrance, which is inevitably located in the long side – as opposed to the gable end of the dwelling. The hut is commonly built with the long side and its entrance facing the road or path. Often the entrance is located in the centre of the long side, following the typical European tradition of incorporating a window opening on either side of the door. The doorway then becomes the focal point of the whole and its decorated and embellished as such, often with colour and sometimes with fretwork. As the hut was usually raised above the ground, steps would be built up to the doorway, cementing the door as the focal point. In many of huts in British colonies, a roofed porch would be added, strengthening the doorway as a feature.

Typical rural house,
St Barthélémy

Later additions included a raised wooden platform on the front long side of the hut and a porch roof, often covering the outside platform. The jalousie or louvred fenestration covering, as opposed to solid shutters, was in use in northern Europe long before it was introduced into the West Indies. These are found on most of the European-style huts as a direct import, usually from France, and are found in the buildings of the European population, unlike the solid shutters of the African-descended population. The English hut was almost exclusively built with a ridge roof of two sloping sides, forming two gable ends with apexes to the roof peak.

The Modular Dwelling

With the advent of the sugar industry and extensive plantations, workers on the French- and British-ruled islands were mostly African slaves, and their accommodation followed the basic concept of a thatched, ridged roof, an entrance in the gable end, and solid fenestration shutters. But labour shortages plagued the plantation economy, and white, European indentured labour was also introduced towards the end of the 17th century. With European workers, some voluntary and others forced, came European styles of hut construction, many solid, fixed structures built for permanence and replicating many features of European domestic architecture.

Plantation workers were often moved around as a matter of necessity. Therefore, a permanent structure was incompatible with the need to move workers around the plantation or from one plantation to another, and a moveable hut style was required. Known as the modular building, the moveable dwelling had been used in some of the plantations in the colonies of North America. It is thought that the trade link between Barbados and the American colonies led to the modular hut's introduction into the British-occupied islands of the West Indies. This style of worker's dwelling spread quickly throughout the English islands from Barbados, apart from St Lucia, which was French-occupied for long periods. The modular hut is a lightweight construction, prefabricated in wood, and twice the length of its width and no more than ten ft wide. It is tall and narrow with a ridged roof, often with barge-boards on each gable.

A door, let into the long side, reached from floor to roof, facing the street with a window on each side of the door. Windows might also be let into the gable ends of the hut. Set on its own platform, the entrance was reached by steps. To increase the size of the modular hut, another identical hut could be added to the rear of the original. When the hut needed to be removed to a location nearer a new working area of the plantation, the entire structure was dismantled, as on Barbados, in flat sections which were reassembled at the new site. In Barbados, this type of worker's dwelling was commonly known as a chattel house.

In Guadeloupe, where the structure of the module is slightly different, the entire strucure was

Wooden frame houses, Antigua

put onto an ox-cart and removed wholesale. In The Bahamas, notably on the Out Islands, where wooden-built houses were traditionally pegged together in a manner typical of the shipwright's craft, the entire building could be dismantled like a kit. This was found useful when the economy of the islands slumped and many settlers dismantled their houses, loaded them onto the decks of inter-island schooners and moved, lock, stock and barrel, to the Florida Keys. It was not uncommon for simple Bahamian houses to be removed to different locations on an island by donkey or mule cart.

The French style of modular building was said also to have originated in the Eastern American states and not, as once thought, in Louisiana. These were square, one-roomed huts with an opening in each side. When three of these square modules were linked together, the space in the remaining corner was used as a porch, with a corner verandah. This style of worker's accommodation was also later popular on Puerto Rico and on Dutch Aruba. On some islands, like those of the Bahamas, if a hurricane took away part of a building, the space would be repaired, not rebuilt, creating some unusual housing designs, some with entire rooms missing.

In all cases, as these simple buildings were constructed mainly or entirely of wood, cooking facilities and those for boiling water were housed in a structure built some distance from the main house, as a fire preventative. This requirement initiated the idea of a backyard or cooking and laundry area, often including a space for domesticated animals.

Materials

Hut construction was often limited to the types of building materials available. These varied from island to island. The basic materials used in the primitive bohío of the Greater Antilles came from one tree, the Royal Palm, while wattle and daub was popular in most of the British Caribbean. In the case of the very early slave huts on some islands like Barbados and the Dutch islands of Aruba, Bonaire and Curaçao, stone took over from wattle and daub where it was easily quarried. In most instances of the Caribbean popular house – the hut, case, cabin, chattel house or module – wood is the main material used for construction. In some cases, the timber frame was overlaid with thatch, wooden shingles, boarding, or, much later, brickwork. A distinctive innovation in such houses on the Bahamas was the addition of a beading, fixed along the lower edge of each board of the building's facing. The boards were cut from Jacksonville pine, cedar or a local tree often known as casuarina. This beading effectively sealed the gaps between each plank, and protected the vulnerable lower edge of the board from rot. Shingles were generally cut from casuarina or from the coconut palm tree trunk. In some cases, the gaps in boarding or shingling were caulked or filled with the copra or fibres from coconut husks, a trick learned from shipbuilders.

Bricks were scarce until well into the late 19th century, and were first introduced as a building material when imported to the Caribbean as ballast on English, Dutch and French ships. The first brick kiln was established on Martinique in the 1690s, producing both bricks and tiles. Roofing tiles were also produced in a factory established in Trinidad de Cuba in the late 1500s. Roofing materials were initially natural, like palm thatch, hay, straw, sugar bagasse, maize or sorghum stalks, or were made of wood shingles. Brick was sometimes used as a roofing material, until tiles or corrugated iron became popular. Only on St Barthélémy and in the Bahamas were roofs pitched or hipped, as on all other islands, the popular house had a ridged or gable roof or, occasionally, a four-sided sloping roof. In some cases, the roof was extended outwards to form a gallery or a porch.

House foundations varied from island to island throughout the Caribbean, except in the case of the moveable chattel houses which generally rested on a bed of stones, to protect the floor from humidity. The primitive Haitian case rested directly on the ground, anchored by wooden posts extending down from the main frame. Some houses rested on concrete or stone pilings, while Puerto Rican modules rested on posts sunk into the ground. Those on St Barthélémy were supported on a base of evenly matched stones.

Cut coral stone blocks supported the pine houses of the Loyalists who emigrated from America to the Bahamas in the late 1700s. Many house designs also took advantage of sloping terrain to create a space under the building, which circulated air and kept out rodents and pests. The rear of the house would rest on the slope of a hillside, while concrete, stone blocks or wooden pillars supported the protruding section.

The Architecture of Production

The early days of mining and agricultural production in the Caribbean spurred the development of various architectural adaptations relating to the processing of crops and minerals. Whether basic shelters in which workers were housed, buildings used for storing or processing a product, or large complexes which combined the requirements of entire plantations, these structures were unique to the Caribbean's essentially agricultural development. There were around twenty major natural industries in the early history of the Caribbean, each one of which left its own architectural landmark on one or more islands.

Aloe Vera and Cochineal

Aloes were in great demand for use as a purgative and as the basis for various lotions. Aloes are an extract of the aloe vera plant, very much like a cactus or sisal plant. Thriving in a dry, barren climate, this profitable product was a mainstay of the islands of the Dutch Caribbean, particularly arid Aruba and Bonaire. Cochineal, the red dye extracted by crushing a minute insect, the *Dactylopius coccus*, was also produced here. This insect lives only on a certain cactus, the Opuntia or Prickly Pear, and must be picked off the prickly leaves by hand. Even the famous red coats of the British army were coloured with cochineal. Flax and sisal, used in making linen and rope, were also grown on these islands, and a tannin was produced from the divi-divi tree, a species unique to the southern Dutch Antilles. The architectural legacy from these industries is to be found in the country estate buildings known as landhuizen and slave huts. There are also large, specially laid-out flat areas where these products were processed.

Cacao

Cacao, indigenous to the Americas, grows as beans inside a large fleshy pod and has to go through several processes before being exported. The pod is split, and the seeds or nibs are removed from the pith, then washed, and sun-dried on vast trays known as *glacis* or *boucans*. These trays, often made of metal, were usually on wheels, with which they could be quickly moved under cover in case of rain.

The cocoa beans were then stored in warehouses for export. Several of the cacao glacis and drying trays still remain. Good examples of the cacao industry's old buildings can be seen on the island of Dominica. Much evidence of the old processing methods can also be found in the Dominican Republic, one of the world's largest producers.

Coconuts

Some early experiments in growing coconuts were confined to Trinidad and St Vincent, which now has one of the world's largest plantations. Coconuts were grown mainly for the meat and husk, which produced copra and coir, and for the coconut oil extracted from the coconut meat. Not only did this process require a large drying area, but extensive warehousing.

Coffee

Coffee was initially introduced into the French Caribbean in the 1720s, but the crop did not develop commercially until Britain reduced its excise duty on coffee in the last quarter of the 18th century. Its legacy includes not only the planters' great houses, but also the factories which processed the coffee from harvesting to dried bean. There still exist old grater mills or pulpers, either hand- or water-powered, the barbecues (*glacis*) or coffee bean drying areas, and the peeling or grinding mills, worked by hand, mule or water. On Jamaica and Guadeloupe, specially built coffee roasting ovens can still be seen. The industry also left another architectural legacy in the shape of the store houses and drying areas, known as boucans. Jamaican Blue Mountain coffee is probably the most famous of the Caribbean coffees, and the best known great house connected with the industry on the island is Charlottenburg high in the mountains. Old coffee processing machinery can be seen at nearby Clydesdale.

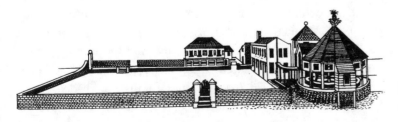

Coffee factory, Dominica, showing glacis

Cotton

On some islands like the Bahamas, the Virgin Islands and Anguilla, cotton was once a thriving industry, mainly supplying the American market. In 1691, for example, there were more than eighty cotton plantations on St Thomas alone. The cotton bolls, once picked, had to be separated from their seeds, cleaned, and baled. This was done in a factory known as a ginnery, often by hand, but later by machinery. One such cotton gin, or processing factory, can be found on Anguilla. There are several old cotton warehouses in the Windward Islands.

Gold

The earliest production buildings were those constructed by the Spanish in the late 1400s and early 1500s for the processing of gold. Some of the first gold mines were excavated on the island of Aruba, which later became Dutch. These were the royal forges, kilns built out of stone, with specially adapted bellows, housings, and run-offs for the molted metal. A structure nearby was used to stamp the gold with its carat value and tribute. Silver was also processed in the same way in these smelting works, usually located near the source of the raw material. None of these smelting works has been found, although the 'Sir Francis Drake manuscripts', the French Huguenot account of his voyages, show what they looked like. Much later, gold processing as recently as in 1916 has left buildings at Balashi in Aruba, constructed for the extraction and processing of the precious metal.

Indigo, Dyewood and Brazilwood

During the 16th and 17th centuries, indigo, the product of the plant Indigofera, was a much-valued blue dye, named 'Indian Dye' by the Spanish who imported it from a few centres in the Caribbean. The extracted dye was formed into blocks and packed into bales before shipping. Indigo, logwood (*Haematoxylon campeachianum*), cinchona and brazilwood were all highly prized as textile dyes, for the extraction of quinine, and for use in paint and varnish manufacture, as were the resins copal and animé. These products were shipped from lumber camps established by the British in Belize as early as the 1660s. Many urban centres grew up around the sawmills for these woods, some of which still exist. The riches made from harvesting chicle, the basis of chewing-gum, from the sapodilla tree also left an architectural mark in Belize. Early shipments of Central American indigo, dyewood and brazilwood were usually transported to Europe via Havana.

Lime and Citrus

Lime and citrus production was important in the Caribbean in the 19th century, when lime juice was at a premium As early as the 1700s, the British Royal Navy discovered that lime juice helped to prevent the vitamin deficiency illness, scurvy. Lime products included citrate of lime, essential oils, the juice itself and limes pickled in sea water. The factories built for producing lime juice were often man- or animal-powered, while the extraction of the lime's essential oils was done by hand on an *écuelle* or special pan. Early lime production equipment and the factories where the limes were processed are now quite rare, and Dominica probably has more remnants of this industry than any other Caribbean island.

Maize and Sorghum

These were both popular crops on the islands of the Dutch Antilles in the southern part of the Caribbean, Aruba, Bonaire and Curaçao. The production of these crops supplemented the expensive importation of cereals. *Magasinas*, old maize and sorghum storage houses can be seen adjacent to many old landhuizen on Curaçao. In the other Caribbean islands, maize was raised to feed slaves, as European settlers preferred wheat flour, imported from their homeland, and later, North America.

Phosphates

Centuries-old deposits of guano, or bird droppings, found on many Caribbean islands, were found to have several uses, mainly as a fertilizer. On other islands, phosphates were natural deposits, like those on Sombrero Island, Anguilla, where phosphate of lime was discovered and extracted from the early 1900s. On Sombrero, the architectural interest lies in the remains of the steam-powered rock crushing machinery houses and the tall chimney, plus what remains of the light railway built there. The uninhabited island of Redonda, off Antigua, was the Caribbean's major phosphate-producing island during the mid-19th century.

Salt

Phosphate factory ruins, Sombrero Island

One of the most easily harvested commodities found in the Caribbean in the earliest days was sea salt, and this mineral was exploited throughout the region. Salt production was a major industry in the history of the Caribbean, as it was an invaluable commodity for the preservation of meats. Some of the major salt-producing islands included the Bahamas, Anguilla and the Turks & Caicos islands, where salt workers, mostly Bermudians, brought with them their distinctive style of house building. On the islands of Aruba, Bonaire, and Curaçao, the warehouses or magasinas, and the huts where the slaves who worked on the salt pans lived, can still be seen. The *salinas*, or salt pans, where the sea water was evaporated to produce the salt, can be seen on many Caribbean islands. One of the largest and longest worked salt pans is that on Dutch Sint Maarten and French Saint-Martin. The old salt pans, storage warehouses, customs houses and slave huts still survive on several islands. As salt was loaded directly onto lighters from the shore before being transferred onto large ships, some of the old salt jetties also exist.

Spices and Herbs

A great variety of spices and herbs emanated from the Caribbean, including ginger, nutmeg and mace, pepper, chillies, cinnamon, annatto seed pods, pimento, saffron, or root turmeric, allspice, cloves, bay, vanilla, tamarind, and sarsaparilla. Most commercial spices were native to the region, but some – such as nutmeg – were imported. Several spices needed processing before being exported, and the factories where some of these were cleaned, separated, grated, graded, dried or processed to extract essential oils can still be found in some islands, particularly on Grenada, known as the 'Isle of Spice'. Mace, the covering of the nut of the nutmeg, had to be separated in special areas, oil of bay had to be extracted in a particular distilling process, as did that of ginger and cloves. Peppercorns had to be specially dried, and each spice or herb needed its own separate storage warehouse. Many of these still stand near the docks in St George's and Gouyave, Grenada. Vanilla is the only orchid which produces an exotic perfume from its pod and bean. They have to be cured to release the pungent odour by steeping in boiling water. The pods are then sweated in cloth, matured, and oven-dried slowly until the white crystals appear on the pod's deep brown surface, showing that it is ready to exude its fragrance. A few of these vanilla-processing plants can still be found.

Sugar

The first commercial foreign crop introduced into the Caribbean, initially by the Spanish and then by the Portuguese and Dutch, was sugar. It was this crop, essentially a large perennial grass, which not only transformed the landscape of most of the Caribbean islands, but left an architectural legacy which is as rich in history as the crop itself was in monetary terms.

The Sugar Plantation

As sugar plantations covered the islands of the Caribbean in a green mantle, the sugar business not only required the plantation owner to plant and harvest the cane, but also to process the cane into refined sugar and molasses and sometimes into rum. Sugar has to be processed within hours of cutting, or otherwise the valuable sucrose begins to dry up. This meant that a factory or mill had to be built on the land, usually located on a convenient artery for transportation. The sugar mill, or *ingenio* in Spanish, was the focal point of every plantation. In the Spanish-speaking islands the sugar cane-processing nucleus was also called the *batey*. This consisted of the engine house, containing the machinery for crushing, grinding and boiling the cane.

Until comparatively late in the 19th century, when mechanical power was introduced, the machinery was operated by manual labour or by a mixture of animal, wind or water power. On some islands, windmills provided the drive; on others, a fast-flowing river might power the mill from a water-wheel; some were mule- or oxen-powered, known as a *trapiche*; but most were originally dependent on the power of slaves. A giant treadmill, worked by up to a dozen slaves at a time, was housed in a shed-like building to one side of the ingenio. The large treadmill turned a conveyor belt on which the cane was fed into the crushing house. The cane stalks, having been trimmed of their leaf tops in the field, cut into convenient lengths and transported from the field by ox-cart, were ground by revolving metal cylinders in the open-sided crushing house, also powered by the treadmill.

In a typical 18th-century sugar mill, the crushing separated the cane juice from the stalk fibres, known as *bagasse*, which was rejected at this stage and often used as cattle fodder or to fuel the fires used in a later stage of sugar processing. The juice obtained by crushing was piped into the boiling house, where it was fed into cauldrons to be clarified with the addition of lime, and then ladled into coppers which converted the juice into molasses. The molasses were then drained off, and raw sugar produced by evaporation in the purging house where it was drained into troughs through large metal funnels, with up to twenty thousand in one purging house. The cauldrons were fired by the bagasse cane waste. The separated sugar was collected in large wheeled boxes, used to transport the raw sugar to the crystallizing pans from which the impurities were drained. The skimmings of the first boiling of the cane juice were used as the basis of rum production. The pans of sugar were finally separated in the drying house. At the top of the sugar pans was the finest white sugar, the second layer was broken sugar, and the third,

Cutaway view of boiling house

the most common, was known in the Spanish islands as *cucurucho* or brown sugar. That dark sugar, moist with molasses, left in the bottom of the pan was known as *mascabodo*. The sugar was then forced into wooden moulds and set in the familiar shape of the sugar loaf or cone.

The thousands of slaves required to tend the crop and cut the cane at harvest time also had to be housed. Thus, the typical sugar estate would consist of hundreds of acres of cane fields, the sugar mill and a slave housing compound, known as a 'barracoon' or barracks. The barracoon was generally built in a quadrangle shape with no windows on the outside and one entrance, closed when all the slaves were housed at night. Inside, the building was sometimes divided into rooms in which an entire slave family would live, or often just partitioned into sleeping quarters. In the centre of the quadrangle was usually a large stone fireplace and boiler for cooking. Nearby would be a hospital and perhaps a nursery for the children of the field workers. Housing for the white workers on the estate and the slave foremen and supervisors was built onto the outside of the large barracoons. Today, barracks of this sort can still be seen in sugar-producing areas of the Dominican Republic, Jamaica or Trinidad.

A bell tower or watchtower was usually located in the ingenio compound to call workers to and from the fields and to keep watch over the work. A fine example of this has been restored on the Iznaga plantation in Cuba (see pages 152–53).

The mill, barracoons and other housing were generally located downwind and out of sight of the owner's mansion, known as the 'great house'. However, a small community of little houses was usually built just out of sight of the family home. This housed the mansion's servants, the blacksmith, stables and storage barns. Located as they were in deep countryside, the sugar barons' mansions often adopted an architectural style which best suited their location and climate. The traditional estate owner's house, or estate manager's house, was generally built in a commanding position on a hill to catch the prevailing breezes and overlooking the mill and the entire domain. The construction of these grand houses was known as the 'Four Winds' design, after their airy structure and location. Many sugar barons did not opt for the traditional architectural style of the merchants and officials who lived in the towns, but designed their own villas to adapt to the country climate.

Most estate owners had town houses of their own, as well as the great house on the plantation. The typical plantation house was a single-storey building, with several high-ceilinged rooms, a verandah at front and back and a rear courtyard for services like cooking. A central patio would be surrounded by a stone-built main building, with a red-tiled roof. One heavy central door would form the main entrance, large enough for a carriage to be driven in, and iron grilles would cover the few external windows, which would be built flush to the walls. Naturally, styles of sugar industry architecture varied throughout the Caribbean, but the general layout of plantations was remarkably similar from island to island.

Thus the processing of sugar gave us a variety of architectural buildings, from the man-powered treadmill, the animal- or water-powered mill, the wind-powered mill, and finally the mechanical mill. Today, it is mainly the remains of a few wind, water and mechanically powered mills which have survived. Very little evidence is left of the boiler houses, apart from the tall chimneys, and in several islands there are the remains of aqueducts, used to channel water, essential to sugar processing. The grounds of the University of the West Indies campus in Mona, Jamaica, contain such a ruined aqueduct. A few old sugar warehouses also still stand on some islands, but most have been modernized.

The development of basic housing was intimately linked with the importance of the sugar business, as were the great houses, villas, mansions, and country homes. The wealth generated by sugar also gave the Caribbean many of its theatres, opera houses, mus-eums, churches and grand official buildings, but most of its old factories, mills and many of its great houses today lie in ruins.

Supplementary Products

Early lime kiln, Prospect Pen, Jamaica

Some processes involved the use of supplementary products. For example, the processing of sugar involved the use of lime, which was also used for mortar in building. The substance was obtained by burning limestone or coral in furnaces. Crushed and burnt coral was found to be an excellent source of lime. Several lime kilns can be seen, either near limestone hills or near beaches where coral was available like those on Aruba or Jamaica. Water was also essential to the agricultural economy and had to be pumped on some islands. Wind pumps were used to raise water, especially on Barbados, where good examples can be seen, or on Salt Cay in the Turks & Caicos, where small, simple water pumps are still in use.

Tobacco

A crop grown throughout the Caribbean and almost as influential as sugar, tobacco has special processing requirements. Drying and curing houses had to be especially made and aligned east to west to catch the maximum amount of sun. They are almost invariably wooden structures with thatch or corrugated iron roofs. These *vegas* or curing houses, vast, high barns, where tobacco leaves are hung to dry and mature, are the most important architectural legacy of the industry. Another reminder of the tobacco industry are the cigar-making factories of Cuba, the Dominican Republic and Puerto Rico. Many other islands also produced tobacco, and the remains of the vast Dutch tobacco warehouses on Sint Eustatius are testament to the universal importance of tobacco. The wealth generated from this profitable crop has also left a legacy of rich planters' villas, as well as the cultural institutions that they sponsored, like theatres and playhouses.

Part Three

What to Look For in Caribbean Architecture

The following is an alphabetical listing of the major features to be found in Caribbean architecture. A short description explains the uses and adaptations of these features.

The unique development of Caribbean architecture has left a trail of telltale features which trace the story of building design and innovation through five centuries. Many of these features are peculiar to certain islands, and some have a fascinating history. Most testify to the exquisite design taste and superlative skills of colonial Caribbean craftsmen using both local and imported materials to create a style that makes a story in itself.

Antepecho

These half height window screens are a traditional Spanish colonial architectural feature, especially when the window looks out directly onto the sidewalk, as in the Cuban city of Trinidad. The guards are usually made of ornamental wrought iron and often built flush with the walls. They are usually quite decorative, and the screens offer protection as well as access to light and air.

Balcony, or Balcón

An outside platform fitted to the wall of a house, sometimes known as a gallery or loggia. It is often open and balustraded and is accessed either from the upper floor through a window, or by means of a stairway from the ground floor. In typical Spanish design, a *balcón* might run around the entire internal courtyard of a house, with access by a stairway from the courtyard or from the internal rooms by means of a 'French window'. Alternatively, a balcony might be fitted to the front of a house, overhanging the sidewalk, and the space below might be adapted into a porch or colonnade. In some cases, the balcony would run right around the exterior of the house. Outside balconies might be open or completely enclosed with a hardwood fretwork screen or louvred shutters, allowing cooling air to pass through, but ensuring privacy and security.

Barrotes

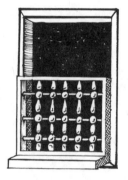

Window screens, which protect the window openings from the street, were sometimes fashioned out of beautifully turned decorative hardwood rods known as *barrotes*. These not only offered protection, but allowed air and light into the room. Later, these were made from wrought iron and became known as *rejas*.

Building Materials

The study of the various building materials used throughout the Caribbean is fascinating because of their origins and diversity. It begins with the round, palm-thatched dwellings of the Caribs of the Guianas known as *kabays*, the timber-built, thatched, stilt houses of the Arawaks called *ajoupas*, and the square, or round, walled, thatched huts of the Tainos, known as *bohíos*.

The first European settlers, Columbus's 39 crew members left in La Navidad on Hispaniola in 1492, had to make use of local materials and the recovered timbers of the wrecked *Santa Maria* to build their stockade. The Spanish initially adopted the Taino style of building, finding it ideally suited to the climate and practical, as all the materials came from one tree, the Royal Palm. Early colonists began to adapt this slightly, covering the interlaced branches of the walls with mud or clay in the building style known as wattle and daub, with a timber frame and palm frond thatch roof in those islands where wood was abundant. The Spanish settlers later introduced the 'Spanish walling' construction method. Masonry fill was used around a timber frame to build the walls instead of the more primitive wattle and daub. Instead of thatch, the Spanish used tiling for the roof, while the floor was usually of lime concrete, made from ground coral rock, replacing the earthen floor of the bohío.

The first stone-built structure, the Church of the Virgin of the Rosary, was built by the Spanish in Santo Domingo in 1496. It was made from blocks sawn from a fossilized coral rock known as *coquina* or ironshore. This material, found mostly in the Greater Antilles, is easy to carve, readily available on the coast and hard-wearing. The Spanish also imported the first European building materials to the New World, the tiles with which they roofed the oldest standing house, the House of the Cord, also built in Santo Domingo, in 1503. The first tile-making factory was in Trinidad, Cuba, and in the 1700s the French began manufacturing their distinctive fish-scale tiles in Martinique.

When the islands of the Windwards and Leewards were settled, the volcanic geology of the islands provided a dark, easily shaped stone, with which many French, Dutch, Danish and English colonial houses were built. A number of islands were also the source of a variety of woods, including mahogany and other precious hardwoods. The Greater Antilles were blanketed with dense forests before sugar was grown commercially, as were a number of the Lesser Antillean islands. Those islands devoid of wood, like some of the Bahamas, the Turks & Caicos, or Aruba, Bonaire and Curaçao, imported beams and timbers, and where possible stone was used.

The mortar used to cement stone blocks together, whether volcanic rock or coral coquina, varied from island to island. Kalk was a favourite as it was simple to make and the raw material was easily available on most islands. A mixture of coral and shells was burned and crushed to make lime for a basic mortar. Kalk ovens, for burning the coral, can be seen on islands like Aruba, and lime kilns on Jamaica. A stronger mortar was utilized in several instances, comprised of a kalk with added molasses and egg whites! Mortar was also used to face stone, rubble masonry work or brick buildings. In some cases, a building material was used made from a mixture of clay and lime, known as marl. Both the English and Danish colonists imported bricks from Europe as ships' ballast, in order to emulate as closely as possible, the buildings of their homelands. The commonly yellow Danish bricks are typically narrower than the English honey-brown or red bricks.

Where wood was prolific, wattle and daub was often replaced by clapboard or weather-board. This consists of overlapping boards covering a timber frame. Many of the houses built in this way were assembled without the use of iron nails, using wooden pegs only, a traditional shipwright's skill. Although these houses were originally thatched with palm, wooden shingles were sometimes used, but corrugated iron roofs became popular in the 19th century. More substantial houses would be built of a mixture of stone on the ground floor, with timber upper floors. These houses would be shingle, tile or, very rarely, slat-roofed.

Ceilings

The most dramatic internal feature of Spain's colonial construction was the use of the Mudéjar, or Moorish, style of ceiling. This usually involved the use of precious woods, like teak, or cedar. Huge beams supported the upper floor, and the spaces between were wood-clad, forming square panels. The panels of some of these Mudéjar ceilings were often hand-painted with floral designs or local scenes, and examples of these, found in the houses, churches and palaces of the Spanish islands, are now very rare. In the French and British colonies, the ceilings of large public buildings, town houses and plantation houses often featured ornate plasterwork, emulating that of domestic architecture. The tray ceiling, shaped like an inverted tea tray, was adopted in some buildings, such as Sam Lord's Castle in Barbados.

Courtyards

Most early Spanish colonial buildings were constructed with a large gateway, closed by huge, heavy doors, through which the occupier could drive his carriage directly into the courtyard. This gave access to an integral carriage-house built into the main structure. Often these large doors were not conventionally hinged, but suspended on a peg and eye device made from iron. The large gateway doors also included a smaller doorway, incorporated into one of the doors, for pedestrian access. This was the forerunner of the *postigo*. Certain features of the enclosed courtyard are typical of many very early Spanish colonial buildings. In order to increase the amount of shade in the cobbled or paved courtyard, trees were often planted in strategic positions. A well often featured in the courtyard, surmounted by an elaborate wrought-iron arch from which a pulley and the well bucket would be suspended. The font-like surround of the well, which was usually of carved stone or occasionally tiled, had a hardwood cover to its opening. Following the Arabic pattern, many wells in Spanish colonial houses were octagonal in shape. Later adaptations in courtyard design sometimes included terracotta spouts protruding from the gullies of the tiled roofs of the surrounding balcony, from which rainwater was caught in large vats. Often these vats were disused oil casks – see *tinajón* (page 67).

The Entresuelo

Occasionally, in some of the grander Spanish buildings external windows or openings were constructed between two floors, letting light into a storeroom or into the servants' quarters. This device was known as the *entresuelo* (literally, between floors) or mezzanine window. This opening enabled goods to be passed into the storeroom or out onto the street without using the main doorways, but it was to be too small for a person to pass through.

Gables

The triangular part of the end walls of a building with a pitched or ridged roof is known as the gable. These can be simple or ornate. Dutch colonial architecture specialized in curvilinear shaped gables. It also produced shaped gables with multi-curved sides, crow-stepped gables with stepped sides, and Dutch gables, which were crowned by a pediment. Dutch gables always slope at an angle of 52 degrees. Hipped gables have the topmost part sloped inwards. Gables were also used to let light into the structure via gable windows, or air through gable louvres. Sometimes the shape of the end gables was echoed in the shape of dormer windows. Barge-boards were often used to finish off the conventional triangular gable. In French wooden-built houses, the barge-boards were often gracefully carved in the gingerbread fretwork so common in 18th- and 19th-century French colonial and Trinidadian architecture.

'Gingerbread'

In many Victorian era wooden buildings, fretwork ornamental embellishments to features such as the gables, verandahs and porch are commonly known as 'gingerbread'. Supposedly derived from 16th-century German pastry-makers, who were famous for their ornately decorated gingerbread creations, the style draws on elaborate wooden latticework. The most imaginative examples of the style are to be seen in Haiti, although Martinique, Guadeloupe and other islands have plenty of surviving gingerbread buildings.

At first, the designs were hand-carved in wood, appearing as decorative trims to the roofs and verandahs of prosperous town houses. These fashionable designs became more ornate in the early 1800s. Wooden gingerbread developed to the extravagant limits that the material would allow. More than 100 designs have been identified, embellishing balconies, gables, eaves and porches – from natural curves and swirls, geometric designs like Greek key patterns, to cutouts of animals, birds, flowers and stars. Gingerbread on some houses echoes the maritime preoccupations of the islanders, with friezes of seagulls, boats and fish. Even entire sheets of wood were pierced and cut out to resemble lace and used as delicate window panels. Two common designs are those called 'ribbon' and 'chain'. Another clever fretwork is the 'Peter and Paul', where interlocking designs cut out as much wood as is left, hence 'robbing Peter to pay Paul'.

In 1865 the mechanical fretsaw was invented. This meant that even more decorative designs could be mass-produced. American machines then began producing fretwork designs which could be bought by the yard. The fashion for 'gingerbread' then spread throughout the Caribbean and the southern states of the US.

Jalousie, or Louvre

This is the name for the slatted wooden shutter or blind, which, when opened, admits air and light but not rain. It can be seen in use over window openings, covering postigo openings, sometimes covering the doorway to a balcony or a verandah, in gables and in roof lanterns. The jalousie slats can be opened or closed, and the word comes from the French for jealousy, thought to originate from the fact that a resident could adjust the slats in order to look out, but not be seen from the outside.

Luceta

Over some Caribbean doorways, the *vitrales*, or coloured glass windows, are not designed in the conventional half-moon shape. In some instances the coloured fan-lights are rectangular in shape, although no less decorative than the mediopuntas. These are known as *lucetas*.

Mamparas

These are interior single or double doors, often with built-in slated fenestration or jalousies. Sometimes they are half-doors or lead out onto a central courtyard. They often have mediopunta or luceta windows which let more light into the interior rooms.

Mediopunta/Medioluna

This is the form of glass fan-light windows usually seen over doorways in the traditional, half-circular, or half-moon fan shape – hence 'fan-light'. Mediopunta design ranges from geometric to floral. They were introduced in the late 18th century, when coloured glass began to be imported into the Spanish colonial

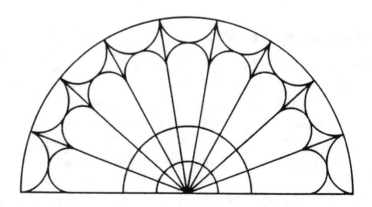

Caribbean. In some cases, the glass would be clear but hand-painted, but often the coloured glass would be opaque, as clear glass was very expensive. Initially, the individual coloured glass panels which made up the basic design of the mediopuntas were divided by bent wooden frames; later, lead dividers were used and the designs became more ambitious. In some buildings, before the introduction of glass, the half-moon shape over a doorway or in an arch opening would have been filled with fan-shaped slats.

The Patio

This is the classic feature of the traditional Spanish colonial home, adapted from the Moorish style of housing. It is generally the term for the central courtyard of a house, the main meeting area, often shaded with trees, and decorated with flowering plants and the site of the well or water butt. Patios vary in size depending on the design of the house, mansion or palace. The more grandiose often feature statues and decorated tiling.

Persianas

From the inside of a house, the light from the windows and open doorways is often controlled by removable wooden slats, or Venetian blinds. In Spanish architecture these are called *persianas*, possibly relating to the Arab origins of regulating light and air in a room. They also ensure privacy while allowing the occupant to see outside.

The Pineapple

This native of the Caribbean grows in the centre of a crown of long spikes once fashioned into Spanish ladies' mantillas. A famous etching shows Columbus being presented with a pineapple on his first visit to Martinique, the first European to taste this fruit. This feature became extremely popular in the architectural embellishments of European and colonial buildings, and became widely adopted as a symbol of welcome. So fascinating is its shape that colonial architects adopted the pineapple, carving them of wood and stone as decorative finials on gateways, buildings and statues.

Porch

This is the name for the ubiquitous covered approach to a building, synonymous with most urban and rural Caribbean housing design. It is occasionally railed in, sometimes raised above the ground, with a planking floor, and throughout the Caribbean few porches will be seen without the ubiquitous rocking chair strategically placed on the verandah to make the most of evening breezes and from which to watch the world go by. Porch styles vary throughout the Caribbean, although most urban and rural workers' dwellings have one. A distinctive English-style of porch is the 'sedan chair' variety, resembling a sentry box and tacked onto the front of a town house, examples of which can be seen in Grenada (see pages 187–88).

Portales

Columned, covered walkways and arcades extending the length of the house frontage, which were a popular feature of colonial architecture, are known in Spanish as *portales*. Many of these can be seen in the grandiose palaces and early official residences on the plazas of the Spanish colonists' earliest towns and cities. In some buildings, the columns supporting the colonnade roof were stone pillars; in others they became an integral part of the building, the columns being fashioned into arches. Later architecture also adopted portales in a more subdued form by adding wooden columned supports to the protective walks as opposed to the stone of early architecture. Sometimes the columns were constructed from finely cast iron pillars or wrought-iron supports.

Postigos

Before the introduction of mechanical fans, several clever innovations were introduced in Spanish colonial house design in order to encourage cooling draughts of air to pass through buildings. Spanish colonial architects adapted Moorish ideas by designing small, barred windows into door structures. These openings in the doors, which allowed the occupier to look out, items to be passed in or out, and cooling breezes to waft into the house interior, are known as postigos. They vary greatly in design and adaptation. Some are just square or oblong openings in the doors, some are miniature doors, cut into the full doors, others might be more imaginatively designed openings. Often shutters and wooden jalousies were fitted to the openings in the double-hinged full or half-doors which allowed privacy but encouraged cooling breezes. Embellishments include elaborate carvings on the doors and postigos, even extending to fretwork carvings forming a screening over some door openings.

Rejas

In Spanish colonial Caribbean architecture, the windows of houses were often ornamented by protective, but decorative, wrought-iron window grilles or screens, known as *rejas*. These are like cages, which stand proud of the window or sometimes from the doorway, projecting out onto the sidewalk. They are often extremely decorative and are fine examples of the blacksmith's skills. Rosettes, scrolls, fans, floral designs, tracery and geometric patterns are all favourites. Some of the best examples of rejas can be seen on houses in Trinidad, Cuba.

Roofs

There are nine distinct, basic types of roof found in Caribbean architecture. The usual style is the pitched roof, with two sloping sides meeting at a ridge along the top. This forms a gable at each end. A hipped roof has a sloping roof at each end. A pavilion roof is hipped equally on all four sides. A lean-to roof has one slope, built against a flat wall. A Mansard roof has a double slope, with the lower steeper than the upper, and a gambrel roof is similar, but with a gablet (small gable) in the top part of each end of the roof. A helm roof is common in spires, with four inclining sides meeting at a

Roofs from left to right: pitched, hipped, mansard and helm.

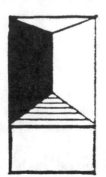

point at the top. A cranked roof is a pitched roof which has a shallow slope over the ground floor, and this rises steeply to the ridge over the first floor, giving a high ceiling in the central part of the house. Bracketed roofs occur where the overhang or eaves are supported by brackets extending from the walls.

Shutters

Shutters are an integral part of Caribbean architecture and come in a variety of designs. The most common is the storm shutter, a featureless heavy wooden shutter, usually side-hinged. In some cases, even doors are storm-shuttered. Shutters can be either side hinged or top-hinged. One form of top-hinged shutter is the Demerara variety, named after the region of Guyana. These very specialized shutters have a latticed window box protruding from the base of the window, with louvered sides sloping up to the top of the window frame. On this sloping frame, a tilting, louvred shutter rests, which can be opened to let in more light and air. Many Caribbean shutters are louvered and either side- or top-hung for this purpose.

Spurs

In the 18th and 19th centuries, when Spain's colonial cities became congested with horse-drawn traffic, house owners noticed that the wheel hubs of carts and carriages damaged the corners of their houses as they plied the narrow streets. Metal sheaths, known locally as spurs, were fixed to vulnerable corners. These are often ornately decorated and sometimes stamped with the date they were installed. There are many examples of spurs in the Spanish-speaking islands. When ancient iron cannon became redundant, these were also embedded, breech up, in the cobbled streets on the corners of buildings to prevent damage to walls, and were sometimes used to divert traffic from pedestrian areas.

Tiles

Red earthenware roofing tiles are a feature of many Spanish colonial houses. In very early times, these specially-made interlocking tiles were imported from Spain. In the early 1500s, near Trinidad in Cuba, a clay pit was discovered which produced the ideal material for making these tiles. A similarly fine clay source was found on Martinique, which became notable as a source of 'fish-scale' clay tiles. Today, the characteristic tiles are still hand-made in furnaces on the outskirts of Trinidad from material dug from those same pits found five hundred years ago. The tiles made here are sun-dried and weather excellently to a rust brown. They provide ideal protection and good insulation in heavy thunderstorms, hurricanes, or harsh sunshine. In many instances, the Spanish and Dutch imported their tiles from Europe. The Spanish favoured their *azuelos*, glazed pottery tiles decorated in bright colours (mostly blue or *azul* in Spanish) and used to clad walls or floors. The Dutch imported their clay tiles for roofing and their famous Delft tiles for cladding. Many English colonial buildings were shingle- or, rarely, slate-roofed, and occasionally shingles were used as wall cladding.

The Tinajón

The Cuban city of Camagüey, originally located on the coast and called Puerto Principe, was once a centre for the importation of precious olive oil from Spain. The oil was use for cooking and lighting and was initially imported in barrels, which tended to break in transit. The city's inhabitants consequently developed vessels from the local clay pits, which made much more reliable containers. A leather skin was tied tightly over the vessel's mouth, which kept the oil fresh and cool because of the nature of the clay. From Camagüey, these tinajones, full of oil or wine and often standing as high as a man, were distributed throughout the Spanish colonies. Quickly, it was realized that the empty tinajones made ideal water storage jars, as they kept water cool by evaporation. They also made ideal water butts for catching rainwater pouring off roofs. These butts can now be seen in many early patios, especially in the islands of the Greater Antilles. Often the wide-mouthed jars were half buried in the ground to keep the water fresh and cool, and placed under guttering spouts to catch rainwater.

The Tinajero

The *tinajero* was basically a mahogany frame which contained a tinajón and acted as a frame for a water filter, ensuring that only clean rainwater entered the vat. A special porous stone, called a drip-

stone and made from a certain type of limestone, was fitted into the surround of the tinajero and filtered the water. Often the clay vat, filter and water holder were housed in a fine wooden cabinet, thus becoming an item of furniture. The tinajero would stand in the corner of a room or in an alcove especially made to house it. The name tinajero then became the word for the cabinet and its contents. Sometimes, two dripstones and a marble bowl would be used instead of the earthenware vessel to catch the purified water. A maid would be responsible for topping up the water from a rain butt, so that pure, filtered, cool water was always on tap. Fine examples of the tinajero and tinajón can be seen many old houses, from Barbados to the Bahamas, but especially in early Spanish colonial houses. The unglazed, clay or earthenware storage jars for purified water were sometimes known as 'monkeys', and in some islands they had a special place, beside a Demerara window, for example, to catch the breezes and keep the water cool by evaporation.

The Verandah

The verandah is an open or usually railed portico or gallery, generally running along the front of a house, with a roof supported on posts, pillars or columns. As with the balcón, access usually comes from an upper room. Some verandahs are freestanding, without supports, and are held up by projecting beams running from the ceiling of the internal room out over the sidewalk, and are sometimes ornately carved. A handrail frequently runs around the outside of the verandah, supported by finely-turned balustrades. Often verandahs were painted in bright colours, although some were made of polished or varnished hardwood. With the introduction of cast iron, ornate wrought-iron verandahs became popular, especially in the French islands.

Vitrales

Arched, coloured glass fan designs can be seen above many Spanish colonial doorways, both interior and exterior doors, which let in sunlight but diffuse brightness. Introduced in the late 18th century, when coloured glass began to be imported for fashionable domestic rather than religious architecture, these windows are known as vitrales. Some are designed in clear coloured glass, others are fashioned with marbled glass. They appear over both main doorways and those opening onto courtyards, balconies or porches. In early times, the design was pieced together with wood between the segments of glass, but later leading was employed. The designs are often beautifully artistic, with floral or geometric patterns.

Wells

Before aqueducts brought water to Spain's colonial houses, wells were located in strategic parts of each town, as were water spouts and fountains bringing natural spring water to the populace. Often these were ornately decorated, and many still operate. In the villas of the wealthy, a well was the central feature of the courtyard or patio. These were often octagonal in shape and built of stone, often faced with ornate, expensive, hand-painted azuelos. The octagonal shape and tiling reflected the Moorish influence on Spanish architecture. In the Arab world, water was such a precious commodity that wells held pride of place in the courtyards of houses and palaces and were invariably finely decorated. A mahogany wooden cover protected the well opening, and above the well a decorative arch, usually in wrought iron, held a pulley from which the well bucket was suspended. The metal arches over wells are now often utilized as improvised plant pot hangers.

Windows

In the early days of colonial settlement, large panes of glass were not only very expensive, but extremely difficult to transport all the way from Europe. Glass windows were also deemed unnecessary in the tropical climate, as in order to keep inclement weather out, wooden shutters were fitted to most window openings and rejas protected the window openings from intrusion when the shutters were open. However, in some very early houses Moorish influence can be seen in the practice of boxing in the entire window opening with a finely pierced wooden covering which could be opened in the same way as casement windows. In the Arab world this window design, known as the *rawashin* (ornamental bay window), or the *mushrabiyah* (ornamental casement), was, and is, a common feature. The piercing of the window screen allowed cooling breezes to enter the interior, whilst protecting from rain and wind. This also prevented strangers from looking into the room. Thus, an unveiled Arab woman could look out through the mushrabiyah without being seen herself. In the latter years of the 16th century, the use of this pierced casement design gave way to simple shutters of persianas – a word derived from Moorish influence on Spanish window design.

Details of Caribbean Architecture

Features of note include beautiful door furniture on the nail-studded doors of churches, palaces and old buildings. These take the form of brass door knockers, some in traditional hand-and-heart designs, gargoyles or crucifixes, embellished peep-holes, locks, door handles, latches in wrought iron and brass, and decorative door hinges.

In some places, the street names and house numbers are made of colourful Spanish tiles. Ornate metal gaslights and delicate iron railings add to the artistic ambiance of the Caribbean's colonial quarters. Decorative hanging lamps are a feature of the Spanish courtyard, as are metal torch-holders fixed to the walls which once held flaming brands to light the streets. Lamplighters in some islands still come round at dusk to illuminate the city squares in a traditional ritual which dates back several centuries. In some towns one can still see the iron rings where horses were tethered, or slaves were restrained.

In the early years of the 18th century Baroque and Rococo embellishments became popular additions to the frontage of many houses of the wealthy and well-connected, and many examples of the plasterer's art can be seen in Spanish colonial buildings in particular. This decorative trend, however, began much earlier in colonial history, at a time when a local or foreign sculptor would be commissioned to carve a coat-of-arms and founding date on a plaque which was fixed above the entrance to a fort, episcopal building or military barracks. Appliqué plasterwork on some buildings depicts cartouches, coats-of-arms, ciphers etc., and often this stucco work decorates the underside of colonnades and verandahs.

A variety of ornamentation is evident in the grand private and civil buildings of the Caribbean's cities. Mostly borrowed from European trends and Classical revival styles, these embellishments include the use of neo-Classical Corinthian, Doric or Ionic columns supporting pediments with decorative acroteria or ornamentation within the angles of the pediment. Finely moulded friezes were often used in conjunction with columnar supports. Often, instead of employing full columns to enhance a building's facade, pilasters were used. These look like flattened columns and are more decorative than of practical use.

Hood moulding, the masonry decoration over doors, windows and porticos, includes small pediments often supported by columns. These were a common feature of 17th- and 18th-century Spanish Baroque architecture, and decorative cornices often enhanced opulent facades or building exteriors. In the early 19th century, the elaborate cutout and scroll work used in the construction and ornamentation of wooden houses, was popular. One of the best examples of this style is the Municipal Museum in Varadero, Cuba. The Gothic revival style of architecture is also much in evidence in Spanish colonial cities. This trend involved the use of pointed arches, slender columns and ribs and vaults, once popular in Europe between the 11th and 16th centuries.

Hood moulding

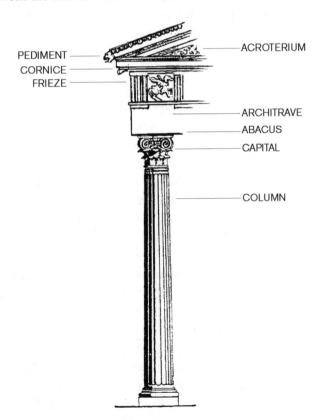

PEDIMENT
CORNICE
FRIEZE
ACROTERIUM
ARCHITRAVE
ABACUS
CAPITAL
COLUMN

Part Four

The Islands

ANGUILLA

This low-lying, narrow, coral island (named after the Spanish word for eel) has few sites of historical architectural interest, but a number of attractive white or colourfully painted private houses, some of which have been converted into commercial use. The original wattle and daub buildings have all disappeared, but some of those built in the 19th century from wooden shingles survive. Several of these are ornately decorated with gingerbread latticework, typical of the embellishment used on many colonial structures of that period in the Caribbean. Anguilla, still a British 'overseas territory', was badly hit by Hurricane Luis in September 1995.

It is thought that the first European settlement on Anguilla, in 1650, was at either Road Bay or the Cauls Pond area, where English colonists grew tobacco. Nothing remains of their early structures, as frequent attacks, first by the Caribs and later by the French, destroyed all evidence of early habitation. By 1796, there were settlements at South Hill and The Valley, where there was also a church. There was also a fort at Sandy Hill. By this time, sugar was the island's main crop. Salt production began in the mid-1700s, and phosphate mining on Sombrero Island started in the early 1800s. The chimney and boiler house of the phosphate factory still stand on the offshore island, as does its 1868 lighthouse.

St Mary's Church in the island capital, The Valley, was built in wood in the late 1800s and replaced by a 1967 model, with a squat, stone tower. The older part of the capital, Lower Valley, has some interesting houses dating from the late 19th and early 20th century,

19th-century lighthouse, Sombrero Island

including a distinctive stone house, built to a Dutch design. Another, wooden house, has a shingle-tiled roof. Here also is the oldest church on the island, the stone-built Ebenezer Methodist Church, with its pitch pine roof, belfry, and Gothic windows.

One of the oldest buildings on the island is the plantation house of Koal Keel, a beautiful, two-storey residence dating from the late 1700s, with a wide verandah and shuttered windows. Its lower floor is stone-built and the upper is built of wood. On Crocus Hill, the basement is all that remains of the old Courthouse, built out of stone and wood in the 1700s. The stone-built lower floor was first a powder magazine and then a prison. The upper floor was a court-house, treasury, post office and customs house, before it was destroyed in a 1955 hurricane.

Near The Valley is the Wallblake Plantation House. Believed to have been constructed in around 1787, it is one of the island's most impressive and oldest houses, dating from when the plantation produced both sugar and cotton. The foundations of this large building are built of stone, mortared together with a substance made of burnt coral, shells, marl and molasses. The wooden upper floor is wood-roofed, and the windows are shuttered. Inside, the tray ceilings are decorated in beadwork. The long, narrow pantry has a flooring of red and black brick tiles. An old, vaulted cistern stands outside, and the twelve-foot wide oven of the bakery outbuildings rises three feet through a stepped chimney. In 1965, the triple-fronted, St Gerard's Church, was built in the estate's grounds by a Belgian Catholic priest, Father John Strychers. It is an unusual structure, sporting a lantern atop the central arch of the facade, which is constructed of multi-coloured local stones and pebbles, as is the altar end of the church. The triple-arched ceiling, shaped like the hull of a ship, is strangely vaulted in three tiers, and lined with precious wood. Open brickwork forms the side walls of the single nave, providing novel ventilation, and the floor is of tiles. Almost opposite Wallblake House is the old cotton ginnery, known as the Factory, the only example on the island. The machinery of the ginnery has been preserved.

At Sandy Ground, the remains of the former salt industry can be seen. There are four wooden buildings here, the main one of which, with a triple-pitched roof, was the grinding and bagging house, where some of the grinding machinery is still kept. The small museum relates the history of salt production on the island. At the north end of the beach is the White House, built in 1902, with stone foundations and lower floor and a wooden upper storey, with a pitched, shingled roof. Gingerbread decorates the first floor verandah, which is supported with wooden pillars and enclosed by a geometric railing. The windows are traditionally shuttered.

East of Sandy Ground is the plantation house of the Road Estate, where sugar and cotton were cultivated. It was built in the early 19th century and was once used as a Manse, hence its current name, the Mission House. At the northern end of Road Bay Harbour, are the remains of an old sugar mill. The ruins of the boiler house and mule-powered mill can be seen here. Another old church is located at South Hill. This is the stone-built Bethel Methodist Church (1878). In the plaster-columned facade, which is flat and decorated by a white star, are twin Gothic-style doors. Buttresses support the walls, and the windows are also in Gothic style. The tiny bell tower is roofed in corrugated iron. In the north-east of the island are the remains of the Flemmings Plantation House, rebuilt in 1890 as a stone-built, school and church. The flooring is made of wood and the gabled roof is clad in shingles. Part of the original building remains, although it was modernized in the 1980s.

Bethel Methodist Church, Anguilla

ANTIGUA

Each of the Caribbean islands has developed its own individual architectural style, usually related to trade or agriculture. In the case of Antigua, the island's predominant architectural heritage results from a history of colonial conflict between England and France. The first English settlers, led by Sir Francis Warner in 1632, were planters, and tobacco was the cash crop of the day. But it was not the soil's fertility that gave Antigua its rich architectural individualism. It was the presence of one of the finest defensible bays in the Lesser Antilles, a natural asset which brought the most powerful navy in the world to Antigua, and with it the English military engineers who built an extensive complex of forts to defend their ships. At one time, Antigua was the most heavily fortified place for its size in the world.

The English had occupied nearby St Kitts for almost ten years before they ventured across the short stretch of water between the two islands in 1632. Scratching a living from the soil, the first colonists initially settled in Old Road, on the south-west coast, but later moved to the region around Liberta, just inland from Falmouth. The word 'road' meant an anchorage or harbour in the 17th century, and Liberta village received its name much later, in 1834, when freed slaves based themselves in the area. The original settlers built a small refuge for women and children on nearby Monk's Hill which later became the citadel of Fort George. The planters turned from tobacco cultivation to sugar growing by 1674, a crop introduced from Barbados by Sir Christopher Codrington.

St John's became the main town, and from 1703 to 1739, Fort James was constructed on St John's Point on the site of an ancient defence work, to protect the capital's harbour. It is in a good state of repair, with several of its 36 cannon and the powder magazine still in place. It once housed a garrison of seventy defenders. Another fort was built north of St John's at Runaway Bay. But it was not until 1707 that the major influence on Antigua's architecture materialized. Frequent skirmishes between England and France carried over into the West Indian colonies, and naval strength became the European powers' obsession in the Caribbean.

Over the next century, Antigua was to serve as Britain's strongest maritime base in the Americas and the seat of government of the 'Leeward Caribee Isles'. Thus, from 1707, Antigua became Britain's most important Caribbean colony after Jamaica. This was the date when the initial development of the great naval complex of English Harbour, across the island from St John's on the south coast, began. English Harbour was to be the headquarters of the British Navy in the West Indies from around 1740 to 1889 and a naval base under Admirals Rodney, Hood, and Nelson. Although another naval dockyard was built in Bridgetown, Barbados, in 1805, it never challenged English Harbour's strategic dominance.

The fortification of the long spit guarding the harbour commenced with the erection of Fort Berkeley (or Barclay), in 1704. Initially, the harbour was used for careening, as British naval ships would sail into the easily defensible bay to have their hulls cleaned and repaired. This work was initially done on the shore of one of the seven small coves which lie inside the large bay. The first wharf was built in English Harbour in 1725 on the eastern side of the inner harbour, where most of the careening took place. Known as St Helena, this dock was located between Commissioners and Freemans Bays and improved in 1728. The eastern dock was later extended to include, in King Yard on the western side of the harbour, quarters for the Commander-in-Chief, a guard house, a boathouse, sail loft, two mast houses, a capstan house, store rooms, a blacksmith's shop, and a saw pit, all enclosed by an encircling wall. The division between the military and naval installations can be seen below Fort Berkeley, where an anchor, carved in the rock, marks the dividing line. The vast naval installation became known as Nelson's Dockyard, from the time that the famous Admiral took command of the Leeward Islands Squadron in 1784 as captain of the 28-gun frigate HMS *Boreas*. The three-year posting was not to Horatio Nelson's liking, and he reportedly dismissed Antigua as 'an infernal hole'. Nelson's Dockyard was eventually abandoned as a naval base in 1889.

Born in Burnham Thorpe, Norfolk, in 1758, Horatio Nelson joined the British Navy in 1770, aged 22. He served in the Caribbean from 1777 to 1780, spending much of his time in Port Royal, Jamaica. In command of the *Boreas*, he arrived in Antigua in 1784 to enforce the Navigation Acts, aimed at preventing illicit trade between the Caribbean and North American colonies. Aged 26, he took command of the Leeward Islands squadron, base in English Harbour, the main British naval installation in the region since 1707. Nelson spent three years in his Leeward Island posting, cruising the islands and spending time in the dockyard during the hurricane season, when smugglers and the French fleet were absent from the Caribbean. It was at the end of this period that he married Frances Nisbet in Nevis. He only briefly returned to the region in 1805 while chasing the French fleet before the Battle of Trafalgar, which cost him his life.

The sail loft and boat repair house, built in 1796, is one of the most famous monuments in the dockyard. Great stone jetties were extended into the harbour, between which small boats could moor, either for repairs or to bring the sails of larger ships for repair. Massive stone columns, twelve feet round, supported the sail loft roof, which would have been fitted with tackle to hoist the sails from the boats up into the loft. The jetties and columns remain, but the rest of the structure was destroyed in an earthquake in 1843.

Copper and Lumber Store, Nelson's Dockyard

After another earthquake in 1871, when the roof collapsed, concrete caps were made for the pillars to prevent erosion.

Many of the Dockyard's other buildings have been restored, like the Prince William Careenage, once the Capstan House, the Galley Bar, once the Cookhouse, and the very English-looking Copper and Lumber Store, which also contained offices and sailors' dormitories. This building was constructed in 1783 to house the copper hull sheathing, which was found to prevent the worm damage and rotting which affected the wooden ships of the time. This large, two-storey Georgian building is brick built, with three tiled roofs, each containing twelve dormer windows. The English-style sash windows are all protected by storm shutters. The shortage of water on the island necessitated the addition of four huge cisterns, built on the outside of the structure to collect rainwater via drainpipes from a specially designed stone parapet, running around the outside of the building's roof. The colonial administration took over the redundant premises in 1906, from when they lay neglected until, in 1950, restoration work began on the store. Partial restoration was completed by 1978, and between 1982 and 1988 the building was converted into a Georgian-style inn and restaurant. The fine Officers' Quarters have also been restored, as has the Paymaster's House, the Shipwright's House and the Admiral's House, which contains a Nautical Museum and the National Parks Authority. The Wardroom is now converted into a restaurant.

The Admiral's Inn, the ground floor of which was once the pitch, turpentine, lead and tar store (the upper floor was devoted to the marine engineers' offices) has undergone excellent renovation work. Now a hotel and restaurant, the Admiral's Inn was planned in 1785, completed in 1788, and redesigned in 1855 from the original bricks which came from England as ship's ballast, as were many other buildings on Antigua, giving them their distinctive British individuality. Brick-lined pits, used for storing barrels of pitch, can be seen on each side of the brick passageway, which forms the entrance. The bar counter, once a workshop bench, is engraved with the names of nautical artisans and British warships dating from 1829 to 1882, including those of the *Fox*, the *Bullfrog* and the *Canada*.

South of English Harbour stands a vast bluff, commanding views over the entire harbour and surrounding ocean. The bluff, known as Shirley Heights after General Thomas Shirley, Governor of the Leeward Islands between 1781 and 1791, was fortified with the installation of the Horseshoe Battery, built facing Fort Berkeley in 1787. This included the blockhouse, barracks, hospital, officers' quarters, and powder magazine. West of English Harbour is Fort Cuyler, overlooking the harbour mouth and Falmouth Harbour. If ever a natural harbour was made to be defended, English Harbour was it. The bay proved its worth, as Nelson's Dockyard was never attacked. The importance of controlling such a large, safe harbour in the Caribbean soon became evident as, during the hurricane season, the enemy, in the shape of the French fleet, had to return to the safety of the Mediterranean ports. In English Harbour's inland bay, meanwhile, an entire fleet could hole up, protected from hurricanes. The prevailing north-east trade winds also meant that the fleet could sail throughout the Caribbean at any time.

Throughout the 18th and 19th centuries, thousands of British ships sailed in and out of the naval port of English Harbour and the commercial port of St John's. The immense maritime activity in which Antigua was involved meant that the island was an attractive and safe proposition to new planters, tradesmen and merchants looking for a secure base from which to do business in the West Indies. St John's became a prosperous centre of commerce and the sugar industry increased its wealth. In its heyday Antigua was the best island in the Lesser Antilles in which to find goods and materials imported from England.

For this reason, much of the island's architecture emulated that of the 'mother country'. Typical of the imperial influence is the magnificent Clarence House, overlooking Nelson's Dockyard and built by English stonemasons in 1787 for Prince William Henry, Duke of Clarence, later to become King William IV. The 'Sailor

King' came to Antigua in his capacity as a midshipman on HMS *Pegasus* and was friendly with Nelson. Clarence House is now the Governor's residence. This fine mansion, which was damaged by Hurricane Luis in 1995, is built on a square floor plan with a symmetrical exterior, over a high, arched stone basement which once held wine and stores. In front of the basement is a double staircase, leading up to the entrance, set in the first-floor gallery, supporting the low, shingled roof. The railed and pillared gallery, which, unusually in English architecture, wraps around all four sides of the house, is shuttered by screens. The railings or balustrades of the balcony are of turned wood, and the internal, high ceilings are timber-clad. Almost devoid of external decoration, the entrance features ornate, wrought-iron brackets, which once held oil lamps. Behind the house in a courtyard are shingled, corrugated iron-roofed, and stone-built outhouses, with warehouse, servants' quarters, laundry and kitchen.

A little further inland is Falmouth where the main attraction is St Paul's Anglican Church, Antigua's first and once a military church when it was built in 1676, when it doubled as a courthouse. It was restored in the 19th century. On top of Monk's Hill, overlooking Falmouth, the fort named Great George dates from 1689. It was completed around 1705, and includes a grand, arched entrance, a barracks, magazine, hospital, 32 cannon sites, and two huge water cisterns, all in seven acres of land. The south-east side of the fort stands 700 ft above the sea. After the Napoleonic Wars, the fort became a signal station but is mostly now in ruins. Further west is the fort on Johnstone Point.

There is much more evidence of 18th-century military architecture around the island. The barracks, on Rat Island, opposite St John's, were constructed in 1741. The vast bulwarks of Fort Charlotte, to the north of Fort Berkeley, were built in 1745, to cover the entrance to English Harbour. Fort Berkeley itself was reinforced so that its 25 large guns could fire from individual, triangular gun emplacements on the spit of land extending into the harbour's mouth. The powder magazine and guard house still stand. On the north-west side of the island on Goat Hill, Fort Barrington, named after an English Admiral who captured St Lucia from the French in 1665, was built above Deep Bay around 1779. This hill, which was fortified from the early 17th century onwards, was the first place that the French attacked when they briefly took the island from the

English in 1666. Fort Barrington was never attacked after its completion in 1779 and became a signal station after the Napoleonic Wars. On the other side of St John's harbour, are the ruins of Fort James, built in 1749 on the site of an earlier fort erected here in 1675. Further south, on the rounded south-west sector of the island, Johnson Point Fort guards the coast almost midway between English Harbour and St John's.

In the capital, St John's, are many fine buildings, incorporating numerous English building styles. Most striking is probably St John's Anglican Cathedral, first built in 1683 and restored twice in 1745 and 1847. The stone-clad, twin-towered cathedral dominates the town. It originally had a squat single tower, with a lantern, but today the new, silver-domed towers have a Baroque look. The cathedral's cool interior is pitch pine-clad, a feature which has helped it to survive earthquakes. It can hold around 2,000 worshippers. The twin, life-size, metal figures of St John the Baptist and St John the Divine at the South Gate are said to have been captured from a French ship *en route* to Martinique and erected here in 1789. The iron railings at the entrance also date from 1789. The cathedral church is now a national monument. The old, smaller, Catholic church is a typical parish church in cruciform design, with a pointed steeple. The central Methodist church, dating from the early 1800s, was extensively restored in the 1970s.

Government House was originally two 17th-century timber-built structures. Its present design dates from 1801, when Lord Lavington, owner of the Carlisle sugar estate, lived here, and it contains a fine example of a Georgian dining room. St John's Police Headquarters building was originally the town's arsenal. Built in 1747, the old Court House in Market Street was once the island's seat of government and is the work of English-born American architect, Peter Harrison. It was built of white stone quarried from one of the north coast islands, was damaged in the two earthquakes of 1843 and 1974, and is now a museum. Used as the offices of the Antigua and Barbuda Historical and Archaeological Society, this is the oldest building in use on the island. Another one of St John's oldest structures is the barracks building, erected in 1735.

Typical of the older period houses are those shops near the waterfront, which have stone-built lower floors, and wooden-clad first floors, projecting out over the sidewalk, supported on narrow pillars. Triple-gabled and corrugated iron-roofed, the houses have

Triple-gabled shop, St John's

typically English sash windows, which, in a concession to the climate, have storm shutters. The lower windows also acted as doors, as they extend to the height of the ground floor. Weatherboarding is common, possibly because of the nautical influence, as early naval dockyards were based at Spithead, Chatham and Portsmouth, all British port towns with a weatherboard architectural tradition. In earlier days, the ground floors were used commercially and the upper storeys as residences. Some of the houses in Redcliffe Quay, where the restored town houses and warehouses are now shops and cafes, display fine gingerbread-decorated balconies. The English flavour of St John's even extends to the cricket grounds, near the Catholic Church, apparently in use since the 1750s.

Elsewhere on Antigua, it is estimated that there were over 170 sugar producing mills, most now in ruins. Thirty-six of these were wind-powered mills, and over fifty were steam-powered. There still exist several old colonial plantation houses and abandoned sugar mills. Betty's Hope, Antigua's first plantation, for example, is a fine restored plantation estate, with two windmill towers, a still house and other mill factory buildings. It is now a museum, with an operative windmill. The name Hope comes from an old English term for an enclosed piece of land or estate, and Betty's Hope was built in 1674 by Sir Christopher Codrington, after whose daughter it is named. Another restored early windmill is that at Harmony Hall, on the south-east coast. Some of the plantation houses have been carefully restored, such as those at Mercer's Creek. However, there are numerous abandoned and overgrown windmill towers across the island, like that at Ffryes Mill.

Antigua's Parham Hill plantation great house originally dates from 1722 and is one of the oldest in the Caribbean. The town of Parham itself is one of the original 17th-century settlements. Many modifications were added to the plantation building in later years, like the first-floor gallery, with its latticework columns supporting the overhanging, steep-pitched, shingle-tiled roof, the leading edge of which has a simple wood fretwork, dog-tooth decoration. The gallery is railed in a wooden geometric design, and the verandah underneath is also edged with the dog-tooth pattern in wood. Part of the upper gallery has a hipped roof. The ground floor verandah is enhanced by a delicate, wrought-iron surround, and the overhanging, wooden floor of the upper gallery is supported by large, decoratively pierced, wrought-iron, curved brackets. The stone walls of the house are painted red, setting off the white tracery and trellis work as well as its white storm shutters and high doors, which open out onto the stone-paved patio. The doors have fine iron medallions and knockers. Both windows and doors have internal, louvred panels. The internal staircase echoes the geometric design of the upper gallery rails. The architectural details of the interior include arched room divisions and doorways, and heavy, timber-beamed ceilings. Parham is also the location of St Peter's Anglican Church, designed in octagonal, Classical Italianate style, and formerly decorated with rich stucco work. It was built by Thomas Weekes in 1840 and once called the most significant ecclesiastical building in the West Indies. It is commonly known as Parham Church.

Weatherhills Estate, originally a cotton plantation and later a sugar estate, dates from 1660, but the existing house was not built until 1890. Typically English in design, the two-storey great house is reached by stone steps leading up to a latticed, corrugated iron-roofed porch. The vast house has three lateral, red, corrugated iron roofs, and its casement windows are storm-shuttered. A verandah runs the length of the ground floor on one side of the house and sports a dog-tooth roof edge decoration. Eight slender columns support the verandah roof. The house is painted in a traditional English white and forest green. Behind the terrace, are the stone-built outbuildings, including stores and a laundry. Fine timber beams form the interior ceilings, and the upper floor ceilings are open to the roof, and timber-clad. The upper part of the dividing wooden walls between rooms comprises latticework clerestory gratings, allowing air to circulate between rooms.

One of the first schools for emancipated slaves' children formed the nucleus of Bethesda village, north of English Harbour. The school opened in 1813, 21 years before emancipation, and freed slaves began building the community from 1834. One of the oldest churches on the island is the Anglican church of St George's on Fitches Creek Bay on the north-east side of the island. Although it has been much restored and remodelled in around 1733, the original structure dates from 1687. Another ancient church is that at St Philips village, in the south-east part of the island, which dates from around 1680.

ARUBA

Although this is the second largest island in the Netherlands Antilles group, the inhospitable nature of the land did not entice the extensive settlement seen on most other Caribbean islands. What early settlement there was, that of small-scale farmers, short-stay miners and merchants, tended to be rudimentary and basic. As a result, few buildings of architectural significance are found on Aruba.

Settled by the Dutch in 1634, this dry, desert-like island, strewn with cactus, offered few benefits to the pioneering colonists. However, the Spanish, who had discovered the island, and then abandoned it to nature, after shipping the indigenous population into slavery, had attracted earlier settlers: the pirates. By 1499, a pirates' lair had been established in the north of the island. This building at Bushiribana, named De Gold Molen, is thought to have been a fortified pirates' inn and, although now a ruin, is the earliest European structure on Aruba. The Spanish erected a cross on a hill near Santa Cruz, a name which indicates the brief Spanish presence. Located in the centre of the island, because of the fear of maritime attacks, Santa Cruz is one of Aruba's oldest settlements. It is believed that the pirates were the first to discover gold at Bushiribana and at Balashi, as the deserted gold smelting works and prospectors' buildings date from the late 15th century. More than

1,350,000 kilos of gold were extracted from these works, and many of the ruins date from the heyday of gold production, around 1824-99. Mining finally came to an end here in 1913.

Although there was a thriving Dutch community on the island by the mid-17th century, and Commandeursbaai (now Savaneta) served as the main port, it was not until 1790 that the Dutch founded the first city in Aruba, Oranjestad (Aruba's oldest settlement, Savaneta, is located in the south, east of Oranjestad). Before that, the settlers made a living from trading slaves with the Spanish, occasionally raiding Spanish ships, and eking a living from the bleak *cunucu* or interior, which they called 'the wasteland'. Aloe vera cultivation, salt production, phosphate mining (begun in 1879 in San Nicolas) and the refining of Venezuelan oil from 1929 onwards followed. Until 1985 Aruba was the site of the world's largest oil refinery.

Wealthy Dutch merchants and traders flocked to Oranjestad in the last decade of the 1700s, building stores, shops and houses remarkably similar to those they left behind in Holland. They built their capital around the Paarden Bay, once named 'Horses Bay', so important was the horse and cattle trade at that time. Many of their tall, narrow, crow-stepped gabled buildings, with their curvilinear facades, and red-tiled roofs, are painted in various pastel shades, with the details picked out in typically Dutch style. Although Dutch colonial architecture is predominant, Spanish features are present, like patios, balconies, and high, wrought-iron railings fencing off the gardens. The oldest public building on the island is Fort Zoutman, built in 1796. The fort was ineffectual as a defensive post, equipped with only four cannon, and the British attacked it and took the island in 1805, holding it until 1816. Between 1810 and 1911, the fort served as government offices. The Willem III Toren, a stone-built tower, was added to the fort in 1868. It was initially a lighthouse, when the petrol light in the spire was lit on King Willem III's birthday in 1869, but later became a clock tower and then a museum. King Willem III's cipher can be seen on the tower. The fort was restored in 1974, and the tower between 1980 and 1983.

One important architectural feature in the city is the early lime kiln, used for producing kalk, a mortar made from burnt coral. Another structure of note is an elaborate-fronted, two-storey building with verandah, dating from 1929. Of passing interest is the floating Schooner Market, and the Wilhelmina Park, with its marble statue of the Queen carved by Arnoldo Lualdi. The canal running alongside the park is crossed by several bridges. There are also a few churches in the capital of moderate interest including the old Protestant and Catholic churches, and the Beth Israel Synagogue. The Protestant church is the island's second oldest building and dates from 1846. Across from the church is an old government building dating from 1911, and the island's public library, once a school and built in 1888. The island's three oldest residences, numbers 21, 27, and 35, Wilhelminastraat, were built in 1877. Back on Shuttestraat, the building number 7 dates from 1937-38, and that at number 8 was built between 1923 and 1925.

Elsewhere, basic and small country houses, with tiles, detailed end gables, porches and shuttered fenestration, dot the landscape. A peculiar feature of many Aruban country houses is the hex sign, usually moulded over the doorway and designed to protect the inhabitants from evil spirits. Santa Anna Church, in the village of Noord, contains a finely carved neo-Gothic oak Dutch altar, communion rails and pulpit, by the sculptor, Hendrik van der Geld, dating from 1870. The original building was constructed in 1766 and was rebuilt in 1831 and again in 1870 and 1886. Father Thomas V Sadelhoff erected the present stone building in 1916. The four German stained glass windows depict Alto Vista's lay preachers or fiscals. There is an ancient cemetery nearby, and the rectory is one of the island's oldest buildings, dating from 1877.

Another delightful chapel is located at Alto Vista, in the north of the island. There has been a place of worship on this spot since Spanish times, hence the name, and this structure was originally built as chapel by the Spanish missionary, Domingo Antonio Silvester, in 1750. Although the Church of Our Lady of Alto Vista dates from 1952, it is built on the site of a church which collapsed in the 1800s. Inside the church is the oldest artwork in the Netherlands Antilles, an ancient Spanish cross.

Gold refining machinery, once installed at Bushiribana to serve the mine at Seroe Gerard, was moved to Frenchman's Pass in 1824. However, the machinery for processing gold at the Balashi gold mill is still in place and dates from 1899. Apart from the Balashi, Bushiribana, and De Gold Molen gold-working ruins, dating from the 1820s, there are few sites of real architectural interest on the island. One unusual import, De Olde Molen, or the old windmill, is, in fact an 1804 windmill, brought from Holland and planted

De Olden Molen, Aruba

behind Palm Beach. There are two striking lighthouses on Aruba, the older one at California Beach, and the other at Seroe Colorado. One interesting feature of the Seroe Colorado lighthouse are the ornate pediments over its twelve windows and entrance door.

THE BAHAMAS

Around 700 islands and a further 2,000 mostly uninhabited 'cays' make up the Bahamas, which, after Columbus' first arrival in 1492, were left to itinerant pirates and buccaneers until claimed by Charles I of England in 1629. In 1647 William Sayle led a group of

English religious dissenters to form a colony on Eleuthera, a venture which was forcibly dispersed by the Spanish in 1684. The unsettled period of the next two hundred years left a legacy of a handful of fortresses. Wrecking, slaving and liquor-smuggling were among the inhabitants' more dubious occupations, and riches were also made from farming, logging, boat-building, fishing, sugar cultivation, sisal and pineapple plantations, sea salt production and the sea-island cotton industry. This last activity thrived during the 18th and 19th centuries until the abolition of slavery, leaving many beautiful plantation mansions and villas. New Providence and Grand Bahama are the most developed and populated islands of the archipelago; the others, known as the 'Family Islands' or 'Out Islands', range from isolated outposts to well-trodden tourist destinations.

It is the strategic position of the Bahamas, scattered between the Caribbean and the south-east corner of the United States, which has always drawn a cross-section of nationalities to settle here. Initially, the Spanish selected a route between Florida and the Bahamas, along which to ship back to Europe the riches plundered in the Americas, highlighting the important location of the islands. Each successive wave of newcomers brought with them the architectural style of their homeland over a period of 300 years. The variety of building styles to be found in the Bahamas is hence both striking and, in some cases, unique.

It is no accident that American colonial buildings rub shoulders with fine English, Georgian-style mansions in the Bahamas, and is the result of the migration of Loyalists from mainland America. After the War of American Independence from 1776, the rebels of the 13 original American states, having obtained their freedom, created a backlash against those colonists who had supported the British in the war. Many thousands of these fled to the Bahamas, re-establishing their plantations and recreating the opulent mansions which they had left in America on the islands. Many were rich cotton planters, but there were also the middle-class, workers, servants and slaves, who built their homes in the style of those in New England, the Carolinas, Mississippi, Louisiana or Florida.

The traditional Bahamanian habit of ship wrecking also led to another architectural development, the network of lighthouses. Each island in the Bahamas had its established pecking order when ships were wrecked off their coasts. Many wrecks occurred more by design than by accident, as the plunder provided a supplement to the islanders' meagre agricultural living and for 300 years wrecking had been a way of life to many Bahamians. To discourage the wreckers, the Imperial Lighthouse Service erected a number of massive lighthouses throughout the islands from the 1830s to the 1870s. These have now become landmarks and tourist attractions, due to the redundancy of the lighthouse with the advent of modern navigational equipment.

New Providence

New Providence is the Bahamas' main island, although not the largest, and Nassau is its capital. The island of New Providence was first settled in 1656, and Nassau was named in 1688, after King William of Orange-Nassau, who became King of England that year. The island's numerous forts and its charming variety of colonial buildings make it architecturally important.

Nassau was formally laid out as early as 1729, just two years before Woodes Rogers (1679-1732), the colony's first Governor, constructed a new barracks for the garrison of Fort Nassau, which was built in 1696. Before this, in 1695, there were several independent buildings in the town, including the church and two public houses, plus around 160 houses. In the early 1740s, the demand for new fortifications led to the rebuilding of Fort Nassau, the building of Fort Montagu, and the erection of Bladen's Battery.

Today's Nassau has a variety of architectural gems, reflecting the prosperity of colonists and Loyalists alike. Before the 19th century most of Nassau's buildings were of timber, but within a few decades it was known as the 'coral city', as so many of its buildings were constructed of white coral limestone. It was with the arrival of 8,000 American Loyalists after the American War of Independence that the town became a city, with the immigrants building grandiose mansions, often after the English Georgian design, not from timber, as in their homeland, but from coral rock. However, they brought wooden embellishments with them, like the jalousied, louvred and latticed-enclosed verandahs, ornate hand rails, high peaked roofs, and the additions of dormer windows.

From picturesque Rawson Square, with its attractive Dolphin Fountain, it is easy to visit the main buildings of architectural significance. Government House, one of the best examples, is reached by a long flight of steps, from Prince Street which lead up Mount

Fitzwilliam. Halfway up the steps is a twice-life size statue of Columbus, erected here in 1830. The magnificent edifice of Government House was begun in 1803, completed in 1806, and rebuilt in the 1920s. It is the finest example of Bahamian-British, Loyalist American colonial-influenced architecture, and is painted pink, with columns, quoins and details picked out in white. The four-columned and pedimented facade of the mansion is typically English Georgian, and its windows are heavily shuttered.

A short distance east is the octagonal Public Library, built by Joseph Eve as a jail in 1798-99. It is though to have been inspired by the Old Powder Magazine in Williamsburg, Virginia. Under its domed and tiled roof, gingerbread fretwork decoration embellishes the second floor, which is built as an all-round verandah or watch platform, supported by sixteen slender columns, with the central bell tower containing fan-lighted windows. The wedge-shaped cells on two floors have stone-concrete vaulting and a single shuttered window. The entrance has a Georgian pediment, and the four windows in each side of the external stone wall are louvre shuttered. This is one of the most remarkable custom-built jailhouses in the Caribbean. The jail became a library in 1879. The cupola and classical design of the nearby Police Station compliment the Library's extraordinary design.

Public Library, Nassau

The gardens nearby are the site of the old Royal Victoria Hotel, built between 1859 and 1861 by the government. Its four-storey twin wings had extensive galleries and a pedimented frontage supported by seven slender columns. This hotel, Nassau's oldest and one of the largest in the Caribbean, was popular during the American Civil War and, later, during the Prohibition period, but was closed in the 1970s.

A few blocks south is the famous Queen's Staircase, 66 brick-paved steps cut into the limestone rock by slaves in the late 18th century. The steps, commemorating Queen Victoria's 66 years on the British throne, lead up to Fort Fincastle, built in 1793, to back up Fort Charlotte. The fort is of distinctive construction, circular in shape, with a bastion shaped like the prow of a ship and supporting six cannon, two of which cover the flanks of the pointed extension, projecting inland. From the 120-foot water tower nearby there is a fine view across the city. The fort, which was never attacked, later served as a lighthouse and then a signal tower.

Governor Lord Dunmore built two forts in Nassau during his period in office (1786-1797), as well as gun emplacements at Fort Winton, Potters Cay and Hog Island. Fort Charlotte, to the west of the city, was built between 1787 and 1794, and was named after George III's consort, Queen Charlotte. Complete with traditional moat, ramparts, battlements, and dungeons, it is the largest fort on the island. It was cut out of the living rock, and the stone from its moat was used to build the upper walls. Elongated in shape, and incorporating Fort Stanley and Fort D'Arcy, two massive, circular bastions face inland, behind a line of gun emplacements facing the sea. Some of the internal buildings were roofed, but most of the fort was carved into the rock. The top floor of the fort was equipped with 24 guns, and another battery, the water battery, was located at sea level and contained another twenty guns. Neither of Dunmore's two forts saw any action.

Also on the west side of town, the British Colonial Hotel occupies the site of the former Fort Nassau, which stood here from 1696 until 1837. The hotel was originally built in 1899, destroyed by fire in 1921 and rebuilt two years later. A statue of Governor Woodes Rogers stands in front of the hotel. On a point opposite Paradise Island, to the east of Nassau, the small Fort Montagu, was built to protect the harbour entrance. This is the oldest of Nassau's three forts and was briefly captured in 1776 by an American force during the Revolution. North-east of Nassau is a building typical of north-ern Caribbean military architecture, the rounded Blackbeard's Tower, said to have been built in the late 1600s and allegedly occu-pied by the notorious pirate. There are two other forts on New Providence island, the late 17th-century fort at Northwest Point, and the ruins of an old fort at South Ocean Beach.

The Public Buildings of Nassau, on Bay Street, are constructed in Classical style, patterned after the colonial architecture of North Carolina, mostly during the Loyalist era. The central building of the three, which house the Legislative Council, Treasury, and House of Assembly, with its columned, pedimented and balconied portico, was built in 1813 by John Fowler. The Senate House is the location of the Monarch's throne, the seat of the Commonwealth's Governor. The two public buildings each side of the central block were built in 1805 by James Tait. All three buildings are harmo-nious in design, with strong quoins and shuttered sash windows. The seated statue of Queen Victoria was dedicated after her death in 1901 and is flanked by two ancient cannon. The Supreme Court building, on Bank Lane, was built in keeping with the classical Tuscan order in 1921, with a strong columned portico under a round-windowed pediment and with louvred-shuttered windows – the only features which bow to the tropical climate.

Nassau's churches reveal a mixture of religions, and therefore of traditional religious architectures. Christ Church Cathedral, on George Street, was Nassau's first Anglican church, pulled down thir-teen years after its construction in 1671 by the Spanish. Since the original's destruction in 1684, four further churches have been built on the site, and today's towered edifice dates from 1837. Its quar-ried limestone block walls are held together almost entirely by their weight. Raised to cathedral status in 1861, when Nassau became a city, it was extended that year to include the sanctuary and part of the chancel, or choir. Its stone-built, island neo-Gothic exterior design is set off inside by stone columns in four early English designs, which support a timber trussed roof. Parts of the church date from 1753, when it became the garrison church. Top-hinged shutters protect the nave's tall Gothic windows, which contain some fine stained glass. The east windows were made in the French city of Nice by a M. Fasi-Cadet and were a gift from an American, and were unveiled in 1949. The other windows were installed in 1995 and designed and made in North Carolina.

The three-storey Deanery dates from 1710, and is said to be Nassau's oldest residence. Its stone-built core, with shuttered fenestration, is enclosed by a latticed and railed balcony, jutting out over the ground floor. The balcony is supported on wooden columns, which rise through the gallery to support the edges of the roof. Nearby are the kitchen and slave quarters in a small, one-storey building to the west of the house. Also on Queen Street, there are some elegant Georgian homes. On East Street, the Church of God of Prophecy is modern in design, built in 1946 as a low, elongated construction, capped by a small, pyramid-roofed bell turret. Tall Gothic-style louvred windows are set off by numerous stepped buttresses. The St Francis Xavier Catholic Cathedral, the first in the Bahamas, built in 1885 and consecrated in 1887, is almost simple Spanish colonial in design, with a steeply pitched tiled roof, roof turret and buttressed tower. The south entrance is plain and buttressed, with an arched doorway under small circular windows. The nearby Priory was Lord Dunmore's official residence, built in 1787, and is a fine example of early British colonial architecture.

St Matthew's Church, one of the oldest in existence in Nassau, is especially hurricane-proof in its low-roofed design by Joseph Eve. Built in 1802 by American Loyalists, its octagonal tiled tower and spire make up for the rectangular simplicity of the main body of the church. The arched entrances are elaborated with raised quoins, and the church's interior is set off by the circular Ionic roof columns of the nave and its large shuttered, arched windows. The cemetery here is of particular interest. St Andrew's Presbyterian Kirk dates from 1810, the Zion Baptist Church dates from 1835, St Agnes Church, with its steeply pitched roof, was consecrated in 1848, and the Trinity Methodist church was built in 1866. In the mid-19th century, the sponge industry attracted a community of Greeks to the Bahamas, and with them came their religion and their religious architecture. The Greek Orthodox Church, 'Annunciation', was built in traditional, domed, Byzantine style in 1932. Its interior is typically ornate, in keeping with the decorative style which dates from the early first century.

The majority of Nassau's residents now live in suburban Grant's Town, founded by freed slaves in 1838, and entered through picturesque Gregory Arch, opened in 1852, but there are several important and distinctive private buildings in Nassau. Most of these are Victorian, but many are built in the style of the Georgian era.

The Jacaranda House, built in the 1840s, has its entire south facing side louvred, with three shuttered windows and attached timber balconies. A curious feature is the chimney stack, with its arched top. The east and west sides have Demerara windows, hinged at the top, while the bottom row are shuttered. Prominent characteristic quoins are picked out in white on the corners of the two-storey house, which is built over a basement floor. The ground floor is reached by a pattern-railed, double staircase, and the main entrance sports fine wrought-iron gates. The nearby Magna Carta building is unusual for its east stone facade and west timber facade, which is louvred with a balcony above the porch. The stone frontage is plain, with shuttered sash windows. Green Shutters, also on Parliament Street, is now a public house and dates from 1865. Oakes House is also very typical of the Victorian period, with a double verandahed frontage supported by slender columns and decorative railings. The top balcony is part-louvred.

Jacaranda House, Nassau

The Balcony House on Market Street is slightly older, around 1790, and has an unsupported, projecting first-floor balcony, built into the eaves and half-louvred above enclosing formal railings. Three small, cantilever curved brackets are all that supports the balcony, which is an integral part of the roof. The brackets are thought to be of shipwright's origin, as shipbuilding was a major industry in Nassau at the time. The house is built of American soft cedar on a masonry base and its simple entrance is reached by railed steps. Inside, the staircase is said to have come from a ship. The Verandah House on the same street has a typical porch and little dormer windows, with top-hinged shutters.

Balcony House, Nassau

Shirley Street, running parallel to the Bay Street promenade, is a delight of old, pastel-painted houses, and Addington House is typical. With a broad verandah and Bahama shutters, it was built in the 1880s. On West Hill Street, the impressive 1860s Villa Doyle is not typical of Bahamian architecture and probably owes its provenance to the mansions of post-Civil War Louisiana. It core is of stone, with prominent quoined corners, and long, double galleries run around the two-storey villa with its bracketed, tiled roof. Also on the same street is The Fold, a two-storey hip-roofed building of simple proportions, with a protruding bay window on the ground floor, supported by brackets, quoined corners and additions to either side. Fenestration is louvre-shuttered and latticed. Graycliff House, a beautiful Georgian colonial mansion nearby, is now an inn and is said to have been the residence of the privateer Captain Gray and dates from the mid-1700s.

On East Hill Street, the pink-and-white Georgian colonial mansion is the East Hill Club, built in the 1840s by American Loyalists. Here, also, is Glenwood House, built in the 1880s, and opposite one of the city's oldest houses, Bank House, dating from the 1780s. On Duke Street is the pretty Princess House, with steps leading up to an enclosed louvred and latticed porch. Its slated roof has dormer sash windows with steep gables. Sand House, now destroyed, was an historic, three-storey landmark on the same street. This building once featured a fully enclosed south facade, and an open north balcony with star-patterned balustrading. The wooden-built, early 19th-century house in Village Road, named The Retreat, is home to The Bahamas National Trust.

Another fine stone and timber building, now demolished, was the Adderley house, with a completely enclosed verandah and lower floor, encased in louvres. Shipbuilders constructed several unusual buildings in Nassau, mainly timber-built like the Timber House in Dowdswell Street, with its completely enclosed, latticed ground floor and balconied first floor. The Cascadilla House, built in the early 1840s, is also typical of the shipbuilder's architectural flair. This house is beautifully simple in design, with little or no embellishments. Its third floor, reached by a small staircase, is thought to have been a lookout. The beautiful timber-framed Red Roofs house on East Bay Street is remarkable for its ornate carved wooden decorations, turned balustrading, latticework, pentagonal porch, louvred windows, fanlight above the front door and fine jalousies. George-side House, on George Street, is a typical stone-built house, surrounded by timber galleries. On the corner of Marlborough Street and West Street is a vast old building, probably dating from the late 1700s and surrounded by timber galleries, supported by carved bracketed posts. The later, second floor, possibly reconstructed, has hip-roofed dormer windows, and the fenestration throughout is sash. Storm shutters protect the main windows.

The Vendue House, to the west of Nassau, the city's oldest house, now the Pompey Museum, was once a slave auction house, named after the French word for 'selling', before becoming a market. The original, single-storey building faced Government House from the dockside end of George Street. It was built sometime before 1769, and its name Pompey derives from that of a slave who lived on the Steventon Rolle estate in Exuma in the 1830s. The present two-storey building has a Corinthian portico with rusticated stone window arches and a typical outside wooden staircase, and was restored in 1992.

Vendue House, Nassau

On Paradise Island opposite Nassau, Versailles Gardens, built by Huntington Hartford, has a 14th-century French cloister, taken from an Augustine monastery near Lourdes. Also in the gardens is a fine marble statue of a reclining nude Empress Joséphine. Father Jerome's St Augustine's Monastery, south of Nassau, is a vast Romanesque complex of cloisters and dormitories, school building, and hall, home to the island's Benedictine monks. There are five country villages on New Providence: Adelaide, Carmichael, Bain Town, Fox Hill and Gambier. These consist of small clusters of wood-built traditional houses and picturesque, simple stone cottages, thatched in palmetto. These were usually built of a timber frame, in-filled with stone known as 'tabby' and then rendered with a lime-based plaster. Timber cross lathes were then thatched. Window openings were unglazed and protected by storm shutters, top, or side-hinged, fixed to the window frame, which fitted into an opening cut into the wall. The doors were simple and timber-planked, hinged into the door frames which were let into the front and back walls.

The Board House at Gambier is typical of later buildings, raised off the ground on stone blocks and reached by little wooden steps. This simple, rectangular dwelling is weather-boarded on a timber frame, with a shingled roof. Window shutters are both top and side hinged. At Adelaide, the St James Anglican Church is of note, built in very simple style in the 1830s, with a steep tiled roof. The later St Anne's Anglican Church at Fox Hill was built on the site of an older church in 1848. The exterior is simple, with rendered walls, but the spacious interior has slender, fluted, cast-iron columns, with ornate finials supporting a heavy, timber roof. The Bacardi company has built a vast rum distillery at Coral Harbour in the south-west of the island. The island has an acute water shortage problem and therefore is dotted by hundreds of wind-powered pumps.

Grand Bahama and Freeport

Neither Grand Bahama Island nor Freeport, its capital, can be rated as of any historic architectural interest. The two earliest historic connections are the possibility of a pirate base here in the 1840s, and the bootlegging jetty, used by liquor-runners during the period of US Prohibition. However, the few modern sites include the ten-acre International Bazaar, with European, Near East and Asian architectural style shops and restaurants dating from the 1960s. The Bazaar is entered through a traditional 35-foot Japanese gateway. This is located next to the Moorish-style Princess Casino, also built in the 1960s as one of the largest in the western hemisphere. In the Garden of the Groves, a botanical tourist attraction, is a tiny chapel built of local stone, intended as a replica of the first church on Grand Bahama. The oldest remains on the island are those of Old Free Town, now an abandoned village. Some of the old cottages of Eight Mile Rock village are attractive, and St Stephen's Church here, dates from 1851.

Eleuthera

This island, named after the Greek word for freedom, was settled in 1647 by members of the Eleutherian Adventurers' Company, who first sought shelter in a 30-foot high cave. Their initial settlement, near the cave, was destroyed by the Spanish in 1684. The island, made up of one long land mass and many islets, is dotted with numerous pretty, early villages with pastel-painted Bahamian-style wooden houses. Typical of these are Tarpum Bay with its tiny church, the picturesque old houses on Spanish Wells, those in The Current, and in The Bluff. Governor's Harbour is the nearest approximation, visually, to the island's earliest settlement, Cupid's Cay, where some of the oldest houses dating from the 1600s, have now been restored. The Victorian village of Governor's Harbour has homes dating back to the 1850s.

The houses in Spanish Wells are stark and basic in design, wood framed and weather-boarded, almost like glorified garden sheds. Picket rails divide housing lots and carved railings embellish the few balconies, which are second-floor overhangs. Sash windows are simply shuttered, and some houses have dormer windows. The roofs of these simple dwellings are shingled and often brightly painted. All the houses are raised off the ground on stone blocks to facilitate ventilation. Some of the houses are more ambitious, with wrap-around verandahs, typically supported by curved and bracketed slender wooden columns, supporting the lower roof of the hipped porch. The roof of the upper storey might be star-shaped, with dormer windows set into the four gables. Curved wooden brackets, typical of the work of the maritime occupants, also support simple gutterings. Chamfered internal columns, as ceiling supports, are also typical of the building details of Bahamian shipwrights' houses. Also on Eleuthera Island is Millers, an old plantation house.

Just off Eleuthera's main island, Dunmore Town is Harbour Island's largest settlement. The island was settled in 1694, and in 1880 Dunmore Town was the second largest settlement in the Bahamas, specializing in sugar refining and shipbuilding. There were once three sugar mills around Dunmore Town, and Monroe's 1797 sail loft was moved from the centre of the town to the water-front. It is now known as the Loyalist Cottage. Some of the earliest of the houses here are two or three storeys high and have typical first-floor verandahs and dormer windows. Many of pastel-coloured saltbox cottages are reminiscent of those in New England. The Methodist Church is the largest in the Family Islands, built in 1843. The Round Heads are fortifications used to protect the settlement from the Spanish, who are said to have used the cannon at the

Battery House. The English-style colonial manor on Barracks Hill was once Lord Dunmore's residence. There is a fine example of a barrel-vaulted family tomb in the town's old churchyard, which was abandoned during a cholera epidemic.

Exuma Islands

Three main islands make up this group, which thrived during the cotton-growing era. Treasured architectural remnants of the industry and its wealthy operators are dotted throughout the islands and date from the 18th and 19th centuries. A hotel occupies the site of an early slave market on Great Exuma, where an obelisk recalls the location's previous use.

In George Town, the miniature town square is surrounded by old buildings like the Library, built on stilts, and the grand, pink Government Building, modelled on Nassau's Government House. On a hill nearby, the simple, slit-windowed, St Andrew's Anglican Church dates from 1802. South of George Town are some 18th- and 19th-century houses in Rolle Town, which has a fascinating, dry stone walled graveyard with some poignant tombs from the late 1700s. It is said that a plantation owner, Lord Rolle, ceded his large estate to freed slaves in 1834, giving his name to Rolle Town and Rolleville, where some ancient cotton plantation ruins can be seen. There are more old houses to the north, in Gilbert Grant, with thatched roofs and English-style walled-in fields. At Hartsville there are some stone-built, pastel-painted 18th-century houses and similar buildings in Rolleville. Steventon was the residence of the cotton-growing Lord Rolle in the early 1800s and one of his five Exuma plantations.

The old Loyalist cotton plantation house of the Hermitage Estate on Little Exuma dates from 1784. A shingle roof covers the entire house and its square pillared verandah. A separate building houses the kitchen and features a brick chimney. A flat-topped cistern to one side of the simple house collected rainwater from the roof. Near the main house are two slaves' quarters, built from sawn coral rock. The door and window openings have red brick 'soldier' or flat lintels, supported by 2-inch thick hardwood planks set into the stonework each side of the opening. The roofs were timber framed, with either thatch or wooden shingle covering. Between the two abutted dwellings, fireplaces were built back-to-back for cooking with a common chimney. There is also an old obelisk on Little Exuma, designed as a navigation aid and erected in the early 19th century in the form of a Tuscan column, thirty feet high.

Other Out Islands

The **Abaco Islands**, a group of ten islands and cays, were first settled in the 1650s. In the 18th century American loyalists arrived, and several of the early buildings on the islands reflect the American architectural style of the period. New Plymouth on Green Turtle Cay is a typical example, with much of the air of an early New England township. The Albert Lowe Museum is an 1840s white-painted, two-storey clapboard house of the island style. Such houses are usually weather-boarded or clapboarded on the outside and timber clad on the inside, with either gable or dormer sash windows lighting the upper floors, and shuttered sash windows in the lower floor. Shingled roofs are typically cranked over a verandah to the front and stores to the back. Kitchens were built separately, away from the main, wood framed, weather-boarded house. The house frames were often pegged together with wooden pegs, and the plank facing is of Jacksonville pine, with typical beading along the lower edge of each board. In the village of Hope Town on Elbow Cay there are numerous examples of New England-style saltbox or sandbox cottages, and an interesting specimen of Loyalist architecture, the Wyannie Malone Historical Museum, dating from around 1875, can be visited. The Loyalist cemetery here has headstones dating from the 1780s, and the old Jail House is a rare example of a stone-built lock-up. On Elbow Cay there is a 120-foot red-and-white striped lighthouse, erected in 1863, a familiar landmark in the region. This is the oldest manned, hand-wound, kerosene-powered lighthouse left in the world. Its light, from 'Bull's Eye' lenses, can be seen from fifteen miles away. The Bahamas Lighthouse Preservation Society is based in nearby Hope Town.

Andros Island's picturesque settlements, with their brightly-painted traditional Bahamian houses, include Love Hill, Nicholl's Town (its largest settlement and noted for its Georgian, colonial-style Administration building) and Staniard Creek. Red Bays Village is a remote community on the west coast of the island, which was formerly a Seminole Indian settlement and which preserves much of the early Bahamian way of life. Old churches exist in Staniard Creek and at Behring Point, were there is an ancient well and a pool used to cure sisal, once cultivated on a local farm.

On **Bimini**, the Anchorage is a fine example of an old Cape Cod-style home, and nearby is the New England-influenced Wesley Methodist Church, built in white clapboard with green shutters and a miniature bell tower in 1858. Ernest Hemingway lived in Blue Marlin cottage on Bimini between 1935 and 1937, and there is the imposing mansion of inventor George Bert Lyon on Paradise Point. The oldest inn on the island is the Compleat Angler, dating from the first decade of the 20th century. Off North Bimini, thirty feet under the sea, some large blocks of dressed stone have been found, of unknown origin, but possibly the remnants of a shipwreck.

Cat Island is the site of a Mediterranean-style miniature Roman Catholic Abbey, with a tall, round bell tower, chapel, study, cloister, sleeping quarters and Hermitage. The complex dates from 1949 and is located on the highest point in the Bahamas, Mount Alvernia (just 206 feet in altitude). Father Jerome, originally an Anglican priest and architect who converted to Catholicism, built the Hermitage by hand. The Bight is Cat Island's main village, and like Bennett's Harbour, the island's oldest settlement, is typically picturesque. One of the oldest houses in the Bahamas, the ruined Deveaux Mansion in Port Howe, was built on Cat Island in 1783 by Andrew Deveaux on land he was granted for having recaptured Nassau from the Spanish. It is one of the finest houses in the Bahamas, and just four of its buildings remain: the kitchen, ablution block and slave quarters adjoining the main house. The main house, two storeys high with six dormer windows in its shingled roof, once had timber galleries overlooking the sea. The floor beams are of local madeira wood, and French craftsmen were imported to decorate the interior. The Loyalist Large House in Arthur's Town is a good example of a typical, square, stone-built villa, based on a stone plinth with a decorated wrap-around verandah, a shingled roof supported by 24 slender wood columns and four dormer windows. Here also are the facade of the old colonial Ambrister House and the ruins of Pigeon Bay Cottage, a 19th-century plantation house. The village of Devil's Point has a number of interesting, low, thick-walled, and brightly-painted old houses, with thatched roofs. Some of the newer houses like those at Old Bight are shingle-roofed and stone-built, with corner buttresses, and timber-framed galleries. At

Old Bight there is also Father Jerome's tiny St Francis of Assisi Catholic Church, featuring a small spire and almost Dutch-looking facade

Crooked Island boasted forty cotton plantations in the early 1800s, and there are two British forts at French Wells and near Marine Farm. Here also is Hope Great House, a fine colonial mansion, and the 120-ft Bird Rock Lighthouse, dating from 1872. Hard Hill, on neighbouring **Acklins**, is the site of an old lookout post, and there are several picturesque and whimsically named old villages on the island, such Delectable Bay, Lovely Bay, Pompey Bay, with its tiny church, and Snug Corner.

The mid-19th century Salt Storage House stands near Matthew Town on **Great Inagua**. The trusses of the roof were originally timber, and the roof itself is metal, covering three bays. Twenty-two huge buttresses support the massive stone walls, and stones were brought from the ruins of Port Royal in Jamaica to build the doorways. This is the largest historical industrial building in the Bahamas. The long, delicately spired St Phillip's Anglican Church was built in 1852 and is stone plastered with a shingle roof and shingled spire. The octagonal font dates from 1897. Near the church are the tiny buildings of St Phillip's Lodge, dating from 1891, and the minuscule Wesley Methodist Church. The remains of the summer retreat of the Haitian King Henri Christophe, built around 1809, stand on North East Point, and his treasure is reputed to be buried on the island.

Burnt Ground on **Long Island** is one of the most typical Out Island villages in the Bahamas, as is Simms, with its thatched houses, a tiny building claimed to be an ancient Spanish church, and a pastel-painted jail. Typical Long Island houses are simple, stone-walled and plastered structures, with hipped roofs and side hung shutters, built without external galleries or embellishments. Shingles replace thatching in many cases. The wooden Methodist Church was built in around 1900 with Gothic influences. It has a shingle roof and a braced timber, free-standing bell tower, with a pointed, shingled roof. The remains of Gray's Plantation House are significant, as is the old cotton gin of Millerton. Near Clarence Town are the remains of the plantation house of Dunmore's Estate. The white twin-towered St Peter's Roman Catholic Church in Clarence Town, was built in 1946 by Father Jerome (See Cat Island) in a style influenced by North African architecture. Father

Jerome also built the slightly less imposing St Paul's Anglican Church here, after a hurricane destroyed the original. The stone-built, timber and metal roofed, Gothic-influenced St Andrew's Anglican Church at Wemyss dates from 1885. It has a gabled rose window and arched bell tower and a typically clear span timber ceiling, as opposed to the trend for Catholic churches to use stone vaulting supported by aisle columns. In Deadman's Cay, the stone-built, metal-roofed, St Athanatius' Anglican Church is English or French Medieval in design, dating from 1929. Built later in 1938, the Church of Our Lady of Mount Carmel at Hamilton emulates those churches built in California or Mexico by Spanish missionaries. Its curved roof and facade are echoed in its buttresses and windows. Built of rendered stone in adobe style, it has a vaulted stone-concrete roof.

San Salvador is the site of Watling's Castle, an old ruined house at French Bay. The building is supposed to have been the work of the infamous buccaneer, Captain John Watling, who was based here around 1680, but research suggests that it was, in fact, a Loyalist plantation house. More plantation house ruins can be found at the towns of Fortune Hill and Sandy Point. Dixon's Hill Lighthouse here was erected in 1856 and is 165 feet above sea level. It is one of the last hand-operated, kerosene-lit lighthouses left in the world. The large cross on the island's east coast commemorates the supposed landing place of Christopher Columbus in 1492, and was erected in 1892. There are three other crosses on San Salvador which proclaim the same event!

BARBADOS

This island is one of the Caribbean's architectural treasure houses, with a plethora of fine British colonial buildings, not least of which are the magnificent churches and public buildings. Barbados' long history of sugar production has also left a rich heritage of grand buildings and typical chattel houses. Almost 350 years of unbroken British rule, ending with independence in 1966, gave Barbados a distinctively British feel, which is reflected in its architecture and its nickname, 'Little England'.

Naming the island after the drooping beard-like aerial roots of the ficus trees, the Portuguese explorer Pedro de Campos dubbed it

Os Barbados in 1536. In 1605, the first English ship, the *Olive Branch* arrived in Barbados, claiming it for the British Crown. The first English settlers, sponsored by Sir William Courteen, arrived in 1625 in the ship *William and John* under Captain John Henry Powell. Courteen and Powell returned to England to recruit more colonists, and a further eighty settlers arrived in 1627, establishing themselves at Holetown (apparently named after the town of Limehouse Hole on the English River Thames). An obelisk now marks the landing place. Another group of Englishmen landed a little further south in 1628 at a place they named Bridgetown, now the island's capital.

St James's Parish Church in Holetown is one of the oldest stone churches in the West Indies; its font dates from 1684 and the church tower's bell is inscribed 'God Bless King William. 1696'. The church was partially reconstructed in 1789 and again in 1874, utilizing the original red coral stonework in a Romanesque design. In 1874, the church was extended an extra twenty feet to the west, when the nave roof was raised and pillars and arches were added. The south porch, with its twin stone pillars and ornamented archway, is said to date from the original design. The squat tower is tiled with a flattened pyramidal roof and is flanked by a tall, rounded turret with a tiled cone-shaped roof. Inside this is a spiral staircase. The central nave, distinctly medieval in feeling, rises above the two side aisles, with quatrefoil windows. Elsewhere, arched windows let light into the interior. A tomb in the churchyard, similar to those elsewhere of the same era, is half buried, with entrance steps leading down to the stone-built mausoleum. This church was sensitively restored between 1983 and 1986.

In Bridgetown, the Anglican St Michael's Cathedral (see page 26), basically Gothic in design, was built between 1661 and 1665, when it was consecrated. It was rebuilt in 1780 after a hurricane, and again in 1789 with lottery-raised money. This cathedral is long and broad and can hold up to 1,600 worshippers. It has a squat, square, castellated tower, and its eastern addition has a roof which resembles the keel of an upturned ship. Inside, the font dates from 1680 and carries the motto, 'Wash the sin, not the skin.' Some of the tombs built into the porch date from 1675. In the 1790s, this church was said to have the widest, barrel-vaulted arched ceiling of its kind in the world. It became a cathedral after Bishop William Hart Coleridge arrived in Barbados in 1825, and it was he who built

Barbados' network of ten 'Chapels of Ease'. Many of these were destroyed in a violent hurricane in 1831 and rebuilt in Gothic style. St Mary's Church dates from 1825, when it was built on what remained of the first St Michael's Church, and also has a squat, Gothic-style castellated bell tower, like that of St Lucy. Georgian elements are also evident, with heavily quoined arches and windows. With its jalousied porch windows acting as a concession to the tropical climate, its interior has a finely decorated vaulted ceiling.

St George's Church, dating from 1780-4, is built in a mixture of styles and has a taller tower, with four pointed finials, reminiscent of the towers of Western England churches. Gothic details include the crenellations, while the arched windows and doors lean to the Georgian. The church is renowned for its altar paintings, and sculptures by Richard Westmacott. This was one of only four parish churches to survive the 1831 hurricane. St Paul's is typical of Coleridge's churches, in the Gothic revival style, with pointed arched windows, buttresses and steep gable roofs.

St Lucy Church, Barbados

'In nothing is the illusion of England so compelling as in the Parish churches of Barbados. They stand alone in the canefields, their battlemented belfries and vanes and pinnacles appearing over the tops of sheltering clumps of trees. Moss-covered crosses and head-stones, or square hurricane graves embedded in the soil, scatter the turf inside the low walls with the haphazard charm of an English graveyard, and the interiors are full of the familiar and evocative aroma of hassocks and hymn-books and pews. Natural disasters have flung them down and the parishioners have built them up again and again, but no hint of these vicissitudes mars their peaceful solid-ity. Nothing but the mid-Victorian stained glass suggests a modifica-tion later than the earliest murmurs of the Gothic revival in the late eighteenth and nineteenth centuries, although, like the plantation houses, they were nearly all rebuilt later than the great 1831 hurri-cane.' Patrick Leigh Fermor, *The Traveller's Tree* (1950)

There are several hundred churches on the island, of varying denominations and architectural styles, and many have outstanding features. The First Baptist Church, for instance, is a 19th-century building, as is St Patrick's Roman Catholic Cathedral, dating from 1848, which was rebuilt after a fire in 1897. It has a fine hammer-beam ceiling. Two churches on the island have graceful spires, those of St Ann's and the Holy Cross. All Saints Church in St Peter parish contains some beautiful stained glass windows, and James Street Methodist church in the city has a rose window and a typically Georgian Palladian porch. St Margaret's in Bridgetown is a converted sugar boiling house.

The Sharon Moravian Church was built in 1799, with a squat-towered entrance surmounted by a pointed-roofed lantern, in typi-cally Low Countries style. Bridgetown's Synagogue was built first in 1654, and again in 1833, after the 1831 hurricane, but was aban-doned in 1929 and has recently been restored. This is one of the oldest synagogues in the Americas, and part of the interior structure has been stripped away to reveal the original roof timbers and coral stone. Country churches of note include the 1837 Christ Church, at Oistins, with its Chase Vault mystery, the 18th-century St Andrew's Anglican Church (rebuilt in 1846) and St Jude's Church with its carved wooden ceiling, dating from 1839, and St Lucy's Church.

Fortifying the Colony

In the 18th century, Bridgetown was developed as one of Britain's three naval dockyards, together with Port Royal, Jamaica, and English Harbour, Antigua. Fort Charles was built south of Bridgetown, on Needham Point, to defend Carlisle Bay. It was the largest of Barbados' forts, but only the ramparts and several 24-pounder cannon from 1824 remain. St Anne's Fort, with its prominent 1804 clock tower, dates from 1704 and has a conspicuous crenellated signal tower. The early 18th-century naval installations included a number of ordnance stores and a mast-pond located in the Garrison Savannah area outside the city. Now the city's race-track, the Garrison Savannah was once the finest parade ground in the Caribbean. The two-storey barracks is formed of a double row of six arches, some completely louvered, providing one colonnade on top of another, fronting the basic, oblong building. Most of the buildings are constructed in typical military colonial style, mainly of brick ballast sent from England.

Shot tower, St Anne's Fort

The old West India Military Barracks, built in red brick, were constructed by the Royal Enginers in 1853. The original barracks, destroyed in 1831 by the disastrous hurricane, were formerly the Naval Dockyard, built in 1805 and which was shifted to its Antigua location. The Garrison Jail, also dating from 1853, is now a museum. The Maya-temple-like, sexagonal structure in the centre of St Anne's Fort is a shot tower, one of the few examples left in the Caribbean. Lead shot was produced in this castellated stone building by dropping molten lead through a sieve from the top of the tower into a reservoir of water deep in the base. The shot tower dates from the early 18th century.

The entire military complex included the General Hospital, or Pavilion Court, at nearby Hastings, and the Quartermaster's Stores, later called the Garrison Theatre. With its Wren-like high clock tower and green-topped dome, the original Garrison Guard House, faces the central parade ground. It is built in Georgian-Palladian style, common throughout the British Caribbean. Beneath the four-tiered, four-sided, clock tower, an ornate pediment dominates the entrance, with an iron roof running the length of the building which shades the interior. This roofing, with its extension over the entrance forming a verandah, is supported by cast-iron columns and ornate brackets. A stone and wrought-iron wall and gateway enclose the building. The collection of cannon outside is the largest in the world, containing thirty cannon dating from the mid-17th to the late 18th centuries. Many stand on metal 'garrison' gun carriages, usually replaced by wooden ones in action. Some of the howitzers here date from 1878.

Other forts on Barbados include Plantation Fort, or Fort St James, in Holetown, which was built in the 18th century. In Speightstown are the remains of the 18th-century Denmark Fort (the town was defended by no fewer than four other defence posts, Orange Fort, Dover Fort, Coconut Fort, and the Heywood Battery, all of which are in ruins). There are also the remains of several early fort sites near Maycock's Bay.

The island also had an intricate system of military signal stations. The famous Gun Hill Signal Station was built in 1818 and is better known for its huge white carved lion than for its buildings which include the hexagonal watch tower, barrack rooms, and magazine. The signal station was once surrounded by a pallisade, and was restored by the National Trust in 1982. The lion was cut out of the limestone rock by a Colonel Henry Wilkinson in 1868. The signal station was later used as a convalescent home for the troops, one of whom was Wilkinson. At Hackleton's Cliff, St Joseph, on the east coast, there is another early military signal station, the Cotton Tower, also owned by the National Trust. The restored Grenade Hall Signal Station, in the north of the island near Farley Hill, is another in the network of the early 19th-century chain of six semaphore towers, and there is another at Moncrieffe, St John.

Planning Bridgetown

Founded in 1628, Bridgetown is allegedly named after an old Amerindian bridge which once spanned the harbour entrance. In the 1640s, Barbados community life centred around the town council. They met in a succession of taverns and privately owned houses until a town hall was finally completed in 1732. However, by 1695 most of the houses of the capital were built of stone and tiles, replacing the early wooden, thatched buildings, which were so susceptible to fire.

Even so, many old Bridgetown architectural treasures have been lost in a series of fires, one of which, in 1766, destroyed a total of 1,140 buildings. From records, paintings and old prints, many of the older buildings had a remarkably strong Dutch appearance, as a result of the Dutch influence on the nascent sugar industry. These buildings had gabled and stepped-gabled fronts and were tall and narrow, crowding down onto the wharves. Most were two-storey, and some three, often with typically Dutch curvilinear gables, a popular feature in Jacobean Europe. Few, because of fires in the mid-19th century, now survive. One, however, appears to date from the late 1660s and is known as the Nicholls' Building. It also has the typical pulley loft in the attic, for winching goods or chattels to the upper floors of the narrow building. There are a few other buildings in the town of a similar style but of a later date. The countryside around Bridgetown was also dotted with wooden-and-stone Dutch-style post windmills, used for sugar-cane crushing.

Although few very old buildings remain in Bridgetown, the Georgian Governor's House dates from 1703. It was known as the 'Pilgrim's House', after the Quaker, John Pilgrim, who first lived on the site. It has a wonderful bow front and is the most elegant and intact building dating from that period on the island. At the top of Queen's Park is a two-storey mansion dating from 1786, which was once the residence of the Commander of the British West Indies Fleet in the Windwards. Other more historic buildings include Washington House from 1750, and Bay Mansion, an 18th-century colonial house, completed in 1784 and built on the original Bay Estate. Here, on the imposing pedimented facade, quoins outline corners and the house's tall, Georgian sash windows. These stand over a triple-arched ground-floor frontage.

Trafalgar Square, actually triangular, was laid out in central Bridgetown in 1874. Nelson's statue, now turned to face inland instead of out to sea, was erected in 1813 by Sir Richard Westmacott, ten years after the Admiral, 'Preserver of the West Indies', died. The statue, without a column, was put up 36 years before the one in London. In the centre of the square is the Dolphin Fountain carved in 1865 to commemorate piped water introduced in 1861. Here also is the 1831 'Olive Blossom' obelisk. The city's grey Public Buildings, including the neo-Gothic Parliament Building, are crenellated, with pointed arches, green louvred windows, red metal shades and roofs. Built in 1872 and 1874, they consist of two long rounded Italian Renaissance-style buildings, with a church-like clock tower. Stained glass windows in the Parliament Building feature British monarchs from King James I to

Queen Victoria. The Montefiore Fountain was donated to the city in 1864, and the Public Library building dates from 1905.

One of the most impressive Victorian commercial buildings in Bridgetown is the centrally located former Barbados Mutual Life building. Set on a block of its own, it rises from a dark stone base in an eclectic style, with an ornate, covered, first-floor iron verandah running around three sides of the building, supported by eighteen curved brackets. The finely decorated verandah roof is itself supported by eighteen thin cast-iron double columns. The central pediment over the second floor, with its arched windows, is dramatically highlighted in bas-relief, complementing the two smaller pediments on either side of the structure. The large pediment is balanced by two three-storey tower blocks, one to each side. These are finished with decorative rails and finials and have vaguely Indian Imperial domes, each one topped by a small lantern.

Street scene, Bridgetown

There are some elaborate town houses in Bridgetown, notably those on Bay Street, with delightful gingerbread fretwork decorations, and the late 18th-century balconies of Swan Street, Roebuck Street, Tudor Street and Baxter's Road. Some houses have ornate cast-iron balconies, and one example dates from 1840. Lynton House is a typically Bajan town house, with a curved parapet and ornate balcony. Castle View is a traditional Georgian house, and the Savoy Hotel, with its verandah addition, dates from around 1800. A few buildings still have old dormer windows in their roofs, and some still have the popular 18th-century brick dentil ornamentation. A good example of the use of quoins and dentil work can be seen on the dramatic frontage of Dacostas Mall on Broad Street, a former Georgian wareouse turned shopping arcade.

Speightstown

Named after a 17th-century member of Barbados' Parliament, William Speight, this town and port became known as 'Little Bristol' during the heyday of the sugar industry. Probably the most significant house in the town is the three-storey Arlington House, with its medieval-looking external staircase. It is thought that these 'single houses', lent their narrow gabled design to those built in Charleston, US, in the late 17th and 18th centuries. Certainly, this 17th-century house is also reminiscent of late medieval English town houses. The grandest official structure is that of the library and post office, with its Georgian staircase and gallery. Built of ship's ballast from Bristol, the three-storey drugstore has dormer windows, a dramatic verandah and has walls 28 inches thick. Classic two-storey shops, with Georgian balconies and overhanging galleries, can be seen on Church Street and on Sand Street, where there are more traditional verandahs and balconies with outside staircases. This is also the site of a 17th-century Manse.

Plantation Great Houses

There are numerous sugar plantation houses in various states of repair throughout the island, although the most famous is in the north of the island. St Nicholas Abbey plantation house is authentic Jacobean in style and dates from 1650-1660, in the reigns of James I and Charles II. This magnificent stone-and-wood mansion was in fact never an abbey (it is reputed that the religious name was nothing more than a snobbish affectation). It was founded by Colonel Benjamin Berringer and soon occupied by Sir John Yeamans, who set out from Speightstown to colonize Carolina in 1663, subsequently to become the third Governor of South Carolina. St Nicholas Abbey remained a plantation house up until the 1940s and is one of the oldest plantation mansions in the Caribbean. It has prominent, raised plaster quoins at each of its four corners, while quoins also flank each of the numerous sash windows, added later in Georgian times to the three-storey building. The house's four ornate chimneys, incongruous in this tropical climate, are important architectural features.

The vertical lines of the building are emphasized by the drainpipes and shaped copper rain hoppers, which drain the steep roof. Three curvilinear or ogee-shaped gables, with decorative stone

St Nicholas Abbey, Barbados

finials, elevate the facade to which a Georgian, arcaded portico was added in around 1746. The gables can be identified to around 1650 (as the popular saying goes, 'curly early, straighter later'). Finials also punctuate the Dutch gables and the two front chimneys. A glazed French door gives access to the portico roof. To the right of the frontage is the kitchen house, with its strong, curved-hooded Dutch-style chimney, and a water cistern. The walled courtyard had a clay tile-roofed bathhouse and multi-seated privy at each of the far corners. The simple interior – which oddly has fireplaces – is set off by a decorative, mastic wood, 'Chinese Chippendale' staircase from 1746 and cedar wood panelling.

Carved mouldings also enhance the arched doorways, beams and cornices. The grounds of St Nicholas Abbey encapsulate all the attributes of one of the finest of the Caribbean's many great houses. The herb garden, stables, coach-house, windmill, water-mill, and sugar boiling house are all in good order.

Just three mansions in this style exist in the Americas. The other two are Drax Hall, also on Barbados, and one of the best examples of its type anywhere, and Bacons Hall, in Virginia, US. Drax Hall, in St George Parish, is located in the centre of the island and is also

Jacobean, with twin, steep-pitched red-tiled roofs. It has a flat-fronted facade at each end of the house, with simple, integral gables and ball finials at each corner. The entrance is similarly simple and covered with a housed-in, tiled portico. Inside, the house contains a carved mastic wood archway and an ornately carved Jacobean staircase. This building is nowhere near as grand as St Nicholas Abbey, but has been dated to around 1653, on a site where sugar was first grown in the 1640s. The 878-acre estate, unusually for the Caribbean, has remained in the hands of the same family since it was founded.

After St Nicholas Abbey and Drax Hall were built, a number of grand plantation houses were soon erected as the sugar trade boomed. Many have extremely interesting – and sometimes unique – architectural features.

A unique example of a hurricane shelter can be seen behind the Georgian Palladian frontage of the Malvern great house in St Joseph. Octagonal in shape, the two-storey hurricane shelter has walls three feet thick. Hurricane damage, particularly to the roofs of large buildings, has always been a considerable risk. There were two bad hurricanes in 1780 and 1831, after which many plantation houses needed extensive restoration. To minimize roof damage, parapets were built around the roofs of many great houses, and some roofs were altered to lower profiles in order to lessen the pitch presented to strong winds. Good examples of these parapets are to be found at Buttals great house and at the ruined Georgian Newcastle mansion in St John. In Buttals, the earlier quoins at the corners of the house were not extended to the top of the parapet, which was added after one of the storms. The same omission can be seen at Harmony Hall. At the classic Palladian villa of the Indian Pond plantation in St Joseph, the original parapet, conversely, does not protect the tiled, hipped roof.

Few great houses have cellars, but the 18th-century Alleynedale mansion, north of the village of Porters, with its three storeys, arcaded verandah and dormer windows, has unusually deep cellars. It is reputed to be haunted by the ghost of a clergyman who committed suicide and was buried in a lead coffin in the cellar. The Byde Mill plantation house has a stone arcade around its cellar, over which is built a wooden verandah at ground level. Halton great house in St Philip also has deep cellars, ventilated by great arches under the ground floor verandah. This house also features a distinctive porticoed entrance and a ten-feet tall Georgian stair window. The Palladian-style Bagatelle plantation house has kitchens built at ground level over the cellars, which were used as a yam store, and its living quarters on the upper floor are in a style known as 'piano nobile', emphasized by a shallow storey above. This house is thought to be almost as old as St Nicholas Abbey and Drax Hall. It was originally named Parham Park House, but gained its new name in 1877 when it was lost by its owner in a gambling debt.

The great house of the Villa Nova plantation, dating from 1834, is one of the most impressive plantation houses of its age on Barbados, and was built by the sugar baron, Edward Haynes. It is surrounded by a gallery that allows cooling breezes to enter the open rooms. Built of light coral stone, the two-feet thick walls of this formal, square-built great house contrast with the fine trelliswork of the gallery. This has a shingled roof, sweeping up into an elegant porch extension over the entrance, which is reached by five stone steps. The front of the porch, which serves as a foyer to the house, forms a curved and pointed gable end and is supported by trellised columns with latticed arches and twin, fluted columns. The porch is marble-floored and the entrance doors are louvred. Interior doors are latticed, glazed, louvred and solid. The external gallery, added in the latter half of the 19th century, is wood-railed in a simple geometric pattern. The entrance door is surmounted by a fanlight, and louvered doors open onto the gallery on all sides. The flat facade of the greathouse is broken by a round, almost tower-like extension, reaching to roof-level, around which runs a protective parapet. Once the home of former British Prime Minister, Sir Anthony Eden, who invited Queen Elizabeth II to lunch here, the mansion is now a 28-room hotel, set in fourteen acres of land.

The bow-fronted style of Villa Nova can also be seen in Government House, the ruined Farley Hill mansion and at the Bay Mansion great house. The upper-floor windows of Villa Nova are covered by half side-hinged and half top-hinged louvred shutters over typically English sash windows. The almost flat roof is parapetted, and a single storey extension forms an elongated stone-built porch addition at the rear of the house. The floor of this extension, and its patio, are in decorative marble of various hues, and its doorway sports a fanlight, echoing that of the main entrance. Two sash windows have no shutters, but are protected by louvred hoods. Trelliswork encases these windows and the arch of the doorway.

Only the frontage remains of the famous 1861 Farley Hill plantation house, where King George V once stayed. It was considered the best on the island in the 1880s before fire finally gutted it in 1965.

Other houses of note include the Francia Plantation House, near Gun Hill Signal Station, dating from around 1900. This has some Brazilian architectural features in imported hardwoods and some locally-crafted furniture dating from the mid-1800s. Of outstanding interest is the Sunbury Plantation House and Museum, constructed in the 1660s and restored later in Georgian style. This house was built from local coral limestone and ballast stone from English sailing ships. Although damaged by a fire in 1995, it is the only plantation mansion that can be toured in its entirety and contains antique furniture, early household items and tools and implements used in the processing of sugar. This fortress-like great house has a 1935 addition, a Barbadian verandah, and another typical Bajan feature takes the form of a recessed panel, used since the 1820s to embellish the walls of many plantation houses. The two-feet thick walls, with plaster quoins at each corner, support a double-hipped roof. Below the two storeys are deep cellars and the domestic quarters. The nearby Oughterson Plantation House has a botanical collection.

Sugar Mills

Old sugar mill windmill towers, of which there were once about 500 on the island, have also been preserved. The best example is the Morgan Lewis windmill, which was built by Dutch Jews from Brazil in the 17th century. It is a simple stone, circular tower, where only the cap moved, as opposed to the earlier post mills, and was used for crushing sugar-cane. The 100-ft tail enabled the operators to point the mill into the prevailing wind. The old crushing gear in the wheelhouse is on view, and this is said to be the largest intact and working windmill in the Caribbean. This site was preserved by the joint efforts of the Barbados National Trust and the World Monuments Watch programmes.

A sugar mill dating from the 1750s is located in the grounds of the 1628 Pollard's Plantation. At Friendly Hall, near Maycock's Bay, there is another disused mill, dating from 1789. A steam engine was installed in the Blowers plantation boiler house in 1882, and this is now the Sir Frank Hutson Sugar Machinery Museum, with exhibits dating back to the earliest days of sugar production on the island.

Houses, Hotels and a College

Out in the countryside and in the suburban towns and villages, there are a number of important sites of architectural heritage. Notable among these is the headquarters of the Barbados National Trust. Formerly in Ronald Tree House, it is now located in the plain but beautiful Georgian Wildey House in St Michael, dating from the 1760s. In prosperous Belleville, the house known as the Great Escape sports an old decorated portico and twin staircase, as do some of the grand villas on nearby Belmont Road. Worth seeing are the grandiose Villa Franca at Hastings, dating from the early 1800s, and the magnificently opulent Trinidadian House in Worthing. Foreign styles also appear at El Sueño, a Spanish-style house built in Worthing in around 1900. Just outside Bridgetown to the east is The Eyrie, probably displaying one of the finest examples of cast-iron tracery work on the island. Also in St Michael, Tyrol Cot (1854) has undergone extensive renovation under the aegis of the National Trust. Today, Tyrol Cot Heritage Village is the four-acre site of the Chattel House Village. Typical Barbadian chattel houses have been re-erected here, as have an early black-

Ronald Tree House, Belleville

smith's shop, a slave hut and chattel house museum. A restaurant has been installed in the stables, which date from the 1840s.

Located on Barbados' east coast, Codrington College is an exceptional example of early 18th-century Classical architecture. Christopher Codrington, Governor General of the Leeward Islands, who was born on Barbados in 1668, bequeathed one of the earliest educational institutions in the West Indies, Codrington College, in his 1702 will. After his death in 1710, the construction began, being completed in 1745. This is a beautiful coral stone-built seminary, with an imposing facade and large, arched portico. The Principal's Lodge is older, dating from the late 17th century, a two-storey stone structure, with carved, triple-arched portico and Renaissance details, dating from 1680. Its distinctive exterior is fitted with top-hinged window shutters, above side-hinged shutters. The College stands in idyllic grounds, where vast Royal Palms line an impressive driveway from the main road.

Further east is Sam Lord's Castle, an 1820 Regency crenellated mansion built on the site of the wrecker, Samuel Hall Lord's original house. This is not only one of the island's architectural treasures, but one of the region's first mansion-hotels. The architect Victor Marson redesigned and developed the house as a hotel in 1942,

Principal's Lodge, Codrington College

adding its twin wings. It is lavishly decorated with ornate, plaster-work ceilings, mahogany columns and embellishments, including an elegant staircase. This building also has a good example of an old turtle crawl, a stone-built turtle pen. One of Barbados' oldest hotels, the Crane Beach Hotel, is an 18th-century coral stone mansion, opened as a hotel in 1887. The Marine in Hastings opened the same year. The very first, however, was the Navy Hotel, opened in the 1780s and now long gone.

Slave and Chattel Houses

The earliest colonial structures on the island were those built of wattle and daub, and palm thatched. When sugar brought its slave trade to Barbados, slaves were housed in more substantial buildings. These were made of coral stone in roughly the same design as the earlier huts. They had a low, hipped, thatched roof, later to be replaced by galvanized, corrugated-iron sheeting. As indentured workers came to Barbados, they too adapted the traditional slave hut to their own needs.

Later, the chattel house was introduced. Early chattel houses were built symmetrical, with ridged or hipped, shingled roofs. They were simple, timber-built structures, with stone steps leading up to a front door. Barbados' distinctive wooden chattel (literally 'moveable property') houses were built of clapboard on coral rock bases above the ground, to avoid vermin, and were initially very simple dwellings, rather like beach cabins. They were either square or oblong and occasionally joined in multiple units, with little external decoration. Other improvements, like gables, allowed ventilation through louvres at front and back.

External decoration gradually emerged in the form of bell awnings over sash, or side-hung, windows, and ornate railings and verandahs were added. Gradually, the shape and design of the chattel houses changed and modified, from garden hut simplicity to complex multiples, with ground floor and sometimes two-floored rear additions, and patios. These houses were traditionally known as 'dollhouses' and were painted in vibrant colours and often profusely decorated with gingerbread fretwork and ornate porches.

When a worker changed employer, he simply moved his entire house from the land of his old employer to that of the new one, often piecemeal or in sections by ox-cart. There are typical estate workers' chattel houses at the Alleynedale Estate, built as basic oblongs but of free-standing stone with pitched roofs, initially shingled but mostly roofed in corrugated iron. Most are built of clapboard. Barbados has preserved many of its early chattel houses, whereas on many other islands they have long since disappeared. Some typical examples of the early Barbados chattel house can be seen at the Four Square Rum Factory and Heritage Park in St Philip.

BARBUDA

There is hardly any building of architectural interest on this small outpost, which offered little in the way of commercial exploitation and was therefore sparsely settled. However, ruins reveal the evidence of attempts at cultivating the island many years ago, and the remains of defences indicate the one-time strategic importance of Barbuda's location.

This tiny, low island, composed entirely of coral limestone, lies just thirty miles north of Antigua, of which it is a dependency. The limestone rock is riddled with caves, of which the Dark Cave, extending 100 yards, and the Darby Cave sink-hole were thought to be Ciboney Amerindian refuges. Evidence of pre-Columbian occupation has been found elsewhere on the island. An English attempt at settling on the island failed in 1628, although the Spanish had visited the island earlier. The few architectural features, apart from the ruins of a large plantation house, include a ruined lighthouse and a still standing look-out tower. Christopher Codrington, whose bequest on Barbados is Codrington College, leased the entire tiny island of Barbuda from the British Crown from 1674 as a private estate for the rental of 'one fattened sheep' per year. Here, for two centuries, he and his successors oversaw the production of livestock, sugar, and later cotton. It was also said that slaves were bred here for work on the plantations on Barbados.

The main settlement of Codrington, in the north of the island, is just a few streets of clapboard and concrete houses. The Codrington family home, Highland House, is now in ruins and was never properly occupied. It dates from 1750 and is now comprised of little more than ruined walls, a water cistern and outhouses. Out on the flat, scrubby island are the remains of several other old plantation buildings. The ruins at the base of Gun Shop Cliff are the remains of a 19th-century phosphate-mining enterprise. The so-called River Fort on the island's south coast is a massive Martello tower, a round 56-foot 19th-century watch tower, modelled on the almost impregnable Mortella Point tower in Corsica, which was adopted as a model for watch towers in Britain, Ireland and Guernsey to deter a Napoleonic invasion. This fortification and watch tower has extremely thick walls, a deep cellar and empty gun platforms, once housing nine cannon. It overlooks the original docking area and is thought to have been built on the remains of an ancient Spanish lighthouse. Another watch tower, further south on Spanish Point, is known as the Castle, but is more probably an 18th-century lighthouse or lookout tower built by the Spanish. Now nothing much remains but the rubble ruins.

BONAIRE

With a topography similar to its neighbour, Aruba, Bonaire is the third largest of the Netherlands Antilles group, and similarly offered few attractions for early settlers. Salt harvesting and small-time farming communities left little of any architectural significance, although the accommodation provided for slaves is of socio-historic interest and is unique to the island.

The Spanish first arrived on this low, flat island in 1499, under Amerigo Vespucci. Spanish slavers later trawled the island for involuntary recruits in 1528 and visited briefly in 1623 to strip what lumber there was from the interior. Bonaire remained abandoned and uncolonized until the Dutch arrived in 1626, finding a country similar to their own, but without the water. The early settlers made crude huts from sun-baked mud and maize stalk thatch, with garden plots hedged in cactus to keep out the voracious goats. They raised cattle and maize and produced sea salt. In the late 1600s, the Dutch established a thriving slave market on the island, building a small wharf, protected by a long coral dyke.

It was not until after a brief period of English occupation, from the early 19th century until 1815, that any real attempt at establishing a capital was made. Even then, the place known as Kralendijk (Coral Dyke) was no more than a schooner landing stage for loading salt and beef produce. The island's largest town has few buildings of architectural note, apart from the Governor's House, which dates from 1837 and was renovated in 1973. It is now Bonaire's Government Building. Kralendijk fish market is located in a tiny, mock Greek temple-like building. The oldest building here is Fort Oranje, built in about 1850, judging by its old cannon. Most of the houses in the little capital date from the early 20th century and are gaily painted and of typically Dutch colonist design, with traditional crow-stepped gables, low, tiled roofs, often painted ochre with white stucco, and with the occasional dormer window.

Oddly enough, the oldest standing buildings on the island are the slave huts on the salt pans, in the south-east of the island. These date from around 1820 and are built of free-standing stone with thatched roofs. The accommodation, each hut housing two people, was temporary and was occupied during the working week, after which the slaves would walk the 17 miles to Rincon for the weekend. Rincon, with its small, pastel-painted houses and gabled church, is the island's oldest settlement. This, the second largest town, is located in the central part of the north-west arm of the crook-shaped island and probably dates from the return of the Dutch in 1816. The slave huts here were built as an alternative to a communal dormitory. Here, also, are three 30-foot triangular ship marker obelisks dating from 1838. These markers guided ships to the jetties, where salt was loaded. There is an old slave-master's house located between the southerly of the three obelisks. At Slagbaai, on the west coast of the island, are some large old *magasinas*, or salt warehouses, and groups of smaller ancillary buildings constructed for the salt trade in 1868. These structures include a Customs House and are currently being restored.

Willemstoren Lighthouse, Bonaire

Further south are more tiny slave huts, with their typical square gables, and the Willemstoren Lighthouse on Southern Point, dating from 1837. Throughout the island there are several *landhuizen* or planters' residences, mostly dating from the 20th century, built and gaily painted in traditional Dutch colonial style. Additional sites of historic interest include the old water mill at San Jose and the ancient aloe oven at Karpata, one of very few remaining anywhere.

BRITISH VIRGIN ISLANDS

The British Virgin Islands comprise around twenty islands and a number of islets, the main islands being Tortola, Anegada and Virgin Gorda. Initially contested between the English and the Dutch, these islands became firmly British in 1672, and supplied cotton, sugar and rum. Still a British colony, the islands are now exclusive tourist resorts, catering to yachting enthusiasts. There is little of any historic interest on the smaller islands, and many of the sites of architectural significance are to be found on Tortola. However, one site, the copper mining ruins on Virgin Gorda, is the only one of its kind in the English-speaking Caribbean.

Road Town, on **Tortola**, is the capital of the British Virgin Islands or BVI. The 'road' in Road Town refers to the 17th-century name for an open anchorage. There are the ruins of three fortresses here: the crude masonry tower of Fort George, to the east of Road Harbour just outside Road Town, and Fort Shirley and Fort Charlotte, both from the 18th century. Fort George was built by the Royal Engineers in 1794. Fort Charlotte was once the island's largest fortification and was also built in 1794, located just south-west of the capital. A few walls, an underground magazine and a water cistern are all that remain of the emplacement. Little more remains of Fort Shirley. The dominant building on the waterfront by the cruise ship dock is the grandiose Government Administration office, with its line of slender arches. The Post Office is in an old arcaded and arched stone-built building.

One interesting relic of the late 18th-century sugar industry is a vast copper boiling vat, made by slaves, on display in the town. The old Sunday Morning Well on Upper Street has a plaque which commemorates the reading of the Proclamation of Emancipation in 1834. The elegant mansion of the Pusser's Rum Store and Pub sports balconies each side of its weather-boarded upper storey, a wide ground-floor verandah fronting the stone-built base and sash windows with blue storm shutters.

On Main Street, many of the colourful wood and stone buildings date from the turn of the 19th century, with gingerbread decoration, like the wooden building housing the Historical Society Folk Museum. Also on Main Street are the Methodist and Catholic churches and the early St George's Anglican church, which rub shoulders with the former jail. Government House is located to the south of Road Town, above Waterfront Drive, and is built in Classical style and painted white with green shutters. A little further on is the Fort Burt Hotel, named after another defensive structure, now no longer visible.

Traditional, single-storey, clapboard, pastel-painted West Indian houses, stores, shops, cafes and restaurants can be seen in most villages in the BVI, with high-pitched roofs of corrugated iron or shingles, window shutters and gingerbread fretwork decoration. Colonnaded arcades and shady, first-floor balconies are added to the larger two-storey buildings. Some early buildings have been restored and commercialized, like the Sugar Mill Hotel, in Little Apple Bay, Tortola, which is located around an ancient windmill dating from about 1650, with factory buildings forming part of the hotel complex.

Out in the country, there are a few traditional single-roomed dwellings, built on stilts above the ground and shingled, with shutters over unglazed window openings and steep-pitched corrugated iron roof, where once was palmetto thatch. The ruins of old sugar estate buildings can be seen throughout the island, like those of William Thornton's estate to the south-west of Road Town. Thornton was born on Tortola in 1761 and was the architect who designed Washington's Capitol building in the US. The tiny Fort Recovery can be seen in the west of Tortola Island, built by the Dutch and dating from between 1648 and 1660. Just thirty feet in diameter, its round tower is well preserved and was re-fortified by the English, who annexed the island in 1672. The old dungeon, actually a small defence post, is located nearby. Old stone steps lead

Pusser's Rum Store, Tortola

Architectural Heritage of the Caribbean

down to what is thought to be a dungeon cell, said to have been decorated by an early inmate's graffiti. In the north of the island near Brewer's Bay, on Mount Healthy, there are the ruins of another old sugar mill and rum distillery. Here, too, is a thick-walled 18th-century windmill, the last standing on the island. In Cane Garden Bay stands the 18th-century Callwood Rum Distillery, where ancient rum-making equipment is on display and early crushers, boiling vats and a still remain in use. In Kingstown village there are the ruins of a pretty little Anglican church, dating from 1833. It was erected for the 600 freed slaves who once settled here.

A retired pirate, named Audain, apparently set himself up as a priest in a community at Cannon Point, just north of Cane Garden Bay. He adopted the church of St Michael's, but quickly reverted to his more lucrative previous occupation. Audain fortified the church and built a bell tower onto its side, from where he could watch shipping movements between Tortola and Jost Van Dyke island. The temptation proved too great, and, as many of his parishioners also had pirateering backgrounds, they lured ships into the nearby bay with misleading lights and plundered them. It is said that Audain would ring the church bell when a likely victim was sighted and that he would even interrupt his services to attack a passing vessel.

In the early 1600s the Spanish found copper on **Virgin Gorda** and established a mine in the south-east of the island. The tall stone chimney, boiler house, cistern and other ruins of the copper mine can still be seen, as it was worked by English miners from Cornwall up until the early 1900s. It is thought that the Spanish first mined copper here, but the highest production took place between 1838 and 1867. The only other historic ruins here are those of Little Fort, and Fort Point near Spanish Town, in the south of the island. Little Fort, with its masonry walls and powder house ruins, was built by the Spanish probably in the early 1600s. The 18th-century Nail Bay sugar mill ruins are situated on the north-west coast of Virgin Gorda, built of coral stone and brick.

The small island of **Jost Van Dyke**, named after a Dutch pirate, has Great Harbour as its main village, containing pretty wooden houses and an old wooden-shuttered church in white and umber, with a red corrugated iron roof and little chapel, featuring a wood shingled bell tower.

As there is no surface water on the BVI, wells and water collection cisterns are a feature of all the islands, and some are quite antique. The BVI's only other architectural structure of any importance is the Queen Elizabeth II Memorial Bridge, erected in 1966 and connecting Tortola to **Beef Island**.

CAYMAN ISLANDS

This group of three islands, of which the largest, Grand Cayman, is 150 miles south of Cuba, offered early settlers little inducement to stay long, being rather barren and isolated. The strategic location of the Caymans attracted a dubious early population, who spent more time at sea than establishing any permanent settlement. Apart from a few fortified sites, there is little of real architectural significance on these islands. The three islands are a British Crown Colony and are famous for their finance and insurance activities. Tourism is also on the rise, and the islands attract divers from all over the world.

Columbus sailed past the islands in 1503, naming them Las Tortugas, or The Turtles. When Sir Francis Drake arrived in 1586, he renamed them The Caimans, or The Crocodiles. Columbus was right; there were many turtles here, whereas Drake's crocodiles were just marine iguanas. Nevertheless, the name Caymans stuck, and it was here that Captain William King landed in 1590. This early attempt to establish a base on the islands failed. However, deserters from Cromwell's army, which had just captured Jamaica, settled on Grand Cayman in 1655.

They found that the Spanish had already erected the island's oldest building, Pedro Gómez's Castle, above Old Jones Bay in 1635. This three-storey, pillared and gable-roofed defence tower was rebuilt in 1765 and fortified in 1780 by the Englishman, William Eden, who named it St James' Castle. The islands officially became British in 1670, and in the early 1700s a group of settlers established the first capital, Bodden Town, and the village of East End. Both are located on Grand Cayman's south coast, and the first dwellings were probably built of semi-permanent wattle and daub, with palm-thatched roofs. In Bodden Town there is an ancient 'U'-shaped defensive wall, totalling four miles in length, dating from those times. Gun Square here, laid out in the early 18th century, contains old cannon. At the entrance to Bodden Town is an example of an 1840s guardhouse. Behind Gun Square, the original wattle and daub Mission House, dating from around 1850, was replaced by a wooden structure and a second storey was added in 1908, when the ground floor was adapted as a schoolhouse.

First named Hogstyes and renamed George Town after King George III, the island's capital, located in the west of Grand Cayman island, has few sites of real historic interest, apart from the ruined Fort George, now restored. Built about 1790 to a very basic design, with limestone and coral rock, its walls were just four and a half feet high and between two and five feet thick. Eight apertures in the walls allowed cannon muzzles to protrude. Nearby, the Emslie Memorial Church dates from the 19th century, but was rebuilt in the 1920s and has a vaulted ceiling with wooden arches. Also in George Town are numerous, century-old, colourfully-painted, one- and two-storey buildings, made of timber frames with lattice or gingerbread-decorated verandahs, wrap-around balconies, hipped roofs and picket fenced gardens, like those on the waterfront and on South Church Street. The single-storey hip-roofed, and porched National Trust building is a fine example of a 19th-century cottage in typical Cayman Island architecture. The Cayman Islands Museum is another specimen of the islands' colonial architecture, with its first-floor balcony, stepped entrance, louvred gable vents, red, corrugated iron roof, and sash windows protected by green storm shutters. This building was once the old Courts Building, constructed in the mid-19th century with a stone lower floor and wooden upper storey. The few older buildings in George Town include the old Marine Buildings, the Peace Memorial Building,

George Town house, Grand Cayman

dating from 1919, the charming Library building and the General Post Office, with its curved facade and covered walkway, which both date from 1939. However, much of George Town's architecture is a hotch-potch of modern, concrete-built, high-rise buildings (the site of the colony's offshore finance industry), while mock Regency and imitation Georgian are *de rigueur*. There are, among these, a few pretty early houses, notably with wrap-around balconies.

Further east from George Town are the ruins of Fort Prospect, built by William Bodden in the early 19th century on Prospect Point, once the islands' seat of government. There is a commemorative monument on the ruins. Gun Bay, on the east coast, has an interesting little church, with a neat belfry. In the interior of the island one is more likely to see traditional Caymanian houses of white clapboard, with gaily painted shutters, shingle roofs, and picket-fenced gardens. It is believed that the curved wooden brackets sometimes seen supporting verandas originated with the shipbuilders of the Caymans, who used to fashion this architectural feature out of American cedar.

At Prospect, the Watler cemetery is of historic interest, as many of the tombs in the dry-stone walled graveyard are house-shaped monuments, with mahogany plaques let into the gables inscribed with the name of the deceased. At Old Savannah, the early schoolhouse is very typically West Indian. Ironwood posts support the poured concrete walls of the one-roomed school, topped by a corrugated iron roof. The schoolhouse stands off the ground, and its window openings are protected by top-hinged wooden shutters.

Elsewhere on the Cayman Islands, there are the ruins of the old settlement of Callabash Spot on Little Cayman, dating from the late 17th century. On Cayman Brac, famous for its Buccaneer's Inn, are the remains of Frenchman's Fort, another early settlement, dating from the 18th century.

CUBA

Cuba, the largest of the Caribbean islands, is steeped in history and full of architectural gems dating back to 1512. This island has arguably more sites of architectural importance than all the other Caribbean islands put together. Some of the world's most interesting instances of early Spanish colonial building still stand in Cuba's cities and towns. In 1959 the Cuban government began a careful programme of preservation in Old Havana, and in 1982 UNESCO designated the old city and its fortifications a World Heritage site. In 1988, UNESCO also declared the city of Trinidad de Cuba a site of World Heritage importance, including the Valle de los Ingenios, or Sugarmill Valley. In 1997, UNESCO also declared the San Pedro de la Roca Morro Fortress in Santiago de Cuba a site of World Heritage significance. The historic centre of Old Havana is also listed on the World Monuments Watch listing of 100 Most Endangered Sites. The Caribbean and Central American headquarters of UNESCO is in Vedado, Havana.

Cuba's forty-year conflict with the US has done much to impoverish and isolate its people, but in architectural terms the blockade has meant that many of the country's towns and cities have escaped the Americanization experienced by other islands. Havana has remained mothballed for several decades, crumbling and in desperate need of resources, yet protected from the worst aspects of insensitive development.

Old Havana

Old Havana alone embraces around 2,750 structures of architectural and historic value. There are a total of 144 buildings which date from the 16th and 17th centuries; 197 date from the 18th century; 460 from the 19th century, 1,959 from the period from 1901-35, and 264 from then until the mid-1970s. In Havana, a total of around 3,000 buildings are of historic or architectural interest, although only around 200 are open to the public. This section will restrict itself to listing and describing the more architecturally significant structures.

The Fortresses

El Castillo de la Real Fuerza (The Castle of the Royal Force) is the oldest fortress in Havana – there are seven in all – and the second oldest in the Americas. Bartolomé Sánchez designed the present fort which was built between 1558 and 1577 on the site of the original which Hernando de Soto built in 1538 and which was destroyed in a raid by the French pirate, Jaques de Sores, in 1555. King Philip II

Castillo de la Real Fuerza, Havana

of Spain commanded the rebuilding of the fort, around 300 yards further south than the original and contributed 12,000 pesos towards its construction. From 1577 until 1762, this fort served as the Governor General's residence.

Its design and position were rightly criticized as the fort was dominated by the high hills on the other side of the harbour's narrow entrance. It was from these hills that French pirates and the English attacked Havana. After the English left in 1763, the fort became a barracks and from 1899 to 1906 it was the repository for the city archives. It reverted to being a military barracks until 1938, when it became a permanent library. The fort itself was restored in 1963. A stone wall twenty feet thick and thirty feet high and a moat surround the structure, fronted by an iron railing protecting the courtyard which contains several ancient cannon. Crossing a drawbridge to enter the fort, one sees the 1579 coat of arms above the entrance which was carved in Seville, Spain. The massive stone bulwarks and red-tiled extension is the nerve centre of the UNESCO World Heritage programme of restoration of Old Havana. The bell tower, built to announce impending attacks, was constructed by order of Governor Juan Bitrian de Viamonte between 1630 and 1634 and is surmounted by a statue of conquistador and Governor Hernando de Soto's wife, and is known as 'La Isabel de Bobadilla de la Havana', 'La Giraldilla' or 'La Havana'. The statue is by Jerónimo Martínez Pinzón, made in 1632 on the request of Bitrian de Viamonte.

The Castillo de los Tres Reyes del Morro, across the bay from Old Havana in Casablanca, is a familiar symbol of the city and is made from great blocks of coral rock in the form of a polygon. It is built on an elevated headland – which is what *morro* means – at the mouth of Havana Harbour. Originally a small white lookout tower, built on the instructions of Governor Diego de Mazariegos in 1563, the fort (or Castle of the Three Kings of the Headland to give it its full name) was established in 1589 to protect Havana and its deep harbour entrance from pirate and corsair attacks in the wake of an attempt on the city by Sir Francis Drake. The design, created on the orders of King Philip II of Spain, was first drawn up in 1588 by the architect Juan Bautista Antonelli, who also designed the Cabana Fort several years later. The King sent 25,000 ducats to the Governors of the Real Hacienda in Havana to pay for the construction. It was built as a replica of a fortress in Lisbon, Portugal. Forty-one years later the building was eventually completed. Sixty cannon still point out to sea, including the huge waterside 'Twelve Apostle' guns, which were often employed against pirate ships and those of the English naval forces which captured the castle in 1762.

The Italian engineer Cristoforo de Roda, Antonelli's nephew, designed a chain barricade to cross the 656-foot wide harbour mouth from the Morro to the Castillo de la Punta on the Malecón promenade opposite. This barrier was installed in the early 17th century, slung between two towers. The Morro was extensively damaged by a mine during the English

Castillo de los Tres Reyes del Morro, Havana

onslaught in 1762, when Havana was taken and occupied by the Earl of Albemarle's forces, and was rebuilt the following year. At its highest point the walls are 180 ft above sea level, ninety ft high and fifteen ft thick, while, to the east, a deep moat protects the castle from landward attacks. Bronze and iron cannon lie scattered, as if recently abandoned, in the grounds at the entrance to the castle. Across the drawbridge, which spans the deep moat, are the great wooden doors and a narrow arched passage which leads out into the castle's interior. A plaque above the arch commemorates the defence of the Morro in 1762 by troops under Don Luis de Velasco, when the English, under Admiral Rodney, overwhelmed the fort after a 44-day siege. The island's Captain General is also remembered here with the inscription 'Antonio Caballero de Rodas, 1879'. Inside its thick walls, the Morro is a maze of cobbled passageways, embrasures with slits for guns, sentry boxes, stairways and ramps that lead to patios, powder magazines and battlements. Apart from the battery of cannon, other artifacts include gun carriage cradles and iron rings in the walls where slaves were once fettered. Just through the main arch hangs an ancient, rusted candelabra. The major fort is built on stepped ramparts containing chambers, galleries, gun emplacements and dungeons, some of which have been converted to house a restaurant named after the Morro's great guns.

After many abortive attempts to take Havana, the English, under Admiral Lord Rodney, the Earl of Albemarle, and George Pocock succeeded in securing the city for the English Crown in 1762. Attacking the Morro from the east, with 44 ships and 14,000 soldiers, the English overwhelmed the 70-gun fort of Captain Don

Luis Vicente de Velasco. They held Havana for eleven months from June 1762 until Charles III of Spain agreed to exchange Florida for Cuba, including trading rights in the northern Caribbean. The spoils of war included 100 merchant ships, 100 bronze cannon, the bells of the city cathedral and the golden statue of Isabel de Bobadilla de Havana from the tower of the Castillo de la Real Fuerza. The Bishop paid a huge ransom in gold to the English in order to protect his churches from vandalism, and the city elders heaped even more gold on their captors, plus, of course, unlimited tobacco and rum!

Originally, the cliffs here were topped by a crude lighthouse, rebuilt in stone in 1764 by Captain General Leopoldo O'Donnell. Today, the fort is dominated by the 1844 lighthouse which is 76 feet high and whose light can be seen 50 miles away – almost in Key West. The squat outline of the fort, together with the finger of its lighthouse, 'El Faro de Libertad – The Lighthouse of Liberty', was electrified in 1945 and is illuminated at night. The Heritage of Havana organization has created the Morro-Cabana Historic Park which includes the Morro Castle and the Cabana Fortress, two of the oldest of their kind in the New World. Exhibitions include one of military architecture.

The massive structure of the Fortaleza San Carlos de la Cabaña is around a tenth the size of the entire area of Old Havana. The fortress was built between 1763 and 1774 by Pedro de Medina, on the 16th-century designs of Antonelli and Silvestre Abarca. It is recorded that the construction cost 14 million pesos and that the King of Spain asked for a telescope so that he could see such an expensive structure from the shores of Europe! After the English used the high position here to bombard the city in 1762, the army realized that the area had to be secured. The Cabaña was the fourth of Havana's defences to be constructed and is the largest Spanish fortress ever built in the Spanish Main. Two French builders were responsible for carrying out the original plans and the fort was named after King Carlos III of Spain. This 2,100-ft long rectangular structure was once considered the most important and impregnable in the New World. Gun emplacements pointed both east and west and the fort could house 5,000 soldiers.

The Cabaña was originally a prison and place of execution for political prisoners until the 1950s, when it became a military academy. A graveyard is located to the south of the fort. The fort is now a historical study centre and museum of military history. When Havana had city gates, a cannon was fired from the Cabana fort twice a day, to signal their opening and closing. Today a cannon shot is still fired from the fort each evening at 9 pm, in a tradition which has been maintained for more than 200 years.

The picturesque Castillo de San Salvador de la Punta, with its seven-feet-thick walls, was completed in 1600. The building of the trapezoid-shaped fort was instigated by the military commander, Diego Fernández de Quinones in 1582. It was an integral part of the fortifications of the city against marauding pirates and attacks by the English Navy and has been restored many times since then. The squat fortress now contains a small museum and a little tavern, the Mesón de la Punta.

The Plaza de Armas or Plaza Céspedes

Originally the Plaza de la Iglesia, because Havana's main 1555 church stood here until it was demolished in the 18th century, this is the oldest square in Havana, laid out in 1519, the inauguration year of San Cristóbal de La Habana. It was initially a parade ground for the Captain General's forces. In 1582, the private houses on the square were demolished to expand it, and in 1776 it was again enlarged to its present size. In 1902, when Cuba became a republic, its name was changed to Plaza Carlos Manuel de Céspedes after the hero of the Independence War of 1868. Restoration work was carried out on the square in 1929 and completed by 1935. Bordered by marble benches and iron railings, the centre of the square contains small fountains and is dominated by a statue of Céspedes, which replaced that of King Ferdinand VII of Spain, erected in 1828 during his restoration (1814-1833) and which was taken down in 1955.

In the north-east corner of the square is El Templete, a neo-Classical, porticoed temple. In 1754, a memorial column to the founding of Havana was sited on this spot. The column, installed by Governor Cajigal de la Vega is surmounted by a bust of Christopher Columbus and topped by a statue of the Virgin de Pilar. The three sides of the column represent the original three states of Cuba. Dating from March 1828 – the year King Ferdinand VII's statue was erected in the plaza, El Templete – or the 'Little Temple', is a six-columned copy of a Doric Greco-Roman temple inaugurated by

Bishop Don Juan José Diaz de Espada y Landa in honour of the city's founding fathers. El Templete was the city's first civic building and is reminiscent of the shrine in Guernica, Spain. The building was the work of the Cuban architect Antonio Maria de la Torre y Cárdenas and contains three murals by the French artist Jean-Baptiste Vermay (1784-1833), a pupil of David. The urn standing in the centre of the temple contains the ashes of the artist Vermay and his wife.

On the north side stands the Palacio del Segundo Cabo, an impressive Baroque limestone palace built between 1772 and 1776 by the Cuban engineer Antonio Fernández Trevejos. It was constructed to house the deputy military governor of Cuba and accommodated dignitaries from 1820 and the Deputy Governor's offices in 1854. The palace also housed the Cuban Senate for the first two decades after independence. In the 1930s it was home to the Academy of Language, History and Arts and now acts as head-quarters to the Cuban Book Fair. Its entrance is through a five-lobed arch in the columned portico, leading to a Spanish-style patio and dramatic two-storey courtyard.

The old Mesón de la Flota (the Inn of the Fleet), on the east side, is now the Hotel Santa Isabel, lovingly restored and luxurious. It was once the Palacio del Conde de Santovenia and the residence of the lawyer and military judge, Doctor Francisco Martínez de Campo. Doctor de Campo's brother, Nicolás, Count of Santovenia, also lived here from 1834. On the succession in 1833 of Princess Dona María Isabel Luisa de Borbon, daughter of King Ferdinand VII of Spain, the Count converted the main facade into a replica of the Tuileries Palace in France. An eleven-arched, twelve-pillared colonnade was created, surmounted by an angel representing 'Virtue' and a knight representing 'Honour'. An inscription above reads 'Through virtue and virtue alone – does one rise to honour's throne'. When the Count died in 1865, a New Orleans Colonel moved in, turning the mansion into the Santa Isabel Hotel. In 1943 the mansion was remodelled as offices, and in the revolutionary turmoil of 1959 it became a nursery and fishing fleet headquarters, before returning to being a tavern and restaurant. Once it was a meeting-house for merchant traders and a restaurant which served the commercial street market.

The impressive Palacio de los Capitanes Generales, the Palace of the Captains General, is one of the most striking late Baroque buildings in Havana, with its facade of ten massive Tuscan columns. The huge bells outside the palace were taken from the watch towers and slave churches of sugar plantations. The wooden pavement outside, the only one of its kind in the New World, is said to have been built to muffle the sound of horses' hooves and carriage wheels while the gentry slept upstairs. Left of the entrance is a marble statue of the seated Spanish King Ferdinand VII, which once stood in the square.

The first building here, which was used by the city's Cabildo or Town Council, was destroyed by a hurricane in 1768. The existing palace was constructed between 1776 and 1791 and served as the residence of Cuba's colonial governors, as instigated by Governor Marqués de la Torre in 1773. From 1791 until 1898 it became the residence of the Captain Generals of the Spanish Guard and later that of the first three presidents. The building was altered by Miguel Tacón in 1834. Between 1920 and 1958 the palace was Havana's City Hall. From then until 1968, the building served as the seat for the revolutionary municipal administration. Restoration work began in 1967, and it now houses the Municipal Museum.

The imposing facade comprises the huge Tuscan columns supporting a first-floor terrace over a paved colonnade and fronts a beautiful, two-tiered, columned courtyard, also in the Tuscan mode, containing early cannon. Sarcophagi under the excavated patio contain the remains of conquistadores, and beautiful local mahogany staircases lead up to the first floor. Even the upper-floor galleries, with doors leading off to grand rooms, have wooden-beamed coverings, supported by great stone arches that rise from the courtyard.

The centrepiece is an exquisite marble statue of Columbus, by Cucchiari. Artifacts from excavations in the building's basement are displayed in the patio, including a strange metal casket with a sword on its lid. On the right hand side is a monument to a lady of court, who was killed in a firearms accident here in 1557. Note the *tinajón*, or water container, and the remnants of the city's first aqueduct. The cannon once announced the opening and closing of the city's old gates.

In anticipation of a visit to Cuba by the Spanish monarchs, one of the rooms in the palace was converted into a throne room, but was never used. The Parish Room of the museum contains religious artifacts, and other halls contain a wide variety of exhibits which trace the history of Havana. The original statue of 'La Giraldilla' is on display here. The Espada cemetery, Havana's first, and its chapel are also located on the ground floor. Named after the Bishop of the time, this cemetery was soon removed to a site a mile outside the city walls. The rooms include the Music Salon, the ballroom (called the Hall of Mirrors with its eight enormous mirrors), the Coffee Room, the Dining Room and the Room of Gold. The Infanta Elalia Room is where the sister of Alfonso XII stayed. On the top floor, Louis XV furniture reflect the lavish lifestyle of the aristocracy from the 16th to the 19th century. To the left of the Palacio de los Capitanes Generales is a 17th-century shrine to the 'Mountain of Mercy'.

The Zambrana House at No. 117-19 Calle Obispo dates from 1570. It is the oldest house in Havana and has some good examples of early *vitrales* above its beautifully carved balcony. On the ground floor there are rings in the walls where slaves were once chained. The Hostal Valencia on Calle Oficios, just south of the Plaza de Armas, is a mid-18th-century, three-floored, colonial mansion, once the home of the Marqués de Sotolorgo, converted into a pretty hotel in 1989. It has a wonderful open courtyard, with a typical octagonal well, Spanish, hand-painted tiled walls and wide, covered, wooden stairways leading up to the two upper floors. Verandahs provide shade for the ground and first floors, supported by elegantly carved wooden pillars, and the red-clay tiled roof shelters the verandah of the top floor. The rooms have Arab-style Mudéjar wooden ceilings, and those on the top floor have balconies with ornate wrought-iron railings.

Plaza Catedral

The ornate, columned facade of the Catedral de La Habana is constructed of *coquina* and limestone and dominates the broad, cobbled Plaza Catedral. It has been likened to 'music turned to stone', and the square has been called 'the finest colonial square in the Americas'. The cathedral is dedicated to La Virgen María de la Inmaculada Concepción and San Cristóbal de la Habana. One of the greatest Italian Baroque-style churches in Latin America, it was built by Jesuits in 1704, rebuilt in 1748 and recommenced when the Jesuits were ousted in 1767, but not completed until 1777.

In 1789, when the old church in the Plaza de Armas was demolished, the status of City Church was transferred to this church, and

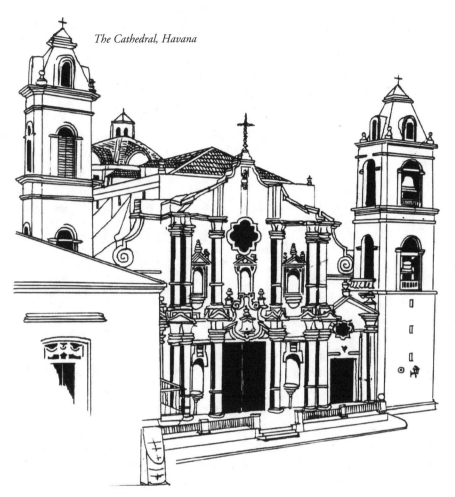

The Cathedral, Havana

it became a cathedral proper in 1799. The exotic Baroque-Tuscan facade of the cathedral, with its five pillared niches and rose window, is flanked by two magnificent towers. Today, only one of the towers has bells, said to contain gold and silver, which enhances their tone. Legend has it that King Charles III threw his gold ring into the largest bell's smelting pot as a regal gesture to the New World. This bell, 'San Pedro', weighing seven tons, was made in Spain in 1763 and the other, 'San Miguel', weighing two tons, cast in Matanzas in 1838. The original bronze bells which hung in both towers were stolen during the English occupation of 1762. The tower on the left side of the facade was built more slender than that on the right so as not to encroach on the nearby, older buildings and the adjacent side street which leads to the Seminary. The great wooden doors open into the main body of the church, which covers almost 400 square feet. Four massive columns each side of the nave divide it from the two aisles, where there are gold and wooden retables and religious paintings. The three aisles, including the nave, lead to eight small lateral chapels. A dome over the vast central crossing lights the cathedral's interior. A huge chandelier is suspended from the cathedral's dome. The main altar is made from Carrara marble and onyx and inlaid with gold, silver and carved wood in the shape of a cupola covering a statue of the Virgin Mary of the Immaculate Conception. The sculptures are thought to be the work of Brancini and the paintings are by Vermay.

There is a small religious museum in the cathedral. The remains of Christopher Columbus are said to have lain here after their removal from Santo Domingo in 1795. His tomb stands in the nave, empty. This is also the final resting-place of several of the city's bishops.

The Seminario de San Carlos and San Ambrosio, a Baroque building behind the cathedral, was erected in 1772 and faces the harbour. It became a seminary in 1774, when the name of the then King of Spain, Carlos, was added to its original name. Three porticoes surround the interior courtyard and its two doors open onto Calles San Ignacio and San Telmo.

The two-storey, tile-roofed Palacio del Conde Lombillo was built in 1737. The arcaded colonnade extends along the entire east side of Plaza Catedral, running under the adjoining building, the Palacio de los Marqueses de Arcos, built in 1741. This was the residence of the Royal Treasurer, Diego de Penalver Angulo, and was later reconstructed as a palace by Ignacio Penalver when he became the Marqués de Arcos in 1762. The ornate bronze balcony surrounds probably date from this period. The Cuban postal headquarters moved into the building in 1825, and the beautiful stained glass windows, or vitrales, were probably installed at that time.

Facing the cathedral on the south side of the square, the Palacio de los Condes de Casa-Bayona is the oldest building in this quarter of the Old City and was reconstructed in 1720 by Don Luis Chacón, the island's military governor. The Count of Casa-Bayona never actually owned this building, but it was named in honour of the Spanish family. In the 19th century the house became the residence of the head of the Royal College of Literature and it is now the Museum of Colonial Art. A testimony to the lavish style of living in the colony during Spanish occupation, the rooms of this museum house marvelous examples of Cuban-made furnishings and other trappings. The newspaper *La Discusión* was once published in this building, and it was also used as a rum distillery. One hall has a precious wood ceiling, another is devoted to furniture from the 17th, 18th and 19th centuries, while further halls contain examples of crystal and porcelain, a collection of everyday household implements and examples of early horse-drawn carriages. The Glass Hall tells the tale of Cuba's unique window and door styles through the exquisite *vitrales*, *mediopuntas*, *mamparas* and *lucetas* on display.

The El Patio restaurant stands opposite the cathedral and is so called because, unlike most 18th-century Spanish mansions, this 1775 villa has no carriage entrance and its doorways lead directly into the open patio courtyard. Arched cloisters surround the cooling central fountain, and a profusion of greenery shades the graceful architecture. This beautiful town house was once the home of Antonio Ponce de León, the first Marqués de Aguas Claras and a relation of the famous conquistador. The house next door may throw some light on the Marquis' title as it was an ancient bath-house, whose clear spring waters once supplied ships at anchor in the nearby harbour. Before the El Patio building was renovated in 1963, there used to be a restaurant called the 'Paris' on this spot and another known as 'El Siglo'. The second-storey balconies look out over the patio and in the front of the house, those of the main upper floor overlook the square.

The cobbled alleyway leading into Plaza Catedral is Callejón del Chorro (Water Spout Alley), which has a plaque on the wall and a fountain spout commemorating the city's first aqueduct. After the city was sacked by French pirates in 1555, a trench was built by royal decree to convey water to the city centre from the Chorrera River, seven miles to the west. One branch of the aqueduct led to this square, and another took water to the Luz Docks. The aqueduct, known as the Zanja Real and running along the line of the alleyway, was constructed by Juan de Tejeda in 1592. It was the first colonial aqueduct in the New World. The trench was rebuilt in 1835 and named the 'Fernando VII' conduit. The plaque marking the termination of the aqueduct was placed here in 1597 on the wall of the former bathhouse. In 1893 the important 'Albear' project brought water to the Old Quarter of Havana and the original aqueduct fell into disuse.

Religious Buildings

The Espiritu Santo, Holy Spirit, church was founded in 1632, although the existing structure dates from the first part of the 19th century. Building was restarted in 1636, and the church has been the subject of extensive restoration, being enlarged to its present size between 1670 and 1674. It is the oldest standing church in Havana, and under the altar is a system of catacombs. Initially, the church was constructed by freed black slaves, and around 1710 Bishop Valdés had the main chapel completed, with a nave and an aisle added later. In 1772 the Pope granted the church the right to offer asylum, an edict which is recognized by a plaque in the facade. Its doorway decoration is typical of Spanish Moorish influence, while the ornate cedar ceiling is more than 120 feet long. The vast mahogany furniture case in the vestry was carved from a single piece of wood and the stained glass and beautiful murals are of particular importance. The altars are 19th-century neo-Classical and the patio is markedly Andalusian. Some valuable oil paintings decorate the walls, such as that by the primitive Cuban painter Nicolás de la Escalera and those by Cabrera Moreno. The *Burial of Christ* is one of the largest neo-Classical Cuban oil paintings. To the left of the long nave is a statue of Santa Bárbara.

Built between 1636 and 1643, the Convento de Santa Clara was the first convent in Cuba. In 1638 the Convent's first nuns arrived from Cartegena, Colombia, and the building was also used as a refuge for maidens who might otherwise be harassed by the port's sailors. There were also public baths and a fountain on this spot. The buildings occupying four small blocks slightly north of the Espiritu Santo church have stucco roofs, exotically carved ceilings and ornate balconies. The garden and courtyard are surrounded by a two-storey cloister, and the main building is topped by an ornate tower, erected at the end of the 17th century by Pedro Hernández de Santiago. The church's interior woodwork was crafted by the master carpenter, Juan de Salas.

The Church and Convent of Nuestra Senora de Belén (Our Lady of Bethlehem) lies between Calles Luz and Acosta, bounded on the east side by Calle Compostela. The church was constructed in 1718, when the convent was also started. The entire block of buildings includes a hospital, church, convent and an educational seminary, where the male children of the poor were taught. Its 130,000 square-foot site is linked to neighbouring buildings across Calle Acosta, on the south side of the convent, by the tile-roofed Arco de Belén, an unusual archway built in 1772. The order acquired one of the country's largest sugar mills, the San Cristóbal factory, which was then worked by 300 slaves, in the early 19th century. The convent and church became an official sanctuary, where pardons and freedoms were granted to slaves. The centre also became an important meteorological observatory, warning the city of impending hurricanes. In 1856 the church and convent were taken over by the Jesuits.

The least impressive, from the outside at least, of Old Havana's churches is La Merced, where construction started in 1755, only to come to a halt in 1792. The church was not finished until late in the 19th century and has a plain exterior, but inside, the frescoes are most impressive.

The Casa Natal José Martí, the birthplace of Cuba's most revered hero, assumes almost religious status and is now a fascinating museum. It is a brick-built house with a tiled roof. The Martí family rented the upper of the house's two floors, and Martí was born here on 28 January 1853. His personal possessions, documents and souvenirs from the War of Independence are on show in this small house in which the hero spent the first four years of his life. The museum was completely restored in 1960 and opened in 1979.

Central Havana

The shady Paseo, or Prado, running up from the Castillo de la Punta to the Capitol building, marks the boundary of Old Havana and is probably the most impressive and picturesque boulevard of its type in the Americas. The Paseo was built first in 1772, modelled on the Prado in Madrid. Originally called the Alameda de Extramuros, or the Public Walk outside the Walls, it later became known as the Nuevo Prado and then the Paseo Isabel II in tribute to the Spanish Queen (1833-1868). Finally, it was named after the hero of Cuban independence, José Martí. Ornate bronze lamp standards light the polished granite promenade, and the mosaic work on the Prado was added in 1927. On each of the cross streets, steps, guarded by bronze lions, lead down each side of the walkway, and carved stone benches are placed at regular intervals. A number of important buildings dating from the 19th and 20th centuries line this thoroughfare and nearby avenues.

The Hotel Sevilla first opened in 1908, and with its plush fittings, Mudéjar-style trappings and gracious decorations, together with its Spanish tiling and treasured statues, was the hotel featured in Graham Greene's *Our Man in Havana*. The ceiling and decorations of the roof restaurant are unequalled in Cuba, and a main feature of the Moorish ground floor is its heavily decorated, arcaded frontage and its beautiful Sevillian patio.

The neo-Baroque Hotel Inglaterra was built in the 1870s by Francisco Fernández, an engineer in the Spanish colonial army and completed in 1875. It was once the Café Louvre, one of the most popular meeting places in late 19th-century Havana. Its Baroque edifice, with columned portals and repoussé iron balconies, includes the famous 'Louvre Steps', a meeting place for pro-independence revolutionaries. The Inglaterra has a Mudéjar interior, an exuberant celebration of Spanish-Moorish architecture. The lobby features early Spanish ceramics, Alicante mosaics, ornamental ironwork, Spanish-style window grilles, stained glass windows, heraldic symbols and carved precious wood doors.

The Gran Teatro de La Habana, built in 1837 as the Tacón Theatre and headquarters of a nationalistic Gallician immigrant society, was re-built in Spanish neo-Baroque style when the magnificent Teatro García Lorca was established in 1915. The theatre then took its name from the famous Spanish writer, Federico García Lorca (1898-1936), and its beautiful facade, dripping with carvings and embellishments, is surmounted by four towers tipped with flying angels presenting the laurel wreath of victory. The National Ballet and Cuba's National Opera regularly perform here, and past performers include Sarah Bernhardt, Enrico Caruso and many other celebrated names through the last 150 years. With 2,000 seats, the Gran Teatro is one of the world's largest theatres.

El Capitolio was constructed between 1926 and 1928 at a cost of US$16 million, and is a more-or-less exact scale replica of the Capitol building in Washington, DC. A total of 2,000 workers and artisans helped build this magnificent edifice which is 600 feet long, has four floors and is surmounted by a gracious dome, the cupola of which is 308 feet high (higher than that of the Washington capitol). The dome is the third highest in the world and the second highest point in Havana. One of its observation points can accommodate up to 150 people. The plans were the work of the Cuban architect Rejean Raymeiro, and much of the bronzework that of the Belgian artist Ricardo Struyf. The neo-Classical building is mainly constructed of a local stone, *capellania*. This stone also faces the rusticated base, below the vast, main-level, columns. It is Cuba's largest building.

The interior was inspired by the Pantheon in Paris, and the eclectic-style interior was based on St Peter's Basilica in Rome. Ten rooms are set aside for events and meetings. The 400-ft-long 'Lost Steps Room', at the top of the first flight of stairs is inspired by a room in Versailles Palace and Raphael's loggia in the Vatican, Rome. Frescoes from Greek mythology decorate the walls of the former House of Representatives, which was designed as a Roman amph-itheatre. Italian Renaissance style was drawn on in the creation of the Yara Room, the floor and walls of which are decorated with 55 varieties of Italian marble. Wood and plaster filigree work decorates the doors and the ceiling, from which hang huge bronze chandeliers. Cabinetwork is in precious hardwoods. The Sevillano Rest-aurant is designed in Spanish Renaissance style with stained glass windows, decorative tiles and murals. Most of the rooms are also decorated in gold.

The Capitol was opened as the seat of Congress during the rule of dictator Gerardo Machado in 1929. At the top of the marble steps the three great bronze doors are decorated with reliefs of scenes from Cuban history. In one, Machado's face was removed when he was deposed in 1933. The interior is gloriously clad in white marble and directly beneath its rotunda and cupola, almost 300 feet high, the 'Star of Cuba' is inlaid in the floor. Directly in the centre of the bronze metal star, under glass, was once embedded a giant 24-carat blue-white 36-faceted Kimberly diamond, itself known as the 'Star of Cuba'. The diamond has been stolen several times and returned, but today it is safely interred in the vaults of the National Bank of Cuba. It is from the space where the diamond reposed that all measurements of distance in Cuba are calculated.

Dominating the main hall is the fifty-ton, 38-foot bronze female statue representing Cuba and named 'La República'. She is dressed as the goddess Athena and holds a lance in one hand and a shield in the other. Created by Italian sculptor, Angelo Zanelli, the statue is plated with 22-carat gold. The magnificent stairway through the embellished bronze front doors is flanked by two fifteen-ton allegorical statues, 'Work' and 'The Virtue of the People', each 23 feet high.

The grand Plaza Hotel, a block or so away, was built in 1903 and converted into a hotel in 1909, displaying its elegant wrought-iron balconies and a lavish, gold-painted lobby. One of its celebrated guests was the Russian ballerina, Anna Pavlova (1885-1931), who stayed here while performing at the nearby García Lorca Theatre. The hotel was completely refurbished and reopened in 1991. Its main internal feature are the vitrales above the lobby bar, depicting Cuba's varied flora.

The former Presidential Palace (and now the Museo de la Revolución) was constructed between 1913 and 1920. This is one of Havana's most ambitious buildings. The Baroque structure, with its columned loggia, tall, pillared facade windows and tower, surmounted by a golden dome and lantern, was originally built to house the provincial government, but in 1917 it was decided to move the presidency here. From 1920 to 1960, the palace was the official residence of Cuba's heads of state. The spectacular interior decoration is the work of Tiffany & Co of New York City. An old *garita* or sentry box, dating from the early 1700s, stands facing the Palace.

Elsewhere in Havana

There are another 200 or more buildings of notable historic architectural merit in central Havana. The Malecón, which curves along the seafront to Vedado, is lined with imposing buildings, revealing a rich variety of balconies and mouldings, but these are in a sad state of disrepair, their colours faded and crumbling under the onslaught of the salt-laden winds. One building is particularly notable for the caryatids that decorate its facade. Numbered and lettered, the grid pattern of Vedado's streets extends north and south of 23rd Street. Here, tree-lined streets and shaded boulevards reveal a rich range of styles from neo-Classical, through Art Nouveau to Art Deco and later trends. Around the Plaza de la Revolución, grandiose modern buildings and monuments celebrate the ideology of Cuba's socialist state. Most of the major government offices are located around this plaza. To the west of Vedado, across the narrow Almaderes River, lies Miramar, Havana's once luxurious suburb. Palatial mansions set in beautifully landscaped grounds, dating from the 1940s and

1950s, now serve as embassy buildings, government offices and official residences. Once these were the opulent homes of Havana's elite, or the holiday houses of America's rich, famous and sometimes notorious.

To the south of the main city, are more residential suburbs of Nuevo Vedado, Cerro and Santos Suarez, with the vast Parque Lenin and the José Martí International Airport on the city's outskirts. Across the bay, to the east, are the more picturesque districts of Regla and Casablanca, with their old churches and mainly 19th-century buildings.

Six buildings particularly illustrate the diversity of the city centre's numerous architectural gems.

Sagrado Corazón de Jesus

Dating from 1914, this Gothic-style church's towering steeple can be seen from all over the city. Created in the Creole fashion which followed the end of Spanish rule, the 'Church on the Reina' is a magnificent testament to latter-day Gothic architecture. Its marble statues, stained glass windows, ornate columns, arches and striking tympanum surpass many contemporary edifices constructed in the Americas in the early 20th century.

Hotel Nacional

Built in 1927, this is one of Cuba's most elegant and prestigious hotels and is designed in a dynamic Classical mould. It is set in landscape, gardens, and the twin-turreted structure facade is one of Central Havana's most prominent landmarks. Inside, the style is Spanish and opulent, with chandeliers and coloured Spanish tiling. This was one of the first, custom-built hotels in the Caribbean and dates back to the period when Havana was a byword for decadence.

Edificio Bacardi

The Bacardi Building, a huge Art Deco tower just inside Old Havana, with mosaics and ornate entrance, is the former headquarters of the Bacardi rum distilling family, who chose to leave Castro's Cuba. Exquisitely coloured glazed tiles and ceramics encase the entire structure like some great 3-D mosaic, and nymph statues decorate the ornate peak. The famous bronze 'bat' Bacardi logo surmounts the vast lantern on top of this, one of Havana's first skyscrapers, which dates from 1930.

Monumento José Martí

Dominating the south end of Plaza de la Revolución is the 497-foot monument to José Martí, (1853-1895) who died in the struggle against Spanish occupation. This *trompe l'oeil* obelisk rises 21 levels above the 55-foot statue of the Cuban hero erected at its base, and was designed in the 1950s by the Cuban sculptor Juan José Sicre. There is an observation platform at the top of what is the tallest monument in the Caribbean.

Universidad de La Habana

The University of Havana was founded in 1728 by the Dominicans, who lived in the Santo Domingo Monastery building, which has stood within the University grounds since 1902. This is one of Cuba's most significant public structures and is constructed in neo-Classical style. This is the largest university building in the Caribbean. The main entrance to these yellow stone buildings is fronted by four massive Corinthian columns.

Cristóbal Colón Cemetery

A major feature of Havana is its vast Christopher Columbus Cemetery in Vedado. This is the largest cemetery in the Caribbean. Here, in this massive, macabre mausoleum, one discovers a host of artistic marvels in marble and granite. Dubbed a 'Symphony in Crosses and Marble' by a local poet, this spectacular cemetery was consecrated in 1871 and laid out between 23rd and 12th Streets, containing the remains of over 800,000 of Cuba's rich, famous, and not so famous, interred in a wealth of artistically sculpted marble tombs and mausoleums. An eighty-foot triple gateway in Romano-Byzantine style has beautifully carved figures of Faith, Hope and Charity in Carrara marble and serves as entrance to the extensive cemetery grounds. It is divided into three porticoes, the central one of which is fifteen feet wide and is closed by ornate wrought-iron gates. From its opening in 1886, the Columbus Cemetery became the place for the wealthy, famous and heroic to achieve immortality in stone. Ever more ambitious monuments were erected as the cemetery grew, the leading Italian sculptors of the day were employed to create masterpieces in precious imported marble and at unlimited expense. Today the site is a treasure house of funereal art. The centrally located Romanesque and Byzantine-style octagonal chapel which can hold 700 mourners, rises to a height of ninety foot and contains a painting of the Final Judgement by José Melero.

The Provinces

There are literally thousands of architectural sites throughout Cuba's towns and cities. The following is merely a selection of some highlights, from west to east.

Pinar del Río

The Museum of Natural Sciences in Pinar del Rio is housed in one of the city's most remarkable structures, the Guasch Palace. This building was constructed in a weird mixture of architectural styles for a much-travelled Spanish doctor, Guasch, between 1909 and 1914. Its varied architectural disciplines, known as 'The Harmony of Disorder', includes Gothic spires, Egyptian motifs, Athenian columns, Baroque embellishments and Moorish fenestration, with decorative sea horses, griffins and strange gargoyles. The José Jacinto Milanés Theatre dates from 1838 and has been rebuilt twice since then, in 1845 and 1898 and fully restored again in the late 1960s. The theatre, built entirely of wood, seats 520 people. Its interior is particularly spectacular, complementing its Greek Revival exterior.

Cárdenas

Not far from the resort of Varadero, this grid-constructed town was once an important sugar centre. The spectacular two-storey steel structure, the Molokoff Market, was built in the shape of a cross by a local citizen named Parodi. Its dome is said to be named after a style of women's crinoline dress which was popular at the time that the market was erected, and which had a similar shape to the fifty-foot-high dome built over the colonnaded structure. The dome was pre-constructed in the US and placed over the market in the mid-1800s. This is the largest iron dome in the Caribbean.

Matanzas

Now a quiet provincial town, Matanzas was once Cuba's second largest city, dubbed the 'Athens of Cuba' because of its vibrant cultural life. It bears the imprint of the many French immigrants who arrived here from the colony of Saint-Domingue. In the centre of the city, the Museo Farmaceútico was the pharmacy of Doctors Ernesto Triolet and the Spanish Juan Fermin Figueroa, who founded the shop in 1882. The business survived until 1964, when the building was converted into a museum. Magnificently preserved with its original interior, it has some beautiful vitrales in Spain's reds and gold (colours which replaced the predominantly tricolor red-white-blue of France on the orders of the Spanish authorities). A large cedar wood display cabinet surrounds the walls and is supported by 22 huge columns, each made from the trunk of a tree and reaching up to the hardwood ceilings from which hang a selection of early German lamps. The original furnishings, fixtures and equipment are on display both in the shop and in the work room behind. Apothecary jars of Sèvres porcelain, mortars in a variety of materials, bottles, cabinets and instruments are exhibited, as are the 55 books of prescriptions made up over more than 100 years.

The Sauto Theatre was built with public subscriptions at the height of the town's cultural boom in 1863 as the sister theatre to the Milanés in Pinar del Rio. Probably the finest neo-Classical building in Cuba, it was completely restored in 1969. Inside, the seats are arranged in three tiers with circular balconies supported on thin brass columns, and the auditorium is decorated with magnificent frescoes and ornate carvings.

Cienfuegos

Several important architectural sites are located in Cienfuegos, founded in 1819 and a city unrivalled in Cuba for its 19th- and 20th-century architecture, influenced by French settlers. Parque José Martí is a fine city square, landscaped with ornate iron lampstands and railings. It is surrounded by some beautiful 19th- and early 20th-century architecture. The bandstand is gloriously opulent, with a pink domed cupola supported by eight Ionic-style columns. The Purísima Concepción Cathedral is a magnificent twin-spired, and pink-domed stone structure. It was completed in 1870, even though the site itself was consecrated in 1867. Curiously, the two bell towers are unevenly matched, and no explanation has yet been put forward for this anomaly. The cupola is octagonal in shape, while the twelve massive windows inside the cathedral are representative of the twelve apostles.

The Museo Provincial (formerly the casino) has a grandiose facade, painted in blue and white and surmounted by a carved pediment above its four-columned entrance porch. This is one of the few buildings that does not have typical Cuban *portales*. The nearby El Palatino Bar is a faithfully restored 19th-century meeting-place with good examples of such portales. Its interior contains some exquisite 19th-century bar furnishings.

The Tomás Terry Theatre is probably the most important building in central Cienfuegos. It is typical of its era, with delicate tracery work, elegant wooden balconies and Romantic ceiling frescoes, and was opened to the sound of *Aïda* in 1890. This grand edifice underwent restoration in 1965. It seats an audience of up to 920, and the floor of the auditorium can be raised to the height of the stage in order to extend the floor area when balls or other cultural or social events are held here. The triple-tiered balconies and boxes are of hand-painted pine and the entire interior is decorated in carved Cuban mahogany. On the ornate exterior, three curious hand-painted plaques form the pediment, and the deep colonnaded facade leads onto the square.

The 1894 Palacio de Valle, just out of town on the Punta Gorda headland, is a fabulous Mogulesque-Moorish construction, now the city's Museum of Decorative Arts. This spectacular palace, with its lavishly ornate decoration and eclectic mix of Islamic and Christian influences, was bought by a Spanish businessman, Alejandro Suero Balbín as a present for his daughter when she married Sr Valle. In the 1950s, the dictator Fulgencio Batista's brother turned the palace into a casino for his nearby Jagua Hotel.

The Castillo de Jagua, across the mouth of Cienfuegos Bay, is a small, but important fortress, founded in 1745 after seven years of construction. The fort was built to protect the settlement from pirate raids and to monitor the activities of smugglers. This is Cienfuegos' oldest building and has been carefully restored. It includes a chapel with a small campanile and is entered by a drawbridge over a dry moat. The traditional wooden houses below the fort make up the hamlet of Perche, founded in the mid-19th century as a fishing village by immigrants from Mallorca and Valencia.

Remedios

One of Cuba's oldest churches, the Iglesia San Juan Bautista de Remedios was built initially in 1570 when this town in Villa Clara Province was an important centre and re-erected on the remains of the original structure in 1692. It was again expanded during the 19th century. This church survived the great fire of the early 19th century, but not the earthquake of 1939, which damaged some of the building. The restoration work, funded in the 1950s by a wealthy local resident, has been most commendably executed and the interior is quite breathtaking. The Moorish-Rococo carved and painted teak ceiling is unique, and the church contains some interesting artworks and carvings on its walls. One statue is the figure of a pregnant Immaculate Virgin. The carved cedar altar is embellished with gold leaf.

Trinidad de Cuba

Founded in 1514 by Diego Velázquez, this delightful colonial gem of a town is now a UNESCO site of World Heritage, and its many ancient architectural features are being preserved for posterity. Since its foundation, Trinidad de Cuba has been a gold-mining town, then turned to tobacco growing, sugar and slavery. In the mid-19th century Trinidad's fortunes declined dramatically and the city became a backwater. Its most important architectural sites are listed.

The cobblestone streets of Trinidad, with old cannon used to protect the corners of houses, have gutters running down the middle of each. Legend has it that a governor of the city once ordered that the streets should slope into the centre so that he could walk down them on the level – his right leg, it seems, was shorter than the left!

Trinidad de Cuba

Plaza Mayor

This main square was laid out in 1522 and is surrounded by several fascinating ancient buildings. This is arguably Cuba's most elegant square, also known as the Antigua Plaza de Trinidad. Ornate, wrought-iron railings ring the square and divide garden areas, where there are a number of decorative iron benches. The plaza, which is raised above the cobbled streets of the square, also contains large glazed urns, which were made locally, and a statue of the Muse of Dance on a pedestal. It is flanked by two Landseeresque bronze greyhounds on plinths. Much of the material with which the plaza was reconstructed was brought from Philadelphia in 1856. At night, the square is lit by early gaslights.

The Parochial Church of Santísima Trinidad

Dominating the elegant main square and set on its own patio, this pretty, cream-coloured cathedral church dates from 1892, although it was the parish church from 1814 and was extended in 1868. This is the only church in Cuba with five aisles (all others have only three) because the white worshippers allowed privileged slaves to occupy the two outside aisles. The church contains some exceptional carvings and mahogany, cedar and acacia Gothic altars. Many of its treasures, including the Christ of the True Cross, were carved in Spain and date from the early 1700s. The niches remain empty, however, as the statues of saints, ordered from Italy, never arrived. This is the only cathedral in Cuba – and one of the few in the world – that does not have a clock tower.

The Inquisitor's House

Almost opposite the church, the house at No. 3 Calle Rosario once belonged to the local head of the Spanish Inquisition, Fernández de Lara, the Chief Inquisitor. Although Trinidad has long been a major stronghold of *Santería*, the Afro-Cuban religion, Roman Catholicism was staunchly upheld by the Inquisition and many unfortunates were burnt publicly at the stake or crucified in the facing square on suspicion of practising Santería. Known locally as the Lara House, this building, dating from 1732, has one of the best examples of typical Trinidadian hand-made tile roofing.

The Romantic Era Museum

Set in the north-west corner of the square, the Museo Romántico was established in the Brunet Palace in 1974. The building itself dates from 1740, when it had only one floor, and has thirteen salons. The aristocratic Brunet family moved in here in 1857and turned it into an elegant colonial mansion. This is the only two-storey building on the square and one of the few in the area, and is fronted by a traditional Cuban colonnade. Furniture, typical of the area and in Romantic style, is on display together with ceramics and 19th-century paintings. The magnificent carved cedar wood ceiling was built between 1770 and 1780. Every detail of the original house has been painstakingly reconstructed, even down to the fine marble floors and the vine design carved in Cuban mahogany on the main staircase. The wooden window screens (*rejas*) with their mediopunto arches were made in 1807. The dining room set is English Victorian, and was made in Cuba in 1835, while the writing desk, enamelled with mythological scenes and dating from the 18th century, is Austrian. There is a wooden toilet dating from 1808 and a beautiful marble bathtub. The porcelain plates in the kitchen date from 1823, and there is a good example here of a *tinaejero*. The long second-floor balcony affords wonderful views of Trinidad's streets.

Guamuhaya Archeological Museum

Located on the south-west side of the Plaza Mayor, this is one of Trinidad's finest houses. In 1801 the house, originally built in 1732, belonged to a Don Juan Andrés Padrón and his family, who hosted the naturalist Alexandre von Humboldt during his visit that year. The house was enlarged in 1835 and contains an extensive selection of Trinidadian architectural features and three main exhibits. The museum here was established in 1976.

Museum of Colonial Architecture

On the south-east side of the main square, this was once the Sánchez family home, originally built in 1735 and painted in yellow instead of the traditional white, as the head of the Sánchez household felt that white was too reflecting in the blazing sunlight. Parts of the walls have been left in the original yellow as a reminder. In the late 1700s the main house was linked with that next door. Pictures and maps here show how Trinidad developed. It contains many Trinidadian architectural features, like the hand-carved and painted wooden ceiling of the older house which is quite exceptional. Exhibits include carved doors and wrought-iron window frames, gas-lit chandeliers and a stockade built to house twelve slaves. One gallery is devoted to sugar plantations and the architectural style of that era. The garden is said to be the most beautiful in Trinidad and the site is supposed to have been occupied for a short time by Hernán Cortéz' house before he left to explore Mexico in 1519. There is an unusual shower here, an old sundial, and a gas generator made in New York and dating from the 19th century.

The Palace of Sánchez Viznaga

This building in typically 19th-century eclectic style, and another of Trinidad's few two-storey buildings, stands on the eastern side of the main square and is not open to the public as it is a private residence. Often referred to as the Viznaga Palace, this was the town house of one of the most powerful sugar barons of the 19th century, Aniceto Iznaga.

San Francisco Convent
(Museo Nacional de Lucha Contra Bandidos)

The reconstructed San Francisco Convent is next to the delightfully converted, ochre-coloured, church tower, just a few steps west of the main square. The museum building, on the site of the old convent itself, is built in Havana Baroque style and was expanded from 1809 to 1813. During the 1890s the convent became a barracks for the Spanish garrison. The tower's cupola collapsed in 1930 and was rebuilt to its original design. The 19th-century bell tower, which dominates the city with its pointed pink dome and clock tower, has 121 granite and wood steps. This belfry was once the highest tower in Cuba. The museum houses exhibits about the US-backed anti-Castro guerrilla campaign in the Escambray mountains.

Across the street is the Municipal Archive, recognizable by the coat-of-arms hanging outside. Opposite, the pink-painted house dates from 1735 and is one of Trinidad's oldest buildings. Next door to is a yellow-painted house, which was apparently built in 1754 by a French pirate, Carlos Merlin, and known locally as the Casa del Corsario. Continue up the street and turn right to find two houses almost opposite each other which have crosses on their walls. These mark two stations in the city's Way of the Cross, a procession re-enacted every Easter. Located almost next door to the Bandidos Museum, the La Canchanchara town house mixes the styles of the 18th, 19th, and early 20th centuries with Mudéjar. It is worth visiting for its pretty little courtyard and cedar-frame roof, and live music is often played here. The Casa de la Trova, on the other side of the Plaza Mayor, is another music venue and is a traditional Trinidadian building dating from 1777. The woodworking on the houses around this area reveals good examples of the Trinidad craftsman's art.

The South of the City

The Iglesia San Francisco de Paula is one of Trinidad's oldest churches and its interior decoration warrants a visit for its unusual motifs. The Ermita de Santa Ana, which dates from around 1712 to 1812, is unfortunately in ruins. Plans are now underway to preserve and restore this impressive old church which flanks the northern side of the Plaza Santa Ana. In front of the Ermita is the pretty square named after the church. To its southern side is the chrome yellow-and-white painted former Royal Prison, built as a defensive fortress and constructed around a large inner courtyard. It is a one-storey building, with two-storey elevations from which the court-yard and the areas surrounding the structure can be surveyed. A parapet around the flat roof allowed prison warders to patrol the entire building. Water spouts of local clay protrude inwards from the flat roof for rain drainage and the collection of fresh water. Around the inner courtyard is a cloister-like, sheltered area surrounded by arches. In the cobbled courtyard are ancient cannon and two large wells. It is now a restaurant.

The Valle de Los Ingenios

Between Trinidad and Sancti Spiritus, this beautiful valley is so important in historical and archaeological terms that UNESCO designated it a site of World Heritage in 1988. In the 1830s, when the sugar-cane business in the Trinidad region was at its height, there were as many as 73 industrial and primitive mills in this valley producing over 80,000 tons of sugar a year. The ruins of fifteen sugar barons' mansions, mills, slave barracoons, slave burial grounds – all evidence of the valley's former prosperity and the labour on which it was based – can be seen dotted around the countryside.

Now completely restored and beautifully decorated, The San Alejo de Manaca Iznaga Villa, a magnificent *hacienda* and planta-tion house, dates from 1750. Its walls are decorated with some interesting maps and details relating to the sugar industry of the 18th and 19th centuries. Outside stands the great bell of the old

The Iznaga Villa and watchtower

watchtower and equipment once used in the production and refining of sugar. The yellow-and-white mansion and its watchtower nearby are surrounded by a small community, the Caerio Manaca Iznaga, where slaves' quarters, part of the mill buildings, a blacksmith's shop and infirmary can be seen.

The building is constructed in the typical 'Four Winds' architectural style of colonial houses. Built on a hill, it is designed so that wherever one is in the building, refreshing breezes are chanelled into its interior. Metal bars protect every window except that of the master's bedroom. It is said that Don Iznaga had a passion for slave girls, and they discreetly entered his room at night through the open window. However, Iznaga was regarded as something of a philanthropist, as well as a connoisseur of local womanhood. He built proper houses, a hospital and a school for his slaves and monitored their health. He also built the first and only slave cemetery in Latin America.

Near the family villa, the 19th-century Torre de Manaca Iznaga was built by the sugar baron family between 1835 and 1845 to keep watch over the slave workers in the expansive sugar plantations. This massive, seven-tiered watchtower was once the highest structure in Cuba, at almost 150 feet. A legend concerns the brothers Alejo and Pedro Iznaga, who bet each other that one could not build a tower higher that the other could dig a well deep. Another story suggests that the competition was for the hand of a beautiful local woman. The well has not yet been found, so nobody knows who won. Some say that the well-digging brother dug his well precisely as deep as the watchtower was high, so neither won the contest. Another version of events claims that Alejo built the tower as a prison for his wayward wife.

Sancti Spiritus

Declared a National Monument in 1978 and targeted in a recent reconstruction programme, the Iglesia Parroquial Mayor del Espíritu Santo was founded in 1522 and built in wood. A parishioner, Don Pedro de Pérez de Corcha, donated a solid gold weathercock to surmount the church's original tower. In 1652, pirates raided the church and stole the cockerel, returning again in 1671, after which it was rebuilt over the following nine years with most of the original materials. The present structure was completed in 1680, although the tower, built in three sections, was not finished until 1764. The cupola was added in the mid-19th century. The ornately carved ceiling with Mudéjar influences in the single large nave is one of the finest in Cuba, and paintings, particularly one of *Christ with Humility and Patience*, religious statues and the polychrome crucifix are all of interest. The church is technically the oldest on the island, as it still stands on its original 1522 foundations. The nearby Colonial Art Museum, a typical early 19th-century colonial structure, once belonged to the wealthy sugar barons, the Iznaga family, and is built in traditional style around a delightful courtyard. There are many distinctive colonial architectural features in the museum, which houses period Spanish-style furniture and decorative items. The Yayabo Bridge, a block away, is the oldest and largest stone bridge in the Caribbean, and is on Cuba's reconstruction programme as a National Monument. It was built in 1815 over the river of the same name with five arches and is Cuba's only remaining stone-arched bridge.

Camagüey

The Santa Iglesia cathedral here is an impressive ecclesiastical building, the city's oldest, and has been reconstructed many times since the mid-16th century. A distinctive bell tower is surmounted by a marble statue, and the cathedral contains a most beautiful inner nave. Nuestra Señora de la Soledad church was finished in 1776 after 43 years of construction. This impressive building has an oddly designed campanile or bell tower, with six sides, and six niches, each containing a bell, and decorated with some of the most exquisite fresco work in Latin America. Its triple-arched frontage is colonnaded in Spanish colonial style. The Teatro Principal was constructed in 1860 and updated in 1926. This imposing building has a suitably theatrical facade, with a grand balcony divided by four pillars over an entrance hall, which is fronted by five doorways surmounted by vitrales. Inside, the theatre has marble staircases and crystal lamps.

Bayamo

The 18th-century Spanish-style birthplace of the Cuban hero of the First War of Independence, Carlos Manuel de Céspedes is a comparatively modest edifice in the undistinguished city centre, even though it is built of marble, taken from a building site in Havana in around 1790. The two-storey town house has a wrought-iron balcony and tall shuttered windows. The Iglesia de Santísimo Salvador, one of the first churches to be established in Cuba, was reconstructed in the 1970s, although much of the interior dates back two or three centuries. Parts of its exterior facade, the columns and cupola to the left of the entrance date back to 1630, and the existing church was consecrated in 1702.

Santiago de Cuba

Cuba's lively second city contains fewer colonial treasures than Havana and is less Spanish in feel, having been home to many French immigrants in the early 19th century. There is also a larger black population than elsewhere on the island, and this is reflected in the city's distinctive food and music.

Built in 1524 and consecrated in 1528, the magnificent Santa Iglesia Basílica Metropolitana is an exceptional celebration of Spanish colonial ecclesiastical architecture. Due to earthquakes, the existing edifice is the fourth to occupy the site. The cathedral's pink-cream edifice is dominated by twin-domed towers and the beautiful sculpture of the Angel of the Annunciation over its four-pillared portico. Inside, there are some interesting church furnishings, including wonderfully carved wooden pews. The hand-carved, precious wood choir stalls date from 1810.

An example of early 16th-century pre-Baroque aristocratic archi-tecture, the house of Diego Velázquez (see page 20) contains all the ingredients of a residence of that period: long, red-tiled roofs, around an interior courtyard, with long window screens; floor to ceiling shutters; Moorish balconies; Mudéjar ceilings; a courtyard well and locally carved mahogany staircases. This is Cuba's oldest villa, dating from between 1516 and 1530..

South of the city, protecting the bay, is the Castillo del Morro, originally the San Pedro de la Roca Fortress and initially built around 1640. That fortification was blown up by the English priva-teer Henry Morgan in 1662 when his forces sacked the city. The existing structure, designed by the Italian architect Antonelli, was built around 1663 and extended in 1710. A moat, crossed by a drawbridge surrounds the landward side of the cliff-top fort, with its vast ramparts, domed bartizans, depots, ancient cannon, dungeons, barracks and a chapel containing a 16th-century wooden cross. In 1997 UNESCO declared the Morro fortress a site of World Heritage, and it is considered to be the best-preserved example of Italian Renaissance military architecture in the Americas. A museum explains the historical scourge of piracy that afflicted Santiago.

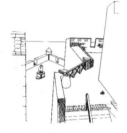

Castillo del Morro, Santiago de Cuba

Six miles west of Santiago, the El Cobre basilica dates from the mid-1600s, when a small church was built on the site (the present cathedral was constructed in the 19th century). This is Cuba's most sacred place of pilgrimage and its full name is the Sanctuario Nacional de Nuestra Señora de la Caridad del Cobre, the National Sanctuary of Our Lady of the Charity of Copper. Built over a copper mine, the church celebrates the miraculous powers of a statue of the Virgin. Set like an architectural gemstone, the basilica is a spectacular Gothic edifice. A tall, pink-domed spire rises up from the white facade, flanked by two smaller spires. A glass case above the exotic marble altar contains the statue of the black Virgin of El Cobre, and stairs lead up to the viewing gallery.

CURAÇAO

The largest Dutch island in the Caribbean, Curaçao has the best selection of architectural examples among the Netherlands Antilles, most of which are directly influenced by the colonial power, Holland. There are almost 1,000 sites on the island of architectural

and historic interest. Cradled by the powerful Dutch West India Company, whose representative, Van Walbeeck, descended on the Spanish cattle ranches on this island in 1634, Curaçao became an important and rich trading base. Peter Stuyvesant was dispatched from the Netherlands to govern the three islands of Aruba, Bonaire and Curaçao in 1643, and by that time, Willemstad, the capital, formerly Spanish Santa Ana, was growing steadily. It was also to become a large naval base and a thriving smuggling and slave centre. Initially laid out as three parallel streets, with 54 town house plots inside a three-sided, protecting wall, Willemstad was a typically ordered Dutch settlement. From the earliest times, the use of wood in architecture was banned, as it was so scarce on all the three so-called ABC islands. The island's buildings were hence constructed, initially at least, from imported brick and locally produced plaster.

Today, there are no fewer than 750 historic buildings in Willemstad. The defensive Fort Amsterdam, the first building, and the barracks area were similarly walled and located nearest the sea. Built in 1642, the fort's features include the pedimented and arched entrance to the classical Governor's residence at the west entrance. The fort, was built to a small-scale, conventional 17th-century design, forming a quadrilateral, with pointed bastions on each corner, the more pronounced facing inland, and presenting a long front of cannon to the sea. The interior barracks block was demolished in 1955 to make way for a hotel. Fort Amsterdam was one of eight forts built to defend the island in the 17th and 18th centuries. At the east end of the fort is the mustard-painted, old Dutch Reformed Church, the Fortkerk, facing into Wilhelminaplein. It is the second oldest church on the island, and was rebuilt in 1796 on the 1763 original foundations.

The Fortkerk was first opened in 1769, and has an imposing double stairway, delicately railed, leading up to first-floor, stylized double entrances. The fenestration is arched and plain plaster-framed and there are two dormer windows on each side of its steep, orange-tiled roof. The elegant lantern and clock, surmounted by a cupola and cross on its roof, date from 1903. There is a museum in the old vestry. During an attack by the British in 1804, a cannonball fired from HMS *Bounty* was lodged in the Kerk's wall. It remains there to this day.

By the early 18th century, there were over 200 houses inside the old walls before the city expanded eastwards into the Pietermaai

The Fortkerk, Willemstad

district. The embracing town walls were demolished in 1861, and Wilhelminaplein, with its statue of Queen Wilhelmina, was laid out in 1862. The building to the right of the square, with its twin staircases of 21 steps each, is the old Stadhuis or Town Hall, now the parliament and high court building. It dates from 1858. The centre of Willemstad is the handsome Handelskade, a long row of early houses facing the harbour channel, known as the Santa Annabai in tribute to the original Spanish name for the town.

With its typically Dutch, narrow, gabled buildings, gaily painted in beige, gold, orange and red, with details picked out in white, the prospect of Willemstad's waterfront must be one of the most incongruous sights of the Caribbean. The orangey-red clay tiles, known as 'dakpannen', came to the Caribbean as ship's ballast, and the reason that so many of the Dutch Antilles' buildings are painted in pastel colours, it is said, is that a governor of Curaçao suffered migraines from the sun's reflection off all the white-painted buildings and ordered that they all be painted any colour but white! With a shortage of building materials, these 18th-century replicas of Amsterdam's houses were built of coral and quarry stone instead of brick, using a mortar of loam, lime and sea sand finished with plaster. Standing on the corner of Handelskade and Heerenstraat is the glorious Penha House, the Julius L. Penha & Sons store, an early merchant house dating from 1708. The four-storey masterpiece of Dutch design has exquisite decorative stucco ornamental plasterwork, almost like icing on a cake, setting off its curvilinear, scroll gables and arched ground floor galleries. These architectural features and the numerous shuttered windows are all picked out in the bright colours of the Dutch West Indies, complemented by its steep roof in orange tiles (see page 31).

Around the corner is an unusual duck-egg blue building and another balconied house painted yellow, the charming 'La Casa Amarilla'. The whole waterfront here is a celebration of multi-coloured facades, with two-, three-, four- and five-storey narrow buildings sporting traditional crow-stepped, curvilinear, and conventional gables, some with dormer windows, others with overhanging frontages, and some with hipped or ridge roofs. The traditional angle of the Dutch gable slopes at 52 degrees. The Stroomzigt House comes straight out of 18th-century Holland, with strong, curvilinear gables, echoed on the dormer windows on its steep, tiled roof, a tall, narrow prospect, with almost featureless walls, staired entrance, and sash windows.

The Mikvé Israel Synagogue dates from 1732 and is an excellent example of Dutch colonial architecture and is the oldest synagogue in the New World, testifying to the arrival of Jews in Curaçao from Spain, Portugal and Brazil. Its simple stone, plastered walls, with four-pilastered facade and arched windows, is fronted by three

The Mikvé Israel Synagogue, Willemstad

curved gables. It has a ceremonial bath, a *mikve*, in the 1780 court-yard museum. The four 24-candle brass chandeliers hanging from the mahogany ceiling in the yellow interior date from between 1707 and 1709. Other treasures include a 17-foot Holy Ark, a torah said to date from 1493, and an 1866 ornamented organ. The sanded floor reminds the worshippers of the Israelites' wanderings in the deserts of Egypt at the time of the Exodus.

Across to the northern side of the colourful floating market, by means of the Waaigat or Wilhelmina Drawbridge, with the air of a Vincent van Gogh painting, is the Scharloo quarter of the city with its European-style architecture dating from 1700 to Victorian times. Once a plantation, this became the expensive quarter of Willemstad. Because of the busy trade with North America in the early 19th century, grandiose classical American architecture influenced the buildings of rich merchants. Sephardic Jews also built their Italianate mansions in the Scharloo district, as the Otrobanda had become a staunchly Protestant area. The neo-Classical buildings here are constructed in a 'U'-shape plan, with a wide, front gallery and a back gallery facing onto a Spanish-style patio. Columns were made of brick, and great attention was taken to details, using plaster, brick, tiling and marble.

The building just behind Scharloo is typical of this period. A stately black-and-white mansion, with curved staircases rising to a first-floor entrance, under a Classical, six-pillared pediment, sports a blue-and-white, wooden cartouche of a ship at sea. On each side of the entrance, tall, arched windows are louvred and emphasized with white mouldings, while the saddle roof is of black tiles. Known as the Roosevelt House, it was donated by Holland to the United States in recognition of assistance during World War II. Towards the end of the 19th century, the more flamboyant South American style of architecture became popular in Scharloo. Here, the octagonal, balconied and staircased Casa Bolívar, built in 1812, is now a museum. The simple domed building is said to have been the residence in exile, of Simón Bolívar, the Venezuelan 'Liberator', and was owned by his sisters. Bolívar's statue stands on Bolivarplein. Nearby, the Bolo di Bruid house is one of Curaçao's most photographed buildings. Near here, in the south-east corner of the Schottegat, is the Autonomy Monument, dedicated in 1954, with six symbolic bird statues, representing the six states of the Netherlands Antilles. To the west of Scharloo, where the Santa Annabaai canal joins the Schottegat, is the old Fort Nassau, which dates from 1796. A restaurant has been installed in this massive building. On the hill is a white marble statue of the Madonna.

> The Queen Emma pontoon bridge links the Punda, or Fort Amsterdam side, with the Otrabanda west across the Santa Annabaai. It dates from 1888 and was designed by the American Consul, Leonard B. Smith, who also introduced Willemstad to electric light and ice. It is formed by sixteen linked barges, or pontoons. One of the earliest examples of means testing came when a small toll was levied on those crossing the bridge, but only on those wearing shoes. However, the poor borrowed shoes to prove that they were not poor, and the rich took off their shoes to avoid the toll! Due to the vast amount of maritime traffic through the canal to the open port waters of the Schottegat, the bridge was replaced in 1939 by a swing bridge. It opens around thirty times a day, and a ferry runs while it is closed to pedestrian traffic.

The modern bridge, the Queen Juliana Bridge, north of the Queen Emma Bridge, was built in 1974 and is the largest bridge in the Caribbean, spanning 1,625 feet and rising 200 feet above the Santa Annabaai. Across either bridge, into Otrabanda, or the 'other side', the architecture is the ornate, 18th-century Dutch Rococo architecture of the Protestant traders who lived here from the early 18th century onwards. The first building permits for Otrabanda were issued in 1707, and by 1774 there were 300 houses in the district. Here stands a monument to the town's most famous early 19th-century hero, Pedro Luis Brion, on Brionplein. South of the plaza of Brionplein is the renovated Rif Fort, or Riffort, dating from 1768 and designed to protect the harbour entrance, together with the Water Fort, built here in 1634. This is reputedly the only fort in the world to boast marine collision insurance. West of the plaza is the 1804 St Annakerk.

Further west of Brionplein in what looks like a Dutch country mansion is the Curaçao Museum. This 1853 building was a one-time Seamen's Hospital, and a Quarantine Station; note the unusual grey, white, red and black geometric colour scheme and an old Dutch 47-bell carillon. This is a classic Curaçao building with twin pointed roofs and raised balconies. The design follows that of an old landhuis, with the original entrance situated in one of its long walls. The entrance was moved later to the end wall and a traditional 19th-century sweeping staircase added. Another fine mansion, typical of those in Otrabanda, is the porticoed Belvedere. Fort Waakzaamheid is nearby, built in 1803 to defend the island against a French invasion. To the north-east is the Beth Haim Cemetery, dating from 1659 and containing more than 2,500 graves and some of the oldest European tombs in the Americas, the oldest dating from 1668. In the Salinja district of Willemstad, is the Landhuis Chobolobo, an old plantation house dating from 1796 and home to the Senior & Co. Liqueur Distillery from 1946. This distillery makes the famous Curaçao liqueur. The north-east suburb of Willemstad is Santa Rosa, and there is a fine parish church here.

Off the Caracasbaai, where cruise ships dock, the large inland expanse of water is named the Spaanse Water, and near here, guarding the entrance to the inland 'sea', is the 18th-century Fort Beekenburg. The nearest real country mansions or landhuizen to Willemstad, east of this, are the estate houses of Parera, and, north of this, the Koingsplein Landhuis, Brever, Groot Kwartier, and Groot Davelaar (built in 1865 and the home of Guzmán Blanco, who became President of Venezuela). The nearby landhuis is Zuikertuintje, dating from 1870. Further out are the privately-owned Girouette, Goede Hoop and Zuurzak landhuizen. The Rooi Catootje Landhuis was built in 1820 and is currently a library. Zeelandia plantation house is now used as a restaurant, and Cas Cora is a botanical garden and zoo.

Further out are numerous old colonial estate houses. Landhuis is the term for the estate itself, including the magasinas, or warehouses, a cistern for water and the stone huts of the domestic servants. The estate revolved around the *kas di shon*, *kas grandi* or great house, although the word landhuis is also commonly in use for the great house itself. Almost all of these plantation houses were built to be defensible and were usually erected on a raised, walled terrace. A hilltop location was often selected to catch the cooling breezes and from which to survey the estate.

Probably the best example of a landhuis, of which there are 55 on Curaçao, is the Brievengat Landhuis, just north of Willemstad and built in the middle of the 18th century. Brievengat is a typical estate building, situated on what was once a cattle ranch and later an aloes and cochineal plantation. It sits, traditionally squat and long, on a raised, defensive-walled base, with access by a wide staircase, leading

Brievengat Landhuis, Curaçao

onto the main patio in front of the house itself. The patio is protected by two square sentry watchtowers, with pyramidal tiled roofs. The main house has white stucco walls, curvilinear gables and an arched entrance sheltered by a gently sloping lower tiled roof. This type of roof is known as a saddle roof, and the main, steep, tiled roof, has four dormer windows and gable-echoing pediments, with massive defensive shutters. Inside, a simple flagstone floor, thick walls and spacious galleries, ensure a pleasant temperature.

North of Brievengat is one of the most spectacular country houses, that of Ronde Klip. Built in the middle of the 19th century on three sides of a raised patio, accessed by a typically funnel-shaped staircase, this grand mansion is constructed on three floors. The massive and solidly built sloping outer walls of the main house and its two wings are fortress-like, with tiny windows high under the eaves. There are hipped, tiled roofs on the main house and the wings and a large pediment on the main roof, facing the square patio. The pediment is supported by six columns from a first-floor verandah, which runs around and above three sides of the patio. The verandah is, in turn, supported over cloister-like galleries, which are formed by 24 arches. This massive structure is vaguely reminiscent of a miniature Hatshepsut's temple at Thebes, in Egypt.

West of Willemstad, are six landuizen: Habaai, the privately-owned Veeris and Groot Piscadera, the Rafael Landhuis, Klein Piscadera and the Blauw Landhuis, dating from around 1700. Further west is the St Michiel district with the remains of its 1713 Fort Sint Michiel guarding the entrance to the bay. Here, there are the two landhuizen of Groot, or large, St Michiel and the Klein, or small, St Michiel Landhuis. Further out to the west are the Malpais Landhuis, Hermanus Landhuis, and the Jan Kock Landhuis, which dates from 1654. The mansion's cellar was used as salt store, and there is a slave prison and bell used to summon slaves back from work on the nearby salt pans. By 1860, this plantation employed over 100 slaves.

Further west are the landhuizen of Sebastiaan, Rif 'St Marie', Cas Abao, San Juan, Pannekoek and the 18th-century Groot Santa Marta and Klein Santa Marta. Klein Santa Marta was built in 1700 and was attacked and plundered by the English in 1805. The pointed roof with triangular tops of the Groot Santa Marta house, built at the end of the 17th century, shows the style of the earliest buildings. Then come the landhuizen of San Nicholas, the 18th-century Santa Cruz, Jeremi, dating from 1880, and the Knip Landhuis, which dates from the late 1600s and houses exhibits of antique domestic appliances. West of the Knip Landhuis is the ancient Westpunt Fort.

Inland to the north-west of Willemstad is the Hato Landhuis, built in the 18th century and once the home of the Director of the Dutch West Indies Company. Nearby is the Weitje Landhuis, the pastel-painted Papaya plantation house and Landhuis Ceroe Grandi, another old colonial mansion. Further west is the Daniel Landhuis, built in 1750 and now a hotel, the privately-owned

Hermanus, Siberie, dating from 1784, and the Ascencion Landhuis, another 17th-century mansion, once a maize and indigo plantation and now used as a naval training centre.

In the far north-west of Curaçao are the two 18th-century land-huizen of Doktersuin, and Savonet. Savonet is typically terrace-raised, with a broadly sweeping roof, ornate gables with fanciful curlicues at each end and shuttered dormer windows. This landhuis was built around 1662 and rebuilt after an attack by British forces in 1806. It now houses an historical museum. Not far from here is the ancient, ruined Zorgvlied estate house. Little survives of the estate buildings, which date from 1716. The walls of the main house, which faces east to west, still stand, as does the porch, but the estate fell into disrepair in 1832. The threshing floor can also be seen, where maishi or sorghum was winnowed, and from which funchi, the staple diet was made. A stark reminder of the early trade of this island is evident in the presence of an old slave post, built from the rare Knip stone.

In the eastern part of the island is the Jan Thiel Landhuis, that of Bottelier, Scheloecheuvel and the three landhuizen of Brakkeput, Brakkeput Rei and Brakkeput Abao. North of the Spaanse Water are the landhuizen of Jan Sofat, Groot St Joris, Choloma and Klein St Joris. On the east side of the Spaanse Water are the 1662 Santa Barbara Landhuis and the ruins of the Fuik Landhuis. The Santa Catarina Landhuis and that of Koraal Tabak are directly north-east of Willemstad, while north of the capital is the Noordkant Landhuis. Most of the landhuizen had small plots of land for their own use or for cultivating certain amounts of vegetables and fruit, usually for local consumption. Known as hofjes, these were espe-cially irrigated, walled-in plots.

Out in the *cunucu*, the parched and desert-like countryside, there are several examples of old slave houses, stone-built and rectangular, with thick, angled walls. They were known as 'straw houses' after the thick layer of crushed maize stalks which formed the thatch and looked like straw. If sorghum stalks were used for the thatch, the house was called a *kas di pal'i maishi*. However, many of these prim-itive buildings now have corrugated iron, zinc, or asbestos 'hoods'. Their walls are thicker at the base than at the top, and their small windows are positioned just under the eaves. In later times, some of these *kas di kunuku* or country houses had walls built of concrete blocks. Near to the main house, a smaller hut was built for laundry work and cooking, and a stone-built and tile-roofed bread oven would be located in the yard. The yard would often be fenced in by a natural barrier of cactus plants. The Kas di Pal'i Maishi, with its sorghum roof, is a replica of these straw huts, built as a museum.

DOMINICA

Dominica's inhospitable, although spectacular, topography ensured that European colonization arrived later than elsewhere in the region. The island was also the last stronghold of the indigenous Caribs, who violently resisted any attempt to establish European settlement. Full-scale colonization did not really take place until the mid-18th century, and the architecture of Dominica was never really developed until that time. The island's tiny capital has a large number of early buildings which have survived numerous fires, and, although Dominica's major fort overshadows the architectural gems of this little island, there are a number of important buildings of significant historical value in the capital and scattered throughout its hinterland.

After Columbus passed by the island in 1493, Carib warriors kept potential European settlers at bay for around 250 years. French would-be colonists and missionaries were driven away, and in 1660 the English and French agreed to leave Dominica to its Carib owners. Nevertheless, the island's proximity to Martinique and Guadeloupe tempted other French colonists, and for much of the 17th and 18th centuries a three-way struggle simmered between English, French and Carib communities. In 1674 the English were responsible for a mass killing of Caribs, at a place now fittingly called Massacre. The 1748 Treaty of Aix-la-Chapelle again returned the island to the Caribs, and attempts at European settlement were forbidden.

However, Dominica's strategic importance made it a coveted colonial possession, and the 1763 Treaty of Paris confirmed British ownership after an invasion two years earlier. Still the Caribs fought off total colonization, retreating to the east coast (where a community remains to this day), while remaining French settlers planted coffee and the British raised sugar-cane. Dominica became an important slave-trading base, but the colonists were harried by itinerant runaway slaves, who took refuge in the impenetrable mountainous interior. This unrest culminated in a French attempt to retake the island in 1795, a move which involved the burning down of the capital, Roseau. It was not until 1805 that Britain finally paid a ransom to France for control of Dominica, the last Caribbean island to become a British colony. Introducing black slaves, the British cultivated sugar-cane on the fertile slopes and began settling the island in earnest.

By the 1730s, the French had begun to define the centre of Roseau by building their timber houses around a market square and erecting a wooden fort nearby. Many of these huts were thatched with reeds which grew along the adjacent riverbed, giving the village its name, 'roseaux', or 'reeds'. However, the village had no definite identity and order until 1768, seven years after the British took the island, when a grid-pattern was formally set out. During the fighting of 1761 many buildings in the town had been razed to the ground, but it was around this time that Roseau became accepted as the island's capital in preference to Portsmouth, located to the north. Roseau was to suffer a further series of devastating fires, as French and British forces used widescale arson to smoke out their adversaries. Fires took place in 1778, 1781, and again, after British occupation, in 1795. Another French-inspired fire swept through Roseau during the Napoleonic Wars in 1805, before Britain finally acquired the island later that year. The wooden shingles of the town's houses were particularly susceptible to conflagration, but it was a river flood that destroyed many buildings the following year, and subsequent hurricanes have also taken their toll.

The wooden upper storeys of houses and warehouses had been consumed, leaving the dark, volcanic stone, lower storeys and foundations as piles of rubble, with which the city was strewn for many years. By the time rebuilding began, the typical dormer windows of colonial town houses had become almost vestigial. Few buildings, especially in the French old quarter, remain from before the mid-19th century, although the stone foundations can still be seen. The Victorian older buildings had retained the traditional thick stone foundations, with Creole wooden upper floors built on top, reminiscent of the original French style.

Some houses were reconstructed in the earlier Georgian style, but most of Roseau's buildings are now two-storeyed, with balconies overhanging the sidewalk, supported on wooden columns. They are often embellished with gingerbread fretwork or delicate ironwork, or with wooden railings in sunburst or floral patterns. Both the windows and doors are usually jalousied or louvre-shuttered. One of the best examples of Dominican architecture in the capital is La Robe Créole Restaurant, a classic stone building with attractive arched windows and doors. Later buildings were constructed in the same style but of stuccoed stone or concrete blocks. Nevertheless, Roseau remains a typical colonial waterfront market town, with traditional, stone-based warehouses interspaced by 'A'-framed Creole houses, old molasses-storage cellars, steep-roofed shops and balconied store-houses. Many of the streets are paved with large cobblestones, carried here as ballast in the 1790s, as were the bricks which embellish several older buildings.

The crucifix and shrine overlooking Roseau was erected near the 18th-century barracks of Fort Morne Bruce in 1924. The fort site and military graveyard of Morne Bruce and King's Hill are reached by the path known as Jack's Walk. Named after James Bruce of the British Royal Engineers, designer of much of Dominica's fortifications, who also lent his name to the village of Castle Bruce on the east coast, the fort's barracks are now used by the police.

Fort Young Hotel, on the quayside to the east of the Old Market in Roseau, is built inside sections of the 1770 fortress, the oldest building in the capital and once the port's main defence. Built by the first British governor, Sir William Young, the fort was completed in 1783 and expanded during the French occupation in the American Independence War years. In the latter half of the 19th century, the police used the fort as their headquarters and it was converted into a hotel in 1964. With the addition of extra rooms, the original lines of the fort are hard to determine, especially as the 1979 hurricane destroyed much of the superstructure, although the thick stonework and numerous gun embrasures are still evident. In the courtyard, the flagstones are original and a number of ordnance pieces dot the grounds.

The only other building of note in this area is the old Post Office, built as the Market House in 1810. The red-trimmed and shuttered building stands on the waterfront at Old Market Plaza and is now the Dominica Museum. Behind, the old Market Square, traditionally cobbled, was once the centre of slave auctions. A wrought-iron, red-painted Victorian memorial marks the block where the auctions took place. The Victoria Monument itself was erected in 1902, and part of the plaza, known as Dawbiney Square, was covered over in

1895, when a local philanthropist left money for its construction. There are the ruins of the old Courthouse on Victoria Street, built in classical Georgian style in 1811 and burned in 1979. The simply designed Public Library was built between 1902 and 1906 with a Carnegie Foundation bequest.

In the 1760s, the British laid out the grid style of the streets in the northern part of the capital. The large, white, green-roofed State House sports a triple-arched, double-stepped entrance and especially tall, narrow, upper windows and high-ceilinged rooms, built to channel cooling breezes. The existing State House was built in 1840, although the original, constructed in 1766 where there is now a lawn has been completely obliterated. A nearby building is the birthplace of novelist Jean Rhys (1890-1979), of note for its age and its fine louvred exterior. This tin-roofed, two-storey building, based on stone-block foundations, is now a guest house. Here also is a small, early monument to Lord Cathcart, who died on the island in 1741. Near the waterfront are several early warehouses, and Roseau's two churches dominate the port.

It was Friar William Martel who built the first church in Roseau in 1732, which was originally a timber-framed thatched building. Another church replaced the first before the present structure of the Catholic cathedral was started in 1800. Its construction involved a strange set of circumstances. Caribs, based in the outskirts of the town, took three months to erect the timber ceiling frame, and convicts from Devil's Island built the pulpit. The cathedral's con-struction is of contrasting volcanic stone and was built in defiance of the lack of support from the Anglican authorities. With no finance provided from public funds, the predominantly Catholic population built the church themselves by carrying stone to the site on the summons of a nocturnal bell. Most of the work dates from 1841, when it was consecrated, and the cathedral's spire was finally completed in 1916.

Catholic Cathedral, Roseau

Today, the Catholic Cathedral of Our Lady of the Assumption (or Our Lady of Fair Haven) is a mixture of Gothic design with romanesque arches, and the interior has finely-carved, Victorian pews. The small west steeple was the last addition to this magnificent building. The top half of the Gothic-style windows are of stained glass, and the lower half are shuttered to allow breezes to enter. Ornate Victorian murals set off the side altars, and a depiction of Columbus features in one of the windows.

Oddly located next to the Catholic Cathedral are the Methodist church and manse. They were erected here in the latter half of the 19th century on land which was not included in the 1865 amendment to the 1766 land grant to the Catholic community. The grey stone, Regency-style, Anglican St George's Church was originally built in 1820, yet its churchyard gravestones date back to the 1780s. Entirely destroyed by hurricane David in 1979, the church was quickly rebuilt, but suffered more damage before the work was completed.

There are few other buildings on Dominica of much architectural or historic significance, but overlooking the small town of Portsmouth are the large fortifications which include the Prince Rupert Battery. Portsmouth was initially selected in the mid-1700s as the island's first capital, and two hundred years ago this small and run-down town was capable of supporting the 400 British warships which once gathered in its deep bay. Fort Shirley was built above Prince Rupert Bay between 1770 and 1815, and the last work on the fortifications was completed in 1826. The fort was designed by the Royal Engineers' Lieutenant, Charles Shipley, under the command of General Thomas Shirley, who later became the island's Governor.

Over the half century of construction, more than fifty military buildings were constructed in the hollow and on the two peaks which comprise the fortifications. The fort had seven gun batteries, seven cisterns, powder magazines, ordnance stores, barracks, a guard house, a parade ground, engineers' quarters, officers' quarters, store houses, two hospitals and a Commandant's House. The central structure was Fort Shirley, located in the hollow, and it was guarded from the sea approaches by 33 cannon, many of which still lie in the grounds.

Thanks to the efforts of local historian Lennox Honychurch, begun in 1982, some of its military buildings have been faithfully restored. The complex includes a museum, built into the remnants of the old powder magazine. Among the volcanic stone blocks used in the garrison buildings' construction are red clay bricks, transported here from England as sailing ship ballast. These can be seen in the arches of powder magazines, in the fabric of ovens and in the cistern walls. The quarries at Grand Savannah, to the south, supplied the pinkish rock used to fashion door and window frames, and volcanic rock was used in the construction as cornerstones, window sills and lintels. Coral limestone and molasses formed the basis of the mortar used to cement the blocks and bricks together, and volcanic stone was used to form the fort's massive ramparts. During a period of French occupation between 1778 and 1783, the fort was substantially expanded, and, at its height, could accommodate 600 regular soldiers and officers. Fort Shirley was finally abandoned by the British army in 1854 after decades of decline. Nowadays, the fort site is just part of the 1,313-acre Cabrits National Park, and towers above the new cruise ship dock, built on the site of the old military dock.

Other 18th-century gun batteries were located along the coast, south of Roseau, down to the cliffs of Scotts Head, named after Captain Scott, who led the British to capture Dominica from the French in 1761. Here are the ruins of the Fort Cashacrou and an old semaphore station. This was the first fort captured by the French General de Bouille, in 1778 during the American War of Independence. Most of the structure of this historic and important 18th-century fort has tumbled into the sea below the promontory of Cashacrou Point. The remains of another of these forts can be seen at Grand Bay. The early church cemetery of Grand Bay is overlooked by the island's oldest crucifix, carved in stone in about 1720. The church has local paintings over the doorway, and its roof has fearsome gargoyles. The bell tower was relocated on the hillside, reputedly so that its peals could be heard over a larger area. Saint Sauveur village has an old plantation house and a tiny church, the pretty village's main architectural feature.

To see examples of the local rural architecture, it is worth visiting the many little villages around the coast, like Soufrière, near Scotts Head, where a pretty, iron-roofed church sports a square bell tower. The imposing, arched entrance, with its roundel window surrounded by quoins, is curiously buttressed by rounded supports, topped by small, decorated domes. The white, crenellated bell tower, picked out in red ochre and echoed in the domed finials of the facade's pillars, contrasts with the dark stone of the solidly built main structure. The church in Vieille Case in the extreme north is similarly built of the dark, heavy, volcanic stone, and is noted for its murals. The island's first Christian mass was reportedly celebrated here by French missionaries in 1646. The yellow-and-ochre little church at Grand Fond village, on the east coast, features a tiny bell tower, quoined corners and decorative finials. The building nearby is ballustraded and staircased in typical Spanish style. Pointe Baptiste, near Calibishie, is a traditional 1930s timber-built home, now available for rent. In the village of Marigot, there are some pretty, brightly-painted, local timber-built houses, many on stilts.

The best preserved early sugar plantation heritage in Dominica can be seen at the Old Mill Cultural Centre, near Canefield airport, on an old estate. This was once the Canefield Estate, the largest sugar and lime plantation on the island. Here there is an aqueduct and water mill wheel, together with a later, steam-driven cane crusher. From here, the road to Pont Cassé, known as the Imperial Road, was built in 1906 and leads towards Castle Bruce, where the cobblestones of Castle Bruce road were laid as far back as 1828. The best preserved water wheel on Dominica is at the ruined site of the Hampstead mill. Other sugar and lime plantations sites are dotted across the island, including that at Riviere La Croix, Blenheim, Stowe, Bagatelle, and the Geneva Estate, near Grand Bay, at one time the home of Jean Rhys.

On the 18th-century Rosalie Estate on the east coast there is another old aqueduct arch, one of the last left on the island, and the remains of the water wheel. Nearby are the ruins of a Norman-style church, and an old crane platform, once used for loading ships' lighters with sugar, limes, cocoa and coffee. The ruins of the Hillsborough tobacco plantation house and the old factory are in the Layou River valley, and at Soufrière there are more sugar mill ruins, as well as those of the famous Rose's lime factory. In the late 1700s, the French built baths for their troops in the sulphur springs behind Soufrière village. The coffee plantation estate house of Bois Cotlette near here is one of the few surviving on the island, but the old buildings of the Sylvania coffee plantation can still be made out near the village of the same name.

At Salybia, the main village in the Carib Territory, there are a number of traditional wooden houses built on stilts, and an example of a *carbet*, an oval, typically Carib communal dwelling. The church here, Saint Marie of the Caribs, has an altar made from a dugout canoe. Its 'A'-framed, sharply pitched roof, is built in Carib *mouina* style, and its facade features a mural of Columbus's arrival in the New World.

DOMINICAN REPUBLIC

Sharing the island of Hispaniola with Haiti, the Dominican Republic reveals a mix of colonial Spanish and African influences together with more modern ones from North America. The country won its independence in 1844 after a 22-year period of Haitian occupation that has soured relations between the two states ever since. Two phases of American occupation followed (1916-24, 1965-66) as well as several repressive dictatorships. Today, however, the Dominican Republic is a functioning democracy and home to one of the Caribbean's fastest-growing tourist industries.

Santo Domingo

The old city of Santo Domingo is a UNESCO Site of World Heritage, an accolade awarded in 1990. Founded in 1498, after the three previous locations were abandoned, Santo Domingo de Guzmán remained the focal point of the Spanish Main for just over twenty years. There are around 25 sites of historic and architectural importance in the old city or *zona colonial*, although there are numerous other interesting buildings in the city which have been carefully restored. It claims a number of firsts – the first hospital, university, fortress and nunnery in the New World.

One of the earliest buildings here is the palace of the Governor, Viceroy Diego Colón (Christopher Columbus's brother). The Alcázar de Colón, sometimes called the Columbus Palace, was built between 1510 and 1514 with massive blocks of coral limestone in Gothic, Mudéjar, and Renaissance styles. The most impressive feature is the two-storey Renaissance facade. Its heavy stone loggias, shaded and pillared, are of Moorish influence, and more Arab influence can be seen in some of the upper-floor windows. This is the first stone palace to be built by Europeans in the Americas and the first two-storey building. It was reputedly built without the use of nails, as even the windows and doors turn on pivots embedded into the stonework. The Alcázar was the Columbus family home until 1577, the seat of Spain's colonial government for sixty years and the centre of most exploratory expeditions in the New World. Its two main buildings contained the Governor's residence, an audience chamber, the treasury, a counting house, a trade office, and a foundry. It was sacked by Sir Francis Drake during his attack on Santo Domingo in 1586, but subsequently repaired. Extensive restoration work was undertaken in 1957, and the Alcázar is now the Viceroyalty Museum. The highly decorative wooden ceiling, or bigas, was donated by the Spanish government. The statue in the plaza is that of Queen Isabela. Steps from the Alcázar lead to a group of eight buildings known as La Atarazana, the warehouse quarter, with a 16th-century ship's chandlery, a colonial arsenal, royal armoury, warehouses and cust-oms houses, now the Naval Underwater Archaeology Museum. Several of the commercial buildings and houses in La Atarazana were built around 1507. Today they house bars, restaurants and tourist shops. A statue of Columbus by French sculptor Gilbert, erected in 1897, stands in Parque Colón.

The oldest cathedral in the Americas, the Basílica Menor de Santa María, was just a wooden church in 1502. It was as early as 1514 when Diego Colón laid the first foundation stone. When the Italian Bishop, Geraldini, arrived in 1519, he began laying out the design for the present cathedral in 1521 after complaining to Emperor Charles V that he was a bishop with no roof. The cathedral, apart from the bell tower, was built between 1523 and 1540. The dedication of the cathedral was celebrated in 1535, well before the building was completed, and in 1546 Pope Paul III elected the church to cathedral status, making in the 'Catedral Primada de América', and the New World's first Christian centre.

The work was directed by the architect Alonso Rodríguez, and encompasses a curious mixture of buildings styles and decoration. The result is almost Gothic-Romanesque, as though the architect was torn between simplicity and overt Plateresque ornamentation. Friezes and statues are set off by the artfully curved roofs. Designed as a late-Gothic basilica in honey-coloured stone, the interior consists of fourteen different artistically-decorated capillas, or side chapels, a baptistry and a choir, leading off the three-aisled main nave. The chapels were added after the main structure was completed and contain some distinguished architectural features. The Capilla Santa Ana, with its Gothic window and Renaissance arch, guards the tomb of Rodrigo de Bastidas. The Capilla de las Animas is an exquisite example of the Plateresque style, and the Capilla de los dos Leones, with the 1524 tomb of Bishop Geraldini, is finely sculpted. Gonzalo Fernández de Oviedo, the great colonial historian and soldier, is also entombed in a side chapel. The nave, which contains a double row of round pillars, eighteen in all, leads to the polygonal presbytery, and the ribbed vaulting above is designed to resemble palm trees. The cathedral's proportions are monumental, covering an area of 30,000 sq feet and fifty feet high. The pressure of the vaulting is lessened by the great flying buttresses on the exterior. The western facade is the most impressive, with a twin-arched porch decorated with Plateresque sculpture. Pillars and pilasters are interspersed with frescoes of saints, and the Hapsburg double-headed eagle coat of arms of Charles V embellishes the centre of the western wall.

The Puerta del Padrón gateway is a feature of the southern transept, although the cathedral is now entered through the northern door. Battlements on the portal are remnants of the city's original fortified wall. The castellations of the perimeter wall are capped in Moorish-style points, and a massive stone archway leads into the courtyard. The huge brick and stone bell tower, containing three bells in diminishing sizes, was added in 1543. The structure has survived numerous hurricanes and earthquakes. Restoration work was carried out between 1872 and 1877, when the supposed bones of Christopher Columbus were found (there are rival claims by Havana and Seville). In 1892, the 400th anniversary of Columbus's arrival, the Spanish government donated the marble tomb in which the remains were placed. They now lie in the Faro a Colón, or Columbus Lighthouse, built to commemorate the quincentenary of the same event. The interior also contains a treasury, a great mahogany throne and statues like that of Bishop Bastida, reputedly vandalized by Drake when he used the building as a barracks in 1586.

The Palacio de Borgella opposite was built during the Haitian occupation of 1822-44. The two-storey building is arcaded with a series of brick-lined stretched arches, and a simple pediment surmounts the whole. The building directly across the Parque Colón, with the impressive tower, is the old Town Hall, dating from the 16th century, but considerably altered in the 1900s.

Door of the Casa del Cordón, Santo Domingo

The Casa del Cordón was built between 1503 and 1509, and is the oldest European-built stone structure remaining in the New World. The House of the Cord was once the residence of Diego Colón and his aristocratic wife, María de Toledo, while they awaited the completion of the Alcázar. It was Francisco de Garay who accompanied Columbus on his first voyage, who had the house built around two courtyards in Gothic design with Plateresque influence. This was where the city's jewels were weighed to pay the ransom demanded when Drake laid siege to the city in 1586. The English sea-dog also used it as his private residence while he pillaged the city. The building is named after the waist cords of Franciscan monks, and the design of one such cord is etched in high relief in stone over the lintel of the embellished portal of the entrance door. This building was restored in 1974 and is now a bank's offices.

Nearby and also on Isabel La Católica is the birthplace of Juan Pablo Duarte, the founder of the Republic, born here in 1813. It is now a museum, celebrating the country's independence struggle. A short distance away is the Casa de la Moneda, thought once to be part of the Royal Mint. Medallions flank the impressive doorway of this building, which dates from 1542, and the medallion above the lintel is said to represent Charles V, who authorized the Royal Mints in the city. The ruins of the old Church of San Antón are located to the west.

The Forteleza Ozama was added to the city's defences in 1507. This is the oldest European fort in the Americas. The neo-Classical entrance to the fort was added in 1787, during Charles II's reign. The statue of Gonzalo Fernández de Oviedo, commander of the fort from 1533 to 1557, stands nearby. Also part of the military complex, is the attractive Casa Bastidas, built in 1512. Named after the conquistador Rodrigo de Bastidas, the arcaded inner courtyard contains a garden and borders another of the city's oldest buildings, the Torre del Homenaje (Tower of Homage). The walls of this tower are seven feet thick and it stands 65 feet high. The lower part of the tower includes an arsenal, the warder's residence and a deep cistern. It was built on the orders of the Dominican Friar and Governor (1502-9) Nicolás de Ovando, and was variously used as a house, prison and torture chamber. It was erected as a watchtower in 1502, completed in 1507 and includes the remains of the Fortaleza Santiago and a powder magazine building. Remnants of the ancient city walls can be seen between the tower and the arsenal, and the waters of the Río Ozama once reached this point. President Trujillo, the country's longest-lived dictator, was responsible for extending the walls to hide the fort from the river estuary.

In 1504, Governor Ovando ordered fifteen religious structures to be built in the city. These included the now ruined San Nicolás de

Bari Hospital, constructed from 1509 onwards. This was the first permanent hospital in the New World, and the basilica-shaped structure was finally completed in 1551. Parts of this colonial edifice had to be taken down in 1909 after earthquake damage, leaving the high outer walls, brick and stone arches and capitals. The building of the Monastery of San Francisco had already begun in 1502 and was completed in 1509. The oldest monastery in the Americas, it was plundered by Drake in 1586, smashed by earthquakes and is now in ruins. It once comprised three sections, the single-aisled monastery church, entered by a massive archway, the main church, or Capilla de la Tercera Orden, or Church of the Third Order, and the Convent, entered by a doorway decorated with Franciscan cords and coats of arms. The entire complex was destroyed by earthquakes in 1653, 1673, and 1751 and used as a hos-pital in 1881. It contains the tombs of several conquistadors, notably that of Bartolomé Columbus, another of Christopher's brothers.

The Dominican Convent, with its rose window, was rebuilt in stone between 1525 and 1535 after the 1510 structure, housing a seminary, was destroyed. Built under the direction of Ovando, the building initially became a monastery in 1521. The first university in the New World, the Universidad de Santo Tomás de Aquino, was then housed here, founded in 1538 and promoted from a theo-logical college by Pope Paul III that year. The monastery church was almost completely destroyed in the 17th century and was rebuilt in the 18th. It is decorated with Sevillian tiles and has Gothic arches and a Renaissance ledge moulding. Its highly decorative west facade portal has elements of Plateresque, late Gothic and Baroque. The interior is also late Gothic, with some Isabeline details, in its five chapels. One of the oldest, the Capilla del Rosario, dates from 1649 and is decorated in a style most unusual for a Christian place of worship. The vaulted ceiling is embellished with a unique cosmological clock, with the twelve signs of the Zodiac for the months of the year, and the seasons represented by Roman gods as four evangelists. Around an image of the sun as God, Saturn stands for Winter, Jupiter repre-sents Spring, Mars Summer, and Mercury Autumn, perhaps recalling European weather in a tropical land where there are no defined

Dominican Convent, Santo Domingo

seasons! In the Gothic apse, the wooden altar, donated by Emperor Charles V, is embellished with the double-headed Hapsburg eagle. From here a door leads to the partly preserved cloisters. It is said that Bartolomé de las Casas, the defender of the indigenous population, delivered his first sermon in the wooden building initially on this site, in 1510.

Three further ecclesiastical buildings stand to the west of the Dominican Convent. The 18th-century Capilla de la Tercera Orden has its stepped, pilastered facade in Plateresque style, while the former Franciscan Church of Regina Angelorum was built between 1537 and 1650. The eastern portal has remained intact during subsequent alterations, and the interior contains two silver-decorated Baroque altars and a wall of silver. Damaged between 1822 and 1844, it has a fine Baroque dome, Gothic arches and beautiful tracery work. Further north-west is the Iglesia del Carmen, built in 1615 and displaying a three-feet-high Madonna in a niche above its doorway.

The Iglesia de Las Mercedes was built between 1527 and 1555 with a late Gothic vaulted roof and single aisle with both Baroque and Renaisssance elements. Inside, the silver-decorated Renaissance altar dates from the 18th century, and the Bishop's tomb was installed in 1644. This church was designed for the Mercedarian Order by Rodrigo de Liendo, and its square brick-built tower and Classical doorway were later additions. The squat church was originally part of a monastery and was plundered by Drake in 1586. Nearby is the Capilla San Andrés, built in 1710 and containing a highly decorated Baroque altar. Further west is the 17th-century Church of San Lazaro, with its Gothic chapel containing yet another fine Baroque altar.

In 1574 building started on the fort and late Baroque church of Santa Bárbara. This church was completed in 1578, was also plundered by Drake and destroyed by hurricanes in 1591 and 1678, only to be rebuilt with towers of odd height at the end of the 17th century. The window in the right hand tower has some interesting fertility symbols. The church shows some Mudéjar features, and an ornate Baroque facade has been built above the triple-arched entrance between the towers. Several side chapels have been installed off the single aisle, and the windows and arches show Isabeline decoration in the form of rows of tiny stone balls. Located in the stonemasons' quarter of the city, this is the only fort-cum-

Santa Bárbara Church, Santo Domingo

church on the island. The 18th-century Santa Bárbara fortress is reached by a flight of steps behind the church.

The Casa de Tostada dates from 1516 and was the residence of the Town Clerk, Francisco Tostada, who arrived in Santo Domingo with Ovando in 1502. The house, with its magnificent inner courtyard, later became the archbishop's residence. The building's twin Isabeline Gothic windows are said to be the oldest examples of their kind in the New World. A simple round column divides the window, which is surmounted by some elaborate tracery work in stone. The two-storey Museo de la Familia Dominicana in the house depicts life in the city in the 19th century.

Calle Las Damas is the oldest street in the city, and is lined with excellent examples of Spanish colonial buildings. The street is so called for the ladies of the viceregal court who paraded along the street, the first cobbled road in the New World. The alleyway known as the Plaza María de Toledo is named after the wife of Diego Colón. Buildings of note here are the Casa Francia, once the residence of the conquistador Hernán Cortés, while he was Town Clerk of Azua, and the house of Ovando, now the Hostal Nicolás Ovando, built between 1510 and 1515, and restored in 1978. The 45 rooms of the house are set around three pretty tiled courtyards, each surrounded by colonnades. It had its own fortifications, the ruins of which are located above the river. The colonial home of the merchant, Francisco Dávila, contains what was once a private chapel, the Capilla de Nuestra Señora de los Remedios, one of the

Casa de Tostada,
Santo Domingo

city's earliest places of worship and entered from Calle Las Damas. The Capilla, where the first colonists said mass, has lateral arches reminiscent of the Castillian-Romanesque style. Friar Antonio Montesinos is believed to have delivered his celebrated mass, condemning the Spanish treatment of the Amerindian population here in December 1511.

The Museo de las Casas Reales (Royal Houses) has plain stone walls, which rise to a parapet with defensive Gothic openings. Its simple doorway advertises the museum's austere interior. On the east facade, above the main entrance, is a fine Plateresque window. The Casas Reales, built in the early 16th century, once housed the Governor, the Captains-General, the Royal Audience Chamber, the Treasury and the Supreme Court. The building has contained a museum since the 1970s and has a superb collection of colonial exhibits. The sundial or *reloj de sol* across the street was built for the occupants of the Casas Reales by General Francisco de Rubio y Penaranda, in 1753. It now stands on a small plinth.

Now the National Pantheon, the domed Convento San Ignacio de Loyola was dedicated to the founder of the Jesuit movement. It is built in a colonial baroque style and was constructed between 1714 and 1743. It was only used as a convent for twenty years until the Jesuits were banished from Spain's New World in 1767, when it became a tobacco warehouse and then a theatre. Inside is a commemorative ceiling mural and a vast bronze candelabra donated by the Spanish dictator Franco. Its wrought-iron doors are said to have come from a German concentration camp. The building became the Pantheon in 1955, when it was restored, and it now contains the remains of and memorials to the nation's heroes. Trujillo has a tomb here, built before his death in 1961, but he never occupied it.

In 1540 work on the city walls began, and they eventually encompassed the entire settlement by 1555. The Puerta de San Diego, once protected by the San Diego Fort, was built into the city wall between 1540 and 1555. This was the city's most important gate and displays the coats of arms of Santo Domingo, Spain and Hispaniola on its east facade, added in 1578. The Puerta San José, with its accompanying cannon, stands facing the Malecón and the Caribbean Sea, to the south of the city, together with part of the old city wall. Further west from this gate are the remains of the ancient San Gil fortifications. North of here is the Puerta del Conde, which was named after Conde (Count) de Penalva, who successfully

Citadelle Laferrière, Haiti

*Fort Christian, Charlotte Amalie,
US Virgin Islands*

Fortifications

Havana Cathedral, Cuba

Parish Church, Mandeville, Jamaica

Churches

Alcázar de Colón, Santo Domingo,
Dominican Republic

Rodney Memorial, Spanish Town, Jamaica

Colonial Splendour

Rose Hall, Jamaica

Farley Hill, Barbados

Schoelcher Library, Fort-de-France, Martinique

Turn-of-the-Century Eclecticism

Ambard's House, Port of Spain, Trinidad

Basic Bohío, Cuba

Thatched Home, Dutch Antilles

Morgan Lewis Windmill, Barbados

Salt Pan Slave Huts, Bonaire

Cottages, Saba

Wooden Homes

Hope Town, Bahamas

defended the city against an attack by William Penn in 1655. This gate was restored in 1976, and the ruins of the Fuerte de la Concepción, part of the city's defences, stand nearby and date from 1543. The Puerta de la Misericordia was named because the city's inhabitants sought shelter under this solid gateway during an earthquake. The brick-built 17th-century Puerta de Las Atarazanas, on the bank of the Ozama River on the north-east side of the city, is named 'la flecha' (the arrow), as it was designed in a wedge shape to make it easier to defend. Near here are the archaeological excavations of the original harbour, with sections of the old city walls.

A monument to celebrate the quincentenary of Columbus's arrival in the New World was the grandiose idea of the Dominican dictator Rafael Leonidas Trujillo in 1929. A competition was organized, and a student of architecture from Manchester, one J. Gleave, submitted his design for a Columbus Memorial Lighthouse in 1931. It won. However, construction was quickly abandoned, money ran out and the plan seemed to have been dropped. But President Joaquín Balaguer (once Trujillo's puppet president) unexpectedly took up the scheme in 1987, channeling vast funds estimated at US$250 million from the poverty-stricken nation's budget into the project. By 1992, the 500th anniversary of Columbus's landing on Hispaniola, the 122-foot high, half-mile long Faro a Colón, was opened across the River Ozama in what had been a crowded slum settlement. Built in the shape of a cross, the massive – and many say grotesque – structure contains Skytracker Xenon searchlights, which project a cross-shaped beam into the night sky, which can be seen from eighty miles away. Inside, an ornate mausoleum contains what are supposed to be Columbus's remains, removed from the cathedral in Santo Domingo. The immense building also contains 21 chapels, six museums and two libraries.

Also across the Ozama River from Santo Domingo are the remains of the city's oldest church, the Virgin of the Rosary, built initially as a thatched wooden structure in 1496 on the site of the original city of La Nueva Isabela. The present Capilla del Rosario was built before 1544, when Bartolomé de Las Casas said mass here, although the structure has undergone numerous renovations.

Outside the zona colonial, Santo Domingo is a mix of leafy middle-class suburbs and shantytowns, including some of the worst slums in the Caribbean. There are some spacious avenues and parks, mostly dating from the 1960s. Of particular interest is the 1930s quarter of Gazcue, with prosperous houses, including some half-timbered Home Counties style homes. The Presidential Palace, painted coral pink and with a neo-Classical portico and cupola, was built during Trujillo's long period in power. More modern buildings, including several excellent museums and art galleries, date from Balaguer's various terms in office. The Museo del Hombre Dominicano is highly recommended and is situated in the Plaza de la Cultura complex along with a theatre, library and modern art collection. Of interest, too, are the many turn-of-the-century popular barrios, many with characteristic *pulperias* or corner stores.

West of Santo Domingo, **San Cristóbal** is the location of Trujillo's Casa de Coaba (mahogany house), with its first floor built entirely of this wood. The house is in bad shape, as is the Palacio del Cerro, a luxurious residence which he never lived in. Both are nevertheless fascinating buildings, dating from the 1940s. Also from this period is the 1946 Iglesia Parroquial. All are due for renovation.

The second city, **Santiago de los Caballeros**, in the north of the Republic is now a bustling commercial centre, but it was once the site of considerable conflict and the building of one of the Spanish colony's first forts. The town was founded in 1495, but little remains of the earliest days, as a 1562 earthquake destroyed the original town completely. There are, however, some examples of 19th-century town houses, and the ruined Jacagua plantation house, just outside the town, is where the first fort was positioned. The Catedral de Santiago Apóstol, with its stained glass window by Rincón Mora, was built between 1868 and 1895. It is in a mixed, neo-Gothic and neo-Classical style, with twin four-storey towers flanking its main entrance arch. The pink-and-white towers are topped by black-tiled pyramidal spires, and each has an entrance arch leading to two of the church's three aisles. Two other fine buildings stand on the central Parque Duarte: one is the neo-Mudéjar style Centro de Recreo club, with its extravagant castellated facade of pointed arches, diamond widows and Spanish tiling. Containing carved wooden-ceilinged halls, it was built in 1894, around the time that the beautiful Palacio Consistorial was erected. Now a museum, this is said to be the best Victorian building in the Republic. A short distance away is the wooden building that houses the Museo Folklórico Tomás Morel. But perhaps the most visible of

Santiago's various structures is the bizarre Monumento a los Héroes de la Restauración, built on the city's highest point

Elsewhere in the Dominican Republic, there are several sites of architectural interest, although the main centre of early Spanish architecture is in the capital. In the Cibao Valley is **La Vega**, and from there one can visit La Vega Vieja (the Old Vega), the ruins of the original settlement built here by Columbus in 1495. These include the remains of an early monastery, whose chapel walls, cloister and a well date from 1502. A little further on is Columbus's Fortaleza Nuestra Señora de la Concepción, with its well preserved tower.

The ruins of the Engombe sugar plantation, the first in the New World, date from the early 1500s, with a master's house, sugar mill and chapel. The Ingenio de Nigua is a reconstructed 18th-century sugar mill, which has a trapiche and an old boiling house, while the nearby Diego Caballero, an older sugar mill, is mostly in ruins. Another early factory, the Batey sugar mill is near La Romana. Also near the sugar town of La Romana is the strange Altos de Chavón tourist village, built to resemble a medieval Italian village. The setting is spectacular, but the taste involved is questionable.

In **San Pedro de Macorís**, founded in 1822 and the Republic's fourth largest town, is the fine Church of San Pedro Apóstol, one of the town's two patron saints. The curiously blank facade, broken only by the single door and medieval-style rose window, is flanked by mitre-topped columns. The church's red-tiled spire rises from a castellated white bell tower, centrally located above the central of three aisles and decorated with Gothic-style gargoyles. The town's grandiose Fire Station is in elaborate Victorian style, built between 1908 and 1913. Its balconied exterior is decorated with finials and topped by a balustrade containing a colourful cartouche. Incongruously perched on top of the building is a spired, columned, octagonal tower, presumably built to serve as a watchtower.

Further east from San Pedro and beyond La Romana, is **San Rafael de Yuma**, site of the fortress-like house of the conquistador, Ponce de León, a solid, stone-built structure with a small doorway and tiny windows located only on the upper floor. It was from this house, where he lived from 1505 to 1508, that Ponce de León helped establish the town of Higüey. Recently restored, this is also the place from where he sailed in 1508 to settle Puerto Rico.

Higüey

Higüey was founded in 1494 by Juan de Esquivel before he moved to Jamaica, and Ponce de León introduced settlers to the region from 1502 until he moved on to Puerto Rico. The two conquistadors installed a miracle-working image of the Virgin Mary, brought from Spain and known as the Virgen de Altagracia or the Virgin of High Grace, in the first church built here. The Virgin is the Republic's patron saint. The pilgrimage church of the Basílica de Nuestra Señora de la Merced, was built here by priest Don Alonso de Pena and his steward, Don Simón Bolívar between 1512 and 1572. It was the main object of pilgrimage until the construction of a newer church on the same site, in 1881. Even this did not prove large enough to accommodate the throngs of pilgrims, and so the Basílica de Nuestra Señora de la Altagracia was built. This new edifice now houses the revered painting. It is one of the most spectacular modern examples of ecclesiastical architecture in Latin America. Begun in 1943, work recommenced after a break in 1952, and the structure was completed by 1971. The basilica's unique design includes a giant, pointed, arched spire in the shape of two hands in prayer, created by French architect, André Jacques Dunoyer de Segonzac. The vast concrete structure is entered through a copper-plated door decorated with reliefs of the Virgin's miracles.

Puerto Plata

Puerto Plata was founded in 1502 on the north coast by Ovando and later became the island's major port as the importance of Santo Domingo waned in the mid-1600s. During this period buccaneers and pirates of several nationalities created chaos in coastal settlements, and much of the population of Santo Domingo dispersed throughout the island to establish or develop new towns. In Puerto Plata, the Fortaleza de San Felipe was built and re-built here between 1520 and 1585. It is the oldest original standing fortification in the New World. The immense and dramatic fort has rounded bastions, dome-topped bartizans overlooking the sea and an imposing gateway. The eastern entrance is flanked by two small towers, and the central keep is now a museum. Above the massive, castellated keep is an observation platform with gun slits, looking down into the wide courtyard with several ancient cannon. The remarkable features of this almost square fort are its doors, just four feet high. Once used as a prison, the fort was at one time overrun by pirates, and the Spanish had to sack their own town of Puerto Plata in 1605 in order to recover it! In 1973 the fort underwent considerable restoration work after a long period of neglect.

The wrought-iron pavilion or gazebo, known as the Glorieta Siciliana was built to a Belgian design in Parque Central in 1872. The park is the location of a number of handsome 19th-century buildings, featuring gingerbread fretwork decoration and wooden pillared porticos. Notable among these are several renovated restaurants and guesthouses. In Calle Duarte, a colonial period house with balustrades and columns is now the Amber Museum. Near Puerto Plata, on Mount Isabel de Torres, is what is said to be the oldest cable car in the Americas. The site of **La Isabela**, Columbus's second settlement in the New World, erected in 1493, lies west of Puerto Plata beyond Luperón. Only the settlement's layout can be seen

Montecristi, to the east of the site of La Isabela, was founded in 1533 by Juan de Bolanos and contains a number of old Victorian wooden buildings, including the imposing Courthouse and an 1890s clock which came from France.

GRENADA

Despite the fires which over the centuries have ravaged the island's capital, where most of Grenada's historic architecture is located, buildings have re-emerged, phoenix-like, from the stone foundations of older buildings. So much so, that some visitors consider St George's to be the prettiest harbour town in the Caribbean. Although it is not as rich in architectural gems as some of its sister islands of the English-speaking Caribbean, a number of fine colonial buildings, including a few plantation houses and ancient forts, are dotted throughout this 'Isle of Spice'. A spectacularly beautiful island, still very much dependent on agriculture, Grenada was the object of international notoriety between 1979 and 1983 when a short-lived radical government was in power. The revolutionary period ended when the popular Prime Minister Maurice Bishop was murdered by hard-line Marxist rivals, ushering in a US invasion that returned the island to quiet obscurity.

Named after the city of Granada by early Spanish explorers and travellers, Grenada was called Camerhogue by its Carib occupants, who were effectively wiped out by French forces in the mid-17th century. The northern town of Sauteurs (French for 'leapers') commemorates the mass suicide of those Caribs who preferred to jump into the sea than be captured and enslaved. The French were the first to properly establish a town, Port Louis, on the island in 1705, naming the settlement Fort Royal when they erected a protective fort. When the British captured the island in 1762, they rebaptized the natural harbour town St George's, building a citadel nearby, now Fort George.

St George's, the small capital of Grenada, is named after King George III and is situated around an almost circular bay, which is an extinct volcano crater. It is built on a hilly outcrop which divides the harbour-side Carenage or inner bay from the Esplanade, facing the Caribbean sea to the west. Stone steps link the main town with Bay Town. The statue at the entrance to the harbour, is a replica of the Christ of the Deeps, commemorating the assistance that the islanders gave to passengers of an Italian cruise ship, the *Bianca C*, which caught fire in the harbour in 1961.

St George's is one of the best-preserved Georgian towns in the West Indies, and the older parts date from the early 18th century. The town was once guarded by six forts. Just two remain more or less intact. Fort George, on the southern peninsula of Fort George Point, dominates the high ground, although the narrow strip of land around the Carenage is also backed by steep bluffs. Buildings therefore rise steeply around the natural amphitheatre that surrounds the harbour. Originally Fort Royal and initially built in the 1680s but revamped in 1705, Fort George has a basic plan, with bastions pointing out towards the sea and two massive landward bastions, huge mortars, guard-rooms and dungeons, all around a central square. The fort's walls are three feet thick, and it was once thought that underground passages linked all six of the capital's forts. A warren of tunnels certainly burrow under Fort George, which is now the police headquarters. Cannon are still in place, and this was the scene of Maurice Bishop's execution by firing squad in October 1983.

The fort's barracks, beautifully restored, are stone-built, two-storey buildings, showing distinctive French influence. The archway entrance to the fort has the date 1710 carved in it. Another building, near Fort George and constructed as French barracks and a prison in 1704, is now the Grenada National Museum. The cells, used when this building housed a gaol from 1763 until 1880, can still be seen. Located on Young Street, this is a handsome building and one of St George's oldest.

The arched Sendall Tunnel, built in 1895 to provide access to the eastern part of St George's (350 feet in length and 12 feet high) runs under the fort to the 1831 yellow brick-built St Andrew's Presbyterian Church. This church, built with the assistance of freemasons, is Gothic in style, with its clock tower and distinctive four corner spires. It is reminiscent of any provincial British church and is known as the Scots Kirk. It is possible that a tunnel was formerly constructed as an escape route from the fort to an earlier church on this site. The present church was last restored in 1884.

There were originally four forts on or near Richmond Hill to the east of St George's, which were begun by the French and completed by the British in the late 18th century. Old Fort is located on Wireless Hill, and has both British and French 18th-century influences. The construction of the ramparted and bastioned Fort Frederick on Richmond Hill was started by the French in 1779 and completed by the British between 1783 and 1791. The remains of the fort are still well preserved, as is the parade ground and its battlements. Fort Matthew, also dating from between 1779 and 1783, is a classic siege fort, located higher up above the harbour. Even further up Richmond Hill is Fort Adolphus, which contained later, more powerful cannon. Military influence can be seen throughout the old town and on the waterfront, with ancient cannon embedded in various points on the streets as bollards.

Up until the British takeover of the island in 1762, the French had established their 'bourg' on the east side of the harbour. However, the most architecturally important buildings during the time of British occupation were constructed on the west side of the bay. Many were a blend of both French and British prevailing architectural trends. The wrought-ironwork along the curving Esplanade is French from the 1750s, and tracery ironwork balconies and latticed window awnings, of Creole influence, elaborate the attractive Georgian buildings.

A typical English feature and more prevalent in Grenada than anywhere else in the Caribbean are the 'sedan chair' porches of several buildings. Although slightly reconstructed, these are best seen on Church Street. In the 18th century two chairmen or porters carried seats in upright boxes supported by two poles, known as

Sedan chair porches,
St George's

sedan chairs, and these were a favourite form of transport for short town journeys. Women of the time were known for their pale complexions, and sedan chairs provided protection from both the sun and short, sharp tropical downpours. The house porches projected out from the front of the buildings into the street, so that sedan chairs could be manoeuvred into the porch, enabling the occupant to alight in shelter. Their construction also allowed sidewalk pedestrian traffic to pass through.

At the end of Church Street is the site of the town's first hospital, built in 1738. Also on this street is St George's Anglican Church, pink-coloured and dating from its rebuilding in 1825. It is noted for its marble altar, frescoes, stained glass, and 18th- and 19th-century English wall plaques of St George. The present clock, with its four faces, was installed in 1904. French-style fish-scale tiles once clad its roof. This was originally the garrison church, built on the site of an earlier French Roman Catholic church dating from 1762.

Beginning at the southern part of the western Carenage, two large two- and three-storey Classical-style houses, with pedimented central units, are of major importance. They are steep-roofed, with ochre-coloured fish-scale tiles, thought to have been imported from the Poterie on Martinique. The stout buildings are uniformly fenestrated, with bell awnings or Demarara top hinged shutters on the upper windows. Large 18th-century brick and stone warehouses jostle for position on the wharf front and further north into the Carenage. They are often two-storey, with arched, goods-loading doors on two levels facing the quayside. The Public Library building, initially a brick-built warehouse and now restored, has been on this Carenage site since 1892. It survived a fire in 1990 which seriously damaged a group of nearby government buildings. These have been restored.

Many of the pastel-painted domestic houses which clamber over the hillside face directly onto the street and not only feature the 'sedan chair' porches, but also include French architectural details. Most of these houses and warehouses are built in pink or honey-coloured London brick, brought over as ballast. Wooden houses were banned in the capital following disastrous fires in 1771 and 1775. At the time, St George's was one of the Caribbean's most important commercial centres and hence home to wealthy merchants and a marketplace for goods imported from England.

One of the oldest surviving buildings is the old Registry Office, near the cathedral, dating from between 1780 and 1790. York House, now the Supreme Court and House of Representatives, dates from its purchase in 1801. The Houses of Parliament are on the upper floor, and the structure may have been named after the Duke of York, who visited the town in the 18th century. This grand stone-built edifice, with its yellow brick-arched lower floor and brick-edged upper floor windows, is fronted by a gateway and wall, topped by typically English spiked iron railings. The upper fenestration on each of its fourteen windows is a combination of vertical- and horizontal-opening glazing, with no shutters or awnings. Two courses of yellow brick along the facade delineate the two floors and the roof's parapet. The nearby market building in Market Square is a conventional metal structure with a red corrugated iron roof, ignored by most market vendors who place their stalls outside on the ground. This square, lined by some 18th-century stone buildings, was once the place for public executions.

Typical commercial building, St George's

Away from the harbour, this tiny capital and its surroundings have fewer than eight churches as well as its vast Roman Catholic cathedral, built on the site of an earlier 1804 church in 1884. The tower dates from 1818, and this church has some pretty stained glass windows and interesting statues. St George's Methodist Church dates from 1820, and is the oldest original church in the capital. The style of building is a combination of English architecture and West Indian colour.

Apart from the old private buildings around the port, with their orange tiles or red-painted tin roofs, the next important historic structure is Marryshow House, a Victorian Creole-style building constructed in 1917. Above this, Government House is the residence of the Governor-General, located to the east of the Carenage and first built in the late 18th century. The present impressive building dates from 1802, with some notable Georgian architecture, but the facade was an unfortunate addition in 1887. Sans Souci, an 18th-century mansion house, stands further up the hill to the east of the town. The pavilion in Queen's Park was erected in 1927.

There is the shell of a single-level windmill tower, with its double broad-arched entrances, above St George's. This is typical of the many windmill remains in the West Indies. The substantial, slightly tapering, tower, made of hewn stone blocks, has its cap, sails and machinery missing, but shows where the sugar-cane was fed in between crushing rollers through one aperture, while the waste or bagasse was taken out of the other. The original cap could be rotated, by means of a long projecting post, to face the sails into the wind. A main shaft from the wind shaft of the sails, connected to the wallower or top cog wheel, was driven by the sails. The upper aperture in the tower gave access to the wallower if it had to be attended to. Likewise, the tower has a long slit down one side, from which the operator had access to the main shaft, should it need repairing. These single-level mills date from around the mid- to late 1600s, as two-level mills took their place from the early to mid-1700s. Although built from roughly cut stone blocks, the stones around the entrance arches have been shaped from volcanic rock.

Not far from St George's, near St Paul's, stands Tower House, a private home built in an eclectic mixture of styles, ranging from Queen Anne to Victorian with a measure of British Raj added. Constructed in 1916, it was originally called St Leonards, apparently in memory of the English seaside town, but when a new owner, coincidentally named Leonard, bought it, he thought it inappropriate to preserve the 'Saint' and so gave it its more prosaic name. Its gardens are particularly exuberant, and the house can be visited by arrangement.

In 1782, Sir Joseph Banks introduced the nutmeg into Grenada. This brought a new prosperity to the island, and numerous spice plantations were established in the following years. Just outside **Gouyave**, the Dougaldston plantation which produces nutmeg, allspice (or pimento), tonka beans and cacao, is built in traditional rural style, with its clapboard walls and tin-roofed buildings. It is still in the hands of the Banks family, and the ancient *boucans* or areas for drying cocoa beans, can still be seen. Unfortunately, the estate is in very poor repair. In Gouyave itself, there are some very typical old Creole houses, and the Anglican and Catholic churches. The sugar and rum factory at the River Antoine Rum Distillery, dating from the early 1800s, is the oldest continual functioning distillery in the Caribbean. Traditional processes, including the original water mill, are unchanged from its 19th-century origins. Dunfermline Rum Distillery, north of Grenville, also still operates an ancient water-powered mill. This is said to be the oldest working water mill in the Caribbean, dating from 1797.

Near **Grenville**, over the Great River, is the triple-arched Paradise Bridge, an impressive stone-built structure, dating from 1831. In the town of Grenville itself, one of the most striking buildings is the 1886 courthouse. Two-storeyed and brick built, its tall win-dows are an unusual combination of sash and Demerara. The flat facade has a pedimented, hipped roof, and the rear has a ballustraded terrace. Three bank buildings and the pretty little Anglican Church are the only other historical structures of any import in the town.

There are many ruins dotted around the island, testifying to Grenada's turbulent past and mixed colonial heritage. Sites on the island include the old Green Bridge over St John's River, the early houses in Belmont village, and the remains of Fort Jeudy, which once protected Egmont Harbour, dating from 18th century. Of interest, too, are the 19th-century army quarantine remains at Goat Point and the early French settlement sites of Grand Marquis and Maigrin. On the island's north-easterly outcrop, facing the small offshore Sugar Loaf, Green and Sandy Islands, are the ruins of an old fort. Near the centre of the island at Morne Fédon is the ruined stronghold of the rebel Julien Fédon, on his Belvidere Estate. It was from here that the free coloured landowner Fédon led a rebellion against the British in 1795. In the 1930s this estate was the largest nutmeg plantation in the world. At Morne Rouge, there are the remains of an early 19th-century leper colony, and off the southern-most tip of the island, on Glover Island, are the remains of a 1925 Norwegian whaling station.

At **Morne Fendue** in the north of the island, the picturesque Betty Mascoll's Plantation House, now a restaurant and guesthouse, is a typical West Indian estate house, built in 1912 of hand cut coloured stones, cemented together with a mortar made of lime and molasses. Other major plantations include the Woodlands and Calivigny Estates, Westerhall, with its ancient mill equipment, Union Estate, and the Waltham Estate. The Samaritham Estate house is a beautiful building, with lattice verandahs, gingerbread gables and decorated roof ridges. Strikingly English are the tall sash windows of this solid, stone-built manor. There are the ruins of an old rum distillery and sugar mill at La Sagesse. This was the site of an early French settlement, Maigrin, the remains of which can just be discerned. On the bay is the 1960s estate house formerly belonging to Lord Brownlow, a cousin of Queen Elizabeth II, and now a guesthouse. There are also the reasonably well preserved ruins of the old sugar mill and boiler house chimney at Black Bay.

Carriacou and Petit Martinique

Two small islands, Carriacou and Petit Martinique, and a number of tiny islets lie between Grenada and St Vincent, and their contribution to architecture is probably restricted to the modern homes of the rich and famous. However, a few remnants of the islands' historic heritage remain, mostly French. Carriacou is criss-crossed with an extensive road system, built by the French in the late 18th century and dotted with forts, many no longer traceable. One fort overlooks Hillsborough, the main town, but its cannon have been removed to Hospital Hill to the north of the town. At Gun Point on the extreme northern tip, there are also some old cannon. The island's Historical Society Museum, on Paterson Street in Hillsborough, is housed in an old cotton ginnery, reconstructed to its 1826 glory. On Main Street, Hillborough, there are three 19th-century stone and timber buildings, originally warehouses. Also on Carriacou are a few old, stone-built, merchant's houses and a number of ruined plantation houses, like the French estate house at La Pointe, and several ruined sugar mills. Belair village not only has French and English ruins, but the best example of sugar mill and windmill foundations on the island. What remains of the first church on the island, the foundations of which survive, is known as the Dover Ruins site. The eighty miles of road on Carriacou were built by the French miltary. South of the island, on little Ile de Caille, there is the ruins of an old whaling station.

GUADELOUPE

The French held Guadeloupe for 124 years from 1635, creating a thriving sugar industry on the island until the British arrived in 1759. Four years later, the French took the island back permanently, apart from another short British term of occupation in 1810. Since then, Guadeloupe has remained French, becoming an integral part of the French Republic in 1946, a *département d'outre-mer*, whose inhabitants enjoy the same status and rights as those in mainland France. The predominant architectural style in Guadeloupe is hence unmistakably French colonial, dating over 360 years.

The territory is in fact comprised of two islands, separated by the narrow strait of the Rivière Salée. Confusingly, the island named Grande-Terre is largely flat and smaller than the other, Basse-Terre, which is more mountainous and spectacular. It also includes a number of small islands – la Désirade, Marie-Galante and Les Saintes, as well as the larger dependencies of Saint-Barthélémy and Saint-Martin

Basse-Terre is the island's administrative capital, although it is smaller and quieter than the biggest city, Pointe-à-Pitre. It is one of the earliest French towns in the Caribbean, having been founded in 1640. Initially, this town was divided in two by the Rivière aux Herbes. North of the river was the commercial centre, called Saint François, and south was the Carmel military quarter, surrounding Fort St Charles. Fort St Charles, sometimes called Fort Louis Delgrès, is the oldest structure on the island, dating from between 1643 and 1667 with 18th-century additions, and is excellently preserved. Its vast fortifications, with huge embrasures, and acres of ramparts, contain a museum of history. The British overran the fort in 1759-63, and occupied it again between 1810 and 1816, when it was known as Fort Mathilde. One of the earliest churches in the French Caribbean was located on the site of the Church of Notre Dame du Mont Carmel, built behind the fort. Basse-Terre's Cathedral of Our Lady of Guadeloupe has a Jesuit facade and was built in 1877 on 17th-century ruins. The Préfecture dates from 1930.

Pointe-à-Pitre is Guadeloupe's bustling main city and principal port, but it has suffered much damage from an 1843 earthquake and subsequent hurricanes. Many of its public buildings are housed in French colonial mansions, like the Musée Schoelcher, which is to be found in an impressive townhouse with a double staircase. The

Shops, Basse-Terre

Musée Saint-John Perse, which commemorates the life and work of the Guadeloupe-born Nobel Prize-winning poet, is also in a well-restored Creole-style mansion, with ornate wrought-iron balconies. The Sous-Préfecture, the Tourism Office and the Chambre d'Agriculture are also housed in prime examples of 19th-century French architecture. The city's cathedral, the Basilique Saint-Pierre et Saint-Paul, was originally built in Empire style in 1847. It features iron balconies and unusual metal columns, and was reinforced with large iron girders because of the damage by three recent hurricanes, earning it the nickname the 'Iron Cathedral'. The yellow-and-white cathedral, with its elaborate metal gingerbread work, contains some interesting, locally designed, stained glass windows. Other sites of architectural interest include the avant-garde building of the Banque Nationale de Paris, the early 20th-century Grand Hotel, constructed in the style of a passenger liner, and the Eglise Massabielle, a handsome 19th-century church.

Typical 18th- and 19th-century Guadeloupean town house architecture is reminiscent of the houses of French Quarter New Orleans. The Maison Hayot on Pointe-à-Pitre's central Place de la Victoire is a typical example. It is a three-storey semi-detached building, with a stone ground floor supporting the wooden upper storeys. Dormer windows add to the roof design, and two rounded, cornered galleries extend from the first and second floor. The galleries are supported by iron scroll brackets and display ornate ironwork railings. The upper gallery is shaded by a canopy, supported by slim columns and formal wall brackets. The rounded corners of the galleries are typical of Guadeloupe. Tall double wooden arched doors lead directly onto the pavement, and the upper-floor windows are louvred. There are a number of stores or commercial buildings in the capital and other towns built in a similar manner, but usually less ornate. Some are built entirely in the local volcanic stone. Early buildings might also have half-louvred windows and storm shutters.

There are several forts of interest on the two islands. East of Pointe-à-Pitre on Grande-Terre is the hilltop Fort Fleur d'Epée, dating from the 18th century, with a drawbridge and moat, dungeons and battlements. Le Moule, also on Grande-Terre, was once the colony's main settlement, and there are remains here of an early fortress. The neo-Classical church at Le Moule dates from 1850, and its town hall has graceful balustrades. On Basse-Terre the fort at Deshaies has all but disappeared, but some rusting cannon still look out to sea. At Pointe Allègre, on the remote northern tip of Basse-Terre, there are fortress batteries and military remains.

Guadeloupe has a long history of sugar cultivation, and many old deserted windmills dot the countryside on Grande-Terre, some still with their chimney stacks intact. At Sainte-Anne, for example, there are the ruins of an 18th-century sugar mill, and the Relais du Moulin hotel is built around one of the old mills. At the Domaine de Séverin between Lamentin and Sainte-Rose on Basse-Terre there is a working water-powered sugar mill and distillery which can be visited. The Musée du Rhum, on the site of the former Reimonencq distillery, is near Sainte-Rose and is also worth a visit. At the old plantation house of Bois Debout in the south of Basse-Terre is one of the best examples in the region of a sugar estate irrigation system. Water is channeled into the large estate grounds from the nearby highlands, and stone-built aqueducts take the water both to the main house, where it is stored in reservoirs and filtered for use in the house and kitchen, and to the mill. The former sugar mill was driven by this water, and the huge waterwheel is still standing in the grounds. The beautiful old plantation mansion has been superbly restored and has gingerbread fretwork trims and geometrically designed verandah rails.

The country estate houses on Guadeloupe are often more ornate than the town houses and were designed to be as cool and airy as possible, making use of galleries and verandahs. The oblong block of the central, two-storey living quarters, formed the basis for external expansion and development. Firstly, the roof might typically have French fish-scale tiles, extended to a wide overhang on all four sides. Little dormer windows might feature on the wide roof, under which a wrap-around verandah or gallery enclosed the entire upper storey. From the wrap-around balcony under the verandah, slender cast-iron, or wooden columns supported the verandah, with decorative, curved finials. These columns were echoed around the verandah, reaching up to decorative support finials under the eaves. Brackets extend under the roof and verandah as extra support. The verandah would be surrounded by ornate iron or wooden rails, and often gingerbread wooden fretwork would add to the embellishment. Doors and windows are commonly louvred, and an entrance porch might be formed by an ornately decorated canopy, sometimes supported with columns and scrolled brackets. Good examples of these houses can be seen in Morne-à-l'Eau, on Grande-Terre. In the villages, many of the houses are much smaller, built of weatherboard with little balconies, shutters and brightly coloured awnings. However, at Trois Rivières on Basse-Terre there is a good example of a country house which was a middle-class villa; with red corrugated iron roof and roof surround, it has a frework-decorated dormer window, which acts as a ventilator for the house interior. The former fishing village of Saint-François is particularly picturesque, with many old wooden colonial houses and an 18th-century church, while Lamentin also has some fine examples of French colonial buildings. Near the 17th-century town of Pointe-Noire is the Maison du Bois, where exhibits trace local building techniques and especially the origins of the gingerbread fretwork patterns used as embellishment on many Caribbean buildings.

An unusual house is to be found at Zévalos, in the flat landscape on Grande-Terre between Le Moule and Saint-François. According to tradition, this plantation house was built from prefabricated parts

Maison Zévalos,
Guadeloupe

that had originally been made in Gustave Eiffel's workshop in Paris. Destined for Louisiana, the ship carrying the parts broke down near Guadeloupe, and the metal pieces were sold at a knock-down price. The elegant grey-painted cast-iron frame was filled in with sand-coloured bricks in the 1880s, while the roof is covered in traditional tiles. The ground floor is comprised of a single large room, punctuated by a row of tall, shuttered French windows. The decorative zinc frieze above the entrance is again evocative of New Orleans, while verandahs run round both the ground and first floors, giving a pronounced sense of symmetry.

Other notable buildings on Guadeloupe include the old Hospital at Saint-Claude, which dates from 1823. At Saint-François is a Hindu cemetery, and there is also a modern Hindu temple at Carangaise, marking the influx of Indian indentured workers after slavery was abolished on the island in 1848. The cemetery at Morne-à-l'Eau has old tombs built like small houses, covered in chequer-board black-and-white tiles, some extremely ambitious in design. Here also are the remains of the 1826 Canal des Rotours, built to drain some of the region's low-lying land.

There are a number of interesting sites on the islands – Marie Galante, La Désirade, and Les Saintes – which lie off Guadeloupe. A number of these are significant fortifications. At Terre-de-Haut in **Les Saintes**, Fort Napoléon was originally called Fort Louis and built in the 17th century, but it was reconstructed in 1867 in Vaubanesque style. It has well-preserved ramparts, barracks and dungeons. From here there is a view across the channel to Fort Joséphine on **Ilet à Cabrit**. This fort was built in the 19th century on the remains of the earlier Fort la Reine established here in 1780. The Grand-Bourg Fort on **Marie-Galante** was built in 1653 by Charles Houel.

These islands also have some attractive old churches, like that at Grande Anse on **Terre-de-Bas**, dating from the 17th century, and the chapel of St Anne in Capesterre, on Marie-Galante. The Sisters of Charity ran the old Leprosy Hospice on **La Désirade**, until 1954, from when it was founded in 1725. Typical of small-island decoration are the geometric wooden railings and pastel shades of the houses in Grand-Bourg on Marie-Galante. Here the town houses have traditional open first-floor balconies, with ornate wood railings and slender pillars supporting a roof which acts as canopy over the balcony. Some verandahs have a seperate roof.

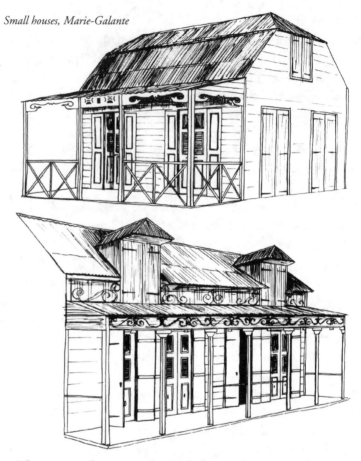

Small houses, Marie-Galante

The sugar industry was particularly active on Marie-Galante, and the Habitation Murat is a Classical French château-type plantation mansion built in the 18th century and rebuilt in 1832. It was damaged in an earthquake in 1843 and there are the remains of a windmill and sugar factory here. The grand, stone-built, tile-roofed mansion of the Murat estate has three arched entrances, reached by six steps, almost as wide as the house itself. Each side of the three-pilastered entrance are wide, shuttered doors, and there are five shuttered windows in the first floor. A circular window in the wide pediment lets air into the upper floor. Moulin des Basses is a restored old sugar mill, and Moulins Roussel, Bonneval, Beauregard and Trianon are other attractive examples of the 100 19th-century windmills on Marie-Galante, many now in a bad state of repair. An interesting architectural feature are the slat-walled (*gaulette*), thatched huts in Anse de Mays, on Marie-Galante. This style of building was common here up until the 19th century.

HAITI

Once France's richest colony, a fact borne out by the wealth of colonial architecture throughout this western part of Hispaniola, Haiti went through a unique and traumatic thirteen-year experience of civil war and foreign intervention, sparked by the world's only successful slave revolution. This not only resulted in the loss by fire of many architectural gems, but it also spawned a plethora of amazing buildings, including the spectacular Citadelle fortress. The oldest European-inhabited island in the Caribbean, it is also its poorest, and much of its early architecture is suffering from neglect. A legacy of dictatorship and political unrest has also contributed to the country's poverty and resulting architectural dilapidation. However, a great number of unique examples of unique Haitian architecture have survived, many with architectural features harping back to French colonialism and combining these with a distinctive Creole style.

Haiti is the site of the first European settlement in the New World, La Navidad, but the initial settlement moved and the first real town, Santo Domingo, was established on the south coast in the present-day Dominican Republic. The entire island was initially Spanish, and much of it was deserted, especially the north coast, which was vulnerable to attacks by pirates. The small offshore island of Tortuga (La Tortue), in particular, was a notorious pirate base and it was from here that isolated parts of Hispaniola were occupied by the French, mostly itinerant buccaneers: Petit Goâve was the first proper French settlement on the western part of the island, and Léogâne, Cap Français, Port St Louis, Petite Rivière and L'Esterre were added when the Treaty of Ryswick officially ceded this part of Hispaniola as Saint-Domingue to the French in 1697. The fortified town of Port-de-Paix stood on the north coast, opposite Tortuga, while Tortuga's most impressive fortress was Fort de la Roche, above Basse-Terre, once a 200 ft-high construction, now in ruins, and built in 1639. Fort d'Ogeron was built in 1667, and its remaining walls and a few cannon can still be seen. The largest ruin on the island is an 18th-century lime kiln, standing forty feet high.

The transformation of Saint-Domingue from pirate outpost to thriving colony took almost a century and involved the importation of up to 15,000 African slaves each year. In 1789 on the eve of the French Revolution, Saint-Domingue boasted no fewer than 3,160 indigo plantations, 3,117 of coffee, 793 sugar plantations, and 789 producing cotton. Little wonder that it was regarded as the most successful plantation colony in the world and was envied by France's European competitors. The French Revolution was to usher in the social transformations that ended colonial rule, for the message of liberty, fraternity and equality was taken up not only by the colony's minority mulatto population, eager to claim equal rights with the white elite, but later by half a million black slaves. A confused period of civil war, foreign interventions (Britain tried to capitalize on the chaos by mounting an invasion) and shifting alliances ensued, which culminated in Haiti's independence in 1804. In 1791, 27,000 planters had fled to nearby Cuba.

It was a new nation 'born in ruins', and few examples of early architecture remain in Haiti dating from before the end of the 1700s. There are, however, some surviving constructions, reflecting French colonial building styles, as well as many ruined forts, a massive fortress and a spectacular palace ruin, both of which date from the early years of independence. These are recognized by UNESCO as World Heritage sites.

Port-au-Prince

The present-day capital of Haiti was not the colony's first town, which was the northern city of Cap Haïtien. Around 1700, a French warship, the *Prince*, used to moor in the bay here, giving the city its current name, but it was not until 1749 that Governor La Caze founded the city as L'Hôpital. By that time, the city's oldest remaining building, the 1720 timber-built Ancienne Cathédrale Catholique had already been completed. Fort National is the city's second oldest structure, dating from the 18th century. As the British took the city in 1793 in the midst of the revolutionary upheaval and the French then returned, only to be ousted during independence in 1804, little building was done in the city.

The succession of wars, fires, hurricanes and earthquakes have destroyed many of Port-au-Prince's historic structures. What remains, among vast areas of shantytowns and crumbling inner-city neglect, dates mostly from the 19th century. The Place des Héros de L'Indépendance, or Champ de Mars, was laid out in the early 1850s. The Eglise Sacré-Coeur is one of the oldest buildings of post-independence Port-au-Prince, dating from the 19th century, although the Fort Mercredi, overlooking the city from the Bolosse suburb, is a little older. The ornate Marché de Fer (Iron Market), with its red corrugated iron roof and twin domed minarets flanking a classical facade, was built France by the same company which constructed the Eiffel Tower in 1889 and should have been delivered to India. Instead, India got the model destined for Haiti.

Most edifices in the city date from the 20th century. One of the earliest is the pink and white Cathédrale Notre-Dame, completed in 1915 in neo-Romanesque style as a copy of the Sacré-Coeur in Paris but without the central dome. The facade is spectacular, with twin towers and a large rose window over five smaller rose windows above the five entrance doors. The 1720 Ancienne Cathédrale in the same grounds is now in a state of near collapse. The Episcopal Cathédrale Sainte-Trinité is notable mainly for its Haitian naive murals (including work by the celebrated Philomé Obin), while the Cimetière Extérieur is noted for its size and sepulchral sculptures. The long, white, triple-domed Presidential Palace was built in 1918 as a copy of the Capitol in Washington. Its four-columned entrance is surmounted by an elegant pediment and the central dome is topped by a cupola. The nearby Dessalines Barracks building, its size testifying to the historic role of the armed forces in Haitian history, was built around the same time.

In Port-au-Prince, official buildings are colour-coded, with government buildings having green roofs and military buildings like the Barracks painted a mustard yellow. The Place des Héros de L'Indépendance in front of the palace contains several statues, including one of the legendary slave leader Toussaint Louverture by Normi Ulysse Charles. Another depicts the *Marron Inconu* or Unknown Runaway Slave who carries a machete and is calling slaves to revolt with a conch-shell trumpet or lambi. It is by the Haitian sculptor, Albert Mangonès and was erected in 1968 during the regime of François 'Papa Doc' Duvalier. The square is flanked by the 20th-century Musée du Panthéon National, the Musée d'Art Haïtien, the Centre d'Art and the mausoleum of Jean-Jacques Dessalines and Alexandre Pétion. The Ministry of Justice building houses the bronze lions which once guarded the entrances to Sans Souci Palace, near Cap Haïtien. The nearby Maison Défly, a prime example of turn-of-the-century architecture, is now the Creole Museum. Built by an army commander in 1896 in typical French Victorian style, this building incorporates rich gingerbread fretwork, balconies, round turrets, steep roofs and gables, with high interior ceilings to allow cool air to circulate. The City University building dates from 1944 and the Technical Institute from 1962; neither is remarkable architecturally.

The 200th anniversary of the founding of Port-au-Prince was celebrated in 1949, with the erection of an exhibition complex near the waterfront area known as the Cité de l'Exposition. Government departments occupy many of the former pavilions, which are now sadly run-down.

The Grand Hotel Oloffson, featured in Graham Greene's novel *The Comedians* and haunt of journalists and would-be Bohemians, was built by a French architect in the 1880s for the son of the country's president, Tirésias Sam. It is a white wedding cake-celebration of late 19th-century tracery and opulence, and the architect has drawn on the best of materials and designs of the era. The mansion is built of brick and stone, and wood is used in all the decorative embellishments. Twin identical balconies front the house with turned wooden balustraded railings, and a wooden awning runs the length of each balcony. Above the awnings, a deep frieze of intricate fretwork allows air to circulate. The entrance, approached by twin, iron railed staircases, is surmounted by a half-turret, forming part of the upper storey balcony and rising to a high, weather-boarded dormer, extending out from the roof. Exuberant

Oloffson Hotel,
Port-au-Prince

gingerbread decorates the dormer gables and the louvred windows. Two smaller dormers provide ventilation, and the roof is edged with gingerbread and ridged with ornate decoration. At each end of the upper floor balcony, twin spired bell turrets project out over the ground floor, exquisitely dripping in fretwork railings and trims. Slender wooden pillars support balconies and the wood shingled roof.

It is in the prosperous Pacot and Pétionville quarters of the capital that some of the best examples of French-Haitian architecture can be found. This district is famed for a number of charming and graceful gingerbread houses, including the famous Cordasco house, the Gingerbread House and the Peabody mansion. However, even the most modest of homes provide the student with architectural interest.

Hilltop House stands high in the Bois Verna residential area of Port-au-Prince. Painted in brown and white, it was built by President Sam in 1898 for his goddaughter. It is approached by a series of stone steps. These lead up to the arched entrance, above which is a square extension, surmounted by a corrugated iron roofed bell spire The exterior is striking in its use of stylized geometric carved woodwork, echoed throughout the interior. Its brick-built lower floor supports the wooden upper storey, which has projecting galleries supported by carved wooden brackets. The roof overhand of the 'skirt' of the bell spire is likewise supported by wooden brackets. Entrances into rooms and the lower floor gallery are through archways, and the floor is tiled in intricate mosaic work. The exterior fretwork design is echoed in the interior balustrade. Arched windows have similarly-shaped shutters.

More colonial villas can be found in the wealthy elite's mountain retreat of Kenscoff, where there are the two 19th-century defensive posts of Fort Alexandre and Fort Jacques, out in the Fermathe Hills. Built on adjoining summits, just Fort Jacques has so far been restored.

Of all Caribbean countries, Haiti's is probably the architectural style in which one can most directly read African origins. The initial impact is made by the stunning and exuberant use of vibrant primary colours in the decoration of local houses, often incorporating African-style designs. Looking closer, one can see African influence in the symbolism deployed in carpentry work, such as the fretwork trims which decorate roofs and balconies. Looking even closer, there is a popular use of finials, often incorporating symbolic religious images. Another prominent feature of Haitian architectural style are the steeple-like pointed roof additions, often built as bell-shaped, corrugated iron peaks. Most are arrowhead-shaped, flattened spires, similar to those on eastern European church and public buildings and on some French châteaux. Some have a flared, corrugated iron 'skirt'.

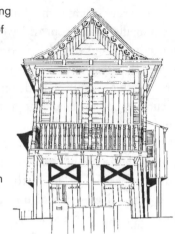

Originally, these peaks appeared on simple huts and were thatched, or shingled. The point of these features is to funnel the hot air in the house up through the hood, thus drawing cool air in through the windows and doors. Sometimes the peaks have louvred, dormer-type projections or are opened at the apex to allow cooling breezes to be funnelled into the home. They often sport finials on every corner or projection, some carved in strange symbolic shapes.

Jacmel

The pretty town of Jacmel lies on Haiti's south coast. It was established in 1698, but its boom years were in the late 19th century, when it was a thriving port and coffee-exporting centre. The red-tiled Marché de Fer, or Iron Market, dates from 1895, its parts having been forged in the Belgian city of Bruges. There are also numerous 19th-century New Orleans-style mansions here, many with imported wrought-iron balconies supported by cast-iron pillars. A good example is the Boucard family house. One of the oldest buildings is the prison, dating from the 18th century, while the Vital family warehouse near the wharf dates from 1865.

The Manoir Alexandra Hotel in the main square of Jacmel overlooks the bay and is a magnificent example of early 20th-century patrician Haitian architecture. It is a strong, stone-built and plastered structure emphasized by the green-painted quoins on the corners of the house, outlining the arches over green and white shuttered windows. The lower windows, built into the thick masonry walls, have built-in wrought ironwork screening and iron bars, both used to let light and air into the interior but preventing unwanted intrusion. The upper windows have half louvres top and bottom and an in-fill lunette in the arch, pierced in a curved sunburst pattern. The ridged roof has arched ventilation openings under the flush gables. Interior panelled tray ceilings contrast with the herringbone precious wood and tiled floors, and the patterned tiles on the upper gallery, which is accessed by louvred French windows. Slender iron columns with ornate cast-iron tops support the two upper-floor galleries of this three-storeyed mansion. A separate building houses the old kitchen, floored with early patterned tiles.

A smaller town house in Jacmel, previously a hotel and once destroyed in a fire, was rebuilt in 1890, and retains its original, monumental interior staircase. Constructed of quarry stone, the window frames of the house are outlined in brick arches, and it has ornate-railed balconies accessed by louvred French windows in arched frames. Arches also divide the rooms of the house, some infilled by double louvred doors. The kitchen is closed off from the courtyard by a solid wooden shutter, and has access to the road through a brick-lined arch, and heavy double doors.

Cap Haïtien

Cap Haïtien, once known as Cap Français and now referred to as Le Cap, is the country's second largest city and the oldest in Haiti, dating from 1670 when it was founded by French pirates. In the heyday of Saint-Domingue's colonial prosperity, it was a cosmopolitan and elegant town. However, the city's architecture has suffered much from destruction, being burnt in 1734, 1798, and fired again in 1802, during the war between the French and their former slaves. It was destroyed again in an earthquake on 7 May 1842 that is reputed to have killed half the town's people. Even so, there are several military structures surviving from the 18th century. Fort Picolet is a classic example, said to have been designed in the very early 1700s by Vauban, Louis XIV's military architect. Both Fort Magny and Fort St Joseph also date from the 1700s.

Cap Haïtien's silver-domed, baroque cathedral, in the centre of the city, was first built in the 18th century, added to in the following century, destroyed in the 1842 earthquake, and rebuilt in its original style in 1942. The triple-gated Barrière Bouteille, or Old Town Gate, dates also from the 18th century, and the fountain in

Town house, Cap Haïtien

the Place d'Armes, and the Town Hall, are relics of French colonial times. There are also a number of houses in typical baroque style with gingerbread fretwork decoration, and a number of Spanish-style buildings in the city, with interior courtyards, porches, arcades, and red barrel-tiled roofs.

To the south-east of Cap Haïtien, there were once a thousand colonial plantations, each with its own *habitation* or great house and slave quarters. All of these buildings are now in ruins, most of them barely detectable. South-west of Cap Haïtien is the site of the old plantation of Habitation Le Normand de Mezy, which include ruined walls and the remains of two aqueducts.

Just outside Cap Haïtien is the site of La Navidad, Christopher Columbus' first settlement in the New World. On Christmas Day 1492, Columbus' flagship, the *Santa Maria*, leading his first voyage of discovery, struck a reef and was wrecked off the coast. It was thus really from necessity that the first European settlement in the Americas was built on this part of the coast, as the crew of the wrecked ship could not be accommodated in the remaining ships, the *Niña* and the *Pinta*, on the return journey to Spain. The wreck of the *Santa Maria* therefore made history for Haiti, although the short-lived base was razed to the ground within a year. Another settlement was established further east, in what is now The Dominican Republic. Although Haiti can claim the site of the first settlement, it was the neighbouring territory which was subsequently developed and where the Spanish colonists built their most impressive New World structures.

Exactly 485 years after Columbus founded the first settlement on Hispaniola, a team of archaeologists, working in Haiti in 1977 came upon the remains of a large Amerindian settlement near En Bas Saline. A later expedition in 1987 found a broken ring of earthworks, around 1,000 feet in diameter. A raised, central mound revealed remains of European pottery and glass and the bones of European animals such as a domesticated pig and those of a rat. Wells were unknown in pre-Columbian culture, and on this site the archaeologists discovered a well containing charcoal dating from around 1500 or before. Experts now deduce that this was the original site of Columbus' first base in the New World, La Navidad, named after the Christmas Day on which it was founded.

Forts

Haiti is littered with the ruins of fortresses, a legacy of its violent past. Some are more accessible than others, and a good area in which to explore them is the southern peninsula. West of Port-au-Prince, on the southern coast and west of Zanglais is the massive Forteresse des Platons, built in 1804 on the orders of Dessalines, independent Haiti's first president. It stands in ruins on a 2,000-ft summit, overlooking the coastal plain. On the north coast of the peninsula is a ruined French fort near the village of Pestel. Other early ruined fort sites in the region include those at Les Cayes where there are the remains of an 18th- and 19th-century fort and also a 19th-century cathedral, with its twin, truncated towers and a number of interesting colonial-style houses. There are the ruins of Fort Télémaque in Jérémie, a treasure house of once fine colonial buildings harping back to the days of coffee wealth, and the city where Alexander Dumas' father was born.

To the north, military buildings include the French colonial fortifications at Port-de-Paix, founded by pirates from Tortuga in 1664, and the ruined fort above the port town of St Marc, which has some delightful colonial-style houses with typical shingle roofs.

The town of Fort Liberté, east of Cap Haïtien on the north coast, is the site of the immense complex of fortifications, the best preserved of which is known as Fort Dauphin. Located on a shoe-shaped promontory just north of the town, this fort was constructed in 1730 and equipped with more than fifty cannon emplacements. It complemented the four other fortifications which defended the bay of Fort Liberté, and its huge blockhouse remains, together with the outlines of barracks and other military buildings.

Several remains of the abortive British occupation are located in strategic outposts of Haiti. The British General Thomas Maitland spent five years trying to wrest Haiti from the rule of Toussaint, finally withdrawing in 1798 after building a series of forts throughout the country. The ruins of a number of these installations stand around Môle St Nicolas, in the island's north-west. On the southern coast, another ancient English battery emplacement faces a ruined English fort on a little island just near the village of Zanglais, not far from the Ile-à-Vache, once the stronghold of the pirate Henry Morgan. On the Ile-à-Vache is the huge ruined fort built by Dessalines in 1804.

Sans Souci and the Citadelle Laferrière

After Dessalines' assassination in 1806, General Henri Christophe (1767-1820), a one-time waiter born in Grenada, proclaimed himself president of the northern part of the country, known as the State of Haiti. Four years later he proclaimed the territory a kingdom and appointed himself King Henri I, setting himself up as an absolute ruler. The first king in the Americas, he created a hereditary nobility and ruled over a feudal society. Among the eight châteaux and nine royal palaces which he had constructed within fourteen years was the fabulous Sans Souci Palace at Milot, with its domed chapel, and four storeys. The palace was begun in 1807 and completed in 1813 as the Caribbean counterpart to Frederick the Great's Potsdam Palace or to rival that at Versailles. The palace was designed to be 'the most regal structure ever raised in the New World' and covered an area of eight hectares. The complex, set inland for fear of naval attack, was an industrial centre and administrative capital. It included a military barracks, hospital, medical school, garment factory, printing shop, distillery, schools, and a chapel. The marble cladding of the galleries has all but disappeared, as the palace was partly destroyed in the earthquake in 1842. It was in this palace that Christophe committed suicide, supposedly with a silver pistol and a golden bullet in 1820 as forces from the southern Republic moved to overthrow him and reunify the country. Sans Souci palace was plundered after Christophe's death.

The massive Citadelle Laferrière, 3,000 feet above the sea, was built over a period of thirteen years. Perched above the Sans Souci palace on the Pic La Ferrière, commonly called the Bonnet de l'Evêque or Bishop's Cap, this 'eighth wonder of the world' has been a UNESCO Site of World Heritage since 1982, as has the palace itself. With twelve-foot-thick walls, and 140-foot ramparts, it was designed to hold a garrison of 5,000 soldiers. In places, the walls are thirty feet thick and 100 feet high. Begun in 1806, it reputedly cost the lives of some 20,000 former slaves in its construction before it was completed in 1819. It is said that the blood of the victims was mixed into the mortar. Three hundred and sixty-five rusting cannon, weighing five tons each (which never fired a shot), await the 45,000 cannonballs, heaped in the three galleries. It was from the top gallery that King Henri apparently ordered a detachment of his soldiers to march off to fall to their deaths, in order to impress a visiting British diplomat with the loyalty of his troops.

The Citadelle is entered through a vast, iron-bound door. The governor's house is located in the central courtyard, surrounded by six massive batteries situated around three towering bastions. Christophe is buried in the Citadelle, with the motto 'I am reborn from my ashes' inscribed above his pyramid-shaped tomb. Four small forts comprise the Site de Ramiers, part of the fortress complex, and located on the ridge behind the Citadelle.

The next best-known of Christophe's edifices are the ruins of his so-called Palais des 365 Portes (named after its original number of doors, windows, and arches) at Petite Rivière de l'Artibonite, where there is also the ruined Fort de la Crête-à-Pierrot, scene of a bloody battle between Dessalines and the French in 1802. At Grande Rivière du Nord, stands another of Christophe's ruined fortresses, Fort Rivière, located on a ridge to the east of the town, while his Crête Rouge fort stands ruined above the village of Limbé. In the hills above the town of Marchand, where the house of Dessalines' wife still stands, are the ruins of seven more massive forts built to defend the town.

JAMAICA

Jamaica's architectural heritage encapsulates the development of many aspects of the Caribbean's colonial rule. After Columbus's arrival in 1494, the Spanish established themselves on the island from 1509, moving from the north coast to San Jago de la Vega (Spanish Town), in 1534. From 1655, the island came under British rule and became one of its most important and richest colonies over several centuries. Some of the island's lavish great houses reflect the prosperity that was monopolized by a small elite of planters and landowners. Yet like many other colonial outposts, it alternated between prosperity and poverty, its most difficult period following the abolition of slavery when falling profits and the frustrated aspirations of ex-slaves resulted in explosive social tensions. Jamaica offers not only a picture of 300 years of British colonial architecture, but an ideal opportunity to study a cross-section of colonial building styles during that period, whether military, naval, commercial, public or private. This section is hence divided according to specific types of architecture, built for different purposes.

Forts

The Spanish were the first to build forts on Jamaica, as early as 1509, but few traces of their construction remain. It is known that they constructed their first fortress in the Sevilla Nueva region, where the remains of Don Juan Esquivel's defensive and administration complex can still be seen near Ocho Rios. The Spanish also built a lookout station on Port Henderson Hill and a stockade at the mouth of the Rio Nuevo, where a memorial stands on the site. However, the north coast was soon abandoned in favour of the southern part of the island, and the earliest forts were neglected as new ones were built to defend new settlements like Spanish Town. There are the remains of an old fort in May Pen, just west of Spanish Town, which might well have been one of these. When the British arrived in 1655, they first targeted the Spanish Passage Fort, located at the mouth of the Rio Cobre, taking this and also the Spanish capital.

The British began fortifying their newly-acquired island from 1655. They chose to settle on a peninsula arm of what is now Kingston Harbour, known as the Palisadoes. The first British defensive post was a small palisade built across this spit of land, protecting the buildings of Port Royal from attack by land. It comprised a wall with a redoubt containing six cannon. As Port Royal was built, a defensive structure was built at the tip of the spit, Fort Cromwell, later to be re-named Fort Charles after the 1662 restoration. Port Royal was also defended by Fort Carlisle, Fort James, Fort Rupert and Fort Walker. These forts now lie beneath the sea, sunk by the 1692 earthquake. Altogether, by the 1690s, Kingston Harbour and Port Royal were surrounded by a total of nine forts, the most heavily defended spot in the British Caribbean. When Port Royal sunk, a fort was built at the end of King Street to defend the settlement of Kingston, but it was torn down in 1870.

By the late 1600s, Port Royal had established itself as the pirate lair of the Spanish Main. The Spanish had called this peninsula Cayo de Carena, as it was here that they careened their ships. With the advent of the English, the site was called Point Cagua or Cagway, possibly a derivative of causeway, reverting to Port Royal when King Charles II was re-instated. Protected by the three bastions of Fort James, Fort Charles and Fort Carlisle, the small township of Port Royal was located on a spit of land, jutting out into the Caribbean Sea. One of the largest buildings in Port Royal was the King's warehouse, known as the Treasury of the West Indies, a vast structure, 230 feet in length, housing cotton, sugar, indigo, tobacco and treasure vaults. One other significant structure was the Church of St Peter, originally the oldest cathedral in the Caribbean, the Spanish Basilica of San Pedro, built in 1523. The houses were two, three and four storeys in height and built of timber, with some 800 taverns, grog shops and punch houses, three markets, and the Marshallsea prison. It was a place of ill repute, the place from where pirates set off to attack Spanish galleons and ports and where they spent their spoils on all manner of debauchery.

In 1692 at eighteen minutes to midday on 7th June, the ocean floor opened up as the result of an earthquake, swallowing two-thirds of the town and killing 2,000 inhabitants. A total of 1,600 buildings were engulfed or sunk, and Fort Charles sank three feet. It is said that a fabulous fortune in gold and jewels was lost when the port was drowned by a massive tidal wave which followed the earthquake. One artifact which survived is a large, silver communion plate, said to have been donated to St Peter's church by Captain Morgan.

The disaster was dubbed divine retribution when it was announced in England. Nicknamed 'the wickedest city in Christendom', Port Royal was rebuilt, but by this time Kingston, the Jamaican capital, was established on the mainland. In 1702, a fire ravaged Port Royal, and a second destroyed the town in 1722. In 1744, the town was also devastated by two ferocious hurricanes. In 1781, another hurricane sunk several ships anchoring off Port Royal. Nature seemed determined to wipe the town off the face of the earth. Today, Port Royal is a tourist attraction and many artifacts from the sunken port are exhibited in the 1819 stone and pre-fabricated, cast-iron Royal Naval Hospital. The old Jail, dating from before the 1692 earthquake, has also been restored.

The basic design of early British forts like Fort Charles included castellated ramparts and bastions, or projecting stanchions, protruding from the corners of the small, basic structure. These bastions allowed the cannon placed in them to cover a 180-degree and often almost a 360-degree arc. A square, or rectangular, internal fort design, with projecting lozenge-shaped bastions at each corner, typified the traditional fortress design, be it naval or military.

Red-brick Fort Charles was built between 1660 and 1696 and was never attacked. Because it was built on the Palisadoes peninsula – land with a sea approach each side, the channel at one end and Port Royal harbour at the other – it was constructed slightly differently, with a rectangular area protected by a straight wall, defended by a double row of cannon (in 1767 there were 104) on the channel side. The Royal Artillery Store, with V.R. 1888 carved over its entrance, under the abbreviations 'ROY: ART: STORE.', was hit by another earthquake in 1907, tilting it over 16 degrees and earning it the name of the 'Giddy House'. This brick-built structure, capped by a flat concrete roof supported the nearby huge Victorian gun emplacements, known as the Victoria and Albert Battery, which were also sunk in the 1907 earthquake. A massive cannon lies near the gun emplacement pits. Towards the end of the 19th century, the British, fearing the military might of the United States, built concrete gun pits instead of forts.

Walls defined the naval dockyard and the military fort, like the old Garrison Wall and Morgan's Line, which defended the east side of the fortifications, where the Half Moon Battery was placed. In 1700, ships moored up to the rings in the fort's lower walls, as the sea once reached the castellated ramparts. This wall was surmounted at each end by a bartizan, or gun turret. On the harbour side of the fort, two arrow-shaped bastions project from the port-side corners of the rectangular fort. In the centre of the fort is the Maritime Museum, fronted by cannon and ordnance pieces. The wooden Nelson's Walkway or Quarterdeck, is another prominent feature of Fort Charles, named after the Admiral who served here as a young-ster in command of the battery for three months in 1779. There is also the 17th-century, beehive-shaped Port Royal powder magazine in Fort Charles, wantonly destroyed in the early 1900s. Its outline can still be traced, however. Altogether, six forts were built in Port Royal after the English occupation in 1655, but the earthquake of 1692 destroyed much of the old town and its fortifications.

Across the bay and reached by the Portmore Causeway is the massive, ruined Fort Augusta, which dates from 1740 and protected the western side of Kingston Harbour. Now a prison, little remains of the original fort, as it was struck by lightening, but the brick patchwork on the old limestone turrets can easily be seen. Near the two-storey Georgian limestone Rodney Arms, once a jail and now a pub, are the remains of the semi-circular Apostles Battery, complete with cannon in the gun emplacements, and an old fort. Further south from here, at the southern end of Green Bay facing Fort Charles across the narrow entrance to Kingston Harbour, the small defence post of Fort Clarence might well have been built on the site of an old Spanish fort, designed to protect Spanish Town. The eastern side of the harbour was defended by Fort Nugent, located

Rodney Arms,
Port Henderson

on Windward Road, and another fort, still containing cannon, a mile to the west. A later addition to Kingston's fortifications was the Martello watchtower, now in ruins, built on the flank of Long Mountain in 1803 to watch for a French invasion which never came. In 1853, a stone-and-cast-iron lighthouse, seventy feet high, was built halfway along the Palisadoes, and it is still in operation.

With renewed naval activity in the 1730s, the naval dockyard at Port Royal was constructed from 1735 onwards. It was built initially with a capstan-house, and then expanded in around 1750 to include a boat-house, mast-house, store houses, blacksmiths' shop and embracing dockyard wall. Later, officers' quarters, a ship-wright's shed and a rigging house – many with dormer windows and wide, overhanging roofs – were added. Today, just the wall and two store houses remain. The dockyard itself was protected by the Polygon Battery.

Further British forts were constructed throughout the 18th century, such as Fort Clarence. Passage Fort, now just a named area, marked the first landing by British forces in 1655 and became Spanish Town's main port until the Rio Cobre shifted its course and Kingston port was built. During the Maroon Wars against runaway slaves from 1690 to 1739, the British built several barrack encampments to combat the guerrillas, one of which can be seen in Trelawny Town. The maroons also built their own fortress, at Nanny Town, but this was overrun by the British in 1734. One of the oldest forts on Jamaica, now just rubble walls, is at the end of Great George Street, in Savanna-la-Mar. In 1755, the British built this fort here on the site of an earlier defensive structure.

Defending Montego Bay, Fort Montego was built by the British in 1750 and still has a battery of three of the original 17 George III cannons. When the cannon were fired in 1762 to celebrate the British taking of Havana, one blew up. The last time the others were fired, in 1795, it was mistakenly at a British warship. On the land-ward side of the fort is the vast powder magazine. At Falmouth, further east, are the remains of Fort Balcarres. Around 1795, the old British fort built from the ruins of Seville Nueva at St Ann's Bay was finally abandoned. It later became a jail, and the iron-grilled windows can still be seen. East of Montego Bay at Lucea stand the octagonal fortifications of Fort Charlotte, where three of its original 23 cannon remain on rotary carriages. Its walls, built in 1761, are six feet thick and the fort served variously as a slave jail, a school and a museum. Near Bluefields Bay on Belmont Point is a privately-built fort, constructed by a plantation owner in 1767 to protect his estate from pirate attack. In 1773, the Morant Bay Fort was built, and it contains three 19th-century cannon. Under the cannon, a mass grave contains the 79 skeletons of those executed in the aftermath of the 1865 Morant Bay uprising, found behind the walls of the old fort in 1965. Port Morant itself was protected by two forts. The ruins of Fort Lindsay can be seen on Morant Point, and Fort William stands guard on the other side of the way.

Later forts were constructed by the British, like the little site in Ocho Rios, which was built in 1777, later used as a slaughterhouse and restored in the 1970s. This is the town's oldest historic site, and still sports four old cannon. In the following year, the northern town of Rio Bueno was fortified with the building of Fort Dundas. Nearby at Runaway Bay, Eaton Hall guest house is built on the remains of an early English fort. Of interest, too, is Port Antonio's ruined 1729 Fort George, with its embrasures for 22 guns cut into ten-foot thick walls. The gun emplacements are original, but the cannon are of a later date. From 1875, the fort became part of Titchfield High School, the parade ground becoming the playground, and the old barracks being taken over by the main part of the school. This was once one of the most powerful forts in the entire Caribbean, and the bastion can be seen at the end of the promontory.

In 1784, the headquarters of the British regiments stationed in Jamaica, Up Park Camp, was established near Cross Roads in Kingston. Five major barracks were also built on the island at the end of the 18th century. The vast military barracks at Spanish Town were constructed in 1791, around the same time as those on Stony Hill, near Port Antonio. A third barracks complex, which dates from 1841, was built in the form of a hill station up in the cooler regions of the Blue Mountain foothills at Newcastle. The government bought the land here from a French planter who had settled to grow coffee in 1789. This military base, established in the hills by General Sir William Gomm in an attempt to reduce the fearful mortality rate from yellow fever, is still in use, and its buildings are constructed on several levels down the hillside, from 4,500 to 3,500 feet above sea level to the flat parade ground. The parade ground displays cannon and the insignia of the Jamaican regiments along its walls. The fourth, the Cornwall Barracks, were constructed in

Moore Town, and the fifth 18th-century barracks were located near Mandeville.

Forts and barracks would also have had military hospitals, similar to that built in 1817 at Port Royal. This Royal Naval Hospital, a large, long, two-storey stone-built block, was constructed around an impressive cast-iron frame, which has withstood 17 hurricanes and several earthquakes. The single hospital block is constructed inside an all-embracing double verandah, about 100 yards long, supporting an overlapping roof. The iron frame components were made in England and shipped to Jamaica. This building is now a Museum of Historical Archaeology, and the old jail to one side dates from before the 1692 earthquake.

Great Houses

For centuries Britain's richest West Indian colony and once the world's largest sugar producer, Jamaica also cultivated substantial quantities of coffee, coconut, citrus fruit, cacao, annotto, cinchona, indigo, tobacco, cotton and pepper. Upon the arrival of the British, Jamaica had been a Spanish colony for 145 years. The Spanish had planted coffee and cacao on the slopes of the Blue Mountains, established *hatos* or cattle ranches around Portland, and started sugar plantations in the few accessible regions. The earliest sugar mill was built to the west of St Ann's Bay at Sevilla la Nueva, in the 1510s, but little evidence of early Spanish plantation architecture remains. Apart from the scant ruins of a Spanish fort here, and those of Peter Martyr's Church, there are mere traces of the island's first sugar mill, and door jambs, semi-columns, stone panels and friezes, which may have come from the first manor house. Before the British occupation, the first European buildings would have been constructed using a masonry filling built around a wooden framework (known as 'Spanish walling'), with a tiled, not thatched, roof.

After the British arrived, agriculture, particularly plantation sugar cultivation, developed prolifically, along with its synonymous architecture. Although plantations varied in size, the great houses or owners' mansions were built at a time when money was no object. Any building materials which were not locally available were imported from Europe, as were the architects, often English but sometimes Italian. As Jamaica established itself as a major source of sugar and indigo, plantations spread across the island. In its heyday, towards the middle of the 1700s, there were no fewer than 430 estates on Jamaica, each with its own processing factory and estate buildings. The great house, usually built on a hill, often looked out over several estates, all belonging to the same master, this concentration of property being reinforced by arranged marriages. Therefore, at one time, there might have been at least 300 great houses of varying sizes and ages scattered across the island. The numerous plantation houses dotted throughout Jamaica cover a wide gamut of architectural styles and reflect the European building trends of the time. In some cases, in order to replicate as closely as possible the English architecture of the era, few concessions were made to the tropical climate. The great house was the main building of all plantations and was where the landowner and his family lived. Today, however, many smaller houses, built for the plantation's manager, the overseer, or even to house processing machinery, might be pointed out as 'great houses'. Many plantations were managed on behalf of absentee owners who resided in England, and the estate manager's house would have been moderate compared to the great houses of the resident owners.

Many of the earlier plantation great houses were constructed around a fortified internal 'blockhouse'. Not only were the occupants conscious of attacks from French or Spanish forces or pirates, but the slave population greatly outnumbered the whites, and insurgency broke out at regular intervals. For five years after the British took Jamaica, Spanish stragglers and maroons continued a guerrilla war against the new settlers. Even when the Spanish were finally routed, the maroons carried on their harassment of British settlers well into the late 1700s. It was hence thought to err on the side of caution to construct permanent, protective homes. Some of the British great houses might have been constructed around earlier Spanish fortified dwellings, and with the early trend for fortification, some of the great houses were even called castles. However, from the outside, most looked like replicas of English country houses and mansions. Of the great houses, mansions and estates mentioned here, some of the more interesting are described in detail, while others may be just ruins or the outline of walls and factory buildings.

The 17th-century Halse Hall great house is a fine early example and one of Jamaica's oldest. Built of stone and timber, it was initially a fortified home for a British soldier, Thomas Halse. The building was constructed on the foundations of the ancient Spanish

Halse Hall, Jamaica

ranch house, the Hato de Bueno Vista, in the Rio Minho valley. Today, it has been fully restored by the Alcoa aluminum mining company. Stokes Hall mansion, in the St Thomas region, is typically fortified and is based on four linked towers, which could also be utilized as defence turrets. It was built by one of the sons of the Jamaican Governor, Luke Stokes, who died in 1660. This is Jamaica's oldest standing house, and although in ruins, its loopholes, used in times of revolt, can still be seen. The National Trust now maintains this 17th-century ruin.

The Seville Estate house is particularly interesting as it is a single-floored, Spanish-influenced structure. Underneath the plaster of its walls can be seen the original wattle and daub, and the roof of this modest great house is shingled. This mansion was built by Richard Hemmings, an officer in Cromwell's army, with many stones taken from the early Spanish church at Sevilla la Nueva. Other early ruins here are a fortified governor's house, built for Juan de Esquivel, and the remains of an ancient Spanish sugar mill. Now a museum, operated by the National Heritage Trust, the sugar mill, drying house, barbecue pit, water wheel, boiling house, aqueduct, and 'busha' or overseer's house, as well as a rare copra kiln, are well preserved. An old coffin stands on the front porch and is said to contain the remains of a slave.

Among the oldest plantation houses on Jamaica, are Colbeck Castle, the Longville great house and the Llanrumny Estate house. Colonel John Colbeck arrived in Jamaica with Penn and Venables in 1655. He built a moated fortress, initially a military rallying point, at St Catherine, and it was from here that he later oversaw his sugar plantation. The so-called Colbeck Castle stands in the centre of what is thought to have been a large, walled, military quadrangle, with defence posts and underground slave quarters at each corner, and the great house in the centre. The grey-brick castle, and its four outbuildings, some of which contain typically military, vaulted chambers, is now in ruins. The corner towers and two of its three arches still stand, and beam slots in the walls show that massive timbers were used in its construction. The corners of its towers are quoined, as are the circular lower window openings and the tall, narrow windows of the top two floors. This is thought to have once been the largest building on the island. This atmospheric ruin – and its tobacco estate – are now maintained by the National Trust.

In the same year that Colbeck built his mansion, Samuel Long founded the Longville Plantation which became the Sevens Plantation, known also as the Seven Hills of Athenry plantation, later settled by Anthony Collier in 1671. The Llanrumny Estate in Morgan's Valley was once owned by the famous pirate turned island governor, Henry Morgan, who established it in 1669. Early in the 18th century the impressively fortified and musket-ball-scarred Stewart Castle was built near Falmouth. Now in ruins, its thick stone walls are designated a national monument and are also looked after by the National Trust.

As the plantation great house became a status symbol in the 18th century and skilled artisans included popular European architectural features in their design, more thought went into their construction. As in Cuba, where the 'Four Winds' style of great house allowed cooling breezes to blow through buildings, the prevailing north-easterly Trade Wind or 'Doctor's Wind' influenced the design of great houses on Jamaica. The main floor became the storey above the ground floor, with verandahs built to channel cooling breezes through the internal corridors, where arched doorways and interior windows maximized ventilation. The great house design began to take on a distinctive identity, not only as an advertisement of its owner's wealth, but in its integral design. Imposing facades or frontages welcomed important and influential visitors, with grand staircases and carved local mahogany doors. Behind the estate house, a kitchen compound, separate from the main house, included a cut stone or brick bake house, with ovens for meat and bread, a smoke house, a 'buttery' and often quarters for staff. The ablutions were often located a distance from the main house. An example of an early latrine can be seen at the restored Green Park great house in Trelawny Parish, where the three-storey bathroom has a space for a three-hole latrine and another for a bath tub.

The Rose Hall Estate plantation house is one of Jamaica's grandest and most famous, and dates from between 1760 and 1780, when it was built by John Palmer, a representative of the British monarch. In the 1820s, it was taken over by his nephew, John Rose Palmer and his wife Annie, the infamous 'White Witch'. Rose Hall was laid waste in the slave rebellion of 1831 and renovated between 1960 and 1966 after it had been disused for around 130 years. The thick, granite-walled house is unusually built on three floors, with a triple roof, a Renaissance-style, double stone staircase, elaborate arches, and a spacious, balustraded, front terrace, built above the ground-floor storage area. The exterior has a porch-like entrance and tall, shutterless, glazed sash windows. The cut-stone and smooth stucco masonry work of the exterior is decorated with prominent corner quoins. For the days, weeks and months of the year, Rose Hall is said to have 365 windows, 52 doors and twelve bedrooms. Low-relief, twin Tuscan columns flank the front doorway, and inside the house has panelling and mahogany beams and floors. The ballroom's silk wall fabric is reproduced from that designed for Marie Antoinette, and the rice paper wall covering design in the dining room features 63 different species of bird. Many of the antiques throughout the house are replicas of the originals which once graced this grandiose mansion, including the doors and mahogany staircase. Originally, the house had semi-circular wings, and had outbuildings to the rear of the courtyard.

John Rose Palmer moved into Rose Hall in around 1820 with his beautiful English-born wife, Anne. Eight years later, he died, leading to a rumour circulated among her servants that she was bewitched and a practitioner of voodoo spells. According to the legend, two more husbands died in suspicious circumstances before Anne began to take slaves as lovers, murdering them when she became bored. She would then order her staff to dispose of the unfortunate suitors' bodies in the sea, linked to the mansion by a subterranean passage. Eventually, the slaves could take no more and Anne was apparently murdered in her bed. Understandably, none of the servants was keen to bury a dead witch, and a planter from a nearby estate took the 'White Witch's' body away and buried it at night. Since then, the legend of Annie Palmer's ghost has haunted Rose Hall. More prosaically, local records suggest that an Anne Palmer did live at Rose Hall, but had one husband and died, the soul of respectability, in 1846.

The Good Hope plantation house dates back to 1755, when it was built on Colonel Thomas Williams' estate, which he purchased in 1742. When the planter John Tharp (1744-1804) bought the main house, in 1767, his interest in architecture led him to construct a series of Georgian-style buildings of wood and stone, found nowhere else on the island. The large Palladian-style entrance to the main house, which leads into the original estate's counting house, has a double stairway, rising to two fan-lighted doors. Elegant columns support the pediment, and two extensions flank the simple design of the main house. These two extensions project each side of the entrance portico, with high, pitched roofs and tall, arched sash windows. Details also include friezes, high-raftered ceilings and hardwood floors. Tharp was one of the wealthiest Jamaican planters, owning the largest estate on the island, combining the property of the Wales, Covey, Potosi, Lansquinet and Pantrepant . estates. The Tharp family parted with the estate in 1867. The slave hospital standing in the extensive grounds dates from 1799, and parts of the original sugar mill, waterwheel and aqueduct also survive. The dungeon once served as housing for 2,000 slaves. Good Hope fell into disrepair in 1904, became a hotel in 1912, owned by an American banker, and was restored in 1993, when the old two-storey coach house was converted into accommodation. In one bedroom in the main house, the original lead and tile-lined bathtub, with its copper water-heating basin, has been preserved. Fruit, flowers and coconut are still grown on the estate, which also has a stable of horses and a few head of cattle.

Good Hope, Jamaica

Marlborough great house in the Manchester region is notable for its Palladian, porticoed, neo-Classical facade, while the Kenilworth great house has oval Palladian windows, edged with light stone. This two-storey limestone mansion, once owned by Thomas Blagrove (1733-1755), is built of two shades of stone, and its arched doorway is reached by a curved flight of steps. Here, the factory buildings dwarf the great house, with a massive rectangular mill house, boiling house and distillery, which once held a gigantic water wheel. This sugar estate factory is one of the best examples of its kind in Jamaica and dates from the 1600s.

Captain George Heron, the great-grandson of a member of the English force of 1655, built Williamsfield great house in 1770 on his 10,000-acre estate. He also built three other great houses in Jamaica, keeping a separate family in each! Holland great house is built over a vaulted cellar and once had a shingled roof, and the early 18th-century, two-storey Blue Hole plantation house, was built for the Waites family, who fled here after the restoration of King Charles. It is constructed of stone and timber and has some intricate gingerbread trim. The sugar mill here still stands, but the boiling house was partly destroyed in the 1831 rebellion. Another early mansion, Edinburgh Castle, was built by a notoriously eccentric and violent Scot, Lewis Hutchinson, near Pedro village in 1763. Circular towers and two loopholed walls are all that remain. It was from these loopholes that the ex-medical student shot more than forty passing travellers, disposing of the robbed bodies down a sinkhole shaft on the hilltop site, which still exists.

Greenwood plantation house, with its fifteen rooms and vast double verandah, was built between 1780 and 1800 and was where Elizabeth Barrett Browning's (1806-61) family lived. The Barretts first arrived in Jamaica as planters in the 1660s, and Elizabeth's cousin, Richard, built the house, although the poet never visited Jamaica. The house is built of timber and huge blocks of fieldstone, some of which was cut in England. It is now one of Jamaica's best museums and antique collections, housing the largest plantation library on the island. Later members of the Barrett family lived in the nearby Cinnamon Hill great house, and the walled family cemetery of the Moulton Barretts can be seen below this 19th-century mansion.

Other notable great houses are those like the Retreat Plantation, which was founded by the Beckford family, who also owned the

Danks and Savoy plantations. Both this and the nearby Potosi estates have some impressive sugar mill and slave house ruins. Near Montego Bay, the Barnett estate, with its fine old mansion Bellfield Great House, was established by Colonel Nicholas Jarrett in 1655. The existing 18th-century house has a stone-built ground floor with defensive features and a colonnaded entranceway. Its upper floor has sand-dashed wooden walls and jalousied sash windows. Verandahs surround the building, which is furnished with antiques. The kitchen is in an outhouse, and the former plantation manager's house is still preserved. The Cardiff Hall colonial mansion also dates from the mid-18th century. Restored in 1994, with the assistance of the Duke of Newcastle, this great house's gateway is protected by two guardhouses with pepperpot roofs. Tombs in the graveyard behind the house date from 1746. Much more recent, but just as imposing, are the ornate, oriental gateways installed on the New Hope Estate, near Savanna-la-Mar, in the 1920s.

Other Jamaican plantation houses of note include those of Bull Head estate, in the centre of the island, Bromley, near Ocho Rios, with its factory and boiling house, the Quebec plantation house, Moses Kellet great house, Rock River estate house and the privately-owned Bryan Castle. The 1790 Marshall's Pen great house, near Mandeville, was once the property of the Earl of Balcarres, Governor of Jamaica (1795-1801). It is entered by a large, cut-stone gateway and is built of stone and timber, with interior wood panelling. The two ruined great houses of the Belvedere Estate, which were destroyed in the 1831 rebellion and one of which has been restored as a hostel and seminary, with a recreated post-eman-cipation heritage village, are open to the public. The Hampden estate house is one of the most striking in Jamaica. This is a working plantation, but its whitewashed great house, with its dark timbers and Mansard roof, is unusual on the island. Dry-stone walls enclose the house, which has original mahogany floors and roofs which extend down, with dormer windows overhanging the balconies. Another unusual planter's mansion is the 18th-century, fortified Prospect Hall great house, with its loopholed walls.

Several great houses are located in the cool uplands of the Blue Mountains, behind sweltering Kingston. Charlottenburg House, once the home of a wealthy coffee planter, still has its slave quarters. The cedar used in the great house's construction came from the estate when it was cleared for coffee growing. Another coffee planter's great house, now a restaurant, is the Blue Mountain Inn, dating from 1754. The coffee from this estate was packed into barrels made at the nearby village of The Cooperage. The Clydesdale coffee planter's house can now be rented and is surrounded by its coffee-drying barbecues and the remains of an old water mill. Strawberry Hill, another former coffee plantation dating from the 19th century, was seriously damaged by Hurricane Gilbert in 1988, but reopened in 1995 as a luxurious hotel and restaurant complex. Also of interest is the restored Craighton great house near Irish Town, currently owned by a Japanese company of coffee-exporters.

Several more estate great houses have been converted into hotels. It is somehow fitting that some great houses are now hotels, as, during the height of prosperity in the 18th century, such houses often served as inns, providing accommodation for 'travellers of quality'. Many are beautifully restored, like the old Jamaica Inn at Ocho Rios and Shafston Estate great house near Bluefields, an atmospheric and subtly restored country house. The Invercauld great house, now a hotel on the Black River waterfront, was built in the late 19th century and is protected by the Jamaican Heritage Trust. The house became the centre for meetings of the Jamaican plantocracy, but was left in ruin after its owner, a Dr Johnson, died. In the 1990s, the great house was converted into a hotel, opening its doors in 1993. Nearby, the Waterloo guesthouse, a typical Georgian structure, was reputedly the first house in Jamaica to have electric lighting. The 18th-century Sign great house is now a holiday home.

The Factories

Built some distance from the great houses, were the industrial buildings of the plantation itself. Today, little remains of the early processing buildings for cacao, indigo, tobacco, cotton and pepper, but there are some striking historic monuments to the sugar and coffee industries on Jamaica. At Sevilla Nueva, the remains of what is thought to be the first, Spanish, sugar mill have been found, dating from the early 1500s.

Upon the arrival of the British, the methods of growing, transporting and processing crops became more streamlined. Most sugar was transported to the factory, by two-wheeled carts. However, on the Potosi Estate, near the Martha Brae River, a 200-foot stone chute was constructed to speed the cane stalks into the mill. This construction, unique to the Caribbean, has a stone stairway each side, where slaves would stand to propel the cut cane down the 'shooter' to the grinders.

Depending on the crop, the nucleus of the factory was the processing buildings, and whatever the crop, it had to be processed, and a source of power was hence essential. There are remnants of these processing and power houses, across Jamaica. At Harmony Hall, in the Trelawny region, is a rare, stone-built, octagonal building, once a mule-mill or *trapiche*, used for grinding sugar-cane. Many of these buildings were wooden, conical structures, none of which have survived. There are mule-mill foundations, however, at Craighton Hall, Fair Prospect, Greenwall, and the Worthy Park estate.

One of the earliest Jamaican windmills, also used to power a sugar-cane crushing plant, can be seen at Greencastle in St Mary parish. This is a primitive stone tower, built in the 'putlog' style, where cross timbers were fitted into the walls as the mill tower was constructed. An example of a single-level, limestone-built, octagonal windmill tower is at Brazilletto, Clarendon parish. Also octagonal in design is the more sophisticated brick-built, two-storey mill tower at Monymusk, also in Clarendon. An older two-storey mill tower, dating from the 18th century, can be found at Lyssons, in St Thomas.

Water mills were also popular, even in areas of Jamaica where water had to be transported. In these instances, aqueducts were built, like the example at the Hope plantation, in St Andrew. Here, parts of the aqueduct, dating from 1758, still operate. Some plantations had mule, wind and water mills. Early waterwheels can be seen at the Good Hope plantation and on the Seville estate, also in the same region. Worth seeing is the huge waterwheel of the former sugar plantation at Tryall, built in 1790, where an aqueduct still carries water to the wheel from the Flint River. This wheel once turned a single three-roll crushing mill, which could be operated by wind power, mule, or even manpower. The sugar works were destroyed in the 1831 rebellion, but the brick chimney was rebuilt in 1834. The ruins at Thetford, St Catherine, contain a double-ramped windmill tower, the outlines of two types of mule-mills, the ruins of a distillery, a bagasse or trash-house and those of a boiling house. The 3,000-acre Barnett Estate is still working and has an old engine-driven mill.

Sugar boiling houses, where the final produce was processed, were an integral part of the sugar factory, The main equipment of the boiling house was the vast copper vats, in which the liquid sugar was boiled and refined. Examples of these vats can be seen at Worthy Park, in St Catherine parish. One of the best 17th-century sugar mills, with sugar boiling house and distillery, is contained within the massive remains at Kenilworth, in Hanover. After processing, the sugar was cured in large barn-like structures, which had to be carefully ventilated. A magnificent example of a most ornate former curing house, once on the Gayle's Valley estate in Trelawny, is the chapel of the Mona campus of the University of the West Indies. With two rows of six windows, each rusticated, the top of the building even boasts a decorative frieze and dates from 1799. Gayle's was a particularly wealthy sugar estate, and rich landowners would even build hospitals for their slaves' welfare. These could also be quite ornate, and good examples can be seen at Worthy Park and Orange Valley Estate. Lime was not only an important building commodity for making mortar, but was also an ingredient used in sugar boiling. Many estates hence had their own lime kilns. Limestone or coral was burnt to make lime in very sturdy stone-built kilns. A good example of an early lime kiln can be seen at Prospect Pen, in St Thomas.

Slave hospital,
Worthy Park, Jamaica

Coffee was introduced into Jamaica in 1728 from Martinique. The processing, involving pulping, drying and peeling, was less complicated than the sugar industry. Pulping was done mechanically in a special pulping or grater house, to remove the twin beans from the pith of the coffee cherry. Although this was often hand-powered, the larger estates, like Clydesdale, used water power to turn the pulping machinery. Drying the coffee beans took place in a barbecue, basically a large, flat platform, where the pulped coffee beans could be laid out and turned as they dried. Barbecues were often walled around and raised above ground level. The coffee beans were then peeled, on a mule-, hand- or water-powered grinder. Clydesdale also has examples of a barbecue, a grinding house, and a coffee storage house, where the beans were kept in especially dry conditions after they had been peeled. There is also a specimen of an old wooden coffee mill house in the Cinchona Botanical Gardens. Both the coffee process and pineapple production can be viewed at the working plantation at Croydon, birthplace of hero Sam Sharpe, at Mavis Bank, a working coffee plantation in the Blue Mountains, at Williamsfield Village, and at the Prospect plantation.

The Churches

The first church in Jamaica was erected by the Spanish at Sevilla Nueva in about 1509, but sadly its stone walls were dismantled to build the Seville great house. Named after St Peter the Martyr, some of its stonework was also used to build the Catholic Church, slightly to the east of the original's site, in 1939. The Spanish moved from the north coast to what is now Spanish Town, or San Jago de la Vega, and a Catholic Franciscan church, the 'Red Church', was built here in 1525, only to be torn down by Cromwell's invading army in the late 1650s.

The Anglican Cathedral of St James replaced the Spanish church, and was built in 1666. It was destroyed in a hurricane in 1712, and the Queen Anne-style structure standing today was built in 1714. It is interesting to note that the church continued in the name of its patron saint, as St James is the English name for Santiago or San Jago. Rebuilt in red brick in a Latin crucifix form, it was restored in 1762. Its tower, and white-painted, double-tiered, octagonal spire, with Corinthian columns, is one of the best examples in the Caribbean and was added in 1817. The timber steeple was added in 1831. This church is the oldest Anglican cathedral outside England and since 1843 has been the cathedral of the Jamaican diocese of the Church of England. Inside, the main features are its beamed ceiling, stained glass windows, fluted wooden pillars, carved wooden pews and choir stalls, and black-and-white chequered floor. Some grave tablets let into the floor date from 1662.

Kingston Parish Church, in the island's capital, was built in 1910 on the ruins of the 1695 original, destroyed in the 1907 earthquake. The oldest tombstone in its cemetery dates from 1699, and in the church is the tomb of the British naval hero, Admiral John Benbow (1653-1702), who died in Port Royal. The bell in the post-First World War tower dates from 1715. Named after Wesleyan missionary, Dr Coke, the original Coke Church was built in 1790 and replaced by the present crenellated, red-brick Methodist chapel in 1840. It was remodelled after the 1907 earthquake. The octagonal St Andrew's Scots church was built in red brick between 1814 and 1819 and altered extensively after the damage done by the earthquake. Once dubbed the 'handsomest building in Kingston', it is surrounded by a gallery supported by Corinthian columns. The original St Andrew's Parish Church dates from 1666, but succumbed to the earthquake of 1692, and the present structure was laid out in 1700, although it was extensively altered in the 1870s. The capital's fifth church is the domed Holy Trinity Roman Catholic Church, with its four minarets built in Spanish Moorish style. The church's pipe organ is said to be the finest in the Caribbean. The Kingston Synagogue has some interesting 16th- and 17th-century gravestones. In Port Royal, St Peter's Church was built of red brick in 1725 to replace the original Christ Church, destroyed in the 1692 earthquake and probably dating back to the 1650s. Original black-and-white tiles pave the floor, but the brick design of the facade is of cement. The beautifully carved organ loft dates from 1743, and the sculptor Roubiliac designed the monument to Lieutenant Stapleton, commander of HMS *Sphinx*, inside. The Parish Church of Hanaover also dates from 1725.

Falmouth was established as a new port town on Jamaica's north coast in 1790 and built on a grid pattern over the following four decades. Its Anglican St Peter's Parish Church dates from 1796, and is vaguely Romanesque in style. Said to be a copy of that in Falmouth in Cornwall, it is built in yellow stone and pebble-dash plaster and has a square tower with a balustrade. With wooden floors and pews, this church is a National Monument. The nearby William Knibb Memorial Church is modern, but built on the site of earlier ecclesiastical structures. The Methodist Manse once belonged to the Barrett family and dates from 1799. Built of stone and timber, this manse has beautiful wrought-iron balconies and Adam-style doorways and friezes.

In Montego Bay, the Parish Church of St James, one of Jamaica's finest, is Georgian and dates from 1775-1782. Built of white limestone, it is designed in the shape of a Greek cross and was reconstructed in 1958 after extensive damage during the 1957 earthquake. Inside is English sculptor John Bacon's memorial to Anne Palmer, said to be Rose Hall's 'White Witch'. Monuments and tombs in the graveyard date back to the 1790s. The original church on the site of the Burchell Memorial Baptist Church was erected in 1824 and destroyed in the slave revolt of 1831. The current building, in red brick, dates from 1835.

Many parish churches were built in Jamaica in the 19th century, and one of the earliest, Mandeville's huge limestone-built Manchester Parish Church of St Mark, was constructed between 1816 and 1820. It has tall, arched windows and a wooden clerestory. Its Manse is one of the town's oldest buildings, dating from 1820. On the north coast, Kettering Baptist

St James Church, Montego Bay

Church at Duncans dates from 1893 and commemorates the missionary William Knibb. There are two churches at Rio Bueno, the 1833 Anglican Church, and a Baptist Church dating from 1901. Ocho Rios' colonial churches include those of the Geddes Memorial church and the Anglican church. St Ann's Baptist Church in St Ann's Bay, was founded in 1827, and the town's Church of Our Lady of Perpetual Help is of Spanish design. Black River's yellow brick Parish Church of St John the Evangelist was founded in 1837. The red-brick neo-Romanesque Anglican Christ Church, the parish church of Portland in Port Antonio dates from 1840 and was the work of the English architect, Annesley Voysey. Its brass lectern was donated by the Boston Fruit Company in 1900, and much of the present structure dates from 1903. The Moravian church of Christiana dates from 1891.

St Andrews Anglican Church in Santa Cruz was built by Duncan Robertson in the 1840s, and St Mary's Parish Church at Port Maria is built of limestone in English style and dates from 1861. The Catholic Church of the Sacred Heart in Seaford Town was established in 1873, and Morant Bay's ochre-painted Anglican Parish Church was built in 1881. The Baptist chapel in Annotto Bay is an imaginative structure, built in 'village baroque' style in red and yellow brick and dating from 1894. St Mark's Church in Brown's Town, was built the following year, of cut stone and wood. This church is a remarkable example of neo-Gothic ecclesiastical architecture. Moore Town, with its Maroon population, has no fewer than seven churches, and the oldest building here is the Anglican Church, with some interesting tombs in its old graveyard.

Prominent Colonial Buildings

Courthouses, seats of learning, administrative centres and early manors, now official buildings, abound in Jamaica. There are six of these historic buildings in the capital, Kingston, a sprawling, mostly modern city of almost a million people. The magnificent Georgian Devon House was built by George Stiebel, one of the first local black millionaires and a gold magnate, in 1881. This is an exceptional example of a grand manor house which adopted many of the attributes of plantation great houses. But this was not a plantation mansion, and the design shows a mixture of Creole influences and Georgian styles adapted to the tropical climate. An elegant, single

Devon House, Kingston

staircase sweeps up to the beautiful wooden facade, with its many-jalousied panels. Finely proportioned, with two storeys and a dormer window centred in the roof, pillared arcades, surmounted by balconies, run down each side of the main structure. Double doors in the centre of the first-floor frontage lead out onto a balcony over the main entrance. The interior is furnished in a variety of colonial styles, some rooms enclosed by louvred verandahs with balustraded decks. Floors are parquet, and the grand staircase is of local mahogany. The entrance hall has the original wallpaper and decorated silk panels, and the ballroom ceiling is Wedgewood in style. Behind a retractable wooden staircase, an illegal gambling den was concealed and can still be seen. The original stables and old brick-built warehouse are now a restaurant and 'Grog Shoppe'. Devon House became the property of the Jamaican government in 1967 and it housed the National Gallery before the collection moved to its present downtown location.

Also in Kingston, the brick and plaster town house, known as Headquarters House, is a good example of 18th-century British colonial architecture, originally built in 1750 by a merchant, Thomas Hibbert. It is thought that four merchants competed to build the best house in order to win a lady's attention. The house has a latticework verandah and three triangular eaves. It was once used by the military and is now the headquarters of the Jamaica National Heritage Trust. The capital also has King's House, now the Governor-General's house, built by the architect Sir Charles

Nicholson on the remains of the old Bishop's Lodge, which was demolished in 1907. Vale Royal is the Prime Minister's residence and was built in 1694 in Queen Anne style as a timber estate house by the planter, Simon Taylor. It was rebuilt in 1909 and restored with its colonial colonnade. This one of the few houses in Kingston which has a lookout tower, built like a dovecote and facing out over the harbour. The Institute of Jamaica dates from 1879, and Mico College, founded in 1834 and one of the world's oldest teacher training institutes, was moved to its present position in 1896. The main building of the college dates from 1909. The old Ward Theatre, the seventh early building of historic importance in Kingston, was built in opulent neo-Classical style in 1907. The blue-and-white Wedgewood-like building was constructed on the site of a traditional theatre by Colonel Ward of the Wray and Nephew rum producing family.

Also in the capital, other houses of note include Gordon House, named after a Jamaican freedom fighter and dating from the mid-1900s, and the Gleaner Building, the 1834 home of the *Daily Gleaner*, the island's oldest newspaper. The Terra Nova Hotel on Waterloo Road, a gracefully balustraded colonial mansion with broad arches, dates from 1924 and during the 1930s was owned by the Myers Rum dynasty. Another historic hotel, located on Jack's Hill, is Ivor House. It was built in the late 1870s as part of the large Woodford Estate by the Rev Hubert Headland Isaacs and it remained in the family until 1926. The old wooden shingles on the roof were replaced in 1931 with galvanized iron, and the side and back verandahs were enclosed in 1947. The building became a guest house in 1985. North of central Kingston is Half Way Tree, an early location going back to the 1600s and a former sugar estate. The aqueducts along the road were built in the 1770s to transport water to the estate. The University of the West Indies was built in 1948 on the foundations of the old Mona Estate house. Near the entrance stands the former Gales Valley estate sugar curing house, now the campus chapel.

Spanish Town

Although sadly dilapidated, Spanish Town still shows traces of a long-gone colonial splendour, initially designed by the first Spanish colonists in 1523. The central administrative square in Spanish

House of Assembly, Spanish Town

Town is one of the most attractive of its kind in the British West Indies. Kings House, a two-storey, red-brick building, with columned and pedimented portico, dates from 1762 and was restored in 1929 after a fire in 1925, leaving the original Georgian facade. It now contains an archeological museum, and in the adjacent Jamaican People's Museum of Craft and Technology is an exhibit of Jamaican architectural techniques through the ages, including a good example of a tinajero or dripstone filter. Kings House stands on the western side of the stately square, facing the 1762 House of Assembly, which is particularly grand with its arched colonnade, brick-built lower floor and balconied wooden upper floor. The original assembly room itself measured forty by eighty feet.

At the south side of the square, Spanish Town's Courthouse dates from 1819, standing on the site of an old English church and an even earlier Spanish Franciscan Abbey. It was gutted by fire in 1986, but had an arched, red-domed, octagonal entrance porch, sporting a fine pillared lantern. Facing this, the Courthouse's dome is echoed in the ornate arched, and pillar-lanterned, red cupola of the Rodney Memorial. The octagonal memorial housing the Romanesque statue of Admiral Lord George Rodney (1718-1792), by John Bacon stands in a sweeping colonnade of twelve classical columns. Carvings on the central 'temple', depict scenes from Rodney's defeat of the French fleet at the 'Battle of the Saints' in 1782. The statue, which features Rodney in an unlikely toga, was completed in 1801, and the cannon which stand either side were taken from the French vessel, Admiral de Grasse' flagship, the *Ville de Paris*.

King Street in Spanish Town has a wealth of old Georgian buildings, and the 1791 two-storey red-brick structure in the southern part of the town, with its vast courtyard, is the old barracks. Nearby, the district prison was built in 1714, and is the largest on the island. The Baptist Church on the old military parade ground dates from 1827. The historic Ferry Inn, just outside Spanish Town, is said to date back as far as 1684.

Courthouses

Historic courthouses feature in most towns across Jamaica. **Port Antonio**'s Courthouse, one of the island's oldest, dates from the 18th century and is a red-brick Georgian structure, with a cupola and iron verandahs. The **Mandeville** Courthouse is also Georgian and is faced in coral stone, with a horseshoe staircase leading up to its Doric-pillared portico. Black River's old courthouse is similarly porticoed. In **Montego Bay**, the Old Courthouse, was constructed in 1804, and The Cage, in the corner of the main square, was once used as a lock-up for slaves found abroad after the curfew. It was built in 1806. Known as the Slave Ring, the old amphitheatre near the courthouse is thought to have been used as a slave market. Just to the south of the courthouse is The Dome, an 18th-century sluice house which once controlled the town's water supply from The Creek.

Falmouth Courthouse was reconstructed in 1926 in its original 1815 Palladian style, including a handsome portico and double exterior staircase. Four Doric columns support the well-proportioned pediment. **Port Morant**'s courthouse was constructed in 1820 and is fronted by a monument to the slave leader, Paul Bogle. **St Ann**'s courthouse was built in 1866 and has a pedimented porch. The port of **Lucea** has an imposing Georgian courthouse, dating from the early 1800s. Its stone arched ground-floor frontage is surmounted by a timber-built second storey and a clock tower built after the style of a German Royal Guard helmet. The tower is supported by Corinthian-style columns and dates from 1817, when it was specially built to house the clock which should have been sent to St Lucia. **Christiana**'s courthouse is one of the more modern and dates from 1896. The courthouse in **Savanna-la-Mar** is notable for the domed, cast-iron fountain dating from 1887, that stands outside. Cast-iron was also the main ingredient of the numerous

Morant Bay Courthouse

clock towers which sprang up across Jamaica between 1890 and 1930. Most imposing of these is the clock tower of **Old Harbour**, the **May Pen** clock tower, that at **Chapelton**, and the one on the market in **Linstead**.

Special Places

Among Falmouth's beautifully preserved collection of restored Georgian and Regency buildings are the Albert George Market, with its curious roof, and the cut-stone warehouses at Hampden Wharf. The Phoenix Foundry is one of the earliest industrial complexes in Jamaica. Falmouth's Georgian buildings include its early Post Office block, and some are distinctive for their stone-built ground floors and wooden upper floors, with wrought-iron balconies and verandahs reaching out over the side-walk, supported on wooden columns.

Post office, Falmouth

More Georgian buildings can be seen in Montego Bay, like the red-brick house at 16 Church Street, dating from 1765, and buildings in Church Street, including the plantation-style police station with its verandahs supported by square, fluted columns. The Jamaica Telephone Company headquarters here is housed in a Georgian, pink stucco building, and there is the double Georgian merchant's home on Orange and Union Streets. There are pretty colonial dwellings at Port Maria, and in Port Antonio, where the 1900 De Montevin Lodge hotel is a delight in red brick and gingerbread fretwork, with carved hardwood interior details. East of Port Antonio is the neo-Grecian Folly, built in 1906 by an American entrepreneur, and abandoned shortly after.

In Lucea, on the north coast, the two-storey Charlotte Inn dates from the late 19th century, and is as simple in design as it is exuberant in decoration. It is a typical middle-class residence of the era. Seven stone steps lead up to the ground-floor open wrap-around balcony, echoed in the upper floor. An extension of the upper floor gallery forms a roof over the entrance porch, leading to a simple, glazed front door. All the house's windows are unusually glazed, and none has shutters. Simple, slender columns support the balcony and corrugated iron roof, and the roof-level porch frontage forms a weather-boarded, front facing gable, rather like a pediment. The columns form intricate tracery brackets where they meet the gallery floor and roof, and the brackets are linked with a gingerbread frieze which runs around the underside of both the balcony and the roof. Trelliswork forms the railings which enclose the lower and upper balcony. Painted in lemon yellow, with white trims and tracery, the entire building stands off the ground on stone blocks. Lucea is famous for its vernacular architecture, some of which goes back to the mid-1700s, and here many of the old timber and limestone buildings sport wide verandahs, clapboard frontages and gingerbread trims. Two houses which should not be missed are Noel Coward's 'Firefly', and Ian Fleming's 'Goldeneye', both on the north coast.

MARTINIQUE

Whereas the majority of early English colonists in the Caribbean aimed to make their fortunes in the tropics and return rich to England, the French settlers tended to view the islands as their home. They quickly laid out substantial towns in the manner of those in France, built for long-term occupancy and with all the cultural trappings of their homeland. Those islands settled by France, and especially Martinique, have a rich architectural heritage, encompassing a variety of buildings, from homesteads to forts, churches and public buildings.

Apart from the eight-year period between 1794 and 1802 when Britain held Martinique, this island has been under French influence since its first colonization by the Norman baron, Pierre Belain d'Esnambuc, in 1635. D'Esnambuc began by building Fort St Pierre, around which St Pierre, the 'Paris of the Antilles', later grew up. But one would be wrong to expect to encounter an almost unbroken succession of French architectural styles from the 17th century to the present day. For one of the worst disasters in the history of the Caribbean hit the island in May 1902, when the volcanic eruption of Mount Pelée wiped out the city of St Pierre and all but one of its 30,000 inhabitants. Had the volcano not erupted, St Pierre would undoubtedly stand as the best example of 350 years of French colonial architecture anywhere in the world. Now, it is sadly famous for the cataclysm that destroyed an entire town in a matter of minutes.

In 1639 a few of the islanders had opted to settle further south around another defence post, Fort Royal, now Fort-de-France, the island's capital. This settlement was established as a commercial centre in 1681. For two centuries, this town remained a cultural backwater compared to elegant St Pierre, and little architectural remains of note date from before the end of the 19th century. Worse, in 1890 a fire almost gutted Fort-de-France, leading to extensive reconstruction programmes.

As with almost all early Caribbean colonies, the oldest architectural remains in Martinique's capital are its ancient forts. Fort St Louis, once Fort Royal, dates from 1638 and extends out onto an arm of the harbour, which it was built to defend. This heavily bastioned fort is in a reasonable state of preservation as it is still in the hands of the army, and contains a maze of passages, ramparts and dungeons. In the 1670s, the fort was enlarged and ramparts were built at both ends of the promontory. Bartizans or turrets project from each angle of the parapets' trace, typical of early design, but much of its present superstructure dates from the 19th century. Low ceiling arches inside are said to have been intended to obstruct any invading Englishmen, who, it seems, were taller than their French counterparts. Several other forts were built later than Fort St Louis, around the 1680s, guarding different approaches to the city as it expanded.

In the 18th century, Fort-de-France was laid out in a geometric plan, with the large La Savane open space being located between

Fort St Louis and the town itself. Two canals, the Monsieur and Madame, run through the city, and it was in the Rivière Madame that the Martinican Gilbert Canque tested his prototype for the first propeller. Two imposing statues stand on La Savane. One, in Carrara marble by sculptor Vital Dubray, is of Napoleon's Empress Joséphine, looking across the bay to her birthplace in Trois Ilets (although it has been much vandalized and even beheaded); the other, in bronze, commemorates Belain d'Esnambuc.

The main building facing La Savane is the Schoelcher Library, named after Victor Schoelcher, the champion of emancipation and the man who decreed the abolition of slavery in 1848. It was designed in 1889 by Henri Pick, a contemporary of Gustave Eiffel, for the Caribbean Pavilion of the Paris Exhibition, after which the entire structure was dismantled and shipped to its present location in 1893. It comprises prefabricated cast-iron and metal components and is surmounted by a large glazed dome which lights the interior. The striking decorative work is picked out in coloured metal panels, and the impressive arched portal, in red, white and blue, is built under heavily ornate gables. A frieze records various events in the emancipation process. High-level arched windows surround the structure, which has been described as Romanesque/Byzantine/Egyptian in style. In 1973, the Schoelcher Library was registered as one of France's historic monuments.

Behind the Library is the Villa Bougenot and the beautifully proportioned Préfecture, with its columned entrance, first-floor balcony and parapet. Arched upper windows set off the pink-and-white facade. A wrought-iron balcony was prudently added to the late 19th-century Bougenot building after lessons learned in the 1890 fire. There are good examples of wrought-iron window screens on the 19th-century Military Commissariat building, which now houses the Departmental Museum. The green-and-white facade is also a pleasing example of early stucco work.

The only other significant public building in Fort-de-France is its Roman Catholic Cathedral. Before the Cathedral of St Louis was rebuilt in iron in 1895 by Henri Pick, six previous churches had stood on the same spot, all succumbing to either fire or earthquake. The present Romanesque structure was erected to the design of Gustave Eiffel (of the Paris tower fame) and had to be rebuilt and refaced to his design again in 1978. The cathedral's soaring buttressed and steel-reinforced spire rises some 200 feet. The church is

Cathedral of St Louis, Fort-de-France

known throughout the Caribbean as the 'Iron Cathedral'. Inside, the cathedral contains some attractive stained glass and iron balustrades.

The real architecture of Martinique, however, lies out on the island, away from the bustling, traffic-clogged city, although a stroll through its narrow streets and tall buildings – unusual in most Caribbean towns – reminds one of the French Quarter of New Orleans, with its pastel-shaded houses, wrought ironwork, gingerbread fretwork and filigree architectural embellishments.

In Didier, a residential suburb of Fort-de-France, for example, there are some beautifully simple two-storey stone buildings from the 1920s, with high-pitched roofs and prominent gables, many with Gothic-influenced wide barge boards, and louvre-shuttered dormer windows. Some have wrought-iron ridge decoration, and some display Haitian-like roof peaks, projecting from the corrugated iron roofs and topped by ornate finials. In Trois-Ilets, across the bay from Fort-de-France, there are some good examples of picture-frame windows, set in the wooden walls with louvred-shutters.

Although in ruins, the relics of old St Pierre can be viewed among the buildings of the modern town, reestablished after the 1902 disaster, with its rebuilt, twin-turreted, long-naved cathedral. A few remains of the old buildings still stand, like the theatre, built along the design of the Grand Théâtre in Bordeaux and seating 800 in its heyday. The old prison can be visited, and it was here that a certain Cyparis, the sole survivor of the disaster, lay in an underground dungeon (he was a habitual drunkard) and avoided the lethal volcanic gases. There are also the walls of 18th-century waterfront warehouses, and an old stone bridge, dating from 1766, also survived the catastrophe. Nearby is the island's oldest church, the 1640 Eglise du Fort, now in ruins. Little, however, remains of the 1635 Fort St Pierre, commemorated by a statue of Belain d'Esnambuc on the original site.

Plantation Houses

There are around a dozen plantation estate houses on Martinique which can be viewed, some restored, others in ruins. Nine of these are of particular architectural interest, either for their age or for their building design. It is interesting to note that their simple and unpretentious structure is both unlike the characteristic decorative or ornate architectural qualities of estate houses on other Caribbean islands and particularly un-French colonial in style. Most, in fact, look as though they have been imported from the farms of northeastern France and are in complete contrast to the elegant, lavishly-decorated town houses of the city. In contrast to the French architect Mansard's double-angled roof style, evolved in the 1630s, the mid-1700s estate houses' roofs in the French Caribbean are generally built with a double roof, where the lower slope flares out, providing shelter from the sun rather than rising steeply.

Probably Martinique's most famous progeny was the local girl who married the Emperor Napoleon, and Marie-Josèphe Rose Tascher de la Pagerie's home, Domaine de la Pagerie, at Trois-Ilets, is a tourist attraction. Joséphine's birthplace, a sugar estate mansion, was destroyed by a hurricane in 1766, but its remains and the chimney of the sugar factory can be seen. The main kitchen still stands as a museum. It is a remarkable replica of an 18th-century Normandy house, and, like most plantation houses on Martinique, is practical and basic, with few Caribbean features. Thick stone walls, heavy shutters and double doors and dormer windows emphasize its solidity, and a notable feature is the tiled roof. The early 18th-century church where Joséphine was baptized in 1763 still stands in Trois-Ilets.

The kitchen, La Pagerie, Martinique

Martinique is said to be the source of the distinctive roof tiling known as 'fish-scale' tiles. These overlapping, round-ended tiles can be seen on roofs throughout the Caribbean wherever the French had a foothold, such as in St George's, Grenada. Near to La Pagerie, is La Poterie, a factory dating from 1694, which produced not only these tiles, but other clay products including bricks. The pottery is on an historic estate which includes a manager's house, slave quarters, administration buildings, kiln and stores.

Le Gaoulé plantation house, on the south coast, is stone built and dates from 1740. It is said to be the oldest standing structure of its kind on Martinique. Its high main facade, sporting two gabled, dormer windows in the red-tiled roof, resembles a Norman country house. However, at the rear, an enclosed gallery under a vast sweep of low roof, also with two dormer windows, gives it a more typical island great house look. Wooden pillars support the overhang of the roof at the rear of the house. Quoins decorate the corners of the house and surround the louvre-shuttered windows. The walls are thick and on two sides are comprised of cemented stonework. The entire ground floor is one vast room.

Pécoul plantation house was built in a square plan in 1760 and is typical of the early French style of great house building. A large, tiled room takes up the centre of the house on the ground floor, surrounded by an enclosed gallery on all sides. The stone-built gallery is red-tiled up to the base of the second floor and has regular window openings protected by storm shutters and louvres. The living room walls are of double thickness, in case of hurricanes, and a wooden belvedere covers the upper floor bedrooms. The walls of the upper storey are tiled. The heavy entrance doors in the front of the house match those in the rear so that one can see right through the house when they are open. The ruins of the mill still contain the old waterwheel, which is constantly supplied by a canal system. Between the watermill and the great house is the barn-like estate manager's office.

Pécoul plantation house, Martinique

La Frégate estate house is a two-storey building dating from the 17th century. Its simple central structure has been surrounded by an enclosed, roofed, ground-floor gallery, with arched windows added in the 19th century. The remarkable steep roof of the main building is covered with fish-scale tiling and the ridge is decorated with ornate clay ornamentation. All the fenestration is semi-jalousied and protected by heavy storm shutters. A small building in the grounds, constructed in the same style as the great house, contains the servants' quarters and stables.

The Beauséjour plantation house dates from 1824 and is timber-clad on a masonry base. Its hipped roof spreads low and wide over enclosed galleries each side of the main house, which were added in the early 20th century. Louvred windows and doors let light and air into the galleries, and dormer windows are set into the terracotta-tiled roof. These tiles came to Martinique as ballast in ships. Gingerbread ornamentation on the eaves and gable windows gives a Victorian feel to this red-painted mansion, as do the ornate louvred windows which separate the main living space from the galleries.

Several of Martinique's magnificent plantation houses are now hotels, like the 19th-century Habitation Lagrange, with its double-turreted facade, or the beautiful 18th-century Manoir de Beauregard in Sainte-Anne. The Saint James plantation house, with its delightful gingerbread decoration, is now a museum of rum production. One of the best-restored Martinican estate houses is that of the Plantation Leyritz, set in the rugged north. Now a hotel, the old outhouses, sugar refining machinery and slave quarters are all preserved here. Other plantation sites include the 1658 Dominican Fond Saint-Jacques estate, which has a sugar purgerie and a chapel, rebuilt in 1769. When Father Jean-Baptiste Labat resided here between 1693 and 1705, he installed the most sophisti-cated rum distilling equipment of its age in the estate. Only ruined walls and part of the original canal system remain.

There are several early churches on Martinique worthy of note, of which the oldest still standing and dating from the 17th century is at Macouba. The Jesuit Church at Le Marin was built in 1766 and has an ornately decorated interior with a multi-coloured marble altar rescued from a wrecked Spanish galleon. At Case-Pilote there is a pretty 18th-century stone-built Baroque church, while Ajoupa Bouillon's church dates from 1848, and at Sainte-Marie the Jesuit-style church was built in about 1850. La Prêcheur is one of the

Church, Case-Pilote, Martinique

oldest villages on the island and contains a number of early, small dwellings and an 18th-century church. This northern village was the childhood home of Louis XIV's second wife, Mme de Maintenon.

But probably the most remarkable – and incongruous – church on the island is at Balata, just north of the capital on the scenic Route de la Trace. This extraordinary church, in its luxuriant tropical setting, dates from 1928 and was modelled on the Sacré-Coeur Basilica in Paris and erected as a World War I memorial. Smaller than the original, it nonetheless copies its Roman-Byzantine shape and white dome. There is also an old Benedictine monastery at Schoelcher, and the northern village of Basse-Pointe has a Hindu Indian temple, testament to the Indians who came here to work as indentured labourers in the 19th century.

Other buildings of note on Martinique include those typical 19th-century houses at La Trinité, in the east of the island, and Paul Gauguin's former house at Anse Turin (now an interesting museum), where the artist stayed in 1887 before moving on to

Tahiti. Nearby Le Carbet takes its name from the Carib thatched huts, although there is little sign of any such buildings and, instead, a small zoo. Finally, one of Martinique's most striking landmarks is the Phare de la Caravelle, a 1861 lighthouse, 450 feet high, on the east coast peninsula. The nearby ruined Château Dubuc owes its notoriety to the legend that its owner used to lure ships onto the treacherous rocks surrounding the Caravelle peninsula with a lantern so as to loot the wrecks.

1920s houses, Didier, Martinique

The historic, isolated outcrop of Diamond Rock, off the south-west coast of Martinique, held a strategic position during the Napoleonic Wars. For several years, French ships had been using the Rocher du Diamant to shelter behind when escaping from the British, who were based on Pigeon Island across the St Lucia Channel from Martinique. Diamond Rock lies a mile off the coast from the village of Le Diamant, across a stretch of water known as the Fours Channel. In late 1803, the British Commander Sir Samuel Hood, decided to capture and fortify the rock. The sheer-sided, 575-foot-high, Diamond Rock was then commandeered by 120 English sailors in 1804 and used as a base from which to bombard passing French vessels. The English built a fort on the rock, hoisting five cannon and supplies up the cliff's face from the ship below. Ships' rope ladders gave access from the shore to the battery, and a bos'n's chair and rope and bucket device transported supplies from ship to rock. Goats and rabbits were bred on the rock for fresh meat. Under Captain Maurice, they named the Rocher du Diamant as a British

Naval warship and it was commissioned as the sloop HMS *Diamond Rock*. This stationary warship so disrupted French convoys for 18 months, that a ship was sent to lay siege to the rock in May 1805. The besieged sailors on the unsinkable 'sloop' held out against French bombardment for three days and two nights. Eventually, the French fleet, arriving from Europe and chased by Nelson's ships, took up the fight. The French Admiral Villaret de Joyeuse arranged for a boatload of rum to run aground on the rock, more than assuaging the parched sailors' thirst. From then on, after a continuous barrage against the rock, the French had no problem storming and taking the garrison, the remains of which can still be seen. Captain Maurice was at first court-martialled in Barbados for surrendering the rock and later congratulated for his efforts against the French by Horatio Nelson. Ships of the British Royal Navy still salute the rock as they pass by.

MONTSERRAT

Note: The eruption of Montserrat's Soufrière Hills volcano from 1995 onwards has covered large parts of the island with volcanic lava and dust, costing scores of lives and creating untold misery. Plymouth has been destroyed, as have many villages and farms. The following short account of the island's architectural heritage serves to remind readers of Montserrat before the volcano and to suggest what one day might be restored.

In 1632, Sir Thomas Warner led a party of Irish and English Roman Catholic immigrants from St Kitts to settle on Montserrat, escaping religious persecution. More Catholic migrants arrived, thanks to Cromwell's deportation of Irish political prisoners. Skirmishes with the French flared intermittently for 150 years until, in 1783, Montserrat was returned to British ownership. It has remained a colony to this day. During the 18th century, this small island became an important sugar producer, with thousands of slaves replacing the original European labourers.

The largest house on the island is the imposing Government House, an 18th-century mansion, completely renovated in 1995. It is a large two-storey Creole-style house, with wrap-around gallery supported by round pillars, and has windows in its three gables, one

Architectural Heritage of the Caribbean

of which is decorated with a shamrock, relating to the Irish heritage of the island. Tiny Plymouth, the capital, named after the Pilgrim Fathers' New England settlement, has two churches, the 19th-century Methodist Church, and the 18th-century St Patrick's Roman Catholic Church.

The old Courthouse dates from the 18th century and is housed in a galleried Creole-style house by the waterfront. The town's typical Caribbean buildings are two-storey, with the ground floor being built of volcanic rock and the upper floor of weatherboard, with louvred and shuttered windows, often gaily painted, and gingerbread fretwork detail and trims. Roofs are often made of corrugated iron, and shady balconies add to their elegance. The arched stonework of the old Georgian waterfront warehouses is topped with wooden upper storeys. Much of the building stones arrived here as ship's ballast from Dorset in England. The old vaulted powder magazine in Plymouth, used as a jail, was built to a French design in 1664 and is one of few of this shape anywhere. There is a war memorial in the town centre, with a bell turret. St Anthony's Church, just north of the town, was dedicated between 1623 and 1666, and much of the stonework dates from 1640. It was rebuilt in 1730. The Montserrat Historic Museum was housed in the tower of an 18th-century sugar mill on Richmond Hill.

The Waterworks Estate house, built in 1741, is almost barn-like, simply built in stone and purely functional. It consists of two corrugated-iron, hip-roofed stone buildings, at angles to each other. A gabled, roofed porch projects from the front of the main building, standing on an open verandah and reached by stone steps. The verandah runs along the left-hand side of the frontage from the porch and is covered by the roof of the second abutting wing. The verandah continues around the side of the second block and around the entire rear of the house. Six storm-shuttered windows run on one level along the front of the entrance. An old canal channels water to the abandoned remains of the watermill nearby, used to grind sugar-cane.

There are a several forts located on the island, like that at Kinsale, built by Governor Briskett above Plymouth in 1664, and Fort Barrington, which dates from the 18th century. Fort St George overlooks Plymouth, with cannon in its two open-plan gun batteries. It was originally built by the French in 1782 and its powder magazine has been reconstructed. The Bransby Point Fortification, with its restored cannon, is another of the numerous defensive posts which surround Plymouth. Out on the island, Harris Anglican Church dates from 19th century, and the Bethel Methodist Church dates from around 1900. Galways Estate sugar plantation, established in the 1600s, is a complete collection of 17th- and 18th-century buildings, with mansion ruins, stables, storehouse, slave houses, a cemetery, boiler house, mule mill and windmill. It was worked for two hundred years, and some of the buildings which date from the 1750s have been partly restored. Old Roads estate was once a plantation house, and Farrels Farm, near the village of Harris, was once a distillery.

NEVIS

Reminded by the white clouds that drift around the central peak of Spanish snow-covered mountains, Columbus named this spectacular island 'Las Nieves' in 1493. It was 135 years after Columbus's visit that permanent settlers were to come to the place the indigenous Caribs called Oualie ('land of beautiful water'). Before they did, however, in 1607 one Captain John Smith built the first European structure on the island, a gallows! He stopped just long enough to hang a few mutineers and then sailed away. The first eighty English planters arrived in 1628, settling in a place they named Jamestown. They built a fortress above the town, Fort Ashby, but Jamestown was engulfed by a tidal wave and earthquake in 1690. As a result, there are few domestic buildings on the island which pre-date the deluge. At one time, there were a total of eight forts along the coast, extending north from Charlestown, the capital. One inhabitant who survived the disaster, 'Redlegs Greaves', went on to become a pirate, while later settlers islanders set about establishing a new capital at Charlestown. It was established on Gallows Bay, the site chosen by John Smith for his executions.

Today Nevis is learning to live from tourism, and many of its former plantation houses have been renovated to provide guests with luxurious accommodation. This tiny island co-exists uneasily with its larger sister, St Kitts, but there have been several attempts to break the connection and establish what would be one of the world's smallest independent states.

The oldest surviving building is St Thomas' Church near Pinney's Beach, dating from 1643 but re-erected several times in the wake of hurricanes and earthquakes, as was the later 17th-century St Paul's Church in Charlestown, probably built after Jamestown fell into the sea. The present church was built in the town in 1890s. The Methodist Church here dates from 1790, while the Jewish Cemetery is much older, going back to at least 1679.

The first public building to be erected here was the coral stone colonial Courthouse, with its little box-shaped, bell turret. It was mostly destroyed by fire in 1874, and there is a library on the second floor where some extraordinary roof trusswork can be seen, as well as the mechanism of the Courthouse clock. The building's tiny square clock tower was added between 1909 and 1910. A typical colonial town house stands a little further up the same street as the Courthouse and was built in 1811. Many of the buildings of this era, and those constructed a little later, are handsome stone town houses, with wooden upper floors and projecting balconies, featuring intricate gingerbread fretwork decoration.

One of the earliest homes is the Alexander Hamilton House, where the future US Secretary to the Treasury and ally of Washington was born in 1757 and lived for five years. The reconstructed Georgian-style stone house, with its original gate and steps, is now the Museum of Nevis History, and further displays are kept in the wooden frame house next door. Perhaps the most impressive structure in this small town's history was the stone-built grand old Bath Hotel, once 200 feet long and 100 feet wide, at the south end of town. The hotel was built by the Huggins family in 1778 over a series of sulphur springs and catered to Nevis's wealthy spa clientele. The bath house is still operational, but the hotel, which even had a ballroom, is in ruins. Its vaulted ceiling, stone corridors and wide verandahs can still be seen. This was the best-known spa in the British Caribbean. During the spa's hey-day, Nevis was known as the 'Queen of the Caribees', so important were the island's visitors and so grand were its plantation great houses. The recently built Nelson Museum nearby houses numerous artefacts from the time Horatio Nelson spent on the island.

The Treasury Building, dating from around 1840, has an elegant frontage, with a fully louvred, wooden first floor which extends over the front of the stone-built ground floor, supported by five slender wooden columns and a single stone wall. It is now roofed in corrugated iron sheeting. Government House, dating from 1909, is a grand two-storey structure, fronted with a wooden pedimented

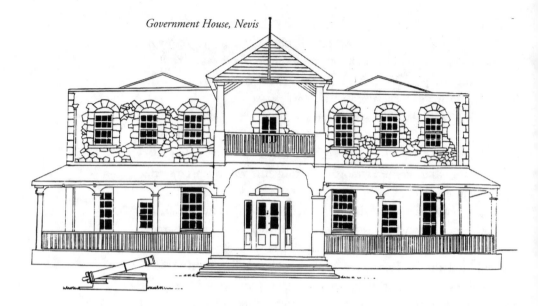

Government House, Nevis

portico and a tin-roofed ground-floor verandah, supported by six slim wooden columns, finialed and bracketed. The seven windows in its simple facade are carefully picked out and outlined in stone, with arched decoration over each.

Fort Charles was built at the southern end the town in 1680. By 1734, it covered an area of six acres and housed thirteen cannon, with two bastions facing the sea and two ramparts and moats on the landward side. The perimeter wall, powder magazine and cistern are all that now remain. Of the twelve open batteries which were once dotted around the island, only that at Mosquito Point and the battery and lookout on Saddle Hill, built in 1740, remain visible.

St John's Church, at Fig Tree Village records the birth of Alexander Hamilton and Horatio Nelson's marriage to Frances (Fanny) Nisbet, in 1787. Tombstones in the graveyard go back to 1682, the date of the church's original construction. The Montpelier Great House, where Nelson met Fanny and their marriage took place, has now been converted into expensive tourist accommodation.

Admiral Lord Nelson's ships would often put in at Charlestown and take water from the wells near Cotton Ground, just north of the town, between 1784 and 1787. Nelson met the widow of Dr Josiah Nisbet, Frances or Fanny Nisbet, at Montpelier House. Fanny was living on the proceeds of her deceased husband's 64-acre plantation on the north coast of Nevis. After a brief courtship, Nelson married the 26-year-old Fanny on Sunday 11 March 1787. The marriage took place in Montpelier House itself. The marriage was recorded in St John's Church in nearby Fig Tree Village, where the church register reads: 'Horatio Nelson, Esquire, Captain of His Majesty's Ship, the *Boreas*, to Frances Herbert Nisbet, Widow.' It was witnessed below the entry by the Duke of Clarence, Nelson's best man. Nelson sailed back to England with his new wife and five-year-old stepson that same month. The romance was not to last, for in 1799 Nelson fell in love with Emma, Lady Hamilton. Fanny lived on until 1831.

The numerous sugar and cotton planters' mansions stand in various states of repair across the island. Two of the earliest are the ruined Montravers estate house, with its old slave prison, and Mount Pleasant great house, both dating from the 1770s. Clay Ghaut and the Montpelier mills were built in 1785, and the John Pinney mill dates from 1790. Near Clay Ghaut, the Old Manor estate house is an excellent example of a late 17th-century great house and has been renovated as an hotel. The Nisbet Plantation House is also splendidly restored and the mill here dates from 1778. The Coconut Walk cattle mill was built in 1804. Its round, stone tower stands some forty feet high and is twenty feet in diameter at ground level and fifteen feet at the top. Another mill is at Golden

Nisbet Plantation House, Nevis

Rock, but the better preserved great house here dates from 1815. Eden Brown Estate was built in about 1740, but was never occupied and is reputed to be haunted. Its grand mansion and sugar mill are now in ruins. At New River village there is a sugar factory dating from 1800, and there are a string of other mills on the island, like Dasents and the windmill at the Zetlands plantation. Three more windmills were built at the end of 19th century: Dunbars, Hanely and Powells. There are also eight steam engines, used in the sugar business, at Hamiltons, Prospect, Cane Garden, Hardtimes, Fothergills, Maddens, Farm Estate and at Round Hill.

Many of the shingle walled cabins or *cases* stand on stilts made from blocks of volcanic stone, with shuttered openings for windows and shingle roofs sporting low peaks. Each peak represented the addition of a new room to the original dwelling. Thought to be one of the oldest wooden house in the Caribbean, the wood-shingled Hermitage plantation house dates from 1740. The original lignum vitae hardwood frame of the central living space can still be seen. Later additions include the square, pavilion-like kitchen building. Four, square-cut pillars support the roof of the tiny porch of this two-storey structure, which is approached by stone steps, leading up to a wide, double, glazed door, and twin windows. A little ginger-bread fretwork embellishes the porch, and an upper-floor sash window is set under the gables of the shingled house front. Side windows have lattice covers and storm shutters. The internal ceilings are timber-beamed, and the upper-floor ceilings are open to the roof, with intricate cross beaming. Louvred doors open onto a side gallery. The many additions to the original house have created a complex of structures in various styles. In front of the house is a large, round, water cistern, fed by pipe from the guttering, and an ancient water filter.

Elsewhere on the island, the few other points of architectural interest include the ruins of the Cottle Church, built in 1824, the first chapel where slaves were allowed to worship with their masters. St James's Windward, near Hick's Village was built in 1679 and contains one of the only three crucifixes with a black Christ in the entire Caribbean. St George's Church at Gingerland was originally built in 1670. Near the airport in the north of the island, the little village of Newcastle contains some picturesque houses. Nearby is the Redoubt, a fort built to withstand Carib attacks in the early 17th century.

PUERTO RICO

There are few places in the world which can rival Puerto Rico's Spanish colonial architectural heritage, and in the Caribbean, the Dominican Republic and Cuba have lacked the resources to renovate their buildings to the same extent. Benefiting from its 'free and associated state' (some say colonial) connection with the US, this third largest island in the Greater Antilles has the best preserved Spanish colonial sites in the Caribbean. The influx of tourist income has also contributed to maintaining not only the capital's historic quarters, but to the conservation of architectural heritage throughout the island. Evidence of Amerindian construction can be seen at Caguana. Colonized by the conquistador Juan Ponce de León in 1508, the island was first named San Juan Bautista, and the bay on which the island's capital was founded was called Puerto Rico, or Rich Port, reflecting the founder's anticipation of the island's wealth. Later, the island's name was exchanged for that of the bay, and the capital became known as San Juan.

San Juan

The old city of San Juan is a UNESCO World Heritage Site, recognized in 1983. UNESCO has named six historic monuments of importance in the old city, which contains around 800 Spanish colonial buildings, of which more than 400 have been restored in recent years. The colonial centre is located on a narrow peninsula and some streets are paved with blue-grey *adoquines* or cobble stones which came to the New World as ballast in Spanish galleons. From its founding in 1510, San Juan was constantly a target for attacks by Caribs, pirates, privateers and various navies. The city was relocated to its present position after the original settlement was abandoned. The old city is situated on a small island and was connected to the mainland by a causeway, the Puenta de San Antonio, for security.

From its inception until the early 1800s, San Juan was first and foremost a military town. Military architects designed the fortifications and city walls, which embraced a seven-square-block area of the islet. Churches, residences and official buildings also grew up here until, in the mid-1800s, space ran out. This part of San Juan was laid out around fine plazas, and virtually all of its earlier architecture remains. As this was a military sector, the central square was the Plaza de Armas.

This was the most easterly of Spain's settlements in the Caribbean and therefore the most vulnerable, although it was protected by La Fortaleza, dating from 1520, and a later, stone-built fort, begun in 1532. The tower and gate date from 1540, when the fort was completed, but most of the architecture dates from the 1800s. The Fortaleza, one of six UNESCO sites, is San Juan's oldest fort, once known as Santa Carolina. It has a mosaic- and marble-lined chapel, medieval towers and stained glass galleries, and contains a mahogany staircase. Once used as a bullion store but primarily the Governor's Palace, the structure was a failure as a fort, and construction of the larger San Felipe del Morro fortification began as soon as the Fortaleza was completed. Drawn by the rumour of two million ducats worth of gold stored in the fort, Sir Francis Drake stormed the Fortaleza from the sea in November 1595. The 25-cannon firepower of the Morro, however, proved too much for Drake's fleet, and it was left to the Duke of Cumberland to take the prize from the landward side in 1598.

The English occupied the Fortaleza for just eight weeks before losses, due to an epidemic of influenza, drove them home. The Dutch, under Boudewijn Hendrikzoon managed to land their forces between the Morro and the Fortaleza in 1625, setting fire to the fort and much of San Juan, before retreating. In 1640, the Span-

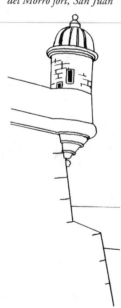

Bartizan at the San Felipe del Morro fort, San Juan

ish began reconstruction of the fort, and, by the 1650s, San Juan became the main Presidio of Spain's New World colonies, with seven forts linked by stone walls surrounding the city. The Fortaleza was expanded in 1800 and again in 1846 and has forty rooms. This is still the Governor's residence, as it has been for more than 400 years, and is therefore the New World's longest inhabited executive residence. A total of 170 island governors have lived here.

The vast Castillo San Felipe del Morro fort on the headland dates from 1540, when the first gun battery was installed. The famous Italian military architect, Juan Bautista Antonelli, devised a six-level gun emplacement, replacing the original 25 cannon in 1589, and the fort was strengthened again in 1591. After the successful defence of the city against Drake's aggression in 1595, the Morro fortress was captured only once, three years later.

The Dutch were repelled in 1625 and the present building was given its final shape and design in 1783. It rises 140 feet above the sea and contains a complex of bastions, underground tunnels and chambers. A moat, now dry, surrounds the fort, and a massive

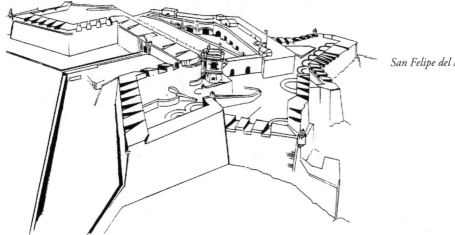

San Felipe del Morro

arched step-flanked ramp gives access to the lower ramparts. This section of the fort is called the Santa Bárbara Bastion. Dome-capped corner watch-turrets (*garitas*) are typical of Spanish military architecture and project from the steep angled stone walls, which are twenty feet thick, giving an all-round view and providing for unimpeded defensive fire. The fort was last attacked in 1898 during the Spanish-American War when the highest point of the fort was destroyed. It has been rebuilt as the Port of San Juan Lighthouse and is a national historic site, administered by the National Park Service. Between the Morro fort and the sea is the San Juan cemetery, with its 19th-century circular chapel.

The massive city walls, another UNESCO site, had six gates and encircle the old city. They were begun in 1630 and form one of the most complete examples of Spanish colonial fortifications left in the New World. Sandstone blocks, cemented together by a mortar of limestone, sand and water, went to build two parallel 42-foot high walls. The gaps between the blocks were filled with sand, and the walls were slanted as a protective measure, ranging in thickness from twenty feet at the base to twelve feet at the top. The walls surround the seven blocks of the old city and are punctuated by fortresses, garitas and city gates. The Puerta de San Juan is the oldest of the town's entrances, dating from 1520, and still protected by huge wooden gates.

The Castillo San Cristóbal, also a UNESCO heritage site, was added to the city's defences between 1766 and 1772 on the site of an older fort, built in 1678. It was then reworked in 1783, rising to a height of 150 feet. This fort guards the eastern side of the old city and is built to a classic design, with five independent bastions, each linked by a moat and a tunnel, surrounding a main keep. Each bastion was designed to be self-sufficient. Cannon are strategically placed around its 27 acres of ramparts, tunnels and arches. The impregnable system of battlements, passages and sub-forts was reputedly devised by two 'Wild Geese' Irishmen, fleeing religious oppression in their homeland. Alejandro O'Reilly and Tomas O'Daly designed their intricate arrangement to ensure that the fort could not be taken until the ramparts were first secured. Henceforth, the fort was never attacked. The San Cristóbal Fort is the second largest Spanish fortification to be built in the New World, just five acres smaller than the Cabaña Fortress in Old Havana.

Fort San Jerónimo was added to the city's defences in 1788. Located at the islet's eastern tip, this fort was damaged in 1797 by an English attack and rebuilt in 1799. It was restored in 1983 and is now a military museum. Outside the walls to the south is the arsenal, dating from 1800, and once the old Spanish naval base. The Bastion de las Palmas on the town walls also protected the city, and the fort of El Cañuelo was built from 1608 on the Isla de Cabras opposite El Morro to command the sea channel.

San Juan's San José church was begun in 1530 and is the second oldest and finest episcopal edifice in the Western Hemisphere. This beautiful but austere building, with its plain white-plastered walls, took a century to construct. Coral stone walls and Romanesque arches support the domes and remarkable vaulted ceilings of the medieval-designed chapel, which are ochre-tiled. Once the convent chapel of the Dominican monastery, San José is one of the best examples of Gothic church architecture in the Americas. The church contains six side chapels, including the beautiful Rosary Chapel. Originally dedicated to St Thomas Aquinas, Ponce de León's family adopted the church as their place of worship, and it was later to be Ponce's last resting-place in 1559. After he died in Florida and was returned to Puerto Rico, the conquistador's remains were interred in San José church before being removed to the city's cathedral in 1908. Ponce de León's coat of arms hangs over the altar, and a 1797 statue stands in the nearby Plaza de San José, cast from English cannonballs dating from an unsuccessful attack that year.

Building of the Dominican Convent next door began in 1523, and this edifice housed the New World's second university (after Santo Domingo). In 1598 the Duke of Cumberland studied here during his brief occupation of San Juan, and the Dutch used it as officers' quarters in 1625. The interior has a spacious patio with double-columned arched cloisters, forming a gallery around the inner courtyard. The library has been restored to its original 16th-century appearance, and the building, now home to the Institute of Puerto Rican Culture, contains an ornate 18th-century altar and early artefacts. To the west stands the attractive Cuartel de Ballajá, the 1864 barracks, stone-built in Classical style with an attractive staircase and large patio. It once housed soldiers and cavalry horses.

The two-storey and balconied house next to the San José church houses the Pablo Casals museum. The famous cellist resided in Puerto Rico for the last 16 years of his life, from 1957 to 1973, and the museum is a celebration of his contribution to cello music. The Casa de los Contrafuertes (the Buttress House) is in the immediate vicinity. So called for the wide buttresses which support the wall next to the plaza, this early 18th-century building is said to be the oldest private house in San Juan. It is now a museum and includes a pharmacy. Just north of the Buttress House is the Callejón del Hospital, or Hospital Alley, one of the last two remaining stepped streets in the old city.

The Governor's mansion, Ponce de León's crenellated Casa Blanca, was built in 1523. The Casa Blanca is a fortress-like residence, built on the site of an earlier wooden-framed structure dating from 1521 by Ponce de León's son-in-law. The conquistador himself never lived in the stone house, as he left on the fatal expedition to search for the legendary Fountain of Youth in Florida. This is one of the city's oldest buildings and is now a museum of archaeology. Furnishings include a throne and contemporary furniture. Ponce de León's descendants lived in the house for around 250 years. Nearby, the Casa Rosa, a beautiful example of Spanish colonial architecture, was built by the military in 1812. The Casa del Cabildo or Alcaldía (the first Town Hall) on Calle Cristo was constructed between 1604 and 1789. It is designed with a double arcade and balconies, flanked by two towers, and has a grand inner courtyard. It was intended to be a reconstruction of the Alcaldía in Madrid. The building has the additions of a double-arcaded facade, coral stone arches and a staircase leading to a huge assembly room, which opens out onto an arcaded balcony. It stands adjacent to the Plaza de Armas, one of the city's oldest squares. The Bishop's Palace, now the Diputación Provincial, dates from the 18th century and also stands on the Plaza de Armas, decorated with 19th-century bronze statues of the four seasons. Once a parade ground, the plaza now contains fountains, bandstands and stores. Also on the square is the old Royal Treasury and the 17th-century jail and barracks, now occupied by the Real Intendencia, a building in neo-Classical style erected in 1851.

The cathedral of San Juan Bautista dates originally from 1521 and had a thatched roof. Work was halted by hurricanes until its Gothic interior was built in 1540. All that remains of the original 1540 structure are its four Gothic-vaulted chapels and the beautiful circular staircase. The interior's main features are this rare wheel staircase and the marble tomb of Ponce de León, brought here from San José church in 1908. The present structure, with its high triple-stepped Classical facade, was built in 1802. Three red-and-white cupolas top the beige-and-white stuccoed edifice.

San Juan Cathedral and El Convento

The nearby Carmelite Convent was constructed in the 17th century and is now a hotel (El Convento), with arched balconies around the inner courtyard, checkerboard tiled flooring and a dining room in the old chapel. The Episcopal Palace originally dates from the 16th century, was burned by the Dutch in 1625 and was rebuilt in 1733. The statues in the Plazuela de la Rogativa, where the Convent stands, commemorate a British retreat of 1797 from the city. The invaders, it seems, mistook a priest and his torch-bearing followers for a band of Spanish reinforcements. The monument was donated to San Juan in 1971. The San Juan Museum of Art and History is housed in the attractive old building nearby, constructed as a marketplace in 1855.

The Capilla de Santo Cristo was built in 1753. A legend surrounds the silver altar, dedicated to the Christ of Miracles. In 1753, two suitors, competing for the love of a local beauty, raced around the city on horseback. One of the youths' horses plunged over the cliff near the site of the chapel, and the young man miraculously survived the fall, although suffering terrible injuries. A witness to the accident promised to build a chapel near the precipice, should the young man's life be saved. Opposite, the Casa del Libro, or House of Books, in an old 18th-century house, contains an exhibit of over 5,000 volumes, some printed before the 16th century. A beautiful Spanish colonial mansion next door houses the Museum of Art of Puerto Rico, while the imposing Aduana, on Plaza de Hostos, is home to the Customs Authority. Almost overpowering the Plaza de Hostos is the Banco Popular de Puerto Rico building, dating from the 1930s. The art-deco facade, complete with eagle cameos, is distinctive for its tall windows with prominent mullions. The Princesa was once a prison, but is now used by the Tourist Board, and the old Spanish hospital, built in 1877, now serves as the City Archives and General Library. It was also once used as the city jail.

The Plaza Colón has a statue of Columbus dating from 1893, faced by the 1832 Tapia Theatre, named after a local dramatist, Alejandro Tapia y Rivera (1826-1882). It was originally financed by a one-cent tax on every loaf of bread sold, but its recent restoration cost 300 times the price of the original building. On the east side of the square is the city's Old Casino, built in around 1890 in the style of a Louis XIV mansion. It has a copper cupola and an elegant ballroom, with an elaborate plasterwork ceiling and twelve-foot chandelier. Not far from the Casino is the Casa Olímpica, or Olympian House, a handsome neo-Classical building dating from 1914.

On Calle Fortaleza is the 18th-century house of a merchant, known as the Casa del Callejón, now a museum. Two separate exhibits occupy this building: the Colonial Architecture Museum contains much information on old San Juan's buildings, and the Museum of the Puerto Rican Family displays the lifestyle of a typical family from the 19th century.

Old San Juan is a delight to walk around. The houses in the old city's seven blocks are pastel-painted in blues and yellows, with white fenestration and doorways. Old iron gas lanterns add authenticity to the steep, narrow alleyways and plazas, paved with adoquines. Houses display decorative wrought-iron railings and balconies, with louvred and sometimes shuttered windows. Inner courtyards are a feature of most of these old town houses, many surrounded by galleries, reached by colourfully-tiled staircases. The Casa San José, now a hotel, is a typical *San Juanero* town house, with three storeys of wooden balustrades around an inner courtyard, reached by a tiled stairway. Inside, the Mudéjar ceilings set off the marble checkerboard tiled flooring and antique furniture. One of these houses, on Calle Luna, is listed as the oldest whorehouse in the New World.

Outside old San Juan, the large urban area includes expensive modern suburbs, hotel strips and sprawling low-cost housing projects. On the edge of the colonial zone, the Capitolio, modelled on the Capitol in Washington DC, with its white pillars, dome and dramatic rotunda, was built by local architect, Rafael Carmoega in 1925. East of San Juan, the cream-and white-San Patricio Church is one of the island's oldest parish churches and dates from 1645. It is the earliest church in continual use on Puerto Rico. The University of Puerto Rico was founded in 1903 in Río Piedras, and the town itself (now part of the urban conurbation) was founded in 1714 with its imposing church of Nuestra Señora del Pilar.

Bayamón is the site of the island's oldest sugar mill, and its interesting buildings on the Barbosa Pedestrian Mall, including the 19th-century Barbosa House, have decorated porches. The Central Park contains some distinctive historical buildings. The neo-Classical City Hall is now a museum, and the Catholic church dates from the 18th century. Shortly before Bayamón on the highway from San Juan is Caparra, the first European settlement founded by

Ponce de León in 1508. There is a museum here, as well as the remains of the original fort.

On the west coast of Puerto Rico is the island's third town, **Mayagüez**, with several sites of architectural interest. The Plaza Colón was set out in 1760 with the foundation of the town and contains 17 bronze statues, including one of Columbus which originally came from Barcelona. The Classical Alcaldía or Town Hall and Roman Catholic Church face the square. Both the domed Yaguez Theatre and the old Post Office are historic buildings, and the Custom House dates from the 1920s.

Picturesque **San Germán**, south-east of Mayagüez, is the second oldest settlement on Puerto Rico. After several attempts at finding a secure location, the first as early as 1512, the town was eventually founded in the foothills of the mountain range in 1573. San Germán was named after the second wife of King Ferdinand, Germaine de Foix, and is the second city to be included in the National Register of Historic Places. Largely unspoilt, the town's charming white colonial town houses surround paved plazas. Dominican friars built the Porta Coeli Church in Spanish Baroque and Gothic style in 1606. Located on Parque Santo Domingo, this is the oldest church site under the US flag and one of the few pure neo-medieval churches existing in the New World. Brick steps lead up to the church, which contains an original palm wood Mudéjar ceiling supported by ironwood beams and an ancient balcony. The vast church doors are of timber surmounted by a pediment containing a batten skylight of the same wood. The pews and altar are all original, and the altarpiece was painted in the late 18th century. The chapel was restored in 1878.

In San Germán are some fine examples of 16th- to 18th-century Spanish houses, once the homes of wealthy coffee barons. They contain some of the best examples of hand-carved mediopuntas, the lacy, half-screen room dividers. There are several recognizable architectural styles: 1850s Spanish colonial, 1880s criollo style, early 20th-century neo-Classical style, 1930s art-deco, and from the 1960s, international style. Once called the two most beautiful homes on the island, the Acosta y Fores House is of traditional criollo timber construction, dating from 1917, with stencilled walls in each room, while the 1920s Juan Ortiz Perichi House, designed by Luis Pardo Fradera, contains a curved balcony and pitched roofs over its multilevel design. The Tomás Vivoni House, named after its architect, dates from 1913 and contains Queen Anne style elements, a tower and gables.

Ponce, the 'Pearl of the South', is Puerto Rico's second largest city, located on the south coast. The city contains some interesting old Spanish colonial style houses and boasts no fewer than 1,000 historic buildings, 600 of which have been restored. Two monumental bronze lions by sculptor Victor Ochoa guard the entrance to the old part of the city. Ponce's central plaza is made up of the Plaza Degetau and the Plaza Muñoz Rivera, with the Spanish-influenced Cathedral of Nuestra Señora de Guadalupe on the site of the original 1670 church. The pillars are Classical, and its twin towers are surmounted by rounded silver domes.

Here there is a beautifully restored neo-Classical town house dating from 1899, the Casa Armstrong-Poventud. It is fronted by caryatid columns and contains a display of furniture through the

Cathedral of Nuestra Señora de Guadalupe, Ponce

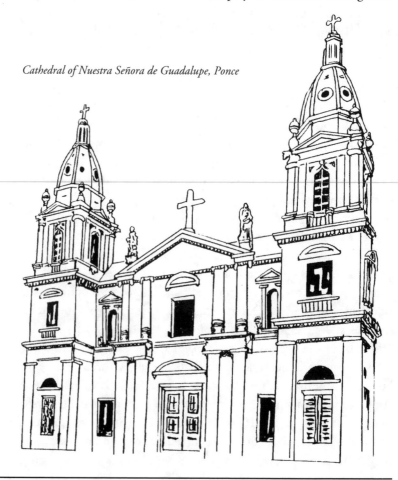

ages. This is the earliest example of neo-Classical architecture in Ponce. The 1911 Casa Salazar, is an architectural gem, combining Moorish and neo-Classical styles, with porch balconies, interior patios, wood and iron columns, vitrales, fixed jalousies, mosaics and pressed-tin ceilings. It is now the Museum of the History of Ponce. The Casa Seralles, is also in neo-Classical style and dates from 1911. The Casa Wiechers-Villaronga is one of the best examples of neo-Classical house styles, crossed with Baroque embellishments such as mouldings and garlands, Ionic columns and art-nouveau railings. It was built by the architect Alfredo Wiechers in 1912. Both Calle Cristina and Calle Mayor are notable for the wrought iron work and decorative balconies of their buildings.

The old Fire Station behind the cathedral dates from 1883 and was built for an agricultural fair. Behind its striking red-and-black facade, featuring arched windows and towers, cornices and crenellations, the interior, with its beautiful staircase, has been lovingly restored. The most important modern structure is the city's two-storey Museum of Art, designed in 1965 by American architect, Edward Durrel Stone, the architect of New York's Museum of Modern Art. It features hexagonal rooms, a patio with a fine wooden central staircase and a fountain. The 19th-century criollo Bertoli Calderoni House contains the Museum of Puerto Rico Music. The neo-Classical Teatro la Perla, fronted by six classical columns, is the work of the Italian architect, Bertoli, and dates from 1864 and was reconstructed in 1940.

On the shoreline are a number of old warehouse buildings, but the wealthy of Ponce built their mansions up on El Vigía hill. A good example is the 1933 Castillo Serrallés, built in typical Spanish revival style with Mudéjar influences around a beautiful courtyard. The interior wood panelling and the unusual dining room, with its heavy carved mahogany and wrought-iron doors, add to the opulence of this classic sugar baron's villa.

Elsewhere on Puerto Rico, there are several architectural attractions, North of Ponce is the old coffee plantation of Hacienda Buena Vista established by Salvador de Vives in 1833. The two-storey estate house, with its exquisite patio, is lavishly restored. The upper floors are entirely of wood, with native *ausubo* (ironwood) beams, and are bordered on three sides by a balcony. The plantation and its machinery were renovated by the Conservation Trust of Puerto Rico in the 1980s. It is now a working museum of the coffee industry, operated by a network of water channels which turn a system of waterwheels, powering the pulping, fermentation, rinsing and crushing machinery. A rice milling machine, cotton gin, and a corn mill were added in the mid-1800s. The entire complex consists of the estate house, corn and coffee mills, a masonry storage shed, which was used as a hurricane shelter, and slave quarters. A similar coffee plantation house, dating from the 1780s, is Hacienda Gripinas, now a *parador* or hotel located in Jayuya.

Puerto Rico contains a good many churches of interest to the architectural historian. The 19th-century Spanish colonial church at **Lares** has an unusually arched roof, and the red-roofed single-naved church of **Barranquitas** has a single campanile lodged to the left of its simple scallop-pedimented facade. The white-and-beige church of San Felipe at **Arecibo** has a single bell tower above the facade and an unusually large cupola at the far end of the nave. **Coamo**, famous for its hot springs, was founded in 1538 and has an 18th-century church with large buttresses and vaulted naves. The elegant masonry house nearby is now a museum. Nearby, the ruins of a hotel built here in 1848 as a spa resort can be seen as part of the newer parador.

In the plaza at **Cayey**, the 1813 church has an unusually long nave, a curious single square tower, and the transept is overlooked by the church's dome. The Cathedral of **Caguas** has been severely damaged by numerous hurricanes, yet its 1856 facade still stands opposite the Alcaldía. The Cathedral of Our Lady of Monserrat at **Hormigueros** is one of the most spectacular in the country. Rising above the town, its stepped, ivory-coloured towers soar up to crimson-red domes, topped with simple white wooden crosses. The sedate church at **Guayama** is perfectly proportioned, with twin, square-topped bell towers, each with four bells flanking a small-domed central portico and facing a broad walkway with its large stone fountain. Here also are some highly decorative old Spanish colonial buildings, with ornate wrought-iron terraces, decorative rejas, and fretwork mediopuntas. Some of the walls of these buildings are opulent with highly sophisticated stucco and appliqué work.

There are eleven important lighthouses around the coast of Puerto Rico and on its offshore islands. Some are of historic architectural interest. On the north-easternmost point of the island at **Las Cabezas de San Juan** is the restored neo-Classical building of El Faro lighthouse, dating from 1882. Exactly diagonally across the island, on the furthest point in the south-west, the **Cabo Rojo** light-house was also built in 1882. The lighthouse at Arecibo has been restored as a museum and dates from the 1890s, as does that at Punta Tuna, which is still in operation. On the tiny island of **Culebrita**, near Culebra, is one of Puerto Rico's oldest stone-built lighthouses; still operational, it dates from 1874. **Vieques**, lying some seven miles east of Puerto Rico is mostly owned by the US military, who use the island for bombing practice and other manoeuvres. Its finest building is probably the plantation great house, known as the Casa del Francés. This beautifully maintained building, with its Palladian frontage and silver roof tiles, looks like a sumptuous New England residence.

SABA

So different from the other five islands of the Dutch Antilles, this tiny speck in the ocean is a sheer volcanic mountain surrounded by cliffs, and therefore was not settled until a party of Dutch came here from St Eustatius around 1640. The earliest buildings were destroyed in landslides and hurricanes, and although the English occupied Saba for some years, no substantial structure was built here until the foundations of the Presbyterian Church were laid in 1775. Some of the earliest buildings surviving on the island are its Dutch-built cottages.

Cottages on Saba are unique in the world. The houses are of a simple, uniform style, built on plinths of volcanic stone, with wooden plank walls and *wallaba*-wood shingled roofs. Often painted white and picked out in primary colours, with red-painted roofs, the basic design was probably initiated by shipwrights, and almost every house is built to a rigid plan. Shipbuilding was once a major industry on Saba, and much of the construction of the wood-work is typically joined with mortise and tenon joints, fitted together with wooden pegs. Often a terrace fronts the house, oblong in shape and single-storey, with a stone-walled garden. The kitchen area is usually of stone, with brick chimneys, and vaulted stone cisterns collect rainwater. The 'rock oven' is a typically Saban feature and is built outdoors for barbecuing pig. Windows are usually of the sash variety and protected by storm shutters, often painted in green and white. Decoration is usually balustrading on terraces and galleries and gingerbread fretwork railings. Occasionally a roofed porch is added to the house front and fretwork decorates the main roof ridge. Many houses also have Dutch, or stable doors.

The Administrator's House, in the island's tiny capital, The Bottom, is a two-storey concrete building, surrounded by a geometric, pre-cast concrete balcony and terrace wall, with a crenellated roof and shuttered windows. It was built in the same style as the original wooden structure, which it replaced in 1972. The orange balls on the gateposts recall the days of the Dutch House of Orange. The Anglican Christ Church here dates from 1790 and has arched windows and doors, with an open rafterwork interior. The stone-built 1919 Wesleyan Holiness Church, also in The Bottom, with its fretwork-gabled roof and squat-towered entrance, looks like a cross between a house and a church. Next to Wilhelmina Park stands a lovely old house with an ornate wrap-around fretwork double gallery and a high-pitched roof. The Roman Catholic Sacred Heart Church was built of stone here in 1934 and has a tiny bell tower on the front gable, with a pyramidal tiled spire. Cranston's Antique Inn is built in typical timber-framed Creole style, with clapboard and gingerbread fretwork gables and ornate roof ridge; it was constructed in about 1815. The Department of Public Works is housed in an early schoolhouse.

The Roman Catholic Church of St Paul's Conversion in Windwardside was built of stone between 1859 and 1860. This is the island's most picturesque church, with a handsome spire, shuttered, Gothic-style windows and mock castellated surrounds on the two windows and door in its simple facade. Gaily painted in typical Dutch yellow and picked out in white, the church's red roof is surmounted by its red-shingled bell tower and spire. The Holy Trinity Church, also in Windwardside, was built in 1877. The Captain's Quarters is a hotel made from two houses, both two-storey, dating from the 1810s. One of them, with a lookout floor, was a sea captain's house. Scout's Place, was a government guest house, now a hotel, dating back to the 1920s. One of the oldest buildings in Windwardside is that which houses the Saba Museum, said to have been built in 1835. It is whitewashed with green shutters and surrounded by beautiful gardens.

The Gate House in Hell's Gate is a hotel with a variation on traditional Saban architecture, as it displays triple pointed gables. Also at Hell's Gate, the 1962 Roman Catholic Holy Rosary

Church of St Paul's Conversion, Saba

Church, has a four-storey stone bell tower, and its stone-built main building has a double gabled frontage, with an arched entrance porch. The only other buildings of historic interest on Saba are the ruins of two old sugar-boiling houses. The road, snaking nine miles across Saba, and one of the most celebrated engineering feats of its kind in Dutch Caribbean history, took islander Lambertus Hassel five years to build, based on his correspondence course in roadway construction. (The Dutch government had said such a road was impossible to build.) It was inaugurated in 1947.

SAINT-BARTHÉLÉMY

St Barts, or St Barth, as this tiny French outpost is fondly called, was visited by colonists from St Kitts in 1648 and those from Brittany and Normandy, in 1660. French pirates also adopted the island as a refuge and a base from where they could divide their plunder and organize raids on passing Spanish, and later English, shipping. The French settlers remained on the island for 124 years, establishing the port of Le Carenage, until France swapped Saint-Barthélémy with Sweden in 1784 in exchange for a number of warehouses in Gothenburg.

This island was the only possession Sweden ever held in the Western Hemisphere. The Swedes renamed the capital Gustavia after their king Gustaf III and gave the island its free port status, hoping that it might become a trading centre like Dutch Curaçao. But the venture was a failure and the Swedes held St Barts for less than a century. The French bought the island back and returned in 1878. Ethnically unique in the Caribbean, St Barts has had an almost exclusively white population, as the islanders had no need for black slaves, due to prosperity in fishing and trading and the absence of the sugar plantations found on almost every other island. The main effect of this history on the island's architecture is that there are no grand plantation houses or agricultural buildings on St Barts, even though the early settlers once raised small amounts of cotton, indigo, and tobacco. Today's inhabitants depend on tourism, and St Barts has a reputation for catering to the rich and famous.

The tiny capital of Gustavia, built at the end of a narrow sea inlet, was protected by no fewer than four forts. The ruins of Fort Gustave have been restored and stand 150 feet above the port, where the main fortress, old kitchens and powder magazine can be toured. At the tip of the harbour's peninsula stands Fort Oscar, still used by the military. Fort Karl still lies in overgrown ruins, and the outline of Fort Anglais can still just be made out. These are the only historic remnants on St Barts, as a fire in 1852 destroyed the port buildings. A remnant of early French stone-built architecture on the west side of the harbour, is known as the 'opera house', but is actually a military garrison building.

However, in the town the few remains of 19th-century stone warehouses lining the wharf and a couple of old Swedish houses

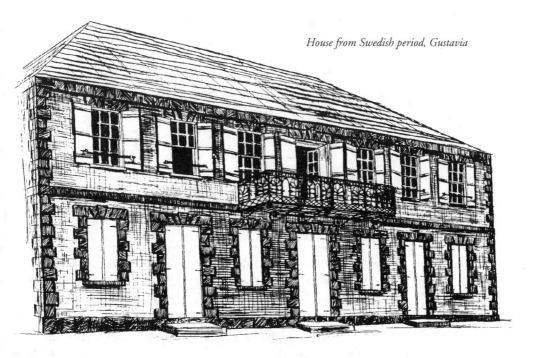

House from Swedish period, Gustavia

have been restored. One of these houses, built in 1841, is in 'Irish Georgian' style, with volcanic rock ground floor and walls supporting a timber-framed first floor. Brick clad, with prominent corner quoins and window surrounds, the parapet is decorated in stonework and the roof conventionally tiled. Just one of ten prefabricated Swedish houses, shipped here in 1830, remains. It is a two-storey timber structure, clad in shingle and board. The old Swedish Customs house in Gustavia's harbour entrance has also been restored.

Just outside Gustavia is the stone-built triangular-roofed belfry of a long-demolished Swedish church, the clock of which has been faithfully restored. Out on the island there are a number of early wood and stone houses and typically French West Indian cases or small houses, like those at Grand Cul-de-Sac, the charming cottages at Les Islets Fleuris and those in St Jean and in Lorient, the island's oldest French settlement. Le Manoir is an original 1610 Norman mansion, shipped out and reconstructed on the island in 1984. The house in front of this is in typical St Barts Creole style.

Possibly of Norman origin, St Barts' unique 'wind houses' are almost prehistoric or Celtic in design. Solidly built of stone and squat, with a low, ridged roof made of heavy timbers clad in wooden shingles, these dwellings are sited so that one blank, thick wall faces the prevailing wind. Inside, these houses are timber framed and have splayed openings in the sloping stone walls, allowing for a small window and door. The stone walls are covered with a mud binding, and finished with a lime wash. Adjoining the oblong dwelling, a stone cistern was built to collect the precious rainwater, fed into the cistern from a peripheral guttering built into the top of the walls around the roof. Gardens were traditionally enclosed in 'blue' stone walls.

ST KITTS

Known as the 'Cradle of the Caribbean' or the 'Mother Colony', St Kitts was the first Caribbean island to be claimed by England, in 1605. However, it was not until 1623, exactly 130 years after its discovery by Columbus, that the first English settlers arrived. Under Sir Thomas Warner, fifteen colonist held the island, until it became divided between the English (St Christopher, or St Kitts) and the French (Saint-Christophe), from 1627 until 1713. Thus, the bulk of the island's historic architecture owes much to both nationalities. For ninety years, the French intermittently held the north and the south of the island, and the British the centre. Despite sporadic hostilities, the truce held. In 1626, the two groups of settlers had joined forces to exterminate the indigenous Caribs at a place now fittingly known as Bloody Point.

The British put their skills into creating an impregnable military stronghold. On the 800-foot high Brimstone Hill, overlooking the Caribbean coastline and named after the faint volcanic odour of sulphur, they decided to build a fort to end all forts, known as the 'Gibraltar of the West Indies'. Five outlying islands can be seen from Brimstone Hill's vantage point: St Eustatius, Saba, St Martin, Saint-Barthélémy and Nevis.

This impressive edifice is constructed mainly from volcanic rock. A vast amount of building lime was also extracted from deposits at the foot of the hill to build miles of ramparts and bastions. The five enormous bastions of the polygonal redoubt of Fort George, with gaps for four giant cannon, face the sea, linked by stone walled ramparts between seven to ten feet thick, with caponiers, or projecting towers. This also enclosed eight smaller bastions, containing seven further cannon, surrounding the arrow-shaped interior. Inside

Brimstone Hill fortress gateway, St Kitts

the 'impregnable' fort were the barracks and the officers' quarters, stone arched, and colonnaded underneath and with wooden living quarters above. Inside was also the parade ground, a 150-ft long vaulted powder magazine, the cook house, mess, hospital, store rooms, a 100,000-gallon fresh water cistern and cemetery – all the ingredients of the most advanced fort of its time. The original plans of the fort can be seen, in the second-floor library of the Old Court House, in Basseterre. The Magazine Bastion, near the entrance at the Barrier Redan, and the Orillon bastions were later added, when the entire site covered 38 acres.

From the high hill here, the English first fired on the French-occupied Fort Charles, a good mile and a half away to the north, causing it to surrender in 1690. In 1706, civilians found refuge in the fort during a French raid, and by 1734 there were 63 cannon defending the fort. Twice the fort was attacked. The first time, before it was completed, was in 1782, when one of the bloodiest land battles ever fought in the Caribbean was waged. The 8,000 French attackers, under the Marquis de Bouille, gratefully captured ten cannon unwisely left at the base of the hill and with these and their own armaments destroyed all except two buildings in the fort. The siege lasted four weeks before the French defeated the 1,000-strong English garrison. In tribute to their bravery, the fort's troops, under Generals Shirley and Fraser, were allowed to leave with flags flying and drums beating. The same honour was granted to the French, when the English retook the fort the following year.

The fort last saw action in 1806 against a French expedition, which attempted a landing at Sandy Point. Gunfire from Brimstone

Hill drove the would-be invaders off. The fort was decommissioned and the garrison withdrawn in 1853. After which, the site was plundered, many of its cannon and stonework being distributed throughout other islands. It was then extensively renovated and declared a National Park in 1985. Fort George now houses an informative museum.

The west coast of St Kitts is especially remarkable for the number of military installations which were constructed along its length. Including Brimstone Hill, no fewer than ten forts protected the island's west side. From Fig Tree Fort in the north-west, these bastions include Sandy Point Fort, Fort Charles, Stone Fort, Palmetto Point Fort, Fort Thomas, Fort Smith and Fort Tyson.

The capital of St Kitts (and Nevis, its sometimes reluctant federal partner), Basseterre, was in French hands when it was founded in 1625. In their 88 years of occupation, the French created a port town unique in the Caribbean. On solid, simple, volcanic stone-built and occasionally brick ground-floor podiums, elegant, timber-framed houses were built in a variety of styles. Large, merchants' warehouses were constructed in the same way, all with traditional French fish-scale tiles. The French built three small forts to defend their capital. One was located on the waterfront and is now completely obliterated. Another, later to become Fort Smith, was built on the east side of the bay of Basseterre, and the third, on the west side of the bay, was renamed Fort Thomas after the mid-18th century governor, Sir George Thomas.

Most of the French colonial buildings in Basseterre disappeared from the date that the English took the island over, and from 1713 onwards, the capital was transformed into a celebration of British Georgian architecture. Due to fires and earthquakes, however, the majority of surviving buildings are Victorian. With the square stone lower floors in place, many of the French-style wooden overhangs and intricate decorations of the upper floors were transformed into the clean-cut lines of Georgian style, with sash windows, storm shutters and pitched, shingled roofs. A great fire in 1867 destroyed much of Basseterre, and most of the town was subsequently rebuilt.

In the aftermath of the disaster, the authorities laid out the octagonal Circus, apparently based on Piccadilly Circus in London. A memorial to a former Speaker of the Legislative Council, Thomas Berkely, stands in the centre of the Circus. It is an ornate Victorian green stone and cast-iron clock tower, with coat of arms and drink-

Palladian town house, Basseterre

ing fountains, erected in 1883. The majority of colonial Georgian-style buildings are gathered around Independence Square, site of the old slave market, and on Fort Street, with its two-storey commercial buildings. The buildings on Independence Square date from about 1790, and the fine stone-built Georgian House restaurant is an excellent example. The Square itself was designed to look like the British Union Flag when viewed from above, with little gates entering each of the eight paths that converge on a central fountain. Another colonial building on the Square, in stone and timber, is now a restaurant and art gallery. The Old Court House was rebuilt to copy the original destroyed in 1867, and nearby is the Georgian mansion of Government House. This building was initially a rectory and has been an official residence since 1882.

Not far away is the twin-towered and spired Roman Catholic Church of the Immaculate Conception, with an exceptional rose window. The church was built in 1928. Probably the most elegant house in the capital is the white-painted presbytery building next door, with its high hipped roof and beautifully ornate first-floor verandah and front railings. Destroyed three times, the present Anglican Church of St George dates from 1869 and is built in traditional English parish church style on the remains of an earlier structure destroyed in the 1867 fire. The original French Jesuit stone-and timber-built church, erected in 1670 and called Notre Dame, had a similar crenellated tower, but was burned down by the British in 1706 and rebuilt four years later. North of this is the square Methodist Church, built in 1825 and restored in the 1920s.

In 1894 the domed black and white Treasury Building was erected on the waterfront as a customs house in front of Old Treasury Pier. It was built of stone, and its columns and cast-iron railings, of typical Victorian design, flank an imposing archway, designed to be the 'Gateway to the Island'. It leads directly into the Circus. Further into the town are some beautiful examples of colonial town houses, with ground floors of cut stone and overhanging first floors, dressed with arched galleries and gingerbread jig-sawed trims. As the town is surrounded by high, volcanic, non-porous stone, rain water floods down into the harbour via ghauts or drains, channelled down the middle of the streets.

In both St Kitts and Nevis a number of old plantation houses have been restored to their former opulence as tourist accommodation. West of Basseterre, is the delightful 1720 residence of the French commandant, now the Fairview Inn. Traditionally built on a volcanic stone podium, the single- and two-storey wooden buildings are roofed with timber shingles. The single-storey building's roof overhangs, creating a verandah, and is supported with ornate timber columns. It is fronted by a wooden-railed balcony. The two-storey building has an elaborate wooden verandah, also supported by twin columns and linked by carved timber panels standing over a railed patio. Windows have side-hinged storm shutters and one top-hinged shutter. Other estate houses, like the Victorian Golden Lemon, which once included a stone-built sugar warehouse, the White House, the Belmont estate, Ottley's Plantation Inn and Rawlins Plantation have been converted into hotels, restaurants and visitor centres. Some, such as Rawlins, which was once the Mount Pleasant estate, have preserved the remains of the boiler chimney, the boiling house, and the windmill tower.

On the west coast is what remains of the first and oldest English settlement in the West Indies, Road Town, dating from 1624, and the location of the 1650s Stone Fort, now in ruins. Here, most buildings are of clapboard, but some stone structures remain, while the Wingfield Manor Estate stands just outside the town. Nearby, the Caribelle Batik Factory was housed in the buildings of the 17th-century Romney Manor until a fire in 1995.

Past Brimstone Hill, at Sandy Point, there were once 65 Dutch tobacco warehouses, until they were destroyed in a fire in 1663. The Roman Catholic Church here has a lovely stained glass window, and the huddle of clapboard and stone residences are in typically

Leeward Islands style, raised off the ground and roofed in tin. Beyond Sandy Point is the promontory of Belle Tête in the part of the island held sporadically by the French for ninety years. Here they constructed another fort near Fig Tree village, now in ruins. Just outside the village of Newton Ground are the remains of another old sugar mill. At Dieppe Bay, the Gibson's Pasture Estate was once a sugar mill and there is evidence of an old French-built fort. There is an old stone-built church at nearby Sadlers village. The ruins of old sugar mills and steam chimneys, abandoned copper boiling vats and crushing machinery can be seen dotted across the island.

In the churchyard of St Thomas Church, dating from the 1600s in Middle Island Village is the tomb of Sir Thomas Warner, the island's founder, under a white-painted, green-roofed gazebo. The tomb carries the inscription 'General of y Caribee'. There are other tombs from the 17th and 18th centuries in this churchyard.

ST LUCIA

Changing hands between the French and the English no fewer than fourteen times, St Lucia's checkered passage through colonial history was also marred by four fires which swept through its capital, erasing many examples of early architecture. A few pockets of old Creole architecture do remain in Castries, although much of the capital has been overrun by modern concrete. However, those early buildings that have survived, perched on their wooden stilts, are among the prettiest in this part of the Caribbean. There are also some spectacular fortifications on St Lucia, and a few plantation houses of particular architectural note.

The origins of the island's name are in some doubt, as claims that Columbus sighted it on St Lucy's Day (13 December) 1502 are not borne out by his log. Nevertheless, after several abortive attempts to establish a European foothold, it was the French who first successfully settled here in 1650. Warfare with the indigenous Caribs and continual inter-European hostility made it a precarious place, and St Lucia did not become an official British Crown Colony until 1814. This alternation of ownership produced a curious mixture of French and English colonial architecture, although, sadly, much of that in the capital has been destroyed, either deliberately or by accident.

Castries, the island's capital, was named after the French Naval Minister, the Maréchal de Castries, in 1784, after it was founded as Petit Carenage in 1650. Plans for the town were drawn up as early as 1746, but these were revised when the town was relocated in 1763. The town has burned down many times since then, latterly in 1948 and 1951. Today, most of the buildings in the grid-patterned town are modern concrete and glass blocks. But a few earlier colonial buildings do remain, notably the line of 19th-century town houses on Derek Walcott Square, and some old wooden French-built houses, with attractive latticework and fretwork-decorated balconies.

One of these, now the Creole-style timber-framed Rain Restaurant, is picked out in green and white. This beautiful example of French colonial town housing has a front-facing gable with a jalousied dormer window, under which are the four side-hinged windows of the second floor. This section is weatherboarded above the charming first-floor verandah, which is supported by four slender wooden columns. Each column is bracketed with intricate filigree gingerbread fretwork. The tall, ground-floor windows are storm-shuttered and face the sidewalk, which runs under the verandah. Two other outstanding buildings are the Marshalls Pharmacy and the attractive Chez Paul restaurant building, dating from 1885. These wooden buildings are typically Victorian French in design, with three storeys and overhanging balconies decorated with gingerbread fretwork.

The Catholic Cathedral of Immaculate Conception was built in Romanesque style, by the architect Pugin between 1894-97, with wooden columns and iron vaulting on a volcanic stone base. It became a cathedral in 1957 and is constructed in a mixture of African and Creole influences, with *trompe l'oeil* columns, a patterned roof and some interesting murals by Dunstan St Omer. Delicate iron arches and braces support the decorated ceiling, and the central altar has four carved screens. The Central Library is constructed of red-and-white stucco and stone in a curious mixture of architectural styles, mingling mock Georgian and late Victorian elements. It dates from the late 19th century. The magnificent red-iron Market Hall was built in 1894 and transferred here from Liverpool, England.

Guarding the much-contended harbour of Castries are the 18th-century, yellow brick barracks and military base of Vigie peninsula, known as Morne Fortune, or Good Luck Peak. More than 38 fortifications were built on St. Lucia over the years from the mid-1700s. Near the summit of Morne Fortune, looming above Castries, Fort Charlotte dates from the late 18th century. There was originally a French fortress on this site, Derrière Fort, erected in 1752 and 1764, but the earliest buildings here are the guardroom, stables and three cells, dating from the late 1770s onwards. The earlier French military installations were built of stone, but the later additions, built around 1794, are British and constructed of red brick. The St Lucia National Trust looks after the restored site, which includes many of the original buildings, barracks, guard rooms and gun emplacements complete with their cannon. The Halfmoon battery was named in 1797 for its obvious shape, commanding a half-circle with five guns. There is an original shot-oven near here, made in 1780. In 1782 the Morne Fortune Battery, known as the Prevost's redoubt, was built, and its gun pits are virtually intact. The 19th-century barrack blocks are typically built with cast-iron frames filled with masonry and plaster, have wide balconies and were constructed between 1829 and 1833. From the plain ground floor of the barracks, steps lead up to the multi-arched, first floor with geometric iron railings. Above, the second floor has a verandah, with cast iron column roof supports. A pitched roof surmounts the whole.

The design of most of St Lucia's barrack blocks is typically 'Army Engineer' Classical, like the Combermere Barracks, built in the middle of the 19th century. The English captured this fort in 1796, and an obelisk, the Inniskilling Monument, commemorates the taking of the hill. A late addition to the fortifications was in 1888, when four ten-inch guns, known as the Apostles' Battery, were installed. The last military positions here were constructed in 1905. The Sir Arthur Lewis Community College is now located here.

In a military cemetery near the fort are the remains of both French and British soldiers who died here from 1782 onwards. Nearby is the handsome Victorian Governor's House, built in 1895 of red stone with white trimmings. A three-storey square tower dominates the entrance, surmounted by a tiled hood, which is topped by a crown-like structure of white-painted cast iron. Demerara windows front the upper storey of this two-storey house, which is reminiscent of an old Victorian public school. It is said to be haunted by the ghosts of numerous governors who died in the building.

South of Castries on the west coast are the tiny fishing villages of Anse La Raye and Canaries, with their charming clapboard houses. Further south is one of the island's oldest port towns, Soufrière, containing many clapboard houses with wooden verandahs and lying in the shadow of the spectacular Pitons. The town dates from 1746, after King Louis XIV donated the surrounding land to the Devaux family from Normandy in 1713. In Elizabeth Square there are some old stone facades, including the four-level volcanic stone tower of the small church, and some French Creole-style homes with typical gingerbread eaves under corrugated iron roofs.

One spectacular example is a three-storey merchant's house, now a shop below a residence. A large cast-iron first-floor gallery gives shelter over the sidewalk, where the tall, ground-floor windows and doors open their shutters onto the street. The balcony is supported by slim metal columns, with ornate finial brackets. Above this, the balcony is surrounded by most lavish iron-gingerbread railings, from which metal columns, again with decorative brackets, support the balcony roof. Above this the third floor is weatherboarded, with well-proportioned fenestration and again embellished with fretwork around the roof, which has delicate dormer windows. The whole is tastefully painted in white and green.

Near Soufrière, the Morne Coubaril sugar estate was fortified by the French, and one of the original cannon remains. Further out from the town are the Diamond Baths, the sulphur baths built on the orders of Louis XVI in 1786 for the French Army, and restored in 1966. Although the original bath house was destroyed in the Brigand War of 1795-9, the catchments remain and two of the twelve stone baths were excavated in 1930. South again lies Choiseul, with its little 1846 Anglican church and typically French Catholic presbytery, with steep, pyramidal corrugated-iron roof, attic dormer windows, encircling verandah and heavy storm shutters. The fishing village of Laborie is where a mysterious tunnel from the old Sapphire Fort opens out to the sea. Near the island's airport is Vieux Fort, the island's second largest town, named after its fortress and the place where sugar was first introduced to the island in 1765. The Moule-à-Chique lighthouse near here is the second highest in the world, standing on a 730-foot hill.

To the north of Castries is Vigie Beach, opposite the deserted nunnery on Rat Island. Further north, Pigeon Island was linked to the mainland by a causeway in 1971, built at a cost of US$30

Victorian French style, Soufrière

million. Nearby there are the clapboard houses and the tiny St Joseph's church of unspoilt Gros Islet. The British fortifications on Pigeon Island include Fort Rodney and cover 44 acres on Pigeon Point, with ramparts and defence lines still visible. The extensive fortifications were restored by the St Lucia National Trust between 1975 and 1979 and are now a National Landmark. They include a two-gun battery, gun slides, barracks, garrisons, a powder magazine, hospital, cooperage, kitchen, bakery, officers' quarters and a signal station, all built between 1778 and 1780. There are more gun batteries like the Musket Redoubt, the Ridge Battery and the Gun Slide, leading up to Signal Hill, and an old lime kiln near the jetty.

There are numerous estates and plantations on St Lucia, like the Dennery Estate, one of the island's largest banana plantations. At Mal Maison, the estate of Marie-Josèphe Rose de Tascher de la Pagerie's father, the buildings are still well preserved, as is the iron water mill wheel, with its crushing rollers, and iron boiling crucibles. There are also the old copra sheds and a copper press once used to extract oil from limes. The girl later to become Empress

Joséphine was born in the former family home at Morne Paix Bouche estate, now mostly in ruins, but the family lived at Mal Maison until 1771, when they moved to Martinique. The old plantation house of Balembouche has one of the island's few remaining old stills and the remains of a magnificent ancient water wheel, once used for driving the sugar mill. At the Invergoll or La Sikwi Estate, dating from 1865, there is a forty-foot waterwheel fed by an aqueduct. The wheel, made in 1878 in Scotland, drove English-made milling machinery which can be seen in the preserved mill house. Other plantation estates include the Soufrière Estate, Cul-de-Sac Estate, Roseau Estate, Morne Coubaril, and the Marquis Estate.

SAINT-MARTIN

The French, northern half of this island, which is shared with Dutch Sint Maarten, was first settled in 1629 by the French, who had challenged Spanish claims to ownership after they erected a small fort on the island in the early 1600s. The Dutch then settled in the south in 1631, attracted by its salt ponds, and the two European groups seem to have coexisted peaceably. Unusually, the Spanish then took exception to this arrangement and returned to retake the island between 1633 and 1648, fending off an attack from the Dutch Peter Stuyvesant that cost him a leg. Eventually the Spanish departed, and a pact in 1648 ceded half of the island to the French, and the other half to the Dutch. Legend has it that the territorial carve-up was settled by a race from the middle of the island between a Frenchman and a Dutchman. The Frenchman, so the story goes, walked faster and claimed more of the island because he drank wine, while the gin-drinking Netherlander was slowed down by his consumption of gin.

Marigot is the capital of the larger French part of the island, and its few old townhouses display typically French colonial wrought-iron balconies. Some, built in stone, have gingerbread-decorated upper-floor galleries, resting on curved, wrought-iron brackets, with railed steps leading up to the entrance. Roofs, painted red with carved wood gables, are stepped over the white-painted galleries, and both doors and windows are shuttered. The Lawrence Wattle house built in 1897 with its attractive fretwork verandah, is typical of the early architecture of this tiny town.

Marigot's oldest structure is the bastion of Fort Saint-Louis, built on the town's outskirts in around 1760. A fort was first erected by the French in 1629 and rebuilt above Pointe Blanche by the Spanish, in 1633. The 18th-century French-built fort is now in ruins, but several ancient cannon still lie around the crumbling walls and ramparts. A restoration attempt was made on the fort in 1994.

Orléans, on the east side of the island, was once the capital and was settled in the 17th century. There are a few examples of early wooden houses in this village and in the pretty hamlet of Colombier. In Cul-de-Sac there is a splendid example of a 1730s country mansion. The few old country estate houses on Saint-Martin are simply built, with a stone ground floor supporting a timber-framed first floor, clad in wooden shingles. The steep roofs often have carved wooden barge boards. The only other historic structure of any note on the French side of the island are the limestone blocks of the ruined Grand Case bridge.

ST VINCENT & THE GRENADINES

Since St Vincent was one of the last islands of the Caribbean to be thoroughly colonized in the mid-18th century, most of its architectural attractions date from the 19th century, after the so-called 'Brigands' War' of the 1790s, in which many early buildings were torched. St Vincent is hence rather disappointing architecturally, although there are a few highlights. The island is an agricultural paradise, however, home to numerous tropical crops including one of the world's largest coconut plantations.

It took until 1797 for the British to overcome the Black Caribs, a mixture of native Caribs and escaped African slaves, who had been wrecked off the coast in 1675. This tough community was determined to resist European colonization. Like other eastern Caribbean islands, St Vincent was also fought over between British and French in the course of the 18th century. By 1719, the French had arrived on the island, only to leave it to the British in 1763. English merchants set up their homes in Kingstown, even establishing the first Botanical Garden in the Caribbean in 1765, laid out by Governor George Melville. A French contingency took the island in 1779, still battling with the itinerant Black Caribs. General Abercrombie eventually routed both the French and the Black

Caribs in 1797 and re-took the island for the British. The Black Caribs were deported *en masse* to the coast of Central America. As a result of this turbulent past, much of the pre-1800 architecture is of French influence, and the later buildings tend to be of British colonial style.

The waterfront of Kingstown, the capital, is lined with a mixture of old stone-built merchant's warehouses and modern shops on cobbled streets. Facing the bay are uniform rows of houses, two or three deep, set out in about 1765 by the first wave of English merchants. The fronts of the volcanic stone ground floors of the colonial houses are overhung by wooden upper floors, supported by vaulted arches over the walkways of downtown Kingstown. In some cases, the Georgian-style commercial buildings lining the streets are totally stone-built, with the ubiquitous tin roofs and the occasional tin window awning, and are arcaded with brick-lined arches. These colonnades are rare outside the Spanish islands of the Caribbean. The roofs were probably shingled initially, and many of the windows are of the English sash style, without shutters or jalousies. Georgetown's main street is cobbled and lined with early two-storey buildings with overhanging balconies. Both the bricks and the street cobbles arrived by ship as ballast.

An outstanding example of St Vincent architecture is the Cobblestone Inn, built as a sugar warehouse in 1814 and later used to store arrowroot. This long and solid two-storey building has a typically red corrugated iron roof and is built of the local dark volcanic stone. Brick arches and pediments are built over the shuttered windows, and an arch which leads through the centre of the building links Upper Bay Street with Middle Street. The pointed lantern on the roof above the arch is shingle-roofed. In the eastern end of the town, where there was once a stream running into the bay, is an unusual paved street, with a drain running down the middle. Also on Upper Bay Street is the police station, dating from 1875, a surprisingly elegant volcanic stone-block building with an unusual tower. The old library is a solid two-storey Georgian building, displaying an unusual twin-storeyed porch surmounted by an ornate pediment. Its six front sash windows are picked out in white and each is topped by curved arches.

St George's Anglican Cathedral is an evocative example of Georgian architecture, built in 1820. It has a castellated clock tower and a stained glass window designed for St Paul's Cathedral in

London. Reputedly rejected for the London Cathedral by Queen Victoria because the angels are wearing red rather than a proper white, it somehow ended up in St Vincent in the 1930s. The three eastern windows are by Kempe and the large south window is of Munich glass. Inside, there are simple pews and an ornate candelabra, said to have been donated by George III. A pale blue gallery runs around three sides of the airy nave. A floor plaque commemorates a General who died in fighting with the Caribs.

St Mary's Roman Catholic Cathedral, also in Kingstown, is an incongruous lucky-dip of architectural styles in dark grey stone and looks as though each part was added randomly by various builders specializing in the eclectic. Those styles which can be identified could be called Romanesque, Gothic, Baroque, Moorish and Renaissance, with a bit of Gaudi and Georgian thrown in for luck! The cathedral is built of volcanic stone and bricks and was started in 1823, enlarged in 1877, 1891 and in the 1930s by Benedictine monks from Trinidad and completed in the 1940s by the Flemish padre, Dom Charles Verbeke. The Belgian seemingly worked from pictures of famous European cathedrals. Small arched turrets mount larger turrets, and numerous interlocking, Romanesque-arched niches contain statues, with supporting battlements and balconies. Gothic spires poke up all over, and fretting decorates any plain stone-work. The interior is rather dull and disappointing in contrast. The rather sombre facade of the Methodist Church opposite, dating from 1841, conceals an interior that includes distinctive, diamond-shaped, latticed windows, colourfully-painted pillars, a circular balcony and a crystal chandelier.

St Mary's Cathedral, Kingstown

Higher up from the town centre are the prosperous colonial mansions of late 18th- and early 19th-century merchants. Government House, built in 1886, is located above the Botanical Gardens, founded as the oldest in the New World in 1765. It contains a breadfruit tree, said to be a direct descendant of the first such tree brought over by Captain William Bligh (of the *Bounty* notoriety) from Tahiti in 1793. Parliament Building is an imposing two-storey stone structure, fronted by a triple entrance arch, roofed in corrugated iron and with a triple arched entrance into the loggia. Raised plaster quoins are picked out in white on the building's corners, around the tall, upper windows with their Demerara shutters, and around the arched, lower fenestration.

West of Kingstown, the British-built Fort Charlotte, dating from 1796 to 1806, is named after King George III's wife. It is reached by a steep causeway and through an arched entrance and stands 636 feet above sea level. The soldiers' quarters have been turned into a museum, and three of the original 34 cannon are still here. Note that the guns face inland, rather than out to sea, telling testimony to the allegedly ferocious nature of the resident Black Caribs. The main battery is a vast structure of local darkvolcanic stone. The fort was decommissioned in 1873, but the barracks are now a museum. A little way down the hill, the old military hospital, now the Womens' Prison, must have one of the best views of any prison in the world, overlooking the Caribbean Sea.

Just to the north of Kingstown, St Vincent's Botanical Gardens are the oldest in the Western Hemisphere, dating from 1765, and are home to the Archaeological Museum, with Carib artifacts on display.

In the interior of the island there are few sites of real architectural interest, although there are numerous attractive tin-roofed village houses and the crumbling remains of plantation buildings and old aqueducts. St Vincent's second town, Georgetown on the east coast, was once a prosperous sugar-producing centre but is now a run-down and gloomy place, where many 19th-century houses and several churches are falling into disrepair. A rare old arrowroot mill, with its rusting wheel, can be seen in Fancy village on the remote and near inaccessible northern tip. South of Kingstown on the Harmony Hall sugar plantation are 19th-century windmill remains. The former plantation great house of Orange Hill, with its long verandah, has been carefully preserved, as have its unusual copra-drying oven in the grounds and the aqueduct, built in 1859. At Barrouallie, there is an example of one of the few remaining whaling villages in Caribbean. This village's architecture is distinctly French in influence, and its police station, one of St Vincent's oldest buildings, dates from the 1700s.

Whaling and the production of arrowroot were traditionally the economic mainstays of St Vincent and the adjoining Grenadines. It was the whaling communities which pioneered boat-building and settlement on several of the islands. One old whaling station stands on Petit Nevis, near Bequia, where a small group of fishermen still harpoon whales with traditional 18th-century methods from purpose-built 26-ft cedar whalers. The indigenous crop of arrowroot was exclusively used to produce a starchy thickening agent until the 1950s, but it now also acts as an ingredient in the production of computer paper. Small farming communities used to produce the starch in the countryside, but nowadays arrowroot is processed in factories in Kingstown.

The military engineer Colin Thomas Browne used Carib and slave labour in 1815 to dig a 300-ft tunnel through solid volcanic rock at Black Point on the eastern coast. This tunnel was used to facilitate the transportation of sugar cane from Georgetown to cargo boats. A man-made cave here was used to store rum before it was rowed out to waiting ships.

On **Young Island**, off Calliaqua Bay in the south of the island, is the well-preserved Fort Duvernette, built in 1800. Reached by a steep staircase of 365 steps cut out of living rock, it has two batteries, one on the summit, and the other forty feet below, featuring ten examples of early mortars and cannon which date from the reigns of George II and George III. Also on Young Island, the Catholic Church is pretty in blue and amber, with Gothic-style windows. Built with weather-boarded walls, the roof is shingled, as is the spire on the little bell tower on the roof.

The Grenadines

There are very few sites of architectural importance on these spectacularly beautiful islands, which run south from St Vincent, linking with those lying to the north of Grenada. The most northerly is **Bequia**, where there are the remains of an old fort on Mount Pleasant, dating from the 1700s, now transformed into a hotel and restaurant. The two-storey, shingle-sided Frangipani Hotel, overlooking historic Admiralty Bay, is housed in a sea captain's family home dating from the late 19th century. This island has some fine examples of pastel-painted, wooden villas, dating from the 1920s and 1930s. The odd settlement of Moon Hole is famous for its contemporary architecture, but is not of historic importance.

Further down the Grenadine island chain after **Isle à Quatre**, **Battowia** and **Balliceaux** comes **Mustique**, where the expensive and exclusive Cotton House hotel is a distinguished example of a coral-built renovated 18th-century cotton warehouse. There are also the ruins of three 18th-century British forts on Mustique. One of these is the hilltop Fort Shandy, overlooking Britannia Bay. A four-bedroom villa has now been built into the ruined walls of the fort. Further south is the tiny island of **Canouan**, whose oldest building is an attractive but abandoned stone Anglican Church located in the north of the island. It was reduced to ruins by a hurricane in 1921. South of Canouan are the **Tobago Cays** and **Mayreau**, where there is a tiny volcanic stone Catholic Church. Near the privately-owned **Palm Island** and **Petit St Vincent** is **Union Island**, where there are the ruins of an old fort on the aptly named Fort Hill.

SINT EUSTATIUS

Known as the 'Golden Rock' because of the trading wealth which passed through this tiny island's port, Statia, as it is frequently called, was first colonized by Dutch settlers from Zeeland in 1636. They immediately secured their settlement by building Fort Oranje, which now boasts three bastions, some of the eleven cannon which fired the first salute to the American flag in 1776, and a wide parade ground. This fort was built on the original site of a previous French fortification erected in 1629. The island changed hands no fewer than 22 times between 1636 and 1816. During this time around twenty forts were built on the island. Fort Oranje is the best example and was reconstructed in 1976. Fort Royal was built later to protect the other end of Oranjestad, the island's capital. The town grew up below Fort Oranje, initially along the waterfront, below steep cliffs. A fire in 1990 devastated part of the fort, which has since been restored, together with its few remaining cannon.

The first buildings on the quayside were vast brick warehouses, built to house slaves and to store goods imported from Europe and New World produce. In the 18th century the island experienced a veritable boom, with upwards of 3,000 ships calling each year. It also did well from smuggling and from supplying Washington's troops during the American War of Independence. But in November 1776 the military commander blundered when he ordered Fort Oranje's cannon to fire in recognition of a ship bearing the colours of the Continental Congress. In retaliation at the island's acknowledgment of the American rebels, Admiral Lord Rodney took Statia in 1781, plundering its warehouses of three million pounds worth of goods. This shows just how much wealth was stored in this tiny Dutch enclave in the late 1700s.

Initially, a single row of stone-built barn-like buildings stretched along the beach, before the Dutch built a dyke, in order to put up a second row of warehouses on the reclaimed land. Some of these warehouses were built of red-and-yellow bricks brought here as ship's ballast. This part of Oranjestad was known as Lower Town, and the merchants' houses were built further up the cliff face in Upper Town. Many of these warehouses and port-side factories now lie beneath the waves, and the ruins of others can be seen along the waterside. Two of these ancient structures have been restored, however; one was the old customs house, and the other an 18th-century cotton gin house. Near here, the steep route leading up into Upper Town is locally known as the Slave Road.

One of the earliest buildings in the exquisitely cobbled Upper Town is the Dutch Reformed Church, built of stone in 1755 and consecrated in 1776. Its notable features include a restored, squat, two-storey square bell tower, with a pyramidal slated roof, doubling as the church entrance. The windows are shuttered with arched storm-shutters but the body of the church is open to the elements. The church has been restored, but initially its tower was painted white and its high wooden roof painted blue. The cemetery has numerous old barrel-vaulted graveyards, once plundered by Admiral Rodney, in 1781 in his search for hidden booty. Even older is the Honen Dalim Synagogue, a two-storey structure dating from 1738. It is part ruined, but is one of the oldest Jewish buildings of its kind in the New World. There are several old houses of note in Upper

Dutch Reformed Church, Oranjestad

Town, like the building called Three Widows Corner, a restored 18th-century private house, and the yellow brick De Graaff House, also from the 18th century. Known also as the Simon Doncker House, it has been restored by the Sint Eustatius Historical Foundation and is now the island's museum. The house has a typical high gallery with slim supporting columns, its interior rooms recreated in 18th-century style. This is where Admiral Rodney stayed while carrying out his methodical retribution. In front of the Three Widows Corner is a typical Statian house with stone foundations, shingled walls and gingerbread fretwork trim. There are two or three other similarly stone and wood-built houses in the town. Other buildings of note include the colonial Stadhuis or Town Hall. In the south of the island is the 18th-century Fort de Windt.

SINT MAARTEN

The smaller, Dutch half of this island was first occupied by rival Spanish, French and Dutch colonists, all vying for possession until the French-Dutch agreement to divide the island in 1648. The

Spanish had already erected forts in two spots, one of them where the town of Philipsburg was to be founded. In 1631 the Dutch arrived and immediately erected Fort Amsterdam on this old fort site. This was the first Dutch fort built in the Caribbean. The Spanish then captured the fort in 1633 and pulled most of the original walls down. The Dutch returned in 1648, reconstructing the fort's ramparts and bastions, which were rebuilt once again in the 18th century. Fort Amsterdam was in use as a military station until the 19th century and as a signal station until the 1950s. It is now in ruins and its cannon are rusting. The British began building their Fort Trigge when they took this part of the island in 1799, returning in 1808 to complete the job. When the Dutch returned in 1816, they renamed it Fort Willem. The fort lies to the west of the town, and there are scant remains of two other forts, Sint Peter's Battery, and Fort Bel-Air.

The capital of the Dutch territory, Philipsburg, was founded by John Philips, commander of the Dutch side from 1735-46 in 1735. He is buried in the old graveyard just outside the town. Nearby there are the 17th- and 18th-century ruins of a brick-built synagogue. The Philips-burg Courthouse on Wathey Square, with its square, shuttered-windowed clock tower, is the town's oldest structure and was originally built in 1793. It has been authentically restored after hurricane damage, both in 1826 and during the 1960s. It was used as a weigh-house, jail, post office and town hall, and was again restored in 1994. The town's museum is housed in a 19th-century West Indian Creole-style building, standing between two *steegies* or alleyways that link the town's Front Street and Back Street. An unusual mixture of designs, this two-storey building is topped by a wood-shingled, triangular-roofed clock tower. Wooden framed, with a roof sloping away from the square tower, the Courthouse's windows are green and white shuttered. A small wooden balcony overhangs the entrance.

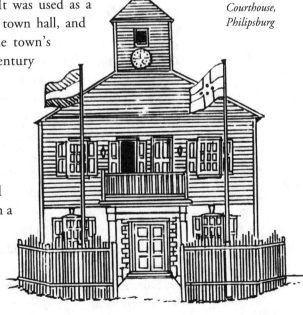

Courthouse, Philipsburg

Just off the town's centre, De Ruyterplein, are some colonial Dutch-style houses, and here there are a few porch-fronted houses painted in pastel shades, with embellished wooden gables. The Passanggrahan Royal Hotel, a former official government guest house, is typical of the architecture here, as is Buncamper House, a beautifully-proportioned early townhouse, with delicate fretwork, front staircase and wrap-around verandah. This is one of the best examples of upper-class architecture on the island. To the east of Front Street there is the original home of the Governor of Sint Maarten. It dates from the 18th century and has been restored. The large Methodist Church in Philipsburg was built in timber in 1851. Based on a stone plinth, the church is clad in shingles, together with its delicate bell tower and spire. The double bank of sash windows are storm-shuttered, as are the Gothic-style windows at the end of the nave.

There are few historic sites outside Philipsburg, apart from the obelisk erected in 1948 to mark the border between the Dutch and French sides of the island, standing north-west of the capital. There are also several run-down remains of early plantation houses dotted across the hilly countryside. The ancient stone plantation house at Almond Grove, in Cole Bay to the west of Philipsburg, was built in 1795 and is now restored as a restaurant.

TOBAGO

This island was the centre of colonial dispute for three hundred year after Columbus's first sighting in 1498. English, Spanish, Dutch, French, Swedes and even American revolutionaries fought over ownership of Tobago from the date that the English first claimed it in 1608. By some calculations, the island changed hands 29 times before it was finally ceded to Britain in 1802. The island's architecture is therefore of mixed origins, but mainly French and English in inspiration. The capital, Scarborough, was not established until 1769, although fortifications like Fort James had already been built to protect early settlers in the island's second town, Plymouth.

Fort James was founded by Courlanders (subjects of James, Duke of Courland, now a part of modern-day Latvia), who in 1642 established six short-lived settlements on Tobago before being ejected by the Dutch in 1658. The present structure is British and dates from between 1768 and 1777. Four of its cannon are still mounted and the barracks still stand. A short distance from here, commemorating the early Baltic settlers, the Courland Monument at Plymouth is a concrete sculpture by Janis Mintiks, erected in 1976. Another commemorative spot in Plymouth is the mysterious tombstone of one Betty Stiven, dating from 1783. The stone is inscribed with the quizzical motto: 'She was a Mother without knowing it, and a Wife without letting her Husband know it, except by her kind indulgences to him'.

The capital town of Tobago, Scarborough, is overlooked by Fort King George, built by the British between 1777 and 1804. In between it fell into French hands, was renamed Fort Castries and then Fort Liberté, and finally returned to the British in 1802. It stands some 400 feet above the town just beyond the hospital. The Division of Tourism has restored the fort complex, which includes a lighthouse and bell tower. The barracks were abandoned in 1854, and the fort fell into disrepair until it was restored and a museum added. The buildings consist of ramparts and redoubts, a domed structure over a well, the old barracks, an ancient 13-inch mortar, a number of cannon and a vast, vaulted-roofed, stone-built powder magazine, with buttressed walls. Some of the fort's buildings, like the officers' mess, are constructed of yellow ballast brick. In the Barrack Guard House there is the Tobago Museum, with good displays of pre-Columbian and colonial artefacts. Further downhill from the fort is the well-preserved stonework hospital, dating from 1819, with great arches for ventilation, and the old 18th-century prison.

In Scarborough itself, at the bottom of the hill, there are a few old stone-built colonial buildings on the harbour, private houses and the House of Assembly on James Park, built in 1825. The railings of Gun Bridge are fashioned from rifle barrels and it is flanked by cannon. The old prison, once a military structure dating from the 1700s, was the site of the repeated hanging of a slave revolt ringleader in 1801 This gruesome pretence was apparently intended to give the impression that the Governor had ordered the execution of all 38 captured revolutionaries. To the west of Scarborough, off Wilson Road, is the site of the old Dutch fort, the first fort to be built in the capital. Also in the town, on Fort Street, is the beautiful balconied rectory of the Methodist Church, built in 1824, and a fine old timber house with multiple gables, an elegant porch entrance, and a wooden-bracketed, pillared and decorative verandah.

Out on the island, there are several sites of historic architectural interest, including the ruins of the 1764 Fort Granby, which once guarded Georgetown, the first English capital of the island, and Barbados Bay. Here is the grave of a soldier, James Clark, dating from 1772. The plantation great house nearby is named 'The Retreat'. The low stone structure of Fort Milford, built by the British between 1777 and 1781, is near the built-up tourist area of Crown Point. It still has one French cannon and five British. Just outside Plymouth, at Black Rock on Great Courland Bay, are the ruins of Tobago's oldest fortress, Fort Bennett, a small military outpost with two cannon.

There are several old plantation houses on the island. Near Fort Bennett is the abandoned Grafton Estate house, and others include Mason Hall, Belle Garden and the Whim plantation great house. The Grafton Caledonia estate was once a cocoa plantation and is now a nature centre. Two great houses have been converted into hotels; the Arnos Vale plantation house, with its deserted sugar mill and a cane crushing water wheel, is one of Tobago's best preserved buildings, dating from 1857. The Richmond Great House dates from 1766 and features a magnificent, extensive wood-planked pediment overhanging its twin-staired entrance, supported by six high, slender pillars. Built above a brick lower storey, the house is basically single floored, with sash windows and high beamed ceilings.

There are several pretty villages in the north east, such as the fishing hamlet of Speyside, where there is a rusting water wheel and the remnants of the old sugar works. Near Charlotteville, the largest village, there is a lookout post which is thought to have been used as a pirate refuge. It is called Fort Campbellton and has a battery of ancient cannon. Here, and in the country villages like Moriah in the west, one can see typical rural dwellings, many built on blocks above the ground for both ventilation and to deter vermin. Often these are

Village house, Tobago

simple timber-framed clapboard huts, with corrugated iron roofing and an added porch. Some are built on sloping ground so that stone columns are needed to raise the structure to a common level. Many of these basic houses are colourfully painted, with fretwork embellishments and perforations on porch shadings, gable vents, and side-hung windows, often without shutters.

TRINIDAD

Port of Spain is the island's bustling capital, and it is one of the youngest of the Caribbean's major cities. For many years after Columbus's first arrival in 1498 the island languished as a half-hearted addition to Spain's territories in the Greater Antilles, with the main town, San José de Oruna, being burned down by Sir Walter Raleigh in 1595. The Spanish moved the capital to St Joseph inland, but later moved back on the coast in 1757. Many Spanish place names from those times survive to this day: Sangre Grande, Mundo Nuevo, Valencia. Sugar-cane, coffee, cacao and cotton were raised by the Spanish during the 1700s, but few Spanish settlers could ignore the gold rush in nearby South America and depopulation became critical. In 1783, Spain implored Catholics of all nationalities to settle in Trinidad, but by 1797 the British had captured the island and began colonization in earnest.

Oil-rich Trinidad is the most cosmopolitan of Caribbean islands and is home to people of African, Indian and European descent. The home of Carnival and calypso, it is a vibrant cultural centre as well as one of the most industrialized of economies. The vast industrial and oil installations around San Fernando are evidence of Trinidad's push towards industrialization in the course of the 20th century.

The earliest building in Port of Spain is Fort San Andrés, built by the Spanish in 1785. It was here that the Spanish astronomer Cosma Damian de Churruca established the first meridian of longitude in the New World in 1792. After the Spanish were ousted, a fire destroyed the city in 1808. Little else, other than stone-built military structures, survived.

Fort Andrés is architecturally unusual as it does not have the thick walls and slender loopholes generally associated with military buildings. The fort's armaments, however, still stand guard over the modern cruise ship harbour. The best preserved fortification on Trinidad, Fort George, is two miles out of town at a height of 1,100 feet. It was abandoned in 1846 and is marked by its guard house, gunpowder store, cells, and six cannon. It is the most impressive and extensive of the island's forts, built during the Napoleonic War and carefully restored. It still displays cannon mounted on gun-carriages around its preserved ramparts. An exiled Ashanti prince, Kofi Nti, is credited with designing the fort's signal station. It is a masterpiece of timber frame design, with wrap-around porch and fretwork-decorated gables on its ground-floor roof, echoed on the roof of its loft-like first floor. It looks more like a cricket pavilion than a naval signal station.

The only other trace of Spanish occupation is Independence Square, laid out by the Spanish as a parade ground. At one end are the three-staged, twin bell towers of the vaulted neo-Gothic Roman Catholic Cathedral of the Immaculate Conception. The church, Port of Spain's first structure to be built after the 1808 fire between 1815 and 1832, is laid out in the shape of a Latin cross. Constructed of blue metal stone from the Laventille Hills, the cathedral once stood beside the sea, until land was reclaimed and it moved back from the shoreline. It contains some English iron framework, Irish stained glass and a Florentine marble altar, with carvings of the Stations of the Cross, and a statue of Columbus. The statue of Captain Arthur Cipriani, a working-class trade union activist of the 1920s, stands in Independence Square.

Nearby, on Woodford Square, which was laid out in 1813 with typically British iron railings, is another neo-Gothic church, the Anglican Cathedral Church of the Holy Trinity, built between 1815 and 1823, with Gothic spires and beautifully carved mahogany altar and choir stalls. The church has a capacity of 1,200, and is worth visiting to see the impressive ceiling, supported by an intricate system of mahogany beams. It is said to have been based on the design of London's Westminster Hall. A marble monument commemorates the Governor of the time, Sir Ralph Woodford. To one side of the Anglican cathedral is Parliament House, known as the Red House. It is a large, green-domed, brick-built, four-storey, neo-Renaissance structure, rebuilt in 1907 after two fires, when Italian craftsmen were brought in to resurrect this impressive structure. In 1897, for Queen Victoria's Diamond Jubilee, the building was painted red, a colour scheme which has remained to this day. Behind it are the Police Headquarters, originally built in 1877 and rebuilt in an almost Anglicized Italianate neo-Gothic style in 1884. The building was gutted in the 1990 coup attempt by Muslim fundamentalists.

However, the architectural 'jewels in the crown' of Port of Spain consist of 'the magnificent seven', a series of mansions standing on Maraval Road by the Queen's Park Savannah. These were built to flaunt the wealth of early 20th-century cocoa barons and other notables, and all, except Hayes Court, date from 1904. From south to north, they are as follows. The 'H'-shaped, ochre-and-blue Queen's Royal College building was built in Italianate and mock-German Renaissance style, although it could fit well in British imperial India. The College has a double row of broad galleries and an immense clock tower. Its arched fenestration is shaded by top-hinged louvred shutters. Next door is Hayes Court, the Anglican Bishop's residence, completed in 1910 and built in a mixture of English and French town house styles. Iron fretwork and a beautiful *porte cochère* or coach doorway are particular features of this classic mansion. Then comes a French provincial mansion, a complicated Baroque-colonial villa known as Prada's House or Mille Fleurs. Once the Mayor's residence, it is remarkable for some delicate wrought-iron filigree and fretwork. Ambard's House (also known as Roomor or the Gingerbread House) is in frothy Creole-French Second Empire style. It was built as an imitation of a Paris château, with cupolas, galleries, dormer windows, towers, spires and pinnacles, although only its tiles are French. The marble used in its construction came from Italy, and its Renaissance-style wrought ironwork was made in Scotland.

The Archbishop's House is Irish in design, with red granite and marble imported from Ireland. The building's many-arched facade contains neo-Romanesque, early Renaissance, Byzantine and semi-Oriental styles. Local hardwood is used in the creation of the interior 'Y'-shaped staircase, panelling, woodwork and floors. To the south is the Archbishop's Chapel and to the west is the Chancery. The Moorish-Venetian-style, four-storey White Hall follows, formerly the Prime Minister's office and described as a 'Corsican wedding cake', but actually an imitation of an Italianate palace in Venetian style. It was built from white Bajan coral, which gave it its name. Next is Killarney or Stollmeyer's Castle, a stone-built, mock-medieval turreted affair in the German Rhinish style and reminiscent of Balmoral Castle in Scotland. It was the first mansion to be built on this site and is constructed from brick and hand-cut local limestone. The interior has a fine staircase, and another leads up into its tower. A lumber shortage meant that the roof beams had to be imported, and Italian craftsmen worked on the ceiling.

Detail of Stollmeyer's Castle, Port of Spain

'The Savannah is a wide green common on the northern side of Port of Spain, where the tropical hills come sidling down to the sea, and around its perimeter there stands a company of legendary Trinidadian mansions. One is gorgeously Gothic, one exotically Moorish, one predominantly blue: but the most stylish of them all is No. 25 Maraval Road, where Mr Morgan lives. It is a big white house surrounded with balconies like an eccentric gunboat on the China Station, and it is encrusted with every kind of ornament, towers and turrets and filigree and wrought iron and balustrades and flagstaffs and weathercocks and all possible fractions of elaboration.'
Jan Morris, *Howzat? and Mr Morgan* (1958)

Just a few other buildings of historic or architectural note are located in and around Port of Spain. These include the Classical-style Princess Building, erected in 1861 to the south of the Savan-nah, and the former Royal Victoria Institute, where the National Museum and Art Gallery is housed in a classic colonial building, opened in 1892 and rebuilt after a fire in 1923. The presidential residence, next to the Botanic Gardens on the northern part of the Savannah, is L-shaped in honour of Governor Longden of the 1870s.

Compared to many other islands of the Caribbean, plantation great houses are few and far between. Some of these mansions are in a state of disrepair, but all demonstrate the opulent lifestyle of the plantation owners, some of whom used these houses as country retreats, having main residences in the city. Two great houses are particularly interesting. There is the eclectic style of Chase Village Great House, embellished with ornate fretwork barge boards above a pillared porch, with filigree-bracketed supporting columns. A heavy, decorative, concrete double stairway leads up to the entrance, and the fenestration is shaded by top-hinged Demerara shutters. Stollmeyer's Plantation House in Santa Cruz dates from the mid-19th century and has rounded-topped dormer windows, with a gingerbread fretworked porch. The porch stands on stilts to facilitate ventilation. Spiked finials set off dormers, gallery gables and the gazebo-like gallery extensions.

Other estate houses include the Spring Hill Estate, and the remains of Lopinot House, an early 19th-century coffee and cocoa plantation house and home to the Comte de Lopinot, who fled Saint-Domingue in 1800. The house has now been restored and is a museum. The well-proportioned estate house has dormer windows in its Mansard roof, which spreads out over a verandah at back and front. The long porch entrance to the centre of the building's front is pitched roofed, with a leading gable. Nearby is a rare example of a cocoa-drying barbecue, with a removable roof. The stone tombs of the Count and his wife stand further from the house. There is another sugar plantation museum in the River Estate house. The three-storey McLeod plantation house at Couva is a magnificent example of a 19th-century Trinidadian great house, with ornate gables and porch, balustrades and decorative window awnings. The Asa Wright Nature Centre, famed for its extraordinary variety of bird life, is located in an elegant 1908 estate house.

The island has plenty of evidence of its mixed cultural and religious heritage. At Sipara, in the south-west, is Trinidad's earliest building. This is the Spanish pilgrimage Church of the Divina Pastora, dating from 1758 and containing a leather-clad image of the Black Virgin. At Mount St Benedict near Tunapuna stands the whitewashed and red-tiled Benedictine Monastery, dating from 1912. The oldest Benedictine foundation in the Caribbean, it offers spectacular views over the sugar-producing Caroni Plain. The little village of Blanchisseuse, in the north, is a typically colourful French Creole community, with elaborately decorated cottages and a small wooden church. Around the east coast village of Pierreville there are a number of picturesque timber stilt houses. The Tapia House here is a good example of the earliest wattle and daub buildings.

With the abolition of slavery, many Indian immigrants were brought work as indentured labourers in Trinidad, and both Muslims and Hindus now have their own places of worship on the island. The Jama Masjid, the island's principal Islamic Mosque, with its slender minarets, is in Queen Street, Port of Spain. The Islamic Jinna Masjid Mosque is in St Joseph and is a centrally domed structure, surrounded by dome-topped towers, over the single-storey main building, which is decorated with ornate arches and flanked by two tall pierced minarets. The Hindu Mandir in the suburb of St James was built in 1963 and consists of a large covered area dominated by an elaborate pierced *sikhara* or tower, with a conical dome. The dome is surrounded by circular columns with decorated finials. In Rio Claro, with its Indian-influenced architectural styles, is a

Town house, Trinidad

Muslim Mosque and a Hindu Temple. In the sugar settlements of the central plain, you will see many Indian-dominated villages, complete with Hindu prayer flags.

TURKS & CAICOS ISLANDS

Unique to the heritage of Caribbean architecture, the domestic buildings of the Turks & Caicos Islands reflect a strong Bermudan influence, brought here by settlers who developed the boat-building and salt harvesting trade on these and some of the islands of The Bahamas. Bermudan salt rakers began arriving in 1678, selling their wares to the British colonies on the North American mainland, principally for salting cod. There are also the remains of American Loyalist plantation houses, dating from the first advent of cotton-growing Loyalists in the islands from Georgia, in 1789. The inhabited islands comprise Grand Turk, South Caicos, North Caicos, and Providenciales, with small settlements on Grand or Middle Caicos, Salt Cay, West Caicos and Pine Cay. Recently discovered stone outlines at Conch Bar, Grand Turk, point to Arawak habitation.

Grand Turk

Cockburn Town is the capital of the largest island, and the 19th-century Bermudan style of architecture is evident in its narrow streets, typically lined with low stone walls and old street lamps. Many of the buildings have walled-in courtyards, built to keep working donkeys in. The best examples of early architecture can be seen in Duke Street (also known as Front Street). These are pastel-painted, timber-framed houses with louvred windows and gingerbread fretwork verandahs. There is a typical two-storey house on the east side of Duke Street, which has a railed porch and upper-floor balcony running the length of the front of the house. A deeply scalloped frieze runs between the two floors, and the balcony displays traditional Bermudan louvres. An external stairway links the porch and the balcony, and the house is clad in beaded weather-board. The roof is built in a style known locally as 'jerkin-headed' and is actually a form of gambrel roofing. Guinep Lodge is the oldest cut-stone house on the islands and is now a national museum.

Here also are ancient warehouses, the shuttered Victoria Library, the old Post Office, the yellow-painted Government Buildings guarded by cannon and the much-renovated Governor's House, called 'Waterloo' because it was built in 1815. Cast-iron building construction arrived on the islands from England around the time of the boom in the salt industry in the 1860s. Many of the cast-iron framed buildings were clad in galvanized corrugated steel sheeting. Further out on the island is St Thomas' Anglican Church, built by Bermudan settlers but then superseded by St Mary's Church (1899) on Duke Street. Two typical early houses are now in commercial use. The Salt Raker Inn, once the home of a Bermudan shipwright, is a classic old island house dating from the 1830's, with wooden walls and the original Bermudan red pine floors. The Turk's Head Inn, also on Duke Street, is located in a handsome, galleried, salt manager's house. It is built of oak, cedar, and Canadian pine, on rock and concrete foundations. Constructed in the 1840s by the same Jonathan Glass who built the Salt Raker, this mansion is in typical ship-builder's style, using no nails and only wooden pegs. The exterior has white trim with green storm shutters and railings, with a red tiled roof, and the entrance has a small porch. Ceilings are made from original ships planking and have ornate mouldings. The original cold-storage cellar remains. Also on Grand Turk, is an old lighthouse, erected in 1852. The lighthouse was cast in iron in England, and shipped to Grand Turk in sections, where it was assembled. The cut-stone lighthouse keeper's hut nearby has interesting heavy buttresses at each corner, and a steeply ridged roof.

Salt Cay has a number of photogenic Bermudan-style stone and wooden houses located in Balfour Town, and the old salt pans or salinas, salt sheds, sluices and ancient windmills. The style of the sturdy, shipwright-built houses on these islands is 'kneed'. No iron nails are used in their construction. Dry stone walls outline properties, some of which show signs of fortification. Mount Pleasant Guest House is a refurbished salt raker's home, built in 1830. The White House, built in the same period of Bermudan ballast stone, is testimony to the wealth generated by the salt industry.

Wind-powered water pump, Salt Cay

Cockburn Harbour is the main settlement in **South Caicos** and has a number of Bermudan buildings, suggestive of the many immigrants who came here in the 17th and 18th centuries. The building known as Highlands is a large 19th-century house overlooking the run-down town. Mudjeon Harbour and Conch Bar are two of the several tiny settlements on the small island of **Grand (Middle) Caicos** and are typical isolated West Indian fishing villages. There are several ancient ruins near Bambarra and Lorimers and some remains dating from Lucayan days. An old paved road links the villages

Whitby and Sandy Point are just two of **North Caicos**'s original plantation settlements, and there are a number of traditional houses in the south of island. Inland, there are a couple of old American Loyalist plantation ruins, like Bottle Creek and Kew. Wades Green Plantation great house ruins are typical of Loyalist architecture, and the overseer's house, kitchen building, slave huts and encircling walls can also be made out. The ruins were excavated in 1989. In the late 1800s, the islet of **West Caicos** had a thriving sisal plantation and a settlement, Yankee Town, today in ruins. There are also the tracks of a small railway, used to transport the sisal. Here are also some distinctive early salt gatherers' single-roomed houses, all abandoned. These have free-standing stone-built walls, covered in coral lime-wash, a thatched, ridge roof and an impressive, imported brick-built chimney at one end of the hut. The dwellings have one crude wooden door and a single window let into the stone wall. The use of stone and brick was due to the lack of wood on the island.

Pine Cay is a private resort and there are no buildings of architectural note here, but on the nearby islet of **Fort George Cay** are the ruins of an old British fort, Fort George, once inspected by Admiral Nelson. The cannon were discarded when British soldiers abandoned the pallisaded fort in 1798. On **Gibbs Cay** the ruins of a French gun emplacement dating from the 1780s can be seen. It was known as Fort Castries.

Providenciales is the biggest tourist centre in the Turks & Caicos, and development has been rapid since the 1960s, with spread-out condominiums and shopping malls. In the 19th century there were three large cotton- and sisal-producing plantations, and older homes can be seen in the three original settlements of Five Cays, Blue Hills and the Bight. The best-preserved ruins of an old Loyalist plantation great house can be seen at Cheshire Hall.

US VIRGIN ISLANDS

The United States Virgin Islands (USVI for short) comprise ten islands and islets, although only three – St John, St Croix and St Thomas – are of any significance. The town of Charlotte Amalie, on the latter, is the USVI's administrative centre. Although the first settlers on St Croix were Dutch and British and despite the fact that the French held the island from 1650 until 1733, the architecture of the islands is predominantly Danish in influence, as it was the Danish West India and Guinea Company which had held St Thomas since 1665 and St John since 1717. These three islands were Denmark's only colonies in the Caribbean, until in 1917 the US purchased them for 'strategic reasons'.

St Thomas

St Thomas is the second largest island in the USVI, and its capital Charlotte Amalie, named in 1692 after the King of Denmark's consort, contains some striking historic sites. These are of unique architectural interest both because of their Danish heritage and because of the wealth of this once thriving commercial centre. No less than half of its buildings are more than a hundred years old. As with most settlement throughout the Caribbean, the forts tend to be the oldest buildings, and Charlotte Amalie's Fort Christian is no exception. The Danes built it in 1671 and named the fort after their King Christian V. The 19th-century modernized additions to this rust-red edifice are incongruous in a fort of its age, with castellated walls, curious lancet-arched windows, a massive clock-towered entrance and stucco work, which give it an almost Moorish-Spanish feel. Behind the castellated Gothic revival entrance, built in the 1870s, the fort itself is traditionally designed with four pointed bastions at each corner. Fort Christian's battlements, once bristling with cannon, defended a large central barracks, twenty other internal structures and a central courtyard area. A total of over 36 cannon protected this fortress, and its walls vary from three to six feet thick. The building has been used variously as a police station and prison, courthouse, Governor's residence and vicarage. For 46 years, between 1706 and 1752, a church stood in the fort. Now, the Virgin Islands Museum is situated in a former dungeon.

In 1874 the green-and-white Virgin Islands Legislature building – opposite Fort Christian – was erected as the Danish police barracks. Now the headquarters of the USVI senate, it can be visited and is a handsome structure, with its ornate, railed double staircase, emblematic stucco panels, narrow pediment, parapet, arched lower entrance, louvred windows and decorative cannon.

Fort Skytsborg was built in 1689 by the Danish West India Company and is known as Blackbeard's Tower because of its

*Bluebeard's Tower,
Charlotte Amalie*

assumed (but unproven) associations with the notorious pirate. This three-storey round tower was converted into an observatory in 1831. Built in rough stonework plastered over, with a brick-arched entrance, this is considered the oldest extant historical structure in the Virgin Islands and is listed as a National Historic Landmark. The other round tower lower down the hill is the 18th-century, Bluebeard's Castle, a Danish fort, supposed inhabited by the celebrated polygamist. Subsequently adapted as a private house and hotel the castellated Bluebeard's Castle has heavily shuttered windows and cannon emplacements on its roof.

Government Hill is traversed by a number of steep stepped lanes. One, known as the Street of 99 Steps (103 in reality and built in the 1700s), leads up to Crown House, a stately home built on the hilltop in the 18th century. East of this is the three-storey brick-and-timber Government House, a gracious colonial edifice in neo-Classical style, with elegant wrought-iron balconies and dating from 1867. It is the Governor's residence, and its staircases are of local mahogany. The red sentry box is also of note. There are a number of colonial 18th-century houses on Government Hill, including Lavalette House, a French sea captain's residence begun in 1819. An Italian architect designed the house with its Spanish influences, which was built with slave labour. This site, which is listed on the Register of National Historic Places, is now the Hotel 1829, completed in that year with an attractive Spanish-style courtyard. The captain's initials appear in the fine wrought-iron railings. Also on Government Hill, the Seven Arches Museum is located in a restored 19th-century house with a separate kitchen and walled garden, once the property of a Danish West Indian craftsman. The gun slots in its wall may indicate its former use as a fortification. On Denmark Hill is Cathrineberg, the Danish Consulate building, dating from 1830 and built in Greek Revival style. Two other early military installations are located on Government Hill. Both were part of a complicated defence system.

Charlotte Amalie has no fewer than five churches and a synagogue. One of the oldest public buildings on the island is the Georgian-influenced Lutheran Church, the Fredrikskerk, built in Danish (narrow) brickwork in 1826 on the site of an earlier 18th-century church. A wide sweeping staircase leads to its imposing arched and fanlighted entrance. Its squat 1871 Gothic-style square entrance tower is castellated, with an arched and shuttered window.

Cathrineberg, St Thomas

The ecclesiastical silver is 18th-century Danish, and the church has a vast mahogany altar and a decorative chandelier. Up Lille Tarne Lane, or Little Tower Lane, the Lutheran Parsonage is a good example of an 18th-century residence and was built in 1725. A fire in 1804 destroyed the original 1744 St Thomas Dutch Reformed Church, which was rebuilt in 1844 with a Classical facade including vast columns and an impressive pediment.

The St Thomas Jewish Synagogue, designed by a French architect, was built a little later, in 1833, but is the oldest synagogue in the US. With hurricane-proof walls, this spacious domed building has sand on its floor, to remind its congregation of the Jewish exodus into the desert. The old Jewish cemetery stands outside the town and dates from 1792. The Roman Catholic Cathedral of St Peter and St Paul was consecrated in 1848 and contains some fine Flemish murals. In celebration of emancipation, the All Saints Anglican Church was erected in 1848, constructed with local stone and yellow bricks brought here as ship's ballast. It features tall, pointed-arched, half-shuttered windows and round gable windows. The Moravian Memorial Church dates from 1882 and has an impressive wooden cupola and a wonderful upper-floor gallery.

The town's Market Square was once a slave market, and in Emancipation Park there is a replica of Philadelphia's Liberty Bell. The former Grand Hotel near the Park dates from 1841 and is a magnificent example of colonial architecture, with its vast columns. It was once a three-storey building until a hurricane struck. An old building, with a flat facade, two large wooden doors and shuttered sash windows on Dronningensgade/Main Street is the birthplace of artist Camille Pissarro (1830-1903). Around this area are a number of reconstructed old warehouses, with some interesting Danish brickwork. Note the delicate cast-iron work on the balconies of the town houses, in particularly that of the 1864 St Thomas Savings Bank in Kronprindsensgade, and on the Baerentzen House on Queens Cross Street. It is also worth noting that many of the merchants' houses have either tiled or slat roofs.

As if to make up for the exceptional number of historic buildings in Charlotte Amalie, there are few other sites of interest in this field on St Thomas. Almost in the centre of the island is the St Peter great house and botanical gardens. The old country dwellings of Frenchtown are also worth a visit, and there are a number of plantation great houses in various states of repair. These include Jim Tillet's old sugar plantation complex, the Wintberg plantation house, the great house at Estate Bonne Espérance, and the remains of the Lovendale sugar factory, now a restaurant. The 19th-century

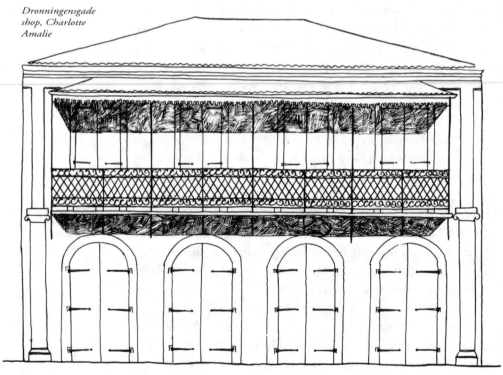

Dronningensgade shop, Charlotte Amalie

Louisenhoj Castle, a private, romantic folly, is located north of the capital. There are early Moravian churches at New Herrnhut and at the 1755 Nisky Mission, which include some interesting half-hip roofed, three-storey buildings. The church at New Herrnhut is plain in external design, with thick walls of solid masonry enclosing a wooden frame to which the hip roof is secured, and unglazed, shuttered window apertures. The interior ceiling is Mansard in design and beautifully timber-lined. The stone farmhouse of Lovendal is also of historic interest.

It was at the coronation of Christian VI of Denmark that two Moravian religious leaders met a black slave from St Thomas and, hearing his description of the island, decided to send a mission to the Caribbean. They arrived in Charlotte Amalie in 1732. The Moravians were accomplished craftsmen and brought with them a range of European styles and techniques. In 1738 they erected their first missionary church at New Herrnhut, an excellent example of early 18th-century rural architecture and unique to the Virgin Islands. The interior wooden ceiling, in particular, is remarkable for its carpentry work.

However, it is on **Hassel Island**, south of the capital, that the most interesting historic military installations can be seen. These date from the early 1800s when the British occupied the island and include the remains of the impressive Cowell Battery, which dominated the south end of Hassel Island. The visitor can also explore Prince Fredrik's Battery on the shoreline below it, the Shippley Battery at the other end of the island and the ruins of around twenty other military buildings, which the Danish expanded from the 1840s. The newer Danish additions to these defence structures include the large magazine, which is still in a fair state of repair.

St John

The smallest of the three main USVI, St John's capital is Cruz Bay, where, in complete contrast to Charlotte Amalie, there is little of historic architectural interest apart from the typical pastel-painted clapboard houses, shops, cafes and bars. The one building of any note in Cruz Bay is the old Danish Battery, but the St John Museum is certainly worth a visit. Two-thirds of this mostly mountainous island forms a national park, the legacy of Laurence Rockefeller, the millionaire philanthropist.

Out on the island there are a few more interesting sites, the best of which is the 1780s Annaberg Plantation. This former Danish sugar plantation on the north coast does not have a great house, but the working building ruins are most impressive. The windmill tower is in a good state of preservation, as are the walls and paved flooring of the sugar factory building, with extensive use of coral blocks on corners, door and window openings. The field workers' cabins were built in the earliest style, with a timber frame and masonry filling, lime concrete floor, and palmetto thatched roofs.

Reef Bay Plantation Great House is spectacular in its isolated ruined majesty. Still hip-roofed, its staired entrance porch, with four massive columns, elaborate banding and arcade of covered terraces, is typically early 19th-century. Remains here include those of a cookhouse, a vaulted oven, servants' quarters, a stable and outhouse. The sugar factory building contains architectural elements of the great house and is in a good state of repair, although its flat brick roof, once supported by heavy timbers, has given way. All the old sugar processing equipment is still here. Other plantation buildings on St John include those of the Lameshur sugar estate, which also raised cotton, Mary Point sugar plantation, Leinster plantation, the factories of Wintberg and Fredriksberg, the windmill tower of the Carolina plantation, the Cinnamon Bay plantation, Caneel Bay Hotel's 18th-century sugar mill, Dennis Bay sugar factory and windmill tower and the Trunk Bay plantation.

Reef Bay Great House, St John

More military installations are located at Coral Bay, where the ruins of Frederik's Fort and its coastal battery can be seen on Fortsberg Hill. This defensive site was begun in 1718, taken over during a slave revolt in 1733 for six months, and burned down in 1826. Near Coral Bay there is the old Moravian Church, dating from the 18th century. The only other site on St John of interest is the Christ of the Caribbean statue, erected near Trunk Bay in 1953.

St Croix

This is the largest and most industrialized of the USVI, and its capital, Christiansted, was laid out by the Danes in 1733 and named after King Christian VI. The entire town has been designated a National Historic District. Again, the town's fort is the oldest building on the island, all the more so as Fort Christiansvaern was built by the Danes in 1734 on the site of a former 1645 French fortification. The existing yellow-and-white building was constructed from bricks brought from Denmark as ballast. It was partly rebuilt in 1772 and abandoned as a fort in 1878, from when it was used as a police station and courthouse. This is the best preserved Danish fort in the Caribbean, and five of its rooms, including the barracks, dungeon, powder magazine, officers' kitchen and battery, as well as its battlements and sally port have been restored to their former grandeur. The double entrance staircase is dramatic and leads up over a lower archway. The black-painted fenestration is interesting for the fixed fanlights and louvred shutters.

Dating from 1747, what could be called the town's oldest public building, the cream-and-white Government House on King Street, was built from two existing merchants' houses and converted to its present use in 1830. It has a handsome arched verandah, a sweeping formal staircase leading to a magnificent courtyard, and a wooden, red-painted, early guardhouse. This massive three-storey building's facade is classical colonial in design, with ornate iron railings. Its inter-arch pilasters, parapet and details are picked out in white, under the crown and cipher of Fredrick VI and the date 1830. Nearby is the house where Nevis-born Alexander Hamilton (1757-1804) worked as a clerk in a merchant's office before going on to be a founding father of the US (now it houses the Little Switzerland shop).

The old Danish West India and Guinea Company warehouse was built in 1749 and is now the Post Office. In a corner of the courtyard, which was once a slave market, is an old guard shelter. The 1735 Steeple Building was the first Lutheran Church here, and the neo-Classical steeple and clock tower on the maroon-and-white structure were added in 1795. It is now used as a museum and has exhibits of the architecture of the region. The Holy Cross Catholic Church, built in the shape of a cross, dates from 1828, and the Lutheran Church was built in 1740.

On Prince Street, the Pink Fancy Hotel opened in 1948 in four buildings, the oldest of which is a typical Danish town house dating from 1780. This beautiful old building has shuttered windows in its wood-built weather-boarded first floor, and the ground floor is of

Steeple Building, Christiansted

stone, with rounded columns supporting the six arches of its fine frontage. The building is listed in the National Register of Historic Places. Another maritime building is the old Scale House (1856) near the wharf, where cargo was once weighed. This is now a tourist information office. There are a number of other warehouses on the waterfront, and the old Apothecary Hall, on Company Street was an 18th-century pharmacy below a residence. The merchants' buildings from this period have living quarters above wide, arched colonnades. The typical colonnades and covered sidewalks are known locally as galleries. These simple, solid buildings have sash windows and storm shutters.

Just outside Christiansted is the Hilty House Inn, with its nearby sugar mill ruin. Built in the remains of a late 18th-century rum distillery, this large villa features a vast Great Room. Also on the town's outskirts is the St John's Anglican Church, and the Friedenstahl Moravian Church, dating from 1854.

Frederiksted, dating from 1752 at the west end of St Croix, has a more Victorian feel about its architecture. This is because, after the 1867 tidal wave and a fire in 1878, started by plantation labourers, which burned the Danish-style wooden upper storeys of the buildings, the stone bases of the houses were rebuilt on in timber, incorporating popular Victorian gingerbread fretwork. The entire town is listed as a National Register Historic District for its many old buildings, mostly dating from the late 19th century. Many of them, like the Frederiksted Gallery on King Street, are two-storey constructions, with retail premises below the residential upper floor. The late 19th-century Fleming Building, on the same street, was built with bricks taken from ruined sugar factories' chimneys. Fort Frederik is inevitably the oldest building in the town, dating from the year the town was founded. The old garrison, barracks, arsenal, canteen, stables, upstairs Commandant's quarters (built in 1760) and courtyard have all been renovated. It was from here that the first official foreign salute to the independent 13 US States was made in 1776. It was also from here that Governor Peter von Scholten was forced to declare emancipation by rebellious slaves in 1848.

The brick-built Customs House, with its 19th-century additions, dates from the late 18th century, as does the police station. An American named Bell built the stone Peterson Public Library on Strandgade in 1880. The three-storey Victoria House, also on picturesque Strandgade, was first constructed in 1803, but after the

1878 fire it was completely renovated, incorporating some intricate gingerbread decoration. The Apothecary Hall was built in 1839, and its lower floor is of cut coral blocks. An intricately latticed gallery accentuates the wooden upper floor with full length shuttered windows. A fine wrought-iron balcony is the main feature of the two-storey gabled Benjamin House next door. The old Danish School dates from 1830, one of eight built on the island for slave children.

The oldest church here is the Holy Trinity Lutheran Church on Hill Street, a handsome Georgian building dating from 1791. The tower's cupola was added later. St Patrick's Roman Catholic Church was built in 1843 of cut limestone blocks, detailed with typically Danish yellow bricks in Gothic Revival style on the site of an earlier 18th-century church. The three-tiered bell tower is a later addition. This church has some interesting local interior woodwork, and the churchyard dates from the 18th century. The priest's residence is the arcaded building nearby. The St Paul's Episcopal Church is a mixture of Georgian Gothic Revival and Classical styles and dates from 1812. The Gothic Revival bell tower of exposed sandstone was added later. Features of the interior include some excellent woodwork and a tray ceiling. Other places of passing interest in Frederiksted are the Old Public Library building and the elaborate house known as Cumberland Castle.

Typical Danish archways front the merchants' houses, and some of the upper storeys are highly decorative, with louvered and shut-

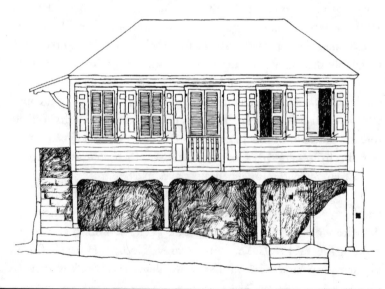

Frederiksted house

tered windows and doors, often with a balustrade of highly ornate wooden fretwork to let air circulate, and with timber cladding, sometimes artfully serrated.

One of the main attractions out of Frederiksted is the restored, elegant, oval-planned, Whim Plantation Great House, built in 1794 and listed as a National Register Historic Site. This great house has curved ends, with cut stone and coral walls three feet thick, parapets and pediments over the windows, and a brick arch over the doors. The structure was surrounded by a unique dry wind moat, which circulated cooling air into the basement and under the floor. Steps lead over this to the entrance. The high roof is shingle-clad, resulting in a ceiling sixteen feet high in all three rooms. A small wing was later added adjacently, also with a shingle roof. Here there are the restored remains of its ancient sugar mill, steam chimney, a circular mule mill (dating from 1750) and a sugar processing factory with all the ancillary equipment, including a still. On display are three types of sugar grinding mills. The dungeon-like outhouses had areas for the blacksmith, cooper, wheelwright, joiner and logger. The original cookhouse is here, as is the old apothecary shop, dating from 1832. Out on the fields is an example of a barrel-vaulted watchtower, which also doubled as a slaves' nursery. Also on the Whim Estate is the Estate Butler Bay great house, one of the most magnificent colonial homes on the islands. The estate workers' village and sugar factory here have been carefully restored.

There are numerous other sugar plantation works on St Croix, some of which have also been renovated or turned into guest houses, but most are in ruins. At one time, there were 400 plantations on St Croix. The remains of the St George's plantation house are worth seeing, with ruins of its old sugar mill and rum factory, a restored slave hut, blacksmith's shop and manager's house. This complex is listed as a National Register Historic District. Little La Grange's 18th-century great house near Frederiksted is a well-preserved example of an estate which was converted from sugar to dairy farming in the 1890s. The La Grange sugar factory, once owned by a Danish Prime Minister, is now restored as a museum, as are the Estate Mount Washington plantation ruins.

The Sprat Hall Plantation House, now a hotel, stands on the western tip of the island. This beautiful great house, built during the French occupation in the latter half of the 1600s, is the island's oldest intact plantation house, and its slave quarters have been

Sprat Hall, St Croix

modernized. There are old stone mill towers at Bodkin and more remains on Jolly Hill and the Mount Eagle estates. One feature of St Croix's plantations is their colourful names. These include Upper Love, Lower Love (with its 112-foot sugar factory chimney erected in the 1880s), Jealousy, Prosperity, Sally's Fancy, Anna's Hope, Hams Bay, John's Rest, Morning Star and Fountain Valley. Golden Grove Estate's great house is on the University of the Virgin Islands' campus and dates from 1890.

There is a collection of historic plantation buildings on the Estate Little Princess, overlooking Christiansted, and Judith's Fancy, now in ruins, was the one-time home of the Governor of the Knights of Malta. There are few remains of the 17th-century château-style great house built here, but the guardhouse is still standing. At Castle Coakey sugar plantation the windmill was supplemented with power from a rare mule mill, protected by a six-sided steep shingled roof. In the 1700s, the great house, built in the style of a Danish farmhouse, stood next to the mill, while to one side of the great house were the slaves' quarters – an early thatched bohío-type dwelling with no walls. The Estate Mount Washington Plantation has been opened to the public and comprises a rum factory, stables and a mule-powered mill. One of the most historic great houses, now The Buccaneer Hotel, was built by the Frenchman Martel, a Knight of Malta, in 1653 on the Estate Shoys. When the Danes bought the island from the French, Governor von Prok turned the great house into a sugar factory, building his home on the estate and erecting the mill, the ruins of which still stand in the grounds. Micheal Shoy bought the estate for cotton growing in the mid-1700s, and the Heyliger Company later began raising cattle here. The Armstrong family operated the cattle ranch from 1922 until they opened the hotel in 1948.

Designed by the Danish architect, Albert Lovmand, in the Classical style, the Diamond school house was built in the 1830s for Moravian missionaries to teach slave children. After emancipation in 1848, this and eight other schools built at that time were used for social functions.

Part Five

Architectural Dictionary

An alphabetical glossary of common architectural terms pertaining to the Caribbean, most of which appear in the preceeding text.

A

Abacus – Upper member of capital, supporting architrave.

Acanthas – Herbaceous plant form often used in architectural decoration.

Acroterium – Pedestal on a pediment, often ornamented, a pinnacle.

Adam-style – After British architect Robert Adam (1728-92), who blended Rococo and neo-Classicism.

Adoquín – Spanish name for cobblestones, often imported from North America as ballast during the 17th-19th centuries, and used to pave streets and courtyards. Often known locally as 'Chinaman's balls' for their smooth, rounded appearance.

Ajoupa – Amerindian house built on stilts.

Antepecho – A half-height window screen, or guard.

Appliqué – Ornamental work laid on some other material or surface.

Apse – Large semicircular or polygonal recess, arched or domed roof at end of church.

Aqueduct – A channel to carry water, often built on arches above the ground.

Arabesque – Decoration with fanciful intertwining of leaves or scrollwork similar to that of Moorish decoration.

Arcade – A series of arches, often in front of a covered passageway.

Arch – Curved structure used as support.

Architrave – Main beam resting on abacus of column. Various parts surrounding door or window. Moulding around exterior of arch.

Arsenal – A building where arms and ammunition are stored.

Artesonado – Wooden ceiling in geometric patterns.

Awning – Covering over the top of a window.

Azulejo – Decorative tiling, often of a typical blue colour, from the Spanish 'azul'.

B

Balcón – Outside walkway of a building, like a balcony, often balustraded.

Baldachin or baloquinto – Canopy over altar or throne.

Ballast – Weight to keep ships on an even keel, often cobblestones or bricks, brought to the Caribbean from Europe.

Balustrade – A low railing either along a balcony or up a stairway.

Baptistry – Part of a church used for baptism.

Barbacoa – Amerindian name for a thatched house built on stilts over water or an open space. Also the name for a modern division of large rooms in old colonial mansions.

Barbecue – Coffee bean drying area in coffee mill, usually a large flat open space.

Barge-board – Ornamental screen, or board, under the edge of a gable, facing the edges of a roof.

Barleysugar – Describing typical twists in generally wooden, turned, columns or supports.

Baroque – Architectural style with curved forms and extravagant decoration, typical in 17th and 18th century Europe.

Barracoon – Slave housing, usually in wooden barrack-like buildings, on sugar plantations. Also, fortified slave compound in Africa. Hence the racist and derogatory term 'coon'.

Barrel vault – Semi-cylindrical vault, usually built of stone blocks or bricks.

Barrote – A window screen, bar or guard usually made of turned hardwood rods.

Bartizan – Turret or watchtower, projecting from the wall of a fort.

Basilica – Oblong hall with double colonnade and apse.

Bas-relief – Sculpture in low relief.

Bastion – Projecting structure commanding walls and foreground.

Battery – Small fortification or emplacement for artillery.

Bay – Principal feature of a building's structure, as in bay-window.

Beading – Small, semi-circular line of decorative moulding of wood or plaster.

Bell awning – Shaped awning, hood, or covering, standing out over the top of a window.

Bigas – Old Spanish word for a decorated wooden ceiling, usually of Mudéjar style.

Bohío – Amerindian word meaning thatched rural house.

Boss – Carved or sculptured projection at centre of ribs, as in centre of vaulted dome.

Boucan – Coffee or cocoa bean drying area.

Bracket – Projecting wooden structure, supporting eaves.

Busha – Local name for a plantation overseer's house.

Buttress – Support built against a wall; a flying buttress stands out from wall.

C

Campanile – Bell tower.

Caneye – Conical Amerindian thatched framework hut.

Canopy – Covering suspended or held over throne, bed, altar.

Capital – Head of pillar or column.

Caponier – A guardhouse, projecting from the walls of a castle or fort.

Cartouche – A scroll on the cornice of a column, an ornamental tablet, often moulded in plaster or carved stone and let into a wall or gateway.

Caryatid – Cast or carved female figure used as pillar to support entablature.

Case – Basic, wood-built hut or house in the French islands of the Caribbean.

Case aménagée – Literally 'fitted out hut' in the French Caribbean.

Casement – Chamber inside the thickness of walls, usually with embrasures.

Castellated – Wall top design, like that on a castle with battlements.

Chamfer – Bevelled edge, formed by cutting off the square angle.

Chancel – Part of church near altar reserved for clergy or choir.

Chattel house – Literally, moveable property, a name given to a small, usually wooden, house.

Choir – Chancel of large church.

Churrigueresque – Of the style of the Churriguera, an 18th-century Spanish architectural family, prevalent in Latin America.

Cinquefoil – Usually with reference to windows, with a shape like five petals.

Cipher – An individual character or monogram.

Cistern – A depression or structure designed to catch, or hold water.

Clapboard – Similar to weather-board, employing wooden exterior wall cladding.

Classical revival – Later adaptation of ancient Greek or Roman styles.

Clerestory – Upper part of nave or transept of large church, containing windows above the roofs of the aisles.

Cloister – Covered walk, often round a quadrangle, with colonnade or windows on the inside and wall on outer.

Colonnade – Series of columns, usually supporting a roof, verandah or upper storey, often with entablature.

Column – Long, vertical, often tapering cylinder supporting entablature or arch.

Cooler windows – Windows which stand proud of the line of the wall, often encased in louvres, also called Demerara windows.

Coping – Capping, or covering of a wall top, designed to shed water and to protect the meeting of the tiles on the slope of two roof sides.

Coquina – Also known as ironshore or black teeth, fossilized coral rock, often used in the construction of early Caribbean buildings.

Corbel – Stone or wooden projection jutting out from wall to support weight.

Corbel table – Projecting course resting on corbels.

Corinthian – Order of Classical architecture, characterized by bell-shaped capitals.

Cornice – Horizontal moulded projection crowning a building or structure, ornamental moulding around wall below ceiling.

Course – Horizontal row of bricks or stones in building.

Cranked – Angled, as in a roofline, cranked over a verandah.

Crenellation – Deployment of battlements and/or loopholes.

Cresting – Decoration on a roof ridge.

Crown – Top part of arch or vault.

Crow-stepped – Steps on the coping or covering of a wall or gable.

Cruciform – Cross shape of church design, with transepts at each side of the main nave.

Cupola – Small rounded dome forming or adorning roof.

Curvilinear – Outline of a gable, or architectural detail, with curved shape.

D

Dado – Horizontal band, usually on a wall, often decorated.

Dakpannen – Name for the orange-red tiles imported to the Caribbean from Holland.

Demerara windows – Long louvres which hinge outwards from small balcony-like protrusions, like window-boxes, often wrought in wooden latticework. These window projections usually incorporate top-hung shutters which can be opened by means of a wooden strut.

Dentil course – Horizontal row of uniformly spaced projecting bricks or stones in a building.

Distress – Method used to make new, usually wooden, furniture appear old.

Dollhouse – Another name fro the Bajan chattel house.

Dormer window – Window built proud of the line of the roof.

Dowel – Pin, usually wooden, used to hold a structure together.

Dry stone – Construction technique without use of mortar or cement.

Dutch gable – Gable end in curvilinear or multi-curved sides, often surmounted with a pediment.

E

Eave – The underside of a roof overhang.

Embossed – Raised ornamentation on a smooth surface.

Embrasure – Bevelling at sides of windows or door, or opening in parapet widening from within, used for firing guns.

Entablature – Part of an order above column, including architrave, frieze and cornice.

Entasis – Imperceptible curve in a column.

Entresuelo – Opening in a wall usually between floors, allowing access for goods.

Escutcheon – In English, a decorative mounting, or shield on a door, or box keyhole, for example. In Spanish *escudo*, or shield.

Estipite – A typical New World style of broken pilaster, or rectangular column, as part of a wall.

F

Facade – Face of building

Fanlight – A window, or opening, usually over a doorway, in the shape of an open fan.

Fenestration – The arrangement of windows in a building.

Fieldstone – Another word for rubble

Filigree – Ornamental delicate tracery work.

Finial – Ornament finishing off apex of roof, pediment, gable, tower-corner or canopy.

Fishpond roof – Roof designed with an integral tank to collect rainwater.

Fish-scale tiles – Overlapping tiles common in French tropical buildings.

Flush – On the same plane or level as surrounding surfaces

Formative Period – The name given to the Spanish colonial architectural styles of the 17th century.

Fresco – Method of painting on wall or ceiling before plaster is dry.

Fretting – Carved ornamental pattern.

Frieze – Ornamented band, often sculptured, between architrave and cornice.

Front house – The front section of a chattel house which has been extended.

G

Gable – Triangular upper part of wall at end of ridged roof. Canopy over window or door.

Gable window – Window located above the roof line of a pitched roof, but with its own small roof.

Gallery – A long room, platform or mezzanine, often on an upper floor, supported on columns or by brackets. Usually facing into the interior of a building.

Gargoyle – Grotesque spout projecting from gutter usually in form of human or animal.

Garita – Sentry box or guardroom.

Gaulette – Wooden slats or boards, forming sides of a house in the French Caribbean.

Gaut – Local name for open drains on St Kitts

Gazebo – Small outside shelter, often open-sided and decorative.

Georgian – Classical Palladian symmetrical style, often Caribbean Georgian.

Gingerbread – Fretwork typical of the Victorian era, embellishing the outside of a house.

Gothic – Church architecture from the 12th to 16th centuries, with typical pointed arches and windows, vaulted roofs and flying buttresses.

Gothic revival – 19th-century revival of above style.

Gragerie – A mill used in the French Caribbean to process cassava.

Groin – Curved line along intersecting vaults.

Gutterhead – Top part of a rainwater down-pipe drain.

H

Hacienda – Farm, estate or plantation (Spanish).

Half-hipped roof – Roof with steeper slopes on the sides than at the ends, which form gables.

Half-timbered – Wooden frame building, where openings are filled with masonry.

Hammer-beam – Term applied to a ceiling, of open timberwork, usually of Gothic design.

Header course – Horizontal row of bricks or stones in a building, with the short sides projecting.

Helm roof – Roof in the shape of a helm or helmet.

Hipped roof – Roof where sides and ends have the same slope from the ridge.

Hofje – Term in the Dutch Antilles for small, irrigated, enclosed plot of land used for growing fruit and vegetables.

Hood moulding – Ornamental moulding over window or door, protruding from the wall..

Hurricane shutters – Solid, plain window shutters, barred in place with a thick slotted wooden bar, sometimes ornate on the inside for show.

I

Ionic – Order of classical architecture characterized by scroll-shaped or spiral capitals.

Isabeline – Ornate architectural style of period of Queen Isabela of Spain (1474-1504)

J

Jacobean – Before Georgian period, style belonging to Tudor or Elizabethan era.

Jalousie – Slatted or louvred wooden shutter or blind over a window or door.

Jerkin-headed – A roof style similar to a gambrel, peculiar to Turks and Caicos Islands.

K

Kabay – Round, conical, palm-thatched Carib Amerindian dwelling. Also *carbet*.

Kalk – Building lime made of burned coral and shells.

Kas di pal'i maishi – Dutch basic slave house, referring to maize or sorghum thatch.

Kas grandi – Dutch plantation great house.

Keystone – Principal block at top of arch holding the structure together.

Kneed – The word for a typical shipwright's house on Salt Cay, Turks & Caicos Islands, and the Bahamas.

L

Landhuis – Country estate house in the Dutch West Indies.

Lancet – Name for a tall, thin window, often pointed like an arrow slit.

Lantern – The structure built on top of a dome, often either housing a bell, a room, or designed to let light in.

Lathe and Plaster – Often woven, thin, wooden strips used to build a wall of double thickness, in-filled with rubble, wood or corn cobs, and plastered.

Latin American Baroque – A Baroque style developed in Latin America, which continued in the region after Baroque had gone out of fashion in the 18th century.

Lattice – A criss-cross patterning used in screening, or the name for a hinged window, or the pattern on a window creating diamond shapes.

Lintel – Horizontal timber or stone over window or door.

Loggia – A roofed, open gallery integrally built as part of a building.

Louvre – Arrangement of sloping boards designed to shed rain outwards but to let light enter. Used mainly on windows and doors.

Loyalist – Style brought to the Caribbean by American immigrants loyal to the British Crown, often traditionally Georgian.

Luceta – A rectangular-shaped light over a door or window opening.

M

Magasina – Old Dutch name for a storage building.

Magazine – Gunpowder and ammunition store.

Mampara – Fenestrated interior door or doors letting in light and air to a room.

Mansard – As in Mansard-roof, where each face has two slopes, the lower steeper than the upper. Also the name for an attic room, mansarde, with a sloping roof. After Mansard, or Mansart, the two French architects, François (1596-1666), and Jules Hardoun-Mansart (1646-1708), archi-tect of the Versailles palace and chapel and the dome of Les Invalides.

Manse – Ecclesiastical residence of pastor, priest, verger.

Mantel – Wood, stone or marble structure above a fireplace.

Marl – A clay and lime mixture used in masonry.

Martello tower – Round watch towers named after the success of those used in Mortella, Corsica, in 1794.

Masjid – Islamic mosque.

Masonry – Construction of stone, brick, tile or aggregates.

Mediopunta/Medioluna – A half-moon shaped light, usually of coloured glass, over a window or doorway.

Mestizaje – Eclectic Spanish colonial mix of influences, European and local.

Mezzanine – A storey intermediate between two main ones, often called *entresuelo* in Spanish.

Mihrab – In Islamic architecture, a niche indicating the direction of Mecca.

Minaret – A tall, slender tower, usually part of a mosque, with balconies for summoning the faithful to prayer.

Moat – A deep ditch, usually water-filled, often found around forts.

Mock arches – Arch shaped decoration, often found over windows.

Mortise – Hole cut in timber to receive a tenon as building technique, as in mortise and tenon joints.

Mosaic – Picture or patterns produced by joining together minute pieces of glass or stone of different colours.

Mouina – An 'A'-framed wooden, thatched structure used as a dwelling by early Carib Amerindians.

Moulding – Ornamental variety of outline in cornices etc.

Mozarabic – Pertaining to Christians in Spain after the Moorish conquest who were allowed to practise their faith in return for allegiance to the Moors. A mixture of Christian and Islamic architectural styles.

Mudéjar – Style of architecture which relates to the Arab or Moorish influence on Spanish architecture, often seen in the style of colonial Spanish ceilings.

Mullion – Vertical bar which separates a window into sections.

N

Nave – Body of church from west door to chancel, separated by pillars from aisles.

Neo-Classical – Revival of the Classical style of architecture.

Neo-Gothic – Revival of the Gothic style of architecture, prevalent in both Spanish and British colonial architecture.

Newel-post – Vertical post providing the main support for railing of staircase.

Niche – Shallow recess in wall to contain statue, vase etc.

O

Obelisk – Tapering monolithic column or monument.

Obverse – Narrower at the base than at the apex or top.

Observatory – Building designed from which to make astronomical, or meteorological observations.

Ogee-shaped – Usually in reference to the shape of a gable – 'S'-shaped.

P

Palladian – Neo-Classical, after the style of 16th-century Italian architect, Andrea Palladio (1508-1580).

Palladian window – Window with three lights and an arch over the central one.

Parapet – Low wall or barrier at edge of roof or platform.

Patio – Inner court open to sky, roofless area belonging to house.

Peak Period – The name given to Spanish colonial architectural styles of the 18th century.

Pediment – Triangular part crowning front of building over a portico.

Pencas – The name for the Royal Palm fronds used to thatch buildings.

Perpendicular – Third stage of English Gothic with vertical tracery in large windows.

Persianas – Slats, often made of wood, which allow the occupant to receive air and light, to look out, without being seen. Like Venetian binds.

Piano Nobile – Upper-storey living quarters, above service rooms or cellars.

Pier – Support of arch or span, pillar of window.

Pilaster – A rectangular column, often affixed to a wall, generally decorative.

Pinnacle – An upright structure, often decorated, usually ending in a spire.

Plateresque – Style of decoration reflecting the delicate filigree workmanship of Spanish silversmiths.

Plaza – Open square or market place.

Plinth – Lowest part of the base of a structure or column

Podium – A continuous base or plinth.

Polvorín – A powder magazine (Spanish).

Portal – Doorway or gateway.

Portales – Columned, covered walkways often running the length of a building.

Porte Cochère – Doorway for coaches, often with a pedestrian doorway set into it.

Portico – Colonnade, roof supported by columns, usually as porch attached to building.

Postigo – Doors with small windows or openings let into them to allow access without opening the larger doors.

Presbytery – Eastern part of chancel beyond the choir.

Primitive Period – Name given to the style of Spanish colonial architecture of the 16th century.

Purgerie – Place in French West Indian sugar factories where sugar is purified.

Putlog – Horizontal beams used to support scaffolding, were fixed into putlocks, or holes in walls used during construction, often left in after building work.

Putto – Figure of child or cherub, Renaissance or Baroque.

Q

Quatrefoil – Usually with reference to windows with a shape like four petals.

Quoin – Prominent stone, emphasising the corner of a building or a window or door surround.

R

Rampart – Embankment raised against a wall or fortification.

Redoubt – Projecting part of a bastion or defence work.

Rendered – The rough plastering of an exterior wall.

Reja – Usually ornate wrought-iron covering or grille, fixed over a window or door.

Relief – Moulding or carving with design standing out from surface, either high or low.

Reliquary – Receptacle for relics, often items associated with saint.

Repoussé – Formed in relief by hammering from behind (ornamental metal work)

Retable – Shelf or panelled frame behind altar for holding ornaments.

Ridge – Line along roof where the slopes of the roof meet.

Rococo – Style developed in 18th-century France, characterized by curved forms, asymmetry and slender proportions.

Rose window – A round window of tracery work, resembling the design of a rose

Rubble wall – Simple masonry building method using roughly hewn stone blocks of varying sizes, sometimes laid in courses like bricks.

Rusticate – Create a rough surface.

S

Sacristy – Repository for church vestments, vessels etc.

Saddle roof – Normal pitched roof with shallower extensions each side.

Sally-port – A gate, or passageway leading underground, from the inner to the outer part of a fortification.

Saltbox – Type of square wooden house, resembling early boxes made to keep table salt.

Sanctuary – Part of chancel between altar railings and east window or screen, containing high altar. Holiest place.

Sandbox – Name given to a house which resembles the boxes where fine sand was kept for drying writing ink, before blotting paper.

Sarcophagus – Stone coffin often adorned with sculpture.

Sash window – Window which can be opened by sliding half the window frame, up or down, balanced by a cord and weight device, the sash, in the casement.

Scroll brackets – The name for scroll-shaped, wrought-iron or wooden support brackets.

Scroll gables – Gables decorated or formed in a scroll design, typical in the Dutch Antilles.

Sedan-chair porch – An English-style, box-shaped porch, often with interior bench seats.

Serrated – Saw-like edge design.

Sgraffito – Graffiti or scratching on surface to produce pattern.

Shed roof – A flat, sloping roof at the back of a small country house over outhouse.

Shingle – Usually rectangular slats of wood used as roofing or walling tiles.

Shot-tower – A tall military structure used to produce lead shot.

Single house – Traditional simple house form imported into the Caribbean from Charleston, USA.

Soldier lintel – Flat, red bricked lintel, with brick ends facing outwards.

Spall – Chip of rock or stone used to fill gaps in wall construction.

Spanish walling – A style of house building with a wooden framework in-filled with stone or brick.

Spire – Tapering structure in shape of cone or pyramid.

Spurs – Often sheaths of metal built around the corner of a building to protect it from the damage caused by carriage wheels. Sometimes cannon or concrete blocks were used for the same purpose.

Storm shutter – Window shutter, usually made solid of heavy wood and either top- or side-hinged.

Stucco – Plaster or cement for coating wall or ceiling surface or for moulding into architectural decoration.

Swags – Ornamental festoon of flowers etc, carved or moulded.

T

Tabby – The name for the stone or rubble in-fill of a timber framed building, used in the Bahamas.

Tapia – Wall in-fill of a timber framed building, as used in Trinidad.

Tenon – See Mortise.

Tester – A canopy over altar or throne, supported from a wall or suspended from ceiling.

Tinajero – A wooden cabinet containing a porous stone through which rainwater was filtered into a small *tinajón*.

Tinajón – A large earthenware jar, originally used to transport oil, placed under guttering spouts to catch fresh rain water.

Tracery – Stone ornamental open-work pattern, as in head of Gothic window.

Transept – Transverse part of cruciform church, north and south arms, as the main nave faced west to east.

Trapiche – A mill for crushing sugar cane, operated by horse, mule or ox power.

Tray ceiling – A ceiling in the shape of an inverted tray, enhancing air circulation.

Trefoil – Usually with reference to a window in the shape of three petals.

Trusswork – An arrangement of roof timbers forming a bracket, or spanning a roof space.

Tuff – A fine-grained volcanic rock used in some Caribbean architecture.

Turned post – Rail, balustrade, post, turned in a lathe, instead of carved.

Turtle-crawl – An enclosed area in which live turtles were kept to be slaughtered for food.

Tympanum – Vertical triangular space forming centre of pediment, or over door between lintel and arch.

V

Valley gutter – A rain drain or gutter running between two roof gables.

Vaulting – Arched roof or series of arches forming roof, radiating out from central point.

Verandah – A portico or gallery usually running the length of an upper floor.

Vega – Wooden, thatched barn used to mature tobacco leaves.

Vernacular architecture – Architecture indigenous to the country or region in question.

Vitrales – Coloured glass panels used as decoration of the lights above doors or windows, introduced in the 18th century.

W

Wainscot – Wooden facing of an interior wall, usually panelled.

Wattle and daub – Wattle is interlaced twigs and branches, and daub is mud or clay plastering, used to create a basic hut wall.

Weather-board – Cladding or structure of a wall with horizontal boards designed to shed rain downwards.

Wind hut – Only found on Saint-Barthélémy, basic thick, stone-built houses, especially designed for the prevailing climatic conditions.

Wind moat – A dry moat built around the base of a building, chanelling cooling air into a basement, or lower floor.

Window walls – Entire walls which can made from a variety of styles of windows, butted together.

Y

Yaguas – Palm frond sheaths, often used to face the walls of bohíos, or thatched huts.

Yam cellar – storeroom, often partly underground, for keeping staple diet for workers.

Part Six

Conservation for the Future

Apart from UNESCO's World Heritage efforts in Cuba, the Dominican Republic and Puerto Rico, many islands now have their own National Trust or heritage organization. These have done much to preserve, conserve, reconstruct and restore the architectural legacy of the Caribbean for future generations.

There remains much to be done to preserve the numerous sites in the Caribbean which are still in need of restoration, and the following societies and organizations are responsible for the architectural heritage of their respective territories. Without their concerted efforts, future generations will lose a unique insight into the past.

Only on Barbados is there a comprehensive heritage visitors' scheme, whereby the National Trust sell passports entitling the visitor to enter any National Trust property on the island as well as several privately-owned old buildings.

Directory

The following organizations welcome enquiries and support from those interested in the region's architecture.

Anguilla National Trust, PO Box 1234, The Valley, Anguilla.
Tel: (264) 497 5297 Fax (264) 497 5571
Axanat@anguillanet.com

The Anguilla Archaeological and Historical Society, PO Box 252, The Valley, Anguilla.

The Antigua and Barbuda Historical and Archaeological Society, Church Street, St. John's, Antigua. Tel: (268) 463 1060. Also PO Box 103, English Harbour, Antigua.

The Bahamas National Trust, The Retreat, Village Road, PO Box N-4105, Nassau, New Providence Island, The Bahamas. Tel: (242) 393 1317 Fax: (242) 393 4978.

The Bahamas Historical Society, Elizabeth Avenue/Shirley Street, PO Box 55-6833, Nassau, The Bahamas. Tel: (242) 322 4231.

The Bahamas Department of Archives, Ministry of Education, PO Box SS 6341, Nassau, The Bahamas. Tel: (242) 393 2175/2855 Fax: (242) 393 2855.

The Bahamas Lighthouse Preservation Society, Hope Town, Elbow Cay, Abacos, The Bahamas.

The Barbados National Trust, Wildey House, Wildey, St Michael, Barbados. Tel: (246) 426 2421/436 9033. Fax: (246) 429 9055. http://www.sunbeach.net/trust

Bonaire Department of Culture, Sabana 14, Kralendijk, Bonaire Tel: (5997) 8868.

British Virgin Islands National Parks Trust, c/o Ministry of Natural Resources, Road Town, Tortola, BVI.

National Trust For The Cayman Islands, The Trust House, Courts Road, PO Box 31116 SMB, Grand Cayman, Cayman Islands. Tel: (345) 949 0121 Fax: (345) 949 7494.

Cayman Islands National Archive, Government Administration Building, Grand Cayman, Cayman Islands Tel: (345) 949 9809 Fax: (345) 949 9727.

Oficina del Historiador, Ciudad de La Habana, Tacón No. 1, La Habana Vieja, Ciudad de La Habana 10100, República de Cuba. Tel: (53-7) 2876/5062/5001 Fax: 33 8183.

Curaçao Monument Council, Inter-Regional Committee Action Willemstad (ICAW), Monument Bureau, Scharlooweg 51, Willemstad, Curaçao. Tel: (5999) 465 4688 Fax: (5999) 465 4591.

Corporation for Urban Revitalization, Monument Conservation Foundation. Belvederestraat 43/45, PO Box 2042, Willemstad, Curaçao. Tel: (5999) 462 8680 Fax: (5999) 462 7275.

Division of Culture, Ministry of Community Development & Women's Affairs, Government Headquarters, Roseau, Commonwealth of Dominica. Tel: (767) 448 2401 ext. 3155 Fax: (767) 449 8446/8220.

Dominica Conservation Association, PO Box 109, Roseau, Commonwealth of Dominica.Tel: (809) 448 4334 Fax: (809) 448 3855 Domcona@cwdom.dm

Grenada Historical Society, St George's, Grenada.

Grenada Board of Tourism, Burn's Point, St George's (PO Box 293), Grenada. Tel: (473) 440 2279 Fax: (473) 440 6637 HYPERLINK mailto:Gbt@caribsurf.com Gbt@caribsurf.com http://www.interknowledge.com/grenada

Union Régionale des Associations du Patrimoine et de l'Environnement de Guadeloupe, BP 82L, Pointe-à-Pitre, 97112, Guadeloupe.

Réhabiliter le Patrimoine Naturel et Historique, 26 rue Ducoste, Port-au-Prince, République d'Haiti. Tel: (509) 22 1219.

Jamaica Conservation and Development Trust, PO Box 1225, Kingston 8, Jamaica. Tel: (876) 960 2848 Fax: (876) 960 2850 Jcdt@uwimona.edu.jm

The Jamaica National Heritage Trust, 79 Duke Street, Kingston, Jamaica.

Bureau du Patrimoine, 43 bis rue Jacques Cazotte, 97200 Fort-de-France, Martinique. Tel: (596) 63 85 55.

Montserrat National Trust, PO Box 54, Plymouth, Montserrat.

Nevis Historical and Conservation Society, PO Box 476, Charlestown, Nevis. Tel: (869) 469 5786 Fax: (869) 469 0274 Nhcs@caribsurf.com

Ponce History Museum, 51-53 calle Isabela, Ponce, Puerto Rico. Tel: (787) 844 7071

Puerto Rico Institute of Culture, Museums and Parks Tel: (787)) 724 5477

St Christopher Heritage Society, Bank Street, PO Box 338, Basseterre, St Kitts. Tel: (869) 465 5584.

St Lucia National Trust, PO Box 525, Castries, St Lucia. Tel: (758) 452 5005/31495 Fax: (758) 453 2791.

The National Trust (St Vincent & The Grenadines), c/o CARIPEDA, PO Box 1132, Arnos Vale, St Vincent & The Grenadines.

The National Trust, c/o Department of Tourism, Ministry of Foreign Affairs, Tourism and Information, Financial Complex, Kingstown, St Vincent & The Grenadines.

The Historical Foundation Museum, Fort Oranje, Sint Eustatius. Tel: (5993) 82288.

Cultural Centre of Philipsburg, Back Street, Philipsburg, Sint Maarten. Tel: (5995) 22056.

Tobago Heritage Committee, Tobago, West Indies. Tel: (868) 639 4441.

Tourism and Industrial Development Company of Trinidad and Tobago Ltd (TIDCO). 10 Philipps Street, Port of Spain, Trinidad. Tel: (868) 623 6022 Fax: (868) 624 8124. http://www.tidco.co.tt

Turks & Caicos National Museum, PO Box 188, Grand Turk, Turks & Caicos Islands. Tel: (649) 946 2160.

Turks & Caicos National Trust, PO Box 261, Cockburn Town, Grand Turk, Turks & Caicos Islands. Tel: (649) 946 2160.

Virgin Islands Conservation Society, PO Box 12379, St Thomas, US Virgin Islands 00801.

Regional Organizations

Caribbean Conservation Association, Savannah Lodge, The Garrison, St Michael, Barbados. Tel: (246) 426 9633 Fax: (246) 426 9635 CCA@caribsurf.com

CARIMOS (Rescue and Promotion of Caribbean Architectural Heritage) P.O Box 1857, Santo Domingo, Dominican Republic. Tel: (809) 682 6593 Fax: (809) 688 6925.

The Caribbean Historic Architecture Trust, (CHART), 2 Aldeburgh Place, Woodford Wells, Essex, IG8 OPT UK.

UNESCO Regional Office for Culture in Latin America and the Caribbean. Apartado Postal 4158, Calzada No. 551, esq. A-D, Vedado, La Habana, Cuba.

UNESCO – Belize, Bahamas and Jamaica, The Towers, 25 Dominica Drive, 3rd Floor, PO Box 8203, Kingston, Jamaica.

UNESCO – Netherlands Antilles, Aruba, Trinidad & Tobago, c/o UNDP, PO Box 812, Port of Spain, Trinidad and Tobago. Fax: (868) 628 4827.

Further Reading

Angus W. Acworth, *Buildings of Architectural or Historic Interest in the British West Indies*. London, 1951.
Ypie Attema, *Sint Eustatius*. Zutphen, 1976.
Sir Kenneth Blackburne, *The Romance of English Harbour*. Antigua, 1959.
David J. Buisseret and Jack Tyndale-Biscoe, *Historic Jamaica From the Air*. Kingston, 1996.

Peter Bynoe, *The Architecture of Trinidad and Tobago*. Port of Spain, 1962.

Morris Cargill (ed), *Ian Fleming Introduces Jamaica*. London, 1965.

Robert Devaux, *Saint Lucia Historic Sites*. Castries, 1975.

Alberto Fernández and Fernando Gómez, *Cementerio Cristóbal Colón*. Havana, 1994.

Frederik C. Gjessing and William P. Maclean, *Historic Buildings of St Thomas and St John*. London, 1987.

Pamela Gosner, *Caribbean Georgian: The Great and Small Houses of the West Indies*. Washington DC, 1982.

Gerard de Groot, *De Nederlandse Antillen*. Baarn, 1978.

Barbara Hill, *Historic Churches of Barbados*. Barbados, 1984.

Lennox Honychurch, *The Dominica Story*. London, 1975.

Pierre Jourdain, *Le fort St Louis*. Fort-de-France, 1946.

Felix Kerr, Willie Alleyne and Henry Fraser, *Treasures of Barbados*. London, 1990.

Earle I. A. Kirby, *The Sugar Mills of St Vincent and Their Sites*. St Vincent, 1973.

J. Lightbourne, *The Story of Fort Christian 1672*. Charlotte Amalie, 1973.

M.D. Ozinga. *De Monumenten van Curaçao in woord en beeld*. The Hague, 1959.

Michael Pawson and David J. Buisseret, *Port Royal, Jamaica*. Oxford, 1975.

Gail Saunders and Donald Cartwright, *Historic Nassau*. London, 1979.

Olive Senior, *A to Z of Jamaican Heritage*. Kingston, 1984.

Suzanne Slesin et al, *Caribbean Style*. London, 1986.

George Tyson, A*n Inventory of the Historical Landmarks of St Kitts-Nevis*. Saint Thomas, 1976.

Philip Wright, *Monumental Inscriptions of Jamaica*. London, 1966.

Books on the Caribbean by the Author

Cuba – Official Introduction. London, 1985.

Cuba – Official Guide. London, 1988.

The Netherlands Antilles. New York, 1989.

The French Antilles. New York, 1990.

The French Antilles and Guyane. 1992

Explorer Caribbean. Basingstoke, 1994.

Globetrotter Cuba. London, 1996.

Cuba – Guide. London, 1998.

Classic Cuban Cookery. London, 1999.

Index of 360 Selected Historic Sites

In most cases individual sites are listed, but sometimes an entire area, town, or village is considered of historic importance.

Notes

Notes

Notes